On the
Edge
of Destruction

On the
Edge
of Destruction

JEWS OF POLAND
BETWEEN
THE TWO WORLD WARS

Celia S. Heller

FOREWORD BY
Nathan Glazer

 WAYNE STATE UNIVERSITY PRESS   DETROIT

Library of Congress Cataloging-in-Publication Data
Heller, Celia Stopnicka.
On the edge of destruction : Jews of Poland between the two World Wars /
Celia S. Heller : foreword by Nathan Glazer.
p.   cm.
Previously published: New York : Schocken Books, 1980.
Includes bibliographical references and index.
ISBN 0–8143–2494–0 (pbk. : alk. paper)
1. Jews—Poland—History—20th century. 2. Jews—Poland—Social conditions.
3. Antisemitism—Poland. 4. Poland—History—1918–1945.
5. Poland—Ethnic relations. I. Title.
DS135.P6H396   1994
943.8′004924—dc20   93–36002

To my grandfather,

Shaul ben Yitzhak Yosef ha-Kohen Rosenman

Your grave unmarked,
Your grave unknown,
Your death implanted in my soul,
For which no solace I can find.

I miss the wisdom of your words,
I crave the joy with which you lived,
I thirst the faith that from you shone,
And made Redemption seem so close.

Contents

Foreword

O*n the Edge of Destruction: Jews of Poland Between the Two World Wars* was first published in 1977. It appears again, sixteen years later, at a time when it would seem all attention on the Jewish communities of Eastern Europe concentrates on their destruction, rather than on their character as living expressions, in culture, in religion, in social life, in politics, of a numerous and varied people. The opening of the impressive Holocaust Memorial Museum in Washington in 1993, along with a similar museum in Los Angeles, and with other museums on the way or promised, only accentuates this contemporary emphasis on the brutal destruction of the European Jews. Yet the destruction should also lead us to pay attention to the character of the Jewish life that disappeared.

It is the special virtue of *On the Edge of Destruction* that it gives such attention to the Jews of Poland, the largest Jewish community in Europe in 1939, the second largest Jewish community in the world at the time, and the origin of a large part of what had become the largest Jewish community in the world, the American. The Jews of the United States had their origins in Warsaw, Lodz, Vilno, Lvov, and other cities and towns of the larger Poland of the period between the wars, which included territories of what is now the Ukraine and Bielo Russia.

Poland had also been the original home of a good part of the Jewish communities of Germany and Western Europe, of Canada and Australia and Argentina. Poland was the motherland of the Ashkenazic Jews, who had spread throughout Europe and the Western World and into the Southern Hemisphere, and had everywhere given rise to vigorous communities of businessmen and professionals and scholars and scientists and political leaders.

The three million Jews of the period of Polish independence between the wars was reduced to a remnant by the savage policies of extermination by the German occupiers. Even that remnant was further reduced by the anti-Semitism of the Polish population, and by anti-Semitic policies of the Communist government. Today only a few thousand Polish Jews remain, a community even smaller than the Jewish communities of the surrounding countries that were also subjected to Nazi policies of extermination. There is hardly a parallel in history to this mass wiping out of a large and vigorous and varied people.

Yet there was much in Jewish life in Poland between the wars that calls for our attention and interest. It is a story surprisingly little known, and there is nothing that tells the story as well as this book. The greater part of American Jews who immigrated from Polish-speaking lands came from Russian-ruled or Austrian-ruled territories, before World War I. They knew little of the vast social changes that were transforming the Jews of Poland in the new independent Poland. They knew certainly of the anti-Semitism—their relatives were often desperate to get out because of it. Even about that one will find a great deal of enlightenment in this book. One will discover just how economic policies were reducing so many of the Polish Jews to destitution; how the educational policies that prevented them from getting higher education worked; what parts of the population, what interest groups, supported the anti-Semitic policies.

But anti-Semitism was only part of the story of Jewish life in Poland between the wars, though it undoubtedly affected everything else. As we well know, traditional religion flourished in Poland, in *shtetl* and city. But Jews responded too to the pressures of the surrounding society. There was a remarkably vigorous Jewish political life, indeed the richest array of Jewish political groups to be found anywhere in the Jewish world: religious and anti-religious, Zionist, non-Zionist, and anti-Zionist, assimilationist and anti-assimilationist, proletarian and middle class, radical, liberal, and conservative: all had their parties, their youth groups, their intellectuals, their newspapers.

One of the most striking features of Jewish life in Poland between the wars was the gradual change in the language of the population. Immigrants from Poland before World War I were Yiddish-speaking, and few knew Polish well enough to use it. The creation of a national Polish state, despite its prevailing anti-Semitism, did spread the knowledge of Polish through the Jewish population, and would in time have created a substantial linguistic divide between Polish Jews in Poland and in the United States and other English-speaking lands, as the common language, Yiddish declined. Indeed, Jews began to participate in Polish culture, and many achieved prominence despite the anti-Semitism of many Polish critics. Jewish life in Poland was much more than *shtetl* life, the life portrayed in the unforgettable photographs of Roman Vishniac. As we learn from this book, a great part of the Jewish population lived in the large cities: they were changing not only their language, but also their outlook on life, as Orthodoxy was increasingly challenged as a way of life by modern social and political movements.

This is a rich and detailed and solidly documented picture of ways of life that have disappeared, cut off long before their time by a unique savagery. Surprisingly, despite the passage of sixteen years, very little has been added in English to the literature on the Jews of Poland between the wars. Vastly more has been added to the numerous accounts of the Holocaust, which does demand, and justifies, all the attention it gets. But the life of the Jews of Poland, at a time when no one could imagine what the future would bring, also deserves attention, unsentimental, clear-eyed, documented, empathetic, and understanding. This is what Celia S. Heller brings to her account of the Jews of Poland between the wars.

Nathan Glazer

Acknowledgments

The names of all those directly or indirectly have helped to make this book possible would make a very long list. Invaluable were the numerous conversations with and interviews of individuals who lived in interwar Poland. I also acknowledge with pleasure my special indebtedness to Dr. Aleksander Hertz, to Professors Arieh Tartakower and Moshe Mishkinski for their comments on and criticisms of the manuscript, a number of which led to revisions in the book. Clearly the final responsibility rests with me. When this book was first conceived, the conversations and discussions with the late Judith Kramer were inspiring. My editor, John Moore, the head of Columbia University Press, proved again, as in my book *Structured Social Inequality,* a staunch ally. I am grateful to Arthur B. Evans, the director of Wayne State University Press, who smoothed the path of this new edition. To my sister, Ann R. Heller, I am grateful for deepening my understanding of the culture of the Orthodox-traditionalists, that large sector of Polish Jewry. I am indebted to Professors Natan Rotenstreich and Elkana Margalit who helped to arrange my access to special materials from the interwar period available only in Israel. Much appreciated is the help in locating materials given to me by Dina Abramowicz, the librarian, and Ezekiel Lifschutz, the archivist of the YIVO Institute for Jewish Research, and that of Bela Weinberg in transliterating of Yiddish and Hebrew terms and titles. Also valued by me is the painstaking work of copyediting done by Leslie Bialler.

I also wish to thank the National Institute of Mental Health and the Memorial Foundation for Jewish Culture for their financial awards.

My greatest thanks are reserved for my parents, Ida and Emanuel Heller, for their limitless moral and intellectual support. To their memory, as well as to that of my grandfather, Shaul Rosenman, this book is dedicated.

C.S.H.

Introduction

World War II marked the most complete destruction of a people in recorded history. On the eve of destruction, the Jewish community in Poland numbered more than 3 million people, and constituted about 10 percent of the population. Today, there are estimated to be only 6,000 to 10,000 in the land. In no European country had such a large number of Jews lived for so long a time. The Polish Jews formed a separate community in the full sense of the word. Many of them adhered to a different culture and possessed highly developed separate forms of social organization. Their way of life was multifarious and pervaded by paradoxes; yet it formed a whole, rooted in their common history and their common existential condition in Poland.

It is incumbent upon the social scientists who witnessed its disappearance to depict a rich way of life that has been destroyed before some of its aspects sink into oblivion and its image becomes further distorted by time. To convey the situation of the Jews in interwar Poland, as well as to reconstruct the main outlines of this complex community before it came to its tragic end, would constitute enough of a challenge. But for me there is yet another reason for writing this book: the hope that it will add to the understanding of those who came out of that community, and their descendants, who are now part of the Jewish communities of other countries.

My aim is thus to reach beyond my academic colleagues to all literate people. As a sociologist, I naturally approach the subject from the perspective of my discipline, but I avoid as much as possible the use of sociological jargon.

The book is nonetheless based on my research and the work of specialists in the interwar period: historians, economists, sociologists, etc. Since most of the materials are in Polish, Yiddish, and Hebrew, my book should also be of value to English-speaking scholars and researchers. It could provide the context of any problem or topic connected with Polish Jewry in the period studied. I have tried to weave together a wealth of material about the general situation of the Jews and how they dealt with it. I mean to address the grand issues that touched most of Poland's Jews and the main currents that engulfed many. In deciding which aspects to omit and how much detail to present, my guiding principle has been to include what was necessary to capture the dynamic and the complexity of the Jewish community.

I have had to omit almost entirely the important matter of regional differences, mostly a legacy of Poland's partition: The Jews in the areas under Russian, Prussian, and Austrian rule had been subject to different influences and fared differently even after independence was won, especially during the early years. But I felt that a general work like mine could not do justice to such variations. I have therefore focused on the basic common features and pointed to regional differences only in those instances where they were so pronounced that no generalization for the whole country could be validly made. Let me also admit at the outset that some of my generalizations apply more to the largest part, central Poland (former Congress Poland) than to other parts, especially Galicia in the South. It may be fairly said, however, that regional differences were progressively reduced in independent Poland.

Some findings, not essential to the exposition but which increase the validity of my generalizations, are stowed away in the notes for each chapter. (In the notes, the titles of Yiddish references—as Yiddish terms throughout the book—are transliterated from the Hebrew script according to the YIVO Transcription

Scheme; Hebrew terms and references according to the Library of Congress Transliteration.)

Between the two world wars, the Jews of Poland bore the earmarks of a conquered population, both in their social status and in their treatment. And yet their presence in that country was not due to conquest but to voluntary migration. They had been invited in the twelfth, thirteenth and fourteenth centuries by the princes and kings in order to build up Polish commerce and Polish cities.

To shed light on this grim transition—from the benign beginning to the terrible oppression in the final decades of the Jews' multi-century presence in Poland—I begin part I with a short historical survey. Especially pertinent as background material for the rest of the book are the last pages of chapter 1, concerned with the second half of the nineteenth century and the beginning of the twentieth. It is then that various ideologies sprung up and political movements developed, which played an important part in the interwar period. The rise of Zionism and of the socialist Jewish Bund are of particular relevance. This chapter is a very compact presentation of the long span of Jewish history in Poland, not easily found elsewhere. It is based on numerous historical works, most in Polish and Yiddish, dealing with specific periods and aspects of this long history.

The declaration of Polish independence from Russia, Germany, and Austria in November 1918 was followed by anti-Jewish violence in many cities, towns, and villages. My portrayal of the Jews' situation in resurrected Poland begins with these events, not so much to document them as to provide insight into the social climate of that country. Polish violence led the victorious Allies to insist that Poland sign the Minorities Treaty, guaranteeing equal rights to national and religious minorities. This event was experienced and regarded differently by the Polish majority than by the Jewish minority. It raised the expectations of the Jews, especially the young; their political leaders proceeded to claim the rights guaranteed by the Treaty. Thus they became the exponents of the advanced idea of cultural and social pluralism. But the Poles in general saw the Minorities Treaty as an unfair imposition from the outside. Poles regarded themselves as the indigenous population with the self-evident right to be there, and they saw the Jews as intruders whose centuries-long presence was due only to the good will of Poles. The social definition of the Jews as strangers and foreigners is thoroughly examined.

Then I proceed to the discussion of the Jews' inferior ascribed status in Polish society, from which few escaped. For with it went the compelling stigmatization, which is described and illustrated. In operating with the equation of different as foreign, the dominant Poles stressed, in addition to the religious differences of Jews, their occupational and demographic (rural-urban) as well as their linguistic and cultural differences. The main outlines of these differences between Jews and Poles are presented, and in this connection the high visibility of the Jews in Poland is thoroughly analyzed. Such analysis provides an illustration for the sociological proposition, often forgotten in societies preoccupied with race, that the high visibility of a group singled out for prejudice and discrimination is not necessarily tied to race.

In the two chapters that follow, I describe the Polish pattern of anti-Jewish prejudice, discrimination, and violence during the interwar period. Also discussed is the development of extreme Polish nationalism and how its triumph was related to Poland's deep economic and political problems, as well as to the inadequacies of the governing elite. I demonstrate how the very presence of Jews in Poland was made into an issue and successfully brought by the Polish nationalist organizations into the center of the political arena. I discuss the economic policies, which imposed hardship on the overwhelming part of the Jewish population, as well as the forms of organized anti-Semitism and terror. Included is a review of the role the influential Catholic Church of Poland played by not containing but rather supporting the organized drive against Jews.

I wish to emphasize, however, that individual and organized opposition by Poles to the campaign of hate did exist, even if it encompassed only a small minority. I do this not only because of my special sentiments for those humane Poles who bravely stood by Jews and opposed the wrongs done to them, but more importantly because their symbolic significance in the struggle of Polish Jews to survive oppression greatly outweigh their numbers.

Chapters 2 through 4 focus a great deal on Poles because they to a great extent determined the Jews' situation—as the Poles were the dominant group, and exercised their power, in accordance with their definitions and norms, over the subordinate Jews. In part II, the concentration is almost exclusively on the actions and the reactions of the Jews to their situation as a despised and oppressed minority. To begin to grasp the complexity, the variety, and meaning of their responses, it is necessary to recognize two striking dialectical features of Jews in the period studied. There was on one hand the growing heterogeneity of the Jewish people and on the other the concurrent sharpening of the tendency among the Poles to disregard such differences and to treat all Jews the same.

In the mosaic of differences among Jews two definite social types may be recognized. I refer to one of these polar types as Orthodox-traditionalist and the other as assimilationist. Each is treated in a separate chapter, not only in order to explicate these contrasting ways, but also to provide greater insight into the dynamics of the rest, the *largest* part of Polish Jewry. The Orthodox-traditionalists represented the pattern from which many, especially the younger, were moving away. The Orthodox-traditionalists were devoted to the conservation without any change of Jewish religio-cultural distinctiveness, and continued in their efforts to cope with their situation in the traditional "Jewish way." Assimilation seemed at some point in the preceding century, especially to those who had embarked on it, to be representing the future of Polish Jewry. But the assimilationists remained a small, deviant group. They tried to escape the Jewish situation by becoming identificationally as well as culturally assimilated. Mostly they identified as Poles, little as Jews. Not much has been written to date about these self-designated "Poles of Mosaic faith" or "Poles of Jewish descent," and the chapter devoted to them is largely based on my own research. Their human tragedy is that despite all of their efforts to make themselves indistinguishable from Poles and distin-

guishable from Jews, they remained subject to categorical treatment accorded to Jews, and failed to become fully integrated into
Polish society.

They persisted to the end on the road toward full assimilation,
but they only proved to the rest of Polish Jewry that assimilation
was not the solution to their minority situation; with minor exceptions, the program and methods of assimilation did not gain new
converts during the interwar period. The primary concern of the
Jews who departed from the Orthodox-traditional pattern was to
create a social structure that would guarantee them equality without the sacrifice of their Jewish identity, would remove the stigma
of being a Jew, and would do away with discrimination and persecution. And the main force in this concern was Jewish nationalism in its many variations.

There was little consensus among the Jews as to how this
equality was to be achieved. The fragmentation was related to the
processes of secularization and acculturation (Polonization) which
continued during the period studied. This of course contradicts the
widely held image of Polish Jewry as being hardly touched by
these processes, in contrast to the Jews of Western Europe. Admit-
tedly, the Jews of Poland had been among the least acculturated of
all Jewish communities. But many especially the young, had been
on the roads of acculturation and secularization when Poland became independent and more were swept by these two processes
during independence.

Between the two crystallized patterns of the Orthodox-traditionalists and assimilationists, a wide spectrum existed of degrees
in Polonization and secularization and in the combination of these
two processes. I treat the variation of the processes in different
classes and age groups. The part played by the Polish public
schools in the rapid growth of Polonization is discussed, as is the
struggle of middle class parents to provide their children with a
secondary education (*gimnazjum*). Neither compulsory nor free, it
represented a strategic point of entry into the intelligentsia.

I also pay special attention to the generational conflict that
resulted from the Polonization and secularization of the young.
The Jewish family in Poland, often romanticized by its survivors as

idyllic, was torn by this sharp conflict. However, the inegrative role of the mother did not simply remain intact, but in some sense became strengthened.

In the final chapter I review how this heterogeneous population resisted oppression. I consider the large number of antagonistic Jewish parties and how their existence hampered unified action. The political issues were overlain with religious and other considerations, so that the interparty and intraparty rivalries constituted a labyrinth for many of the Polish Jews of the period, let alone for one who tries to untangle those issues today. I aim to make sense of the main issues without oversimplifying the political scene. One set of issues, which had surfaced earlier, continued to dominate—the question of the ultimate solution to the Jewish problem: Zionism versus Socialism. The new set of issues that were created with Poland's independence revolved around whether or not and how to participate as ethnic parties in Polish parliamentary politics. Jewish public opinion shifted from wide support of such participation at the beginning of independence to complete disillusionment with it in the last years before World War II. By then most Jews realized that, contrary to what was originally preached and forecast by their leaders, having Jewish representatives sit in the Polish parliament did not do the Jews much good. At the same time their aspirations to emigrate to Palestine suffered a heavy blow, with England's proclamation of the White Papers closing the doors of their ancient homeland. Trapped in hostility—undermined economically and harassed by the Poles to get out of Poland—they had nowhere to go. The last years were marked by the politics of despair. The Jews shifted their orientation from national to local electoral politics, trying to effect on the local level the decisions which governed their everyday life. On the national level, the politics moved toward mass protest into which were drawn many who had formerly abstained from political action. There was also some movement in the direction of self-defense against the pogroms and terror fomented by the extreme Polish nationalists. In both the protest and defense, Jewish unity began emerging but, alas, had no time to unfold.

Now that I have outlined what the book addresses itself to,

some readers might be asking the very question put to me by a few friends and colleagues while I worked on this book: is this a historical or a sociological work? I must admit that I found this question at first a bit unsettling because I saw no reason why I should pigeonhole my work in this manner. After some reflection, I realized that this question was in good part related to the fact that most contemporary sociologists confine their studies to the present, and yet the fathers of sociology dealt with past phenomena, as, for example, Max Weber's *The Protestant Ethic and the Spirit of Capitalism.* For me history and sociology are not so separate as some contemporary sociologists make them out to be, for I lean toward C. Wright Mills's conception of sociology as the history of today. I also share the sentiment of the distinguished historian, Edward Hallet Carr, who in *What Is History* remarked that "the more sociological history becomes and the more historical sociology becomes, the better for both."

Of course, as a sociologist I was guided in my work by the concepts, theories, and generalizations developed by sociologists, particularly in the study of comparative ethnic relations. Chronology is not the organizing principle of this book, and in this sense it differs from the popular conception of historical writing; but I do pay attention to events, which many sociologists concerned with social structure tend to ignore. I am dealing with a subsociety in the process of rapid change, and the study of social change cannot be separated from that of events. The changes in the situation of the Jews and their responses to the changes could not simply be deduced from the structure of Polish society and of the Jewish community. They were also closely linked to certain crucial events: the pogroms at the beginning of independence, Poland's signing the Minorities Treaty under pressure, Marshal Piłsudski's return to power in 1926, the rise of Nazism in Germany, the death of Piłsudski, and England's issuance of the White Papers on Palestine.

In dealing with the past, I have tried not to impose upon it the opinions of the present. I have also made an effort to avoid the idealization—the kind of sentimentality that marks lachrymose writings about the shtetl. (Frequently the heterogeneous and complex interwar Jewish community of Poland is erroneously equated with the nostalgic image of the shtetl.) I have been guided by the conviction that to pay tribute to this community is to tell its story with forthrightness and integrity. If I have succeeded, perhaps it was because, born in this community, I loved not its ideal representation, but the people in it with their faults as well as their virtues, their failures as well as their successes.

In short, I have done my best to convey reality, using the best data available, as well as other information that I have gathered through interviews of survivors. Research for the book involved a systematic review of the extensive interwar literature—in Polish, Yiddish, and Hebrew—dealing with specific aspects of Jewish life in Poland between the wars. However, certain aspects of the period have not yet been adequately researched, especially the case of the assimilationists in Poland. I conducted ten in-depth interviews with surviving members of assimilationist families, some of which I tape recorded. I have also made use of some diaries as well as a number of published memoirs and autobiographies. I rely on them for subjective insights into the period rather than for a rendition of objective reality.

For other aspects which required primary research, I have examined some of the Jewish daily press (written in Yiddish and Polish). I have also analyzed census data. My greatest find was the autobiographies and diaries of young Jews; they had been collected in Poland during the 1930s by YIVO, the Jewish Scientific Institute in Vilno. Over 600 such documents were in the possession of YIVO before the war broke out. When the Nazis occupied Vilno, they removed them to Germany. After the war, 302 of these were found near Frankfurt. With the aid of the U.S. State Department and Military Government, they were brought to YIVO in New York, where its headquarters had been transferred in 1940.

I consider myself fortunate to have had access to these and am grateful to YIVO for its generosity. Reading these documents was like hearing voices recalled to life. In analyzing these documents, however, I was careful to discern fact from fancy. These autobiographies supplied illustrations for findings derived from other data. I quote from these autobiographies and diaries (which I

translated from the Yiddish and Polish in which they were written), as well as from the interviews I conducted, in order to bring
some of the fleshless findings to life.

Some of my formulations are more tentative than others. I
nevertheless present them without surrendering scholarly scrupu-
lousness, confident that they will be further validated in the future, as other scholarly studies of particular aspects of Jewish life
appear.

Perhaps an explanation is now in order about the rule used
concerning the names of Polish cities and towns. Those few well
known by their Anglicized names—such as Warsaw and Cracow—
are thus referred to in the book. When first used, the Polish equivalent is given in parenthesis. In all other cases, the cities and
towns are referred to by their Polish names.

With all this said, let us proceed to the story of the Jews in
Poland during the penultimate period of their existence, prophe-
tically designated in 1937 by a *New York Times* correspondent as
the time when modern anti-Semitism was "turning the recurrent
Jewish tragedy in that biggest Jewish center in the world into a
final disaster of truly historic magnitude." *

* Otto D. Tolischus, "Jews Face Crisis in Eastern Europe," *New York Times*, February 7, 1937.

PART I
THE SITUATION
OF THE JEWS

POLAND IN 1938

(Marked on the map are only the localities discussed or mentioned in the book.)

I
Historical Perspective:
Tolerance and Hate

Between the "war to end all wars" and the one that spelled their doom, the Jews of Poland bore the marks of a conquered population in their social status and in the treatment accorded to them. Yet their presence in Poland was not due to conquest but to voluntary migration; they had arrived there in medieval times at the invitation of princes and kings, who had expected that they would be of aid in developing Polish commerce and building Polish cities. These contrasting facts of their condition in the period before the Holocaust and their origin in Poland are crucial to the understanding of the rare social constellation which I shall examine in this book.[1] Experts on comparative ethnic relations tend to connect the situation of a minority at a given time and place with the way it became a minority. The contrast is drawn between immigration and conquest, or voluntarism and force. In the United States, the situation of European immigrant groups is contrasted to that of Negroes and Indians; and the implication is clear: their origins as minorities differ and much of the contrast in their present situation can be traced to that difference in origin.

But take twentieth-century interbellum Poland and compare its two largest ethnic minorities, the Ukrainians, whose presence in Poland was due to conquest, and the Jews, who had arrived as immigrants. The Jews were treated no better than the Ukrainians. A historical perspective may help reveal how the invited guests became an oppressed and suffering minority (from the Jews' perspective) and were hated as foreign intruders (from the Poles' perspective).

Jewish traders are mentioned in chronicles dating back before 963 A.D., when the oldest Polish state, that of the Piasts, is mentioned in historical sources. Centuries later, Jews inhabited every corner of the Polish Kingdom. This kingdom came to extend from Courland in the north to the Dniester in the south, from the Oder river in the west to the Dnieper in the east. It became the Commonwealth Kingdom of Poland and included many areas whose indigenous population was not Polish but in the main Lithuanian, Belorussian, or Ukrainian. The Jews came here mostly from western and southwestern Europe and were of Ashkenazi culture. In the twelfth century, after the Second Crusade, when the conditions of the Jews in Germany worsened greatly, some Jews came to Poland from the Rhine and Danube provinces. They arrived in greater numbers in the thirteenth century. The persecution of Jews during the Black Death (1342–50), which they were accused of carrying, brought a wave of immigration from Bohemia as well as Germany. From both places immigration continued in the second half of the fourteenth century and first half of the fifteenth. Jews from Austria came at the end of the fifteenth and beginning of the sixteenth century.

The importance of Jewish immigration for the economic development of Poland was first realized by the medieval Polish princes. Prompted by the desire to cultivate commercial and industrial activities in their dominions, these princes welcomed settlers, mostly Jews and Germans, from more advanced parts of Europe. Poland was a rural country with many forests and only a few thinly populated towns when the Jews and Germans were invited there as trailblazers of urbanism. The development of towns in Poland was mainly carried out by Germans. The towns were granted autonomy, the privilege of living according to the German Magdeburg Law. Thus Polish towns followed the German model: They were German in their mode of life as well as origin. The Jews were encouraged to settle in these towns and did so in large numbers.

A great potential for economic development existed in Poland and the Jews proved adept at realizing it. Thus they began as a "complementary population," supplying the skills that were weak or absent in Poland. As is generally known, the Church of the Middle Ages forbade the lending of money for interest, but money-lending was required for economic development. Polish sovereigns favored the immigration of Jews, who were able to serve as intermediaries between lenders and borrowers. The landed nobility needed money to develop intensive agriculture on their large estates, and they received it from the Jews. During the thirteenth and fourteenth centuries Jews were found among the administrators of the mint and the salt mines. Between the fourteenth and sixteenth centuries, the services of Jewish bankers proved indispensable for the expansion of trade. Consequently, in an agricultural country of two fixed estates—owners of soil and tillers of soil—the Jews represented a rising urban middle class. This salient historical point must be kept in mind for an understanding of the position of the Jews in twentieth-century interwar Poland.

The first to react against this position of Jews was the Church, which tried to prevent social intercourse between Christians and Jews. Christianity had not come to Poland until 966, and the Church seemed to fear that the presence of a prosperous population of a different faith would prevent it from taking deep root. The canonical law, passed by the Church Council of Breslau (Wrocław) in 1267, clearly indicates this to be the chief factor in the Church's anti-Jewish activities. "In view of the fact that Poland is a *nova plantatio* [a new planting] in the body of Christianity," reads clause twelve, "there is reason to fear that her Christian population will fall an easy prey to the influence of the superstition and evil habits of the Jews living among them, the more so as the Christian religion took root in the hearts of the faithful of these countries at a later date and in a more feeble manner." This was given as the reason for passing a canonical law aimed at a separation of Jews from the rest of the population in the oldest Polish diocese of Gnessen (Gniezno). "For this reason," proclaims the law, "we must strictly enjoin that the Jews residing in the diocese of Gnessen shall not live side by side with the Christians but shall live apart . . . in some section of the city or village. The section inhabited by the Jews shall be separated from the general dwelling place of the Christians by a hedge, wall, or ditch." It orders Christians, under the threat of excommunication, not to "invite Jews or Jewesses as their table companions or to eat or drink with them," or to "dance or caper with them at their weddings or banquets." The canonical law further provides that "in order to be marked off from the Christians" Jews must wear a specially shaped hat. The hat seemed an insufficient badge of identification, and in 1279 the Church Council ordered that a red cloth be sewed on the left side of garments of Jews.

The clergy was not strong enough to enforce these artifical barriers. They did, however, try to agitate the people by fabricating myths of evil acts by Jews; the only anti-Jewish outbreaks that took place in the Kingdom of Poland before the fourteenth century were those organized by the Church. In these outbreaks the Church found ready allies among the townspeople, who had acquired from the German burghers a malign image of Jews. When Polish merchants arose in Poland, it was to their interest to oppose the Jews.

Here then is the beginning of a basic change in the situation of the Jews—from that of complementarity to competition. With the development of towns in the second half of the fourteenth century, the Polish merchant class became strong enough to attempt an organized struggle against the Jews, with whom they were competing commercially; and the Church supplied them with inspiration and arguments.

The first use of the blood libel in Poland took place in 1399 in Posen (Poznań), economically the most developed part of Poland. A rumor was spread that the Jews had bribed a Polish woman to steal three hosts, which they stabbed, and that blood had spurted forth in confirmation of the Eucharist dogma. The Archbishop of Posen instituted a trial and the verdict was the burning alive of the rabbi and thirteen elders. In addition, the Jews were punished by an "eternal" fine which they had to pay to the Dominican Church.

(This fine was exacted until the beginning of the eighteenth century.) Eight years later (1407), Cracow (Kraków) was the scene of an organized massacre, plunder, and burning of Jewish houses, when a priest made a public announcement that Jews had murdered a Christian child.

The Polish merchants were growing stronger, and by the second half of the fifteenth century they were powerful enough to force concrete measures limiting the rights of the Jews. During that time all larger towns (Posen, Cracow, Lvov) compelled the Jewish communities to conclude "voluntary agreements." According to those agreements, Jewish merchants were limited or, as in the case of Cracow, excluded from commerce almost entirely. Following the precedent of spatial segregation advanced by the Church, some of the municipalities run by Polish burghers limited the areas of the city where the Jews could reside. Occasionally a municipality excluded Jewish residents entirely, among them Warsaw (Warszawa) from which all Jews were expelled in 1483.

In the middle of the next century, however, the Jews returned to the outskirts and those parts of Warsaw which were under the direct jurisdiction of the magnates, rather than the municipalities. This privilege, called *jurydyka* (jurisdiction), of having whole sections of towns outside the jurisdiction of municipalities and under the authority of the nobles had been granted by the King and the Diet. These nobles were often protectors of Jews. Later, for example, the Jews settled in Mariensztat, on the outskirts of Warsaw, in the *jurydyka* of Count Potocki.

The princes, and later the kings of Poland, who welcomed the Jews (realizing their value for the economic development of the country), shielded them from the wrath of the Church and the rising Polish merchant class. But the protection of kings and nobles, although important for immediate survival, came to be a factor second only to economic competition in the growing hostility toward Jews. As early as 1264, Prince Bolesław of Kalisz, known as the Pious, had issued a charter, *Privilegium*, defining the rights of Jews within his dominions. Its three main provisions placed Jews under the jurisdiction of the prince, protected the interests of Jewish creditors against their Christian debtors, and granted the Jews a large measure of autonomy in dealing with disputes among themselves.

In exchange for the right to pursue commerce, the Jews were to pay fees and taxes directly to the princes's treasury. The first clause of the charter provided that in both civil and criminal cases the testimony of a Christian against a Jew could be accepted only if confirmed by the deposition of a Jewish witness. It was followed by a clause guaranteeing the Jews inviolability of their person and property. A Christian who murdered or wounded a Jew had to answer for his crime before the princely court. If he murdered a Jew the offender would lose his property; if he wounded a Jew, he had to pay a fine to the Prince. The kidnapper of Jewish children for the purpose of baptizing them was to be severely punished.

The provisions of this charter give us some insight into the type of offenses against Jews the anti-Jewish agitation of the Church had led to. However, in the thirteenth century Catholicism in Poland had not yet acquired sufficient strength to inflict serious damage on Jews, who lived in relative safety under the protection of the princes and kings. Even in the fourteenth century, when the Polish merchants became an additional force against the Jews, the king protected the Jews in the interest of economic development of the country. Thus King Casimir the Great (Kazimierz Wielki, 1333–70) ratified the charter of Bolesław of Kalisz and extended its operation to all provinces of the kingdom. In view of the hostility of the municipalities controlled by the Polish merchants and the Church, the king amplified the rights of the charter. He removed all legal cases involving Jews from the jurisdiction of the municipal and Church authorities, and placed them under his own jurisdiction. Also, he granted the Jews the rights to reside in cities, towns and villages; to free transit; to rent and mortgage estates; to lend money. In contrast to the policy of the Church, he encouraged Christians to associate with Jews. "If a Jew enters the house of a Christian," says Casimir's charter, "no one has a right to cause him any injury or unpleasantness." Under his rule, a new township was founded near Cracow, bearing his name, Kazimierz. It was inhabited by Jews and became one of the centers of Jewish life in Poland. Casimir the Great's attitude toward the Jews was mainly part of his policy to attract foreign settlers whom he considered useful for the development of Poland, although historical evidence also indicates he had some personal sympathy for Jews. His protective policy led to the economic advancement of Poland, including the tremendous growth of cities. Perhaps the consequences of this policy are best expressed in the common Polish saying, "King Casimir found a Poland of wood and left behind a Poland constructed of stone." And the consequences of his personal sympathy for Jews are expressed in the exalted position he occupied in Jewish folklore. The image of the good Polish king in whose eyes the Jews found favor lived on and was loved through centuries by Jewish folk, especially Jewish children, as long as there was a Jewish community in Poland.

Some of the kings that followed were unable to withstand the pressure of the Church and the Polish merchants. The first of these was Yagello (Jagiełło), under whose reign the blood libel and burning of Jews in Posen took place. As a convert to Catholicism, he proved his adherence to the faith by frequently yielding to the Church. This deference continued throughout the Yagellonian Dynasty. The third of that dynasty, however, King Casimir IV (1447–92), decided to rule independently and confirmed the rights of Jews granted by Casimir the Great. During his reign the ecclesiastical attitude toward the Jews found influential expression in Cardinal Zbigniew Oleśnicki of Cracow and the cardinal's chronicler, Jan Długosz, later archbishop of Lvov. When the King lost one of the battles with the Teutonic knights, the Cardinal interpreted it as a punishment for favoring the Jews and denounced him. The King yielded and withdrew the privileges of Jews as "opposed both to divine right and law of the land." However, it was a short-lived repeal and the rights of the Jews granted by Casimir the Great persisted.

The anti-Jewish forces of the Church and the burghers were joined in the sixteenth century by some members of the gentry, the *szlachta*. They aspired to positions in civil service and resented the fact that the collection of royal revenues had been turned over to Jewish contractors. (The kings and magnates found the Jews to be more efficient and reliable in running their estates.) At the Piotrków Diet, 1538, where the gentry asserted itself, a constitution was adopted with a separate section on Jews. It denied the Jews the right to be contracted as revenue collectors by the high nobility. From the provisions of the Piotrków constitution we gather that despite the efforts of the Church and the Polish burghers, some Jews in the Kingdom of Poland had reached a high level of acculturation. "Whereas the Jews, disregarding the ancient regulations," declared the constitution, "have thrown off the marks by which they were distinguishable from the Christians, and have arrogated to themselves a form of dress which closely resembles that of Christians, so that it is impossible to recognize them, be it resolved for permanent observance: the Jews of our realm . . . in whatever place they happen to be found, shall wear special marks." But the King, Sigismund I (Zygmunt Pierwszy), had ruled four years before the Piotrków Diet that Jews did not need to wear any distinguishing marks on their clothes. Despite the Piotrków resolution, the King's decision prevailed.

Soon another element of the Polish population, the artisans, joined in the fight against the Jews. As Jews were being forced out of commerce and contractual positions, they shifted to handicrafts. The Polish guilds excluded the Jewish artisans and tried to force them to work for their coreligionists only. In self-defense the Jewish artisans started forming guilds of their own at the beginning of the seventeenth century. Also, to win over the Polish clients, the Jews began to produce more standardized and lower-priced goods. This led to further resentment by Polish artisans who looked down on these products as shoddy. (The term "Jewish work" became synonymous with cheap and trashy products.)

Fewer in number than the Polish artisans but quite influential among the anti-Jewish forces of the seventeenth century were the Polish physicians. Again the basic factor in this antagonism seemed to be economic competition. Jewish physicians were greatly respected in Poland. When the Jews were expelled from Spain, a number of Jewish physicians had arrived in Poland and became the attendants of Polish kings and high nobility.

And finally we come to the historical roots of the anti-Jewish feelings among the bulk of the population, the peasantry. These feelings are tied to the middleman position of the Jews, vis-à-vis the peasants. The Jews served the nobles well in the day-to-day running of their estates, mostly in posts that were rather minor and of limited authority. But as the peasants started awakening, they tended to blame the Jews, with whom they had more frequent contact than with the noble owners and administrators of the lands. Thus their wrath was turned against the Jews, whom they saw as their oppressors.

Until the middle of the seventeenth century, the two most powerful institutions of Poland—the Church and the Crown—differed fundamentally in their attitude toward Jews. The former, in the interest of strengthening and maintaining the Catholic faith, pursued a policy of hate, violence, and discrimination. The latter, in the financial interest of the Crown and in the economic interest of the country, manifested a measure of tolerance and protection. Yet, this very protection became another factor in the development of further hatred of Jews among the Polish population. Economic competition with the Jews and the intermediate position of Jews between peasantry and gentry were additional factors which turned specific groups against the Jews.

Still, as compared with fellow Jews in the rest of Europe, those in Poland considered themselves relatively well-off and secure, before the catastrophe of 1648. Some among them seized the opportunities that the economically underdeveloped country contained and became quite wealthy in new occupations they created. Among them were those who prospered as financial agents and tax collectors of the Crown and the nobles. A few ran the Polish salt mines and administered the mint. Of special importance were those who prospered in commerce; even with the growth in number of Polish merchants, the Jewish merchants, thanks to their long experience in commerce and their ties to Jewish communities abroad, were often able to overcome obstacles placed in their way by Polish merchants and the Church. But the bulk of the Jewish population was not wealthy. It is estimated that by the middle of the seventeenth century there were about half a million Jews; they constituted five percent of the total population of the

Kingdom of Poland (which included the Grand Duchy of Lithuania, associated with the Polish Crown). Most of the men among
them were petty traders and artisans who lived in modest circumstances at best. And the legal status of all, whether rich or poor,
was that of *servi camerae*, servants of the treasury.

Jews accepted this status, as well as the hostility of the people
among whom they lived, as part of their fate. Their ultimate hope
lay not in the change of their status and situation in Poland but in
God's redemption of the Jewish people. This prevailing view is
expressed in the words of a great Polish-Jewish scholar, Rabbi
Solomon Luria (1510–1573): "Jews in these times can have neither much prosperity—in order that they should not become too
haughty—nor too much tribulation—in order that they should not
perish. All the nations come to an end but not the Jews."

In extremely rare cases, Jews would take the only avenue
available for escaping their inferior status, that of conversion to Catholicism. Under the Elective Kings (starting in 1573), both Polish
law and custom favored conversion. The converts were sponsored
by noblemen, were well received, and even enobled. There may
have been some reservations against the upstart convert, but by
the second and third generation all differences tended to disappear. Yet very few Jews chose to escape their inferior status by ceas-
ing to be Jewish. Jews interpreted conversion as the death of a person as a Jew. Therefore, the family of the convert sat in deep
mourning (*shiva*) for seven days.

In accepting their minority situation as unalterable and ines-
capable, Jews achieved an extraordinary measure of unity and solidarity that made it possible for them to accommodate to conditions
with a minimum of social disorganization. Within the framework
of their situation, they built their own closely knit society and developed an elaborate culture; both were firmly rooted in Jewish
tradition. Jewish traditionalism was the cumulative product of the
best minds of the Jewish people, who had been trying to keep the
people physically and spiritually intact since Roman times. These
prescriptions of the learned men were infused with life by a people
who in following them were able to maintain an inner dignity
despite the slights they were subjected to. The importance of this

living tradition, which provided the Jews with strength to cope with their situation, is the key to understanding the development of the Jewish community. Few minority communities throughout history have reached the degree of social and cultural autonomy that the Jews of Poland had achieved by the seventeenth century. Furthermore, they won official recognition for their self-government.

The basic unit and very foundation of the self-governing structure was the local community (*kehilla* or *kahal*) within the confines of a single city or town. (Many included Jews from nearby villages.) This formal organization functioned on the basis of Talmudic Law and custom. It raised the taxes to be paid to the king (a head tax to the king's treasury was imposed on Jews in 1552) and to maintain the community organizations and services. From its treasury it paid the rabbi (*rav*) whom it hired. The community ran its own court for Jews involved in disputes with one another and operated a set of administrative, religious, educational, and charitable organizations and facilities. Foremost among them was the synagogue, referred to as *Bet Hamidrash* (house of study) or *Bet Hakeneset* (house of assembly). It was not a place confined to the realm of the sacred. For the Jews the synagogue was the center of community life: of study as well as prayer, of assembly as well as study. Here, too, court was often held in disputes involving Jews only.

The kehilla exercised a high degree of control over the life of the Jews. And yet the chief disciplinary measure that it had at its disposal, excommunication, was very rarely used. Its control was rooted in wide consensus, for the very Talmudic Law and custom on which it based itself was considered legtimate and proper by those subject to its control. The executives of kehilla represented the Jews before non-Jewish authorities and administrative and judicial bodies. However, Jews seldom resorted voluntarily to the use of Polish institutions. The consistent avoidance of Polish institutions led to the emergence of a super-kehilla organization.

The local kehillot were joined into district councils which eventually became transformed into provincial councils under the rule of the *Va'ad Arba' Aratsot*, the Council of Four Lands. The four lands were Great Poland (principal community: Posen), Little Poland (Cracow), "the Lvov land" (later known as Eastern Galicia) and Volhynia (Ostróg, Krzemieniec). The Grand Duchy of Lithuania, had its own council, similar in structure and function to that of the Council of Four Lands. The Council was the supreme legal, judicial, and executive body of Polish Jewry. It manifested the greatest degree of Jewish autonomy within a regional or national framework ever attained by Jews in Europe. This Council represented the Jews in dealings with the king, the state, and other formal administrative organs.

Along with the development of their communal structure came the advancement of Jewish culture in Poland. The period from 1580 to 1648 is known as the Golden Age of the Jews in Poland. It is therefore pertinent to recall that until the fifteenth century the Jews of Poland were considered to be culturally inferior to most Jews in Europe—even more backward culturally than the Jews of Germany. (Among the Ashkenazic communities, those of Northern France and Lithuania ranked high. But these, too, ranked below the Sephardic communities of Spain, Provence, Italy, and Greece.)

To gain even a cursory insight into the nature of this culture, it must be understood that its builders planted themselves firmly in the ancient traditions of the Jewish people, from which they derived inspiration and hope. The literature they produced, as Abraham J. Heschel aptly describes it, was written by Jews for Jews. No apologies were offered to philosophers and historians, no praises were sought from princes or non-Jewish writers. Jewish writers did not spend their energy on the rebuttal of hostile prejudices.

The two most celebrated writers were Solomon Luria and Rabbi Moses Isserles. Solomon Luria (1510–1573) was a great scholar, whose fame and influence extended far beyond Poland; he was a passionate champion of the Talmud as the source of Jewish Law. His magnum opus, *Yam shel Shlomo*, is a superb attempt to treat Talmudic Law systematically.

Rabbi Moses Isserles of Cracow (1525–1572) was the leading intellectual of that era; he produced glosses to and modifications of the *Shulhan Arukh* (the codification of law and custom compiled by Joseph Caro), incorporating Ashkenazi traditions and practices into the older ones. This monumental work served as a common behavioral guide for the Jews in Poland and constituted an important unifier.

The contribution of Jacob Ashkenazi (1550–1623?) cannot be put on the same intellectual plane as that of the above two scholars; however, he too extended the knowledge of the Law by making it accessible to women who, unlike Jewish men, did not understand Hebrew. He accomplished it through the *Tse'enah Ure'enah*, the translation of the Pentateuch into the vernacular, Yiddish. This work, which appeared at the beginning of the seventeenth century, was read by women throughout the length and breadth of the land and came to be known as the women's bible.

The study of the Law was not confined to intellectuals but was an integral part of the Jewish male role. Through it man was to satisfy his innate thirst for knowledge, for the Law was the fountain of life. In it he would also find consolation and joy. In accordance with this conception, every male was expected to engage in the study of the Torah, each in accordance with his capacity. Thus universal education for men was a fact among the Jews of Poland before it became a goal in the advanced "civilized" countries. Each city and town had its primary schools, private *hadarim* and community Talmud Torahs, maintained mostly for the children of the poor. In addition, there was an extensive network of higher schools, *yeshivot,* devoted to advanced studies of the Talmud and the vast literature that had grown around it. These academies were not confined to training prospective rabbis but were widely attended by youths, except for the very poor. And even among the latter class, the gifted, sponsored by the community or wealthy individuals, often found their way into the yeshivot.

The pedagogic method that was extensively used in the yeshivot was that of the *pilpul,* developed by Rabbi Jacob Pollak of Prague and Cracow (1460–1532?) and promoted by his pupil, Rabbi Shalom Shakhna (1500–1558) of Lublin. This new adaptation of the dialectic method, (which had originated in the ancient academies of Babylonia) aimed at cultivating and sharpening intellectual acumen and wit; it relied mainly on a search for subtle similarities in divergent elements and for differences in similar ones. Although opposed by some prominent scholars because of its negative consequences, such as casuistry and "hair splitting," it triumphed as the chief method of Jewish higher learning and it left its imprint on the Jewish intellectual pattern of later centuries, even when Jewish intellectual life in Poland became highly secularized.

Thus, the Jews in Poland responded to the growing hostility of the population among whom they lived and to the barriers imposed on them by proudly accepting—indeed cultivating—their differences. They were highly visible in their distinctive dress and language, and easy targets of hostility and derision. But this hostility and derision only confirmed for them the righteousness of their own ways. They were sharply set off from the dominant population in their religion through centuries when religion became a dominant force in Poland. The Jews dealt with their minority situation in Poland by forming a close society of their own, highly organized to meet their needs. Theirs was a largely stable society, deeply rooted in tradition and slow to change. It was a very traditional society, both objectively and subjectively: subjectively, the members regarded its existence as based on a body of knowledge and values handed down from generation to generation; objectively, the social organization and social behavior were based on and reflected the values and norms inherited from the past.

The traditional base was of such strength that even extreme blows from the outside did not shatter it. This is shown by the massacres of 1648–49, which accompanied the uprising of the Cossacks, led by Bogdan Chmielnicki, in the Ukraine (which had been acquired by Poland after its union with the Grand Duchy of Lithuania in 1569). Tens of thousands of Jews were killed, entire Jewish communities were destroyed, whole provinces in which Jews concentrated were left without means of livelihood. It was the greatest holocaust that Jews had suffered since the time of their dispersion. And yet it was interpreted by Jews in the traditional manner— put within the framework of Jewish suffering in exile. No new political lesson was drawn from those events. On the contrary, the lesson drawn was an old moral one: They could shorten their suffering only by adhering more closely to their own ways. Thus, additional prayers were composed and fasts proclaimed.

During the period that followed a growing interest in mystic teaching of the Zohar spread. In it numerous bright young Jews found comfort and solace. It culminated in the messianic movement of Shabbatai Zevi (1626–1676), who proclaimed himself the Messiah in 1665. Eventually most of the followers became disillusioned after the false Messiah embraced Islam. But some persisted in their faith and formed a separate sect.

A century later the vast majority of the Shabbatean sect followed the self-proclaimed messianic leader, Jacob Frank (1726–91). He was the founder of a Jewish sect named after him, the Frankists. Many members of this sect were led to Catholicism by Jacob Frank. The King himself, in an elaborate ceremony on November 18, 1759, sponsored Frank's baptism. In Lvov alone, 500 Frankists converted. Many also converted in Warsaw. The total number of converts is thought to be in the thousands. There is no other instance of such a mass conversion in Poland. The conversion—which brought more people of Jewish extraction than ever before into the ranks of the Polish nobility—marked the end of the Polish liberal attitude toward new converts and their descendants. After that time the Jewish past of converts was treated as a stigma.

Note especially that the above unprecedented event in the history of the Polish Jews took place in the eighteenth century, the period of Enlightenment in the West. The eighteenth century, which meant striking progress for Western Jews, brought rapid deterioration in the conditions of Polish Jews. Poland was on the decline and the Jews suffered greatly because of it. It is estimated that there were about 600,000 Jews in Poland, including Lithuania. An increasingly large number, were becoming impoverished. Many, left without a steady source of livelihood, came to be known as *luftmentshn* (people of air). A census of the period shows more than half of Jewish men to be without a specific occupation. While this might be an inflated figure, it nevertheless points to the dire economic circumstances in which the Jews found themselves. At the same time, the Polish authorities were pressuring the Jewish community with increased taxation. This resulted in the weakening of the kehillot, which were left without means to serve the growing numbers of people who needed help. With it came a moral decline in the quality of their leadership; no longer were leaders those who best symbolized community values, but rather those who had come into office through economic power and through the help of Polish authorities. The impairment of the kehillot spelled the weakening and eventual disappearance of the super-kehilla organization. In 1764, the Polish Diet deprived the Council of the Four Lands from its tax-collecting function. It ruled that Jews were to pay the head tax directly to the state. The next year the Council ceased to exist.

The mood of despair that swept the Jewish people was also, apart from the economic burdens and unworthy leaders, produced by the frequent accusations and trials for ritual murder which took place in Poland in the first half of the eighteenth century.

Jews were trying to cope with their situation by leaving the large cities, the citadels of anti-Jewish hate and violence, and moving to small towns, where they lived with the approval of the gentry; for the nobles, the presence of Jews meant additional income. Others fled the cities for villages. In the villages about 80 percent of the Jews were concentrated in three occupations. The most important and most wealthy of the three were the *arendators*, who rented land from the Polish nobles, as well as the various rights to taxes and dues. Then there were the *kretshmers*, the tavern-keepers in villages and on the roads. The poorest were the *shenkers*, mostly employees of the *arendators* and *kretshmers*. At the close of the eighteenth century, about 80 percent of Poland's Jews lived in small towns, *shtetlekh*, and villages. Jewish life in Poland after that became synonymous to many in the Western world with the particular pattern found in the shtetl.

It was to the smaller towns, more than to the cities, that a movement spread in the last quarter of the eighteenth century which curbed despair and held out hope to the poor and oppressed. It arose in the Polish province of Podolia and its founder was Israel

Baal Shem Tov (1700–1760), a man of great charisma who became a legendary figure and whose "miraculous" cures in the name of God became legendary deeds. Hasidism proclaimed faith and emotional expression of Jewishness to be above learning and erudition. Joy and ecstasy transformed religious worship into an escape from the dreariness and fears of everyday life. No wonder that the common people flocked to the *tsadikim* (righteous), the charismatic leaders, who banished their worries, freed them from feelings of inadequacy because of their lack of learning, and inspired them in song and dance to celebrate the fact of being Jewish. The courts of many of the prominent *tsadikim*, which later developed into seats of dynasties, were not located in cities but in small towns, such as Ger (Góra Kalwarja), Kock, Kozienice, and Mezrich (Międzyrzecze), etc. Despite the strong opposition of the rabbis and other learned opponents of Hasidism, who came to be known as *mitnagdim*, large portions of the Jewish population were won over to Hasidism by the beginning of the nineteenth century. It became the dominant force among Jews, except for those of Lithuania. There the illustrious scholar and moral guide, Elijah ben Solomon Zalman, the Vilno Gaon (1720–1797), successfully opposed it. Elsewhere, the opposition of the rabbis subsided. A sort of coexistence of two religious institutions emerged: the rabbi (*rav*) was the religious functionary, the expert in religious law, while the *tsadik* or *rebe*, the hasidic leader, was the mentor of the fold. Eventually a synthesis also occurred between hasidic expressiveness and rabbinical learning. It is exemplified by the action of the Rebe of Ger, the hasidic leader who restored Talmudic study. This synthesis, with strong hasidic elements, remained prominent in Poland, especially in the small towns and among the older generation, until the very extinction of the Jewish community by the Nazis.

Hasidism was an indigenous movement and it swept Polish Jewry. In contrast, the other major Jewish movement of the same century, the *Haskala* (Enlightenment), which won over the Jews of Western Europe, drew its inspiration from European Enlightenment. Although Hasidism brought about major changes in the Jewish community, it did not alter the traditional attitudes of that community to the outside world. In contrast, the central goal of the Enlightenment was to change the nature of the relationship between the Jews and the dominant society. Hasidism accepted the tradition that only peripheral (chiefly economic) contacts should be made with the Poles; the Enlightenment aimed at fuller participation in and social integration into non-Jewish society. Those inspired by Enlightenment aspired to become part of the new enlightened society which they thought was in the making in Europe.

The antithesis between these two movements, one indigenous and the other inspired by the outside, throws light on why the Enlightenment came so late to Poland (after it had passed its high point in Germany) and failed to take hold among the Jewish masses. It reached Poland after its partitions (which took place in 1772, 1793, and 1795) and fared differently in different parts. After the Congress of Vienna in 1815, much of former Poland came under Russian rule as the semiautonomous Kingdom of Poland, also known as Congress Poland. It is to be distinguished from the part of Poland under direct Russian rule, the region known as Lithuania-Belorussia. The Haskala scarcely existed as a movement in Congress Poland, but was much more prominent in Lithuania-Belorussia. It was most influential in Galicia, which was under Austrian rule. The founders of the Galician Haskala were mostly from wealthy families—Nachman Krochmal from Żółkiew, Joseph Perl from Tarnopol and Shlomo Yehuda Rapaport from Lvov.

Krochmal was the author of *Moreh Nevukhei Hazman* (Guide to the Perplexed of our Time), which was concerned with the historical manifestations of Judaism. He is considered to be the spiritual father of nineteenth-century Jewish nationalism. Rapaport was known as a determined opponent of the German *Wissenschaft des Judentums* because of its assimilationist character. The Galician followers of the Enlightenment (*maskilim*), in contrast to the German ones, retained Hebrew as the language of modern Jewish scholarship; they also stressed the cultural importance of the mastery of German as the language of European culture. Outwardly, there appeared little to differentiate the early Galician maskilim from the traditionalist Jews—they wore beards and traditional Jewish attire; but they combined secular worldly knowledge with learning of the Torah. They were convinced that such knowledge would lead to the shedding of superstitions and strengthening of the moral values of the religion.

Some leading maskilim of Congress Poland also valued and held on to the Jewish tradition. One was Abraham Stern, who combined mathematics with a profound Talmudic erudition. (He was the inventor of a threshing machine and a calculator.) Another was Chaim Selig Słonimski of Warsaw who, like Stern, remained an observant Jew but devoted himself to scientific studies. More often, Haskala led to sharper breaks with distinctive Jewish patterns. The maskilim of Congress Poland tended to criticize Jewish society from the perspective of enlightened Western society, measuring Jewish institutions against the institutions of Western society, which they accepted as the norm. Thus, Jewish institutions seemed deficient to them, an attitude that marked the beginning of the erosion of Jewish pride.

The pronouncements and activities of the maskilim were viewed with apprehension by the traditional leaders and elders of the Jewish community, to whom they represented the dissolution of the traditional society and the abandonment of the Jewish people by Jews. Traditional leaders saw Enlightment as the first step toward conversion, and this prophecy was partially fulfilled. The children or grandchildren of many leading maskilim converted to Christianity. The Słonimskis are a case in point: Antoni Słonimski, the prominent Polish writer and grandson of the strictly observant maskil Chaim Selig Słonimski, was born Christian. Among the maskilim of Congress Poland there was a prominent wing which aspired to full assimilation with Polish culture and full integration into Polish society. It is to the Haskala then that one can trace the origin of the assimilationist group in Poland (which began in the nineteenth century and is tied to Poland's struggle for independence), as well as of modern Jewish nationalist movements.

With the disappearance of Poland as an independent state in 1795, Jews fared differently under the jurisdiction of the various partition powers. Jews in Galicia, under Austrian rule, fared best in terms of political rights and protection under the law, since Austria allowed a large measure of cultural and political autonomy to the nationalities under its rule. A smaller number of Jews in the Posen region and in Pomerania came under Prussian jurisdiction. They were politically worse off but economically in a better position than the Galician Jews. But the greatest number of Jews found themselves under Russian rule and their situation, both economic and political, was by far the worst.

In all parts of Poland the Poles, suffering from the decline of their country, became more than ever conscious of the existence of a Jewish problem. A new awareness spread among them of a population in their midst that possessed an autonomous communal life, a separate language, a different religion, and customs strikingly dissimilar from those of Poles. There was a general preoccupation with this Jewish population, with its relation to the national and spiritual aspirations of the suffering Polish nation. Prevailing attitudes ranged from dislike to hate of the Jews, on whom the responsibility for Poland's plight was placed. Generally, the Jews served as a convenient scapegoat for Poles. This found expression in the provisions concerning Jews, part of the plan for the codification of Polish law that was presented at the Diet by Chancellor Andrzej Zamoyski. The plan called for the confinement of Jews in separate parts of cities and towns and the expulsion of those Jews who were without an occupation. Luckily, the whole plan for the codification of Polish law was rejected by the Diet in 1780.

But there were also some distinguished Poles of the time who became especially friendly toward the Jews. They saw similarities in the fate of the Polish and Jewish peoples. Generally, these friendly Poles hoped to reform and Polonize the Jews. Foremost among them was Tadeusz Czacki, a historian, economist, and statesman. In the important post that he occupied in the Polish Treasury (1786–92) he was responsible for the supervision of the affairs of the Jewish communities. His first-hand contact with Jews lead to his sympathetic understanding of their situation. This reflects itself in the treatment he accorded to Jews in his book, *Treatise on Jews and Karaites* (Vilno, 1807), as well as in his pamphlet, "Reflections on the Reform of Jews," which appeared in 1788.

Maciej Butrymowicz, a representative to the Polish Diet, was also friendly to the Jews. In 1789, before the second partition of Poland, his sympathetic pamphlet, "The Way to Reform the Jews in Poland," appeared. The author blamed the failure of the Jews to Polonize on the Poles themselves, who treated them as a "foreign and separate nation . . . removed them from the right of citizenship, put special taxes on them, and viewed their religion with disdain." At the same time, said the author: "Having done that, it was demanded that the Jew carry his chains with dignity and kiss the hand that put the chain on his neck." *

The preoccupation with the Jewish question is seen in the deliberations of the Four Years' Diet, 1788–1792, which was summoned to rescue Poland from impending ruin. Although the nobles were largely opposed to any changes in the status of the Jews, various proposals were presented. Some aimed at greater restriction of the rights of Jews, but the liberals, who were very vocal, championed equal rights for Jews as a way to reform them; reform in this instance meant making Jews resemble Poles culturally and socially. The liberals were headed by the aforementioned Maciej Butrymowicz, Tadeusz Czacki, as well as Hugo Kołłątaj, Jacek Jezierski, and Tomasz Wawrzecki. None of the proposals were acceptable to the representatives of Polish Jewry. Obviously Jews opposed the reactionaries' proposals to restrict their rights. But they also opposed the liberals' proposals to end the autonomous power of the kehillot, to compel Jews to change their distinctive dress, to send their children to Polish schools, to limit the number of holidays they observed, and to limit the age of marriage.

Their opposition was expressed in the petition to the King Stanisław Augustus Poniatowski, who was friendly to the Jews. It was presented to the King by his Jewish plenipotentiary, Abram Hirszowicz. As a result, the King's secretary, Scypion Piattoli, de-

---

* Hilary Nussbaum, *Żydzi w Polsce, Historya Żydów od Mojżesza do Epoki Obecnej*, vol. 5 (Warsaw, 1890), p. 338.

vised a compromise plan, which among other things called for the continuation of the kehillot (but with the language of their deliberations changed to Polish) and the continuation of separate Jewish schools (but in which the teaching of Polish would be compulsory).

However, none of the reform plans were adopted at the Four Years' Diet. The only provision concerning Jews that was passed was that they, like the other inhabitants, could not be arrested without a court warrant. With the advent of the second partition of Poland in 1793, all attempts at legal reforms concerning Jews collapsed.

And after the partitions, some of the ideologues of Polish independence, influenced by Western democratic ideas, appealed to their "Israelite brothers" or "people of the Old Testament" (*Starozakonni*), for help to resurrect a Poland where all citizens would be equal irrespective of their religion. Thus, the nineteenth century marks among the Poles the beginning of the idea of separation—in the case of Jews—of religious belief from national identity, which never came to fruition in the independent Poland of the twentieth century. But in the nineteenth century some Polish Jews, especially from among the rich, responded to the above promise and expected its fulfillment in an independent Poland, free of anti-Semitism. They supported with money and fought in the Polish insurrections. Berek Joselewicz (1770–1809), who participated in the Kościuszko uprising and died defending Poland's independence, became their hero.

Many Jews, particularly in Russian Poland, were becoming pauperized in the nineteenth century, but a small number became rich. This growth of wealthy Jewish families is tied to the beginning of industrialization, in which some Jewish families played an eminent role. The emergence of a new rich Jewish bourgeoisie in large cities, such as Warsaw and Lódź, which started at the beginning of the nineteenth century, reached its peak between the two Polish uprisings, 1831 and 1863.

The assimilationist movement began in Poland in the 1820s among some of these bourgeois families. Among them were the wealthy merchant and banking families, such as the Natansons, Toeplitzes, Kronenbergs, and Wawelbergs. Although there were regional differences in the movement, an overall pattern was apparent. The immediate reference group of those who chose to assimilate, the "progressives" (*postępowi*), were the wealthy, assimilated Jews of Germany and France. By attacking the Talmud as the source of superstition, some of the intellectuals among the progressives aimed at complete religious reform. High on their list of reform was the replacement of yeshivot by modern seminaries, and they established a Rabbinical Seminary (*Szkoła Rabinów*) in Warsaw. The post of director was offered to the prominent maskil Abraham Stern; he turned it down, since he opposed religious reform and thought that the school would produce rabbis not truly devoted to their religion. A less observant and more acculturated maskil, Antoni Eisenbaum, filled the post.

The department of Hebrew and Bible was entrusted to Abraham Buchner, who years later wrote a German pamphlet entitled The Worthlessness of the Talmud (*Der Talmud in seiner Nichtigkeit*, 1848). Not one graduate of this Rabbinical Seminary became a rabbi. But a number of the graduates occupied prominent places in Polish cultural life. The editor of the first encyclopedia in the Polish language (*Encyklopedia Powszechna*), Maurycy Orgelbrand, was a graduate of this school.

The center of the progressives' activities on behalf of religious reform was the German Synagogue on Daniłowiczowska Street in Warsaw, founded by a German Jew in 1802. (This was the forerunner of the famous synagogue on Tłumackie Street, opened in 1878, which was still traditional but with sermons in the Polish language.) In Lvov the Committee for a Progressive Synagogue began meeting in 1840 in the home of Dr. Emanuel Blumenfeld. It resulted in the founding of the Progressive Synagogue, into which in 1898 an organ and mixed choir were introduced. These symbols of drastic departure from the traditional service made it an anathema to the Orthodox. Despite the efforts of the progressives, the religious reform movement did not succeed in becoming institutionalized in Poland, as others did in Germany, England, and the United States. This is an important fact bearing on the distinctive pattern of secularization among Polish Jews, especially in the interwar period.

The assimilationist Jews accepted the definition of the Jewish problem as it was formulated by Polish intellectuals, albeit by those sympathetic to the Jews. These Polish intellectuals held that the solution lay in the Polonization of the Jews, which was the road to their equality in citizenship. And the small number of Jews who believed this, the progressives, proceeded to assume that Jews could and ought to become Poles of "Mosaic faith," *wyznania mojżeszowego*, different from others only in the private realm of religion (which, too, had to be substantially reformed). By disengaging themselves from traditional Jewishness, they thought that they would enter a life more abundant, for they found the Jewish community narrow and confining. They therefore renounced Jewish separatism in Poland and proclaimed the goal of Polonization of the Jewish population. These "Poles of Mosaic faith" began to participate in the major patriotic and cultural activities, which were aimed at promoting Polish culture under foreign rule and reviving Polish independence. Many wealthy Jews gave financial support to the clandestine army and the young joined as volunteers in the revolts. (Later we shall see that in the interwar period the assimilationists pointed with pride to their kin who had fought in these revolts.)

In the cultural and scientific life of Poland, especially in Warsaw, sons of these wealthy bankers, industrialists, and merchants occupied an important place. Among the distinguished Polish scientists of that time were Jakub Natanson, professor of chemistry, and Ludwik Hirszfeld, professor of anatomy. That Jews were able to figure prominently in the cultural life of Poland was in large measure due to subsidies by rich Jews of some of the literary and scientific journals, as well as outright ownership of large publishing houses and major Polish newspapers. Henryk Natanson owned one of the largest publishing houses; Nathan Gluecksberg owned the largest. The newspaper *Gazeta Polska* was owned by Kronenberg and *Gazeta Handlowa* by Kempner. Ludwik Natanson, upon his return from medical studies abroad, founded in 1843 the im-

portant weekly journal of medicine, *Tygodnik Lekarski*. The influential periodical *Kłosy*, so central to the Polish cultural life of that
day, was published by Salomon Lewenthal.

I have called the Jews who chose this course in the nineteenth century "assimilationists," to indicate that for them assimilation was both a conscious program and a method of solving the
Jewish problem in Poland. Their choice was the promise of individual freedom at the cost of dissolution of the Jews as a group. However, the Polish bourgeoisie feared that the granting of citizenship
to Jews would further strengthen the Jews' economic position and
so opposed it violently. In their attacks, they did not spare the assimilated Jews, whom they labeled "the Jewish autocracy" and
charged with damaging the country through economic exploitation
and detrimental influence on Polish culture. Nevertheless, in
1863 the Jews of Congress Poland were granted full rights of citizenship, including the right to vote, by the Marquis Alexander
Wielopolski, the head of the civil government in the Kingdom of
Poland, on behalf of Alexander II of Russia. (These rights had
been granted earlier in the province of Posen, under Prussia, and
later, in 1867, in Austrian Poland.) But then came the failure of
the Polish uprising of 1863, in which some Jews fought valiantly.
It was followed by the Czar's revoking the rights of Jews granted
by Wielopolski.

The result was the strengthening of Polish loyalty among
many Jews, especially the assimilated. After the dashed hopes of
freedom, young Polish patriots turned away from romantic nationalism and toward the ideas of positivism. They now saw the solution to Poland's weakness and ills in the economic development of
the country. Among the advocates of positivism, assimilated Jews
figured prominently. Inspired by its ideas, they viewed the future
with optimism. After all, wrote one of the leading assimilationists,
Leopold Kronenberg, to the Polish writer Józef Ignacy Kra-
szewski—into stock market transactions, religious or racial considerations do not enter.

In their enthusiasm for Polonization and the zeal with which
they pursued it, the wealthy bourgeois families weathered the first
broad reaction that set in against the ideas of economic positivism.

The Polish conservatives accused the positivists of betraying the venerable Polish ideal of nationhood. The Church condemned them as weakening the religious fibre of the nation. To radicals, influenced by socialist ideas, positivism was the philosophy of economic exploitation. And the populists asserted that under the cloak of economic positivism, people who were not Poles—Jews and Germans—became enriched while the Polish people remained impoverished.

The assassination of Czar Alexander II in 1881 was followed by anti-Jewish violence in Congress Poland, as well as in Russia. The eminent assimilationist historian, Dr. Hilary Nussbaum, in dealing with the events of the day pointed to the decisive role played by the Polish press in arousing the hate of Poles against Jews. The press, he said, "in seeking out the negative and harmful sides" of Jews, hammered into Polish heads contradictory accusations against them: that the Jew was spreading both superstition and atheism, that the poor Jew was a burden to the country and that the rich Jew became rich at the expense of the Polish people. Anti-Jewish sentiments flourished and the atmosphere of the 1880s was charged with hate and violence. The words of the Polish novelist Eliza Orzeszkowa, written in 1881, testify both to this atmosphere and to the fact that Jews did have some Polish defenders.

> In case of outbreaks, which are very probable among us, we have decided to defend and protect with all our might the wronged ones. The stupid and dark masses will probably embark on crimes and madness. But let at least a handful of Polish intelligentsia protest before mankind and history not only with words and deeds, but with our lives. I for one and a few more are ready, even if we are to perish, to stand between the raging wave and the doors of the victims.*

The defenders were few. They did not perish although they stood bravely by the Jews; however the Jews suffered violence and humiliation. If this wave of anti-Semitism, including pogroms, was

* Cited in the introduction by G. Pauszer Kłonowska to Eliza Orzeszkowa, Z Jednego Strumienia (Warsaw, 1960), p. 6.

an important factor in containing the spread of assimilationism in other strata of the Jewish population, as Nussbaum asserted, it did not reverse the process among the wealthy assimilationists. By then they were economically well entrenched and felt secure. For example, Ludwik Natanson, the formal head of the Jewish community in Warsaw, issued an appeal after the pogrom of 1881 in which he declared that the only remedy for anti-Semitism is for Jews "to come closer" (*zbliżyć*) to the Polish people, to give up their distinctive language and dress, "the external signs which create division" between Jews and Poles. The assimilationists, and especially their ideologues, interpreted the Polish reaction against them (which according to their credo should not have taken place) as a temporary setback on the road to progress through assimilation. This interpretation is worth noting, for it became a standardized explanation among the assimilationists and reappeared again and again until World War II, and even in communist Poland. According to the assimilationists, anti-Semitism was a foreign import, alien to the Polish spirit and contradictory to a traditional Polish tolerance. Assimilation was among other things a debt of gratitude that Jews owed to Poland, which had embraced them when other nations were rejecting them. The Jewish masses' resistance to this "progressive" course was attributed by the ideologues of assimilation to ignorance, superstition, and the fanaticism of the rabbis. And they set before themselves the task of "civilizing" the Jewish population, Polonizing it, and ridding the religion of superstition.

This stance of the assimilationists comes through clearly in the note on which Hilary Nussbaum finished the final volume of his five-volume history of the Jews in Poland:

> The progressives, undiscouraged by the accusations against their faith and race, do not cease to march without fear on the road of progress, nurturing humanist ideals, fulfilling faithfully the responsibilities of citizenship, and showing themselves worthy of the rights which were granted to them. They do this despite the fact that from *time to time* their rights are curtailed.[*]

[*] Hilary Nussbaum, *Żydzi w Polsce, Historya Żydów od Mojżesza do Epoki Obecnej*, Vol. 5 (Warsaw, 1890), p. 448. Emphasis and translation mine.

But the Jewish masses suffered during such periods and could not accept the benign interpretation which allowed the assimilationists to cling to assimilation. The anti-Semitic agitation and the pogrom of 1881 destroyed for them the idea that becoming like the people among whom they lived would save them.

The credibility of the assimilationists was undermined by the growing anti-Semitism. The assimilationists had succeeded in occupying prominent offices within the Jewish community of Warsaw, Lvov, and a few other big cities. Ludwik Natanson held, for a quarter of a century (1871–1896), the post of president of the Warsaw kehilla. These assimilationists tended to be viewed as intermediaries between Jews and Poles, but the tide turned against them as the Jewish population lost confidence in them and saw them as betrayers of their interests. That many of the assimilationists were converting to Christianity by the end of the century must have played a part in this loss of trust. For example, the foremost banker and railroad builder, Leopold Kronenberg, converted, as did both sons of the publisher Samuel Orgelbrand, Hipolit and Mieczysław.

Advancing anti-Semitism put the brakes on assimilationist tendencies in Poland and strained the tenuous links between the assimilationists and the Jewish people. Rejection of assimilation, however, did not mean that the cracks in the traditional structure were mended and that the traditional pattern of life had been restored. On the contrary, it continued to be assaulted from new and broader bases. The number of Jews in rural areas was decreasing, forced out by Czarist orders. The growing urbanization and proletarianization of the Jewish masses produced increasing secularization, especially among the young. Jewish workers were flocking into trade unions and organizing strikes to fight against the inhuman conditions that prevailed in the large industrial establishments, especially the textile mills of Łódź, owned by Jewish industrialists.

The Jewish population was becoming strongly politicized through union organization and political movements. The second half of the nineteenth century signified the rise of modern Jewish nationalism in Poland. It culminated at the end of the century in two major movements, the Zionist and the Bundist. Both fought for the right of the Jews to live as a distinct national entity. The first wanted them to achieve this by returning to the ancient homeland; the latter by struggling for it in their centuries' old homeland. These movements attracted some youths of middle class background who had become disenchanted with the idea of assimilation. Their ranks swelled with the influx of a large number of working class youth. These movements in turn acted as strong agents of secularization and were tearing youths of all social classes away from the traditional pattern of life. They represented the first major attempts to organize the Jewish population for secular and independent political activity.

The socialist Bund insisted that Jewish workers involved in a revolutionary struggle for socialism had a right to continue being Jews and a duty to recognize the specifically Jewish problems, not faced by Polish workers. As for the Zionist movement, its ideology proclaimed that the only solution of the Jewish question in Poland, as elsewhere, was in a mass exodus and the achievement of national sovereignty in their ancient homeland. This solution followed from the Zionist premise that the social definition of Jews as undesirable strangers, and its accompanying anti-Semitic manifestations, were inevitable results of the Jews' not having a land of their own. For Jews were a nation and, contrary to the fallacious conception of the Enlightenment, not simply a religious denomination. The appeal of Zionism, especially to the young, lay in its promise of a national renaissance of the Jewish people. Most Jews in Poland spoke Yiddish and some were already linguistically acculturated to Polish or German. But enthusiasm was kindled to transform Hebrew, which had remained alive as the language of daily prayer and religious scholarship, into a spoken language. Zionism held out the promise that the Jewish people could restore for themselves the normal conditions of national existence, of which they had been deprived for two millennia. This promise fired the imagination of the young: they were excited by the idea of a land of their own; they were inspired by the idea of a Jewish cultural revival, in which religion, if at all, would be only one form of creative national expression; and they were prompted by the no-

tion of socially regenerating the Jewish people, who, according to
Zionist theorists, had been forced into an anomalous occupational
structure in exile. Their slogan became the "productivization" of
the Jews by creating large strata of farmers and workers in place of
the petty traders. Manual labor, which until that time had been
looked down upon as a mark of low social status, was glorified as a
salutary social and psychological force, to be regarded with pride.

The Zionist movement manifested itself in numerous political
shades, including extreme socialist radicalism. But the socialist
Bund was opposed to all forms of Zionism, including socialist Zionism. It held that Zionism meant running away from the problem,
for Palestine could not solve the Jewish problem. And yet Zionists
and Bundists had a certain profound similarity, in addition to that
of being nationalists. They shared a disdain for the traditional Jewish attitudes of accommodation and nonviolent resistance, which
had proved so functional for Jewish continuity in the past. They
both advocated militancy, believing that Jews should be ready to
defend themselves and fight for their rights.

The similarities of the two movements, which visualized
themselves as diametrically opposite and fought each other relent-
lessly, were keenly perceived by the traditionalists, led by the
rabbis and rebes. Both movements were seen by them as undermining traditional Jewish life in one of the few places where it
remained intact. The rabbis and rebes believed that it was incumbent upon them to keep the Jewish people from falling prey to the
illusion that the solution to their basic problem could come in any
way but through God. They rejected Zionism not because it advocated a return to Zion (they too longed for it), but because the
movement placed its trust in secular means to return the Jewish
people to their ancient homeland. Such illusions, they feared, were
likely to bring more tragedy, as the false Messiahs had done in the
past. Some rabbis, however, embraced Zionism, among them the
founders and leaders of its religious wing, Mizrachi.

Soon to the other sins of which the Jews were accused by
Poles were added Jewish nationalism and radicalism. The accusations of radicalism, the fears that the Jews were planning to destroy from within the Polish heritage which the Poles had pre-

served bravely under foreign rule, became acute as some assimilated Jews moved into leadership positions in the Polish Socialist Party, the Social Democratic Party of the Kingdom of Poland and Lithuania (the forerunner of the Polish Communist Party), and the Communist Party. For example, Herman Lieberman, Emile Haecker, Stanisław Mendelsohn, Feliks Perl, and Bernard Szapiro were prominent in the first; Rosa Luxemburg, Jan Tyszka (Leo Jogiches), and Józef Unschlicht in the latter; and Adolf Warski (Warszawski), Henryk Walecki, and Jerzy Ryng (Heryng) in the last. Poles were hardly aware that such individuals were mostly devoid of a Jewish self-identity.

After the revolution of 1905 came a new wave of anti-Semitism, which reached its crescendo in 1912. Its specific target were the "Litvaks," who had come to Poland to escape Russian anti-Semitism. They concentrated in industrial cities, such as Warsaw and Lódź, where some of them prospered. The intelligentsia among them played a major part in spreading the ideas of Jewish nationalism to Poland. The Litvaks were accused both of Russifying Poland and spreading the subversive doctrine of a separate Jewish nationality on Polish soil.

In 1912 hatred erupted during and following the election campaign to the Fourth Imperial Duma, the parliament of Russia. How illusory the right of citizenship was for Polish Jews was proven then. The city of Warsaw had a right to one deputy in the Duma, to be elected by a general electoral college of the city. The citizens of Warsaw voted for the members of this electoral college and a number of Jews were elected. The Jewish electors in turn voted overwhelmingly for the Polish Socialist candidate, Władyslaw Jagiełło, a nonentity in the political arena until then, to represent Warsaw. They voted for him despite the warnings of the prominent assimilationists that they vote for the candidate of the Polish National Bloc, Professor Jan Kucharzewski, a well known moderate. However, since he had formerly been a member of the National Democratic Party (*Endecja*), he was perhaps erroneously associated in the minds of the Jewish delegates with anti-Semitism. As the vote of the Jewish delegates was responsible for Kucharzewski's defeat, the vote caused resentment and bitterness on the part of the Polish population that had supported the Bloc. The anti-Semitic wing of the National Democratic Party became strengthened. This party, established in 1897 by members of the radical intelligentsia, went through a number of splits in 1907–10, when many intellectuals and representatives of organized labor left the party. In order to maintain their strength among the Polish masses, the party increasingly relied on anti-Semitic slogans. These slogans proved especially effective as the Jewish population was increasing both in numbers and proportions in the bigger cities. The natural increase of Jews was larger than that of Poles. Also, the Litvaks added visibly to the growth of the Jewish population.

Anti-Jewish excesses erupted when the results of the vote for the representative to the Duma became known. A boycott of Jewish enterprises throughout Poland was proclaimed by the leader of the National Democratic Party, Roman Dmowski (1864–1939). He published an inexpensive daily, *Gazeta Polska*, dedicated to fostering the economic and social boycott of Jews. The masthead's slogan, "patronize your own," rapidly became the slogan of the land: in Polish, *Swój do Swego po Swoje*. Simultaneously with the economic boycott, a campaign was launched in the press against the Jews, accusing them of being Poland's enemies and of betraying Polish interests.

Thus, resentment and hate raged against Jews in the remaining years before Poland gained its independence as a result of World War I. Anti-Jewish attitudes, feelings, and activities constituted a strong link between diverse elements of the Polish nation. But Jews were divided in their response. Large numbers continued to find shelter and solace in their religion and in their old traditions. No longer bound legally to their distinctive dress, they clung to it as a mark of their Jewishness. However, growing numbers, especially among the youth, rejected the religion and the old ways, turning to national ideologies as guides for forging new ways. The abandonment of distinctive dress often became to them a mark of emancipation. It was a time of sharp divisions as to what constituted Jewishness. But it was also a time of the upsurgence of Jewish national consciousness, which filled the voids of collapsed religious faith. Rebuffed by the extreme nationalism of the Poles, young Jews responded with a nationalism of their own. But by the beginning of World War I, the dominant Polish sentiment was expressed in their popular slogan: "On the banks of the Vistula there is no room for two nationalities." In an atmosphere epitomized by this slogan was ushered in the penultimate period in the centuries' long coexistence of two peoples.

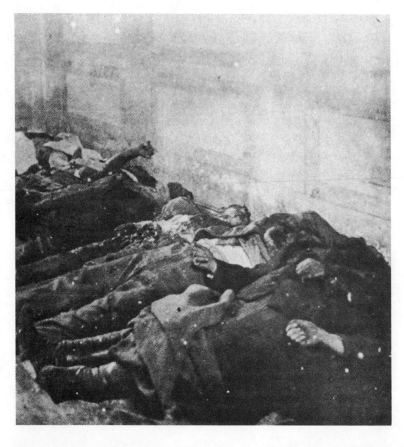

*The declaration of Polish independence in 1918 was followed by
pogroms in many places . . .*
CORPSES OF VICTIMS, PIŃSK, POLESIE PROVINCE, 1919 (YIVO INSTI-
TUTE FOR JEWISH RESEARCH)

II
The Social Definition
of the Jews in Poland

"We thought it would all turn out very differently."
"What? The Russian Revolution?" asked Zachary.
"Not only the Russian Revolution—everything!"
And, half to himself, he added with a sigh:
"The liberation of Poland—
don't you understand?" *

Polish independence was ushered in with a wave of fierce anti-Semitism, a gruesomely fitting inauguration of the kind of treatment that Jews would receive in the independent Poland. The declaration of Polish independence in 1918 was followed by pogroms in many places. As soon as the Germans withdrew from Warsaw, signs calling for a boycott of Jewish stores appeared throughout the capital of free Poland. Such events brought disillusionment to those Jews, particularly the young among them, who—stirred by the ideas and slogans of Polish freedom—worked and fought for its independence. Reality was piercing their long-nurtured dream of the beloved *ojczyzna,* fatherland, in its resurrection purified of the old malady of anti-Semitism. For them, as

* From the fictional conversation between a Warsaw Jew, Hurvitz—a Polish patriot involved in the clandestine Polish independence movement—and the Russian Jew, Zachary Mirkin who visited him after Poland gained its independence, in: Sholem Asch, *Three Cities,* (New York: G. P. Putnam's Sons), 1933, pp. 898–99.

for the masses of Jews who had no such illusions, peace did not bring respite.

The suffering of the Poles under the scourge of war was compensated by the rebirth of their country's independence: thus the Polish people often interpreted the experiences of World War I, for they saw in their suffering the price they paid for Poland's freedom. The greater agony of the Jewish people during World War I could not be interpreted in this manner, since it was followed by violence and oppression. During the war, Jews were blamed by the soldiers on each side of the conflict for helping the other side. This accounted for the extra measure of brutality meted out to Jews. In independent Poland the situation of the large Jewish minority—over 3 million in number and constituting a tenth of the total population of the country—was, in some respects, essentially no different than in partitioned Poland. Regional differences in their situation—in the former Russian, Austrian, and German parts—continued for some time. But these differences were becoming greatly reduced as shifts in population resulted in mingling of people from different regions and as Polish institutions grew stronger year after year. Throughout Poland the Jews fared worse in the period between the two world wars than in the independent Commonwealth Kingdom of Poland before its decline.

It would be senseless for me to try to convey the horrors of the violence against Jews during World War I and the immediate postwar period to those of the Holocaust and post-Holocaust generations who have become accustomed to the sight and sound of the ultimate of horrors. Neither do I aim at a historical documentation of events. The figures of killed and injured, although they seemed horrible in the period they occurred, even then failed to communicate the "terrible condition of apprehension and anxiety" under which the Jews found themselves.[1] In the hope of providing an insight into this condition, I can present excerpts from autobiographies and diaries of young Jews, collected in the 1930s.* They

---

* In the Introduction is found a brief explanation of how these biographies and diaries were collected by the YIVO Institute for Jewish Research in Vilno and how they survived World War II. For a fuller explanation, see: Moses Kligsberg, "Child and Adolescent Behavior Under Stress—An Analytical Topical Guide to a Collection of Autobiographies . . . in Poland," *Terminal Progress Report*, YIVO, Institute for Jewish Research (New York: 1965).

The pogroms brought disillusionment to the young who were stirred by the ideas and slogans of Polish independence . . .

A POGROM SURVIVOR, KIELCE, NOVEMBER 5, 1918 (YIVO INSTITUTE FOR JEWISH RESEARCH)

afford a glimpse of the *subjective* side of these events that generated the social climate in which the Jews had to make their first adjustment to living in independent Poland.

From Recollections of Violence

Here is a view of the pogroms with which some Poles celebrated their freedom, as a young man describes his experiences in his home town near Cracow, when he was eight years old:

> The pogrom began. They broke down doors and windows.
> . . . They took everything they could carry. . . . they rushed
> like demons. We cried, we hid in cellars and in barns but we
> were ready for death. The pogrom didn't subside; it grew. The
> gang leaders who gave directions were well-dressed men. The
> more we pleaded with them for mercy and the more they felt
> like masters of the situation, the madder they became. . . . We
> cried for our martyrs: for the slaughtered fathers, sons and
> brothers. . . . I ran to the woods [to find shelter]. I was
> afraid. In every Pole I saw a murderer.[2]

Such violence was common in the first period of Poland's new existence. A mission from Britain collected documentation showing that pogroms and anti-Jewish excesses were committed in one hundred towns and villages during the short period of three months, November 1918 through January 1919.[3]

The period of pogroms was followed by violence meted out against Jews by the invading Red Army. The cruelty of the soldiers of the "glorious revolutionary army" shocked those young Jews who sympathized with the noble goals of the Russian Revolution. The pathos of these events comes through in an entry in the diary of a seventeen-year-old high school girl. Typical of many among the rising young intelligentsia, she was from a relatively well-to-do family, enamored with Polish literature and culture and sympathetic to the Russian Revolution:

> Hell broke loose at home. Father cannot control his pain
> because of the murder and robbery of so many Jews. And he

> considers me the culprit. . . . I hear the voice of my father, full
> of pain: "We Jews suffer everywhere, from pogroms, from rob-
> beries. Oh God! Have we sinned so greatly, that you are punish-
> ing us so heavily? And it is because of you," he said almost with
> hate to me. "Here you have your socialists, your Bolsheviks,
> who rape, murder, and steal! This is your socialist freedom: the
> poor Jew is the victim, he is made responsible. . . ." I couldn't
> listen anymore. I thought that the rushing blood would split my
> head. I wanted quiet. I wanted to forget the world.[4]

When Poland was attacked by the Red Army in 1920, some
Jews—persistent in their Polish patriotism—volunteered to serve
in the Polish army. They, like some Jewish soldiers and officers
who were part of the regular army, were detained instead in the
military camp in Jabłonna, where they were kept in separate bar-
racks in the "Jewish section" and treated as potential traitors.[5]
Because of the radicalism of some of the secularized younger Jews,
all Jews became suspect of sympathy with the Bolsheviks. Also, in

When Poland was attacked by the Soviet Union in 1920, Jewish
soldiers and officers of the Polish Army were detained in the mili-
tary camp in Jablonna, treated as potential traitors . . .
SOME OF THESE SOLDIERS, AFTER THEIR INTERNMENT, AND THEIR
FRIENDS (YIVO INSTITUTE FOR JEWISH RESEARCH)

the governmental bodies set up by the Bolsheviks in the territories occupied by the Red Army, Polish communists of Jewish background figured prominently in both higher and lower ranks. That these communists were as ruthless in their dealings with the local Jewish population as with the non-Jewish, Poles were unaware. To them Jews were cooperating with the enemy. Also, they tended to be ignorant of or quickly to forget those instances where, in towns heavily populated by Jews (like Lomża) Jews old and young fought bravely against the Bolsheviks. The Jewish press ran full page ads on the part of various Jewish organizations, urging Jews to help in the defense and reconstruction of the country and to buy war bonds.[6] But at the same time, a part of the Polish press prominently projected the image of the Jews as sympathetic to the Bolsheviks and aiding them whenever possible.[7]

As soon as the Russian Army withdrew, having been defeated by the Poles in a stunning victory, Polish soldiers, aided by civilians, turned against the Jews. Allegations were made about the treachery of the Jews who supposedly had helped the Bolsheviks in many ways. Rumors were flying about Jews clandestinely pouring boiling water on the heads of passing Polish soldiers, about Jews maintaining secret telephone connections and feeding the Bolsheviks information concerning the whereabout of the Polish arms, or about Jews guiding the Bolsheviks in the robbing of Poles. Earlier in a letter to Paderewski, dated May 4, 1919, in which Piłsudski described his victorious entry to Vilno, he wrote: "With great effort I prevented a pogrom which simply hung in the air."[8] A favorite sport of some soldiers was to catch Jews and forcibly cut their beards.

Terrorism against Jews was rampant on trains and in railroad stations.[9] In some captured areas, kangaroo courts were speedily set up to try Jews for treason and their verdicts resulted in the killing of those tried. How far-fetched the accusations of Jewish betrayal were is illustrated by the killing of the ultra-Orthodox rabbi of Płock, Hayim Schapiro, who was arrested while praying on his balcony wearing his *tephilin* (phylacteries) and extending his hands to heaven. He was accused of giving signals to the Bolsheviks.[10] The shock that Jews experienced when Rabbi Schapiro was executed on such a preposterous charge is illustrated in the description of the event in the diary of the then seventeen year old girl, quoted above:

> Those who kill, murder, rob, have government protection but innocent people are shot. I didn't cry but, oh, how my heart ached. Rabbi Schapiro was shot. I am not a clerical sympathizer, but how could one accuse this religious fanatic, who didn't know a word of Polish or Russian? [of aiding the Bolsheviks.] He was shot, the father of eight children. Why? Why? If there were a God . . . he would not allow the spilling of this innocent blood. At two o'clock they read the verdict to the rabbi and at three he was shot. Jews wanted to put up much money as bail, until a delegation could get in touch with Warsaw [appeal to the government]. But the beasts were thirsty for blood. The rabbi was composed. He said to one Jew: "I am dying innocently but I am glad to serve as a scapegoat for all Jews. Don't forget my children." And when he was going to be shot, he took off his rabbinical hat, wrapped himself in his prayer shawl, and recited *Shema' Israel* [Hear, Oh Israel . . .] He fell. I still hear today my father crying. I would have never thought that in this slight man, in this rabbi, there would be such a strong spirit. At three o'clock he was killed and already at three-thirty there were announcements all over town. The Poles read them, laughed and applauded. The pain of my father, a believing Jew but not fanatical, is indescribable. And I feel so sad.[11]

The anti-Jewish violence immediately after the end of World War I appears to have been largely spontaneous. It was followed by more planned violence, inspired and often led by a major political party, the National Democratic Party popularly known as the *Endek* party or *Endecja*, whose anti-Jewish activities prior to independence we touched on in the preceding chapter. Whether spontaneous or planned, the later violence was an extreme expression of the general reaction of Poles against the growing claims and demands for equality by the Jews.

Claims of Jewish Equality vs.
Claims of Polish Superiority

Independent Poland came into existence, after a century and a half of foreign rule, "because of a combination of unpredictable coincidences." [12] Foremost among them was the concurrent defeat by the Allies of two of the three powers that had partitioned and ruled Poland, Germany and Austria, and the weakening of Russia by revolution. The peace terms dictated by the victorious Allied and Associated Powers—none of whom had taken part in partition of Poland—included an independent state. Under the sovereignty of the new state were to be placed not only Poles but other large ethnic groups with distinctive language, culture, and religion. But "Western opinion had been shocked by reports of anti-Jewish riots and massacres in Poland," at the end of war and the beginning of peace. These happenings "were denied by the Poles, whose veracity therefore incurred suspicion." [13] Under these circumstances, the Allies decided to make the guarantee of the equal rights of minorities, and specifically the Jews, a condition of Poland's independence. Poland signed the Minorities Treaty on June 28, 1919, the same day that it signed the Versailles Treaty guaranteeing its independence. (For the Allies, the Treaty was signed by the United States, the British Empire, France, Italy and Japan.)

The Minorities Treaty contained detailed provisions for the rights of minorities. It consisted of twelve articles, some applying to all minorities and some to specific minorities.[14] In the first article of the Treaty it was stipulated that the clauses in articles 2 through 7 were "fundamental laws" that could not be altered by Poles. (These were incorporated later into the Constitution of 1921.) [15] Foremost among these were the elementary rights to life, liberty, and freedom of religion (Article 2). The last of these clauses provided equality before the law and equal civil and political rights:

> Differences of religion, creed or confession shall not prejudice any Polish national in matters relating to the enjoyment of civil or political rights, as for instance the admission to Public employment, functions and honors, or the exercise of professions and industries. . . . (Article 7)

To quote from the other important articles applying to all minorities in Poland:

Polish nationals who belong to racial, religious or linguistic minorities shall enjoy the same treatment and security in law and in fact as the other Polish nationals. In particular they shall have an equal right to establish, manage and control at their own expense charitable, religious and social institutions, schools and other educational establishments, with the right to use their own language and to exercise their religion freely therein. (Article 8)

Poland will provide in the public educational system in towns and districts in which a considerable proportion of Polish nationals of other than Polish speech are residents adequate facilities for ensuring that in the primary schools the instruction shall be given to the children of such Polish nationals through the medium of their own language. This provision shall not prevent the Polish Government from making the teaching of the Polish language obligatory in the said schools.

In towns and districts where there is a considerable proportion of Polish nationals belonging to racial, religious or linguistic minorities, these minorities shall be assured an equitable share in the enjoyment and application of the sums which may be provided out of public funds under the State, municipal or other budget, for educational, religious or charitable purposes. . . . (Article 9)

Not to be overlooked are the two of the articles pertaining specifically to the Jews:

Educational Committees appointed locally by the Jewish communities of Poland will, subject to the general control of the State, provide for the distribution of the proportional share of public funds allocated to Jewish schools in accordance with Article 9, and for the organisation and management of these schools.

The provisions of Article 9 concerning the use of languages in schools shall apply to these schools. (Article 10)

Jews shall not be compelled to perform any act which constitutes a violation of their Sabbath, not shall they be placed under any disability by reason of their refusal to attend courts of law or to perform any legal business on their Sabbath. This provision, however, shall not exempt Jews from such obligations as shall be imposed upon all other Polish citizens for the necessary purposes of military service, national defense or the preservation of public order.

Poland declares her intention to refrain from ordering or
permitting elections, whether general or local, to be held on a
Saturday, nor will registration for electoral or other purposes be
compelled to be performed on a Saturday. (Article 11)

These excerpts show that under the Treaty rights were not
only granted to individuals but also to minorities as distinct legitimate groups. The Treaty also provided international guarantees to
assure that Poland would fulfill its obligations to safeguard these
rights. Thus the provisions of the Treaty held out the possibility of
a large measure of cultural and social autonomy for Jews and the
other ethnic minorities in Poland.

As soon as the Treaty was signed, the modern political leaders
among the Jews proceeded to behave as if the minorities' rights
specified in the Treaty were their de facto rights. Thus they became the exponents of the advanced idea of cultural and social
pluralism, coupled with patriotism and loyalty to Poland. But re-
born Poland was an economically backward state in which a semi-
feudal mentality continued to prevail. The ideas of pluralism en-
compass a respect for cultural and religious differences within the
same society. They postulate that not only can unity exist in such
a society but that the unity based on diversity is of advantage to all
concerned. Such ideas did surface in Poland during the nineteenth
and twentieth centuries in the concept of religion as distinct from
nationality and in the various conceptions of Polish federalism, but
they failed to take hold among most Poles. And, as we shall see in
the next chapter, the attempts to incorporate them into the political structure of the resurrected state largely failed. The leadership
of the "new" Poland, in contrast to neighboring Czechoslovakia,
did not prove itself able to rise to the challenge of steering the nation along the new paths of pluralistic democracy and modernity.

The Poles in general did not share the fundamental principles
of the Treaty they signed. They saw the Treaty as an unfair imposition from the outside. Even the assurances of Clemenceau,
one of the chief architects of the independent Poland, that there
would be no interference by the powers in the internal affairs of
Poland, did not satisfy them.[16] The ideological interpretation of the

events leading to independence that soon took hold among the Poles was that they had won their independence through their bravery and patriotism. Outside might had violated their sovereignty and honor: Poland, the traditional country of tolerance, was made to sign a treaty implying the opposite.

Poles saw this as national humiliation. And the Jews were regarded as the chief culprits since representatives of East European Jews and of Jewish organizations in the West, especially some influential American Jews, were among the foremost champions of the Minorities Treaty.[17] Resentment ran especially high when representatives of Polish Jewry began calling the government to task for not living up to the provisions of the Treaty.[18] Polish honor was felt to be particularly wounded when criticism of Poland spread abroad. Although the Poles resented such criticism, they continued to violate the provisions of the Treaty with greater righteousness than before. Shortly after the Treaty was signed, a number of official missions came to Poland to investigate reported violations. Sixteen months after the Treaty was signed, Louis Marshall wrote to the Secretary of the Polish Legation in Washington:

> The reports that come from Poland from disinterested observers, not Jewish, satisfy me that, notwithstanding the acceptance by Poland of the terms of the Minorities Treaty signed by its representatives, Mr. Paderewski and Mr. Dmowski, at Versailles on June 28, 1919, the letter and spirit of this treaty have not been observed, and that the Jews continue to be subjected to all manner of hostility and discrimination.[19]

The Honor of Poles and the
Caste Situation of Jews

The defiance of the terms of the Minorities Treaty they signed was not generally regarded by Poles as a violation of Polish honor. On the contrary, these acts were to them acts of courage to restore Polish honor violated by the Treaty. What then was this Polish honor? One must realize that in the Polish hierarchy of values, marked by an aristocratic tradition, honor ranked very high.[20] The rhetoric of Poles, especially of the rulers and the intelligentsia, was filled with allusions to Polish honor. But honor was seldom used to judge their own acts toward people weaker than themselves. Rather, it expressed itself in an acute sensitivity to how they were treated by others. Polish honor was delicately balanced and easily wounded. It was tied to a special quality which every Pole inherited as part of his Polish birthright and which he was to guard constantly against violations by outsiders, especially inferiors. And the Jews were considered the outsiders, the strangers in their midst. They were also considered the epitome of inferiority.

The chief elements of the prevalent social definition of the Jews in Poland were their foreignness and inferiority. By demanding equality, let alone the way they did it, Jews defied this definition and were perceived as offending Polish honor. The secularized Jews' behavior vis à vis the Poles often impinged on the old caste-like structure, challenged its assumptions, and violated the hitherto governing caste etiquette.

Caste, as defined by Max Weber, is a closed status group.[21] The Jews of Poland were such a group—closed and with the shared status of compelling inferiority. Their caste situation, which emerged in the middle ages and continued throughout the period of Elective Kings and during the partitions, persisted after independence was gained.[22]

Here I must digress to discuss the appropriateness of the concept of caste, because of two important controversies concerning it. One is the debate over its use in a racial context, largely waged in connection with its employment in relation to blacks in the United States.[23] Of more direct bearing is the argument waged prior to the Russian revolution, when Lenin spoke about the Jews in Russia and Poland as a caste:

> Of the ten and a half million Jews in the world, somewhat over half live in Galicia [Austrian Poland] and Russia [including parts of Poland], backward and semi-barbarous countries, where the Jews are *forcibly* kept in the status of a caste. The other half lives in the civilized world, and there the Jews do not live as a segregated caste (italics supplied).[24]

When Lenin made his statement, he was criticized by some Jewish intellectuals, who maintained that the Jews were a nation, not a caste. Similarly, the use of the term for Negroes in the U.S. has been criticized; they are a race, not a caste. But in my view a distinct national, racial, or religious group in a given society—just as a distinct stratum within the same nation, race, or religion—can be forcibly placed and kept in a caste position through various means. In such cases, it is proper from a sociological perspective to speak of an ethnic or race caste stratification system. It is the nature of the relationship, not the basis of differentiation, that makes it a caste system.

The concept of caste is extremely useful in understanding the situation of Jews in interwar Poland, just as it is in understanding the situation of Negroes in the United States before the Civil Rights struggle.[25] The rigidity of the social line between Poles and Jews came very close to that of the color line in the United States. The failure of the Jewish assimilationists in Poland—like the failure of the mulattoes in the United States—to be recognized as an intermediate category between Jews and Poles, testifies to the rigidity of the line (see Chapter 6). True, the Polish line had no legal basis—in contrast to the Jim Crow laws in the United States—but it was firmly rooted in Polish custom and the Polish psyche. Polish norms required that any association between individual Jews and Poles must not imply social equality of Jews and Poles as groups. As a member of the Jewish group, one was an object of contempt and ridicule, and occasionally of pity. Sometimes, when known personally, an individual Jew's positive traits would be recognized. "Even though he is a Jew, he is a decent human being," was a common expression in such cases. However, the Jew who claimed or implied in his behavior that Jews in general were the social equals of Poles transgressed the basic tenet of the caste system: the inherent inferiority of Jews. Such an action tended to produce in Poles a psychological reaction of distaste, disgust, and contempt. It would trigger in the mind of the Pole, and quite often in his speech, the caste labels for the Jew which symbolized his inferiority: *parszywy żyd, parch* (mangy Jew), *gudłaj* (distinctive, very derogatory term the origin of which is not known), *cebularz* (onion-eater), etc.

Generally Poles expected Jews to behave subserviently to them. Jews were conscious of these expectations, as they excelled in getting around them and, among themselves, poked fun at them. The latter is illustrated by a widely known Jewish tale. A Polish nobleman, during the reign of Catherine the Great, ran into a Jewish peasant's house to escape the Russian authorities searching for him. The Pole asked for a place to hide and the Jew hid him in a pit at the bottom of his big oven. After the Russians left the vicinity, the Jew came to tell the Pole that he was safe. "Jew, take off your hat," were the first words that the Pole addressed to the Jew. "Jew, take off your hat," or an equivalent, was often used as a shorthand signal to brace oneself, or advise others to do so, before assuming the posture of inferiority in encounters with Poles. Through the centuries in Poland, such subservient behavior became habitual among Jews, as it did among Negroes in the United States. The traditional Jews in interwar Poland swiftly donned the mask of inferiority; their sense of Jewish worth, and their not infrequent sense of humor, allowed them to play the inferior role with a minimum of psychological pain inherent in the situation (see chapter 5). The secularized Jews, especially the young, were contemptuous of such behavior as undignified and demeaning, and often defied it. Their break with the pattern was seen by many Poles as impertinence and arrogance.

By amassing wealth or possessing it, individual Jews did not violate the caste line. In the eyes of Poles they behaved very much in accordance with the norms, for historically business pursuits were considered the Jews' caste function; no matter how rich the Jew might be, his inferior status was not altered, although his wealth was often resented. Even such achievements as education—not considered a Jewish caste function—were usually not sufficient to lift him completely from his lower caste position. In this position Jews were fixed by a rigid rule of ascription and from it they could not legitimately move out, except perhaps by conversion. No matter how Polonized, affluent, educated, and mobile Jews became, the inferiority of their birth was not obliterated. This "inherent" inferiority to Poles they shared with all other Jews. If an individual's parents were Jewish, he was generally considered to be a Jew, no matter how Polish his ways or how loudly he proclaimed himself a Pole.[26] The term "Pole" was generally reserved for Christians and was seldom, if ever, applied by them to Jews. Even such expressions as "Poles of Mosaic faith" or "Jews-Poles" did not gain wide usage.

Thus with the lower caste position went compelling stigmatization: The attribute of being a Jew was believed to be deeply discrediting as well as persistent. Even when their Jewishness was invisible, the fact of their origin still sufficed to justify treating them as stigmatized beings.[27] The stigma of Jewish origin, hańba pochodzenia, stuck stubbornly to those with any Jewish mixture and could rarely be entirely erased. The lengths to which many Poles went to hide any Jewish mixture, and how devastated they felt if discovered, becomes comprehensible only when one keeps this in mind.[28] How strong the stigmatic quality was is reflected in the "unmasking" of the Jewish ancestry of political opponents, which was frequent in the left and the right. Another manifestation of the pervasiveness of the stigma is how Poles reacted to the rare instances of their children marrying completely Polonized Jews, ready for Catholic conversion. It is interesting, for example, to note the numerous arguments that a well-known Polish writer, Stanisław Witkiewicz, used in the letters to his son to persuade him not to marry a Polonized Jewish girl from a wealthy home. Ironically, he was known in Poland for his enlightenment and liberalism. Witkiewicz—who had befriended Sholem Asch and whom Asch called his "teacher and guide"—warned his son about the inherent conflict that would inevitably erupt in such a marriage:

> Between you and her a gap will open immediately . . . because the feeling of racial and social superiority, of historical superiority, will erupt impulsively in you and in her will erupt the feeling of contempt which Jews have for the rest of humanity. . . . Think of it, what will you do when she bears you half-a-dozen little Jews, your children? [29]

The very term *Żyd*, Jew, reflected the stigma and was charged with negative emotional content. It sounded jarring to Polish ears and brought forth a feeling of distaste. Polish writers when introducing in their work a Jewish character, actual or fictional, who was not to play the role of the villian would use the terms "a nice Jew" or "decent Jew," since "Jew" alone would clearly indicate the opposite.[30] Occasionally, in personal contacts with Jews, more educated Poles would substitute "of the old Testament," "of Mosaic faith," or "Israelite," expressions that came into being in the nineteenth century but did not gain wide usage. More often, in an attempt to mitigate the negative connotations of "Jew" well-meaning Poles would use "little Jew" or "little Jewess." In such instances, they would be shocked and puzzled when reprimanded by young modern Jews for the use of these condescending terms.

Assumptions and convictions of Jewish inferiority flourished despite ample objective evidence of the contrary—an example of W. I. Thomas's theorem, which in its applicability comes close to a sociological law: "If people define things as real, they are real in their consequences." The Jews were literate people in a country with a high rate of illiteracy; they greatly surpassed the Poles in their concern and help for the needy members of their community; their rate of criminality and delinquency was much lower (this contrasts with the frequent association of minority status with a high rate of criminality and delinquency); they excelled in Polish schools in much larger proportions than Polish children. Despite discrimination, Jews made contributions to Polish science, learning, and culture much above what their number in the general population would warrant. But such facts, if noticed at all, were explained away and the Jews in general continued to be treated as inferiors.

Jews Considered Foreigners

The Jews were also treated as foreigners in Poland. Like their inferiority, their basic foreignness was assumed to be everlasting. Think of it: Here was a population that had been in Poland almost since the country's historical beginnings. Here was a people whose contribution to the development of Poland was much greater than its proportion in the total population. Moreover, in contrast to the other large ethnic groups—Ukrainians and Belorussians—who wanted secession, Jews demanded at most equality in a Poland that honored their right to a pluralistic existence. No Jews asked that a portion of the land in which they had lived for many centuries be ceded to them. Yet Jews were considered foreigners. Poles regarded themselves as the indigenous population, and so considered their right to be there as self-evident. But they still regarded the Jews as intruders whose presence in Poland was due only to Polish good will.

One should bring to mind that in Poland "alien" (*obcy*) was synonymous with "different." Of long historical significance was the religious difference. True, the nineteenth century marked the beginning of the idea of separation of religious belief, Jewish, from national identity, Polish. But it never came to fruition in independent Poland. "To be Polish is to be Catholic" was the prevailing conception among the Poles. In other respects too—culturally and socially—the Jews were still quite different from the Poles when Poland became independent. Furthermore, modern Jewish leaders, invoking the Minorities Treaty, were bent on perpetuating and developing Jewish culture—albeit mostly secular—not on obliterating it.

Some would argue that the Poles' attitude was therefore natural, since it is part of the human psychological makeup to react to differences with suspicion or hostility. But this argument does not provide an adequate explanation. Is it not also part of human psychological makeup to be attracted to and be excited by differences? The point is that the social definition of the Jews which evolved utilized the former human potential and neglected the latter. In some other countries such a narrow definition gave way under the impact of capitalist development and democratic ideology. But in Poland these social forces were weak, and the narrow definition of Jews was strengthened by the growing Polish and Jewish nationalism. Consistent with the social definition, the common attitude of Poles was, "Jews are a foreign body in Polish society. They are different from us. They irritate us with their foreignness and distinctiveness. We do not like them and we do not want them to have anything to say in Poland." [31] In equating *different* with *foreign*, some Poles stressed the religious differences of Jews, others their linguistic and cultural differences, still others their demographic and economic differences. However, most shared the central assumption that the differences were basically unalterable, even if, on the surface, they might appear changed. Although in contrast to Germany no uniform or highly structured racist ideology was ever constructed in Poland, nevertheless nineteenth-century European racial doctrines did influence the conception of Jews. They were generally considered a distinct race in the following sense: a group different from Poles because of their innate, immutable characteristics—physical, mental, emotional, and spiritual. And in the 1930s, Nazi influences strengthened the racist elements in the Poles' conception of Jews.

Cultural Differences

Before outlining some pronounced cultural differences between the Jews and the Poles, I want to raise two warnings. In focusing on the cultural differences, we must not forget that these differences were becoming substantially reduced. From a historical perspective, the process of acculturation—Polonization—was proceeding at a considerable pace. Acculturation gained such momentum at the end of the nineteenth and beginning of the twentieth century that neither anti-Semitism nor the Jewish nationalism of the interwar period contained it, although they may have slowed it. The second reminder is that, in dwelling on the cultural differences between Jews and Poles, we should not lose sight of the great cultural differentiation within the Jewish population itself. In independent Poland the Jews were far from culturally homogeneous. Although it is perhaps an extreme illustration, there were some Jews who could not communicate with fellow Jews because of the absence of a common language. Jews whose native tongue was Polish could not speak with, and some could not even understand, monolingual Jews whose language was Yiddish. Between the two extremes of virtual absence of acculturation and complete assimilation were various degrees and types of acculturation.

These two phenomena—increasing Polonization and increasing internal differentiation within the Jewish population—will be dealt with in some depth and detail in the second half of the book. But they have to be mentioned here to avoid a misconception that could easily arise from focusing on how different the Jews were from the dominant group. For, indeed, the large majority of Polish Jews were notably distinctive in their culture during the period studied. Large portions of the Jewish population adhered to a Jewish way of life, markedly different from that of the Poles, "without reservation and without disguise, outside their homes no less than within them." [32] As a whole, the Jews of Poland were among the least acculturated of all European Jewish communities of that time. Therefore, unless one remembers from the preceding chapter that the process of purposive acculturation began late in Poland but made deep inroads and unless one recalls how short the interwar interval was, one might arrive at a mistakenly static and homogeneous image of Poland's Jews. (Such an erroneous image was often characteristic of the Poles' view of the Jews in independent Poland.)

Take two of the most obvious cultural differences, hairstyle and dress. The traditional clothes of Jews were markedly different from the European clothing of urban Poles and the folk costumes of the Polish peasantry. Some of the older generation, especially in the larger cities and among the higher strata, had changed their traditional appearance at the end of the nineteenth and beginning of the twentieth century (or their parents had earlier in the nineteenth century). In independent Poland, increasingly, the younger generation was shaving its beards and abandoning its distinctive manner of dress. In some cases the process was gradual. It is rather well conveyed by an informant from a small town, who had worn traditional dress as a child. "You know, the first step was to shorten the *kapote* [the black caftan] and the next to wear a European suit with a Jewish hat. The final step was to start wearing a European hat too. There were many young men . . . who wore European suits and Jewish hats." [33]

Other young people abandoned the traditional dress all at once, as a break with "old-fashioned" patterns and as sign of emancipation and modernity. Among them, and among secularized Jews in general, a strongly negative attitude toward the traditional appearance was spreading. They saw it as a badge of backwardness and regarded it with disdain or shame. Had the Jews of Poland not been killed off by the Nazis, the traditional garb would probably have disappeared within two generations, except among a small minority. But in the interwar period, on the streets of Poland, in any city or town, it was still common to see men, women, and children in traditional dress.

As with clothes, so it was with strict observance of religious orthodoxy, which the traditional clothes symbolized. Although it was breaking down, especially among the young, it was still widespread (see chapters 5 and 7).

The same pattern can be seen in linguistic acculturation—which swept the upper stratum in the nineteenth century and moved to the middle strata at the beginning of the twentieth century—became the dominant trend among the middle-class youth in independent Poland who attended secondary schools. In the lower strata, Polish was also gaining, because of compulsory public primary education, but more as a second language.[34] Had Poland not been defeated and had Jews lived on there, within two or three generations Polish would have probably replaced Yiddish as their predominant language. But in the interwar period, Yiddish was the main language of a large majority of the Jews in Poland and often the only spoken language among adults of the lower strata. Yiddish was especially prevalent in the small towns. There, Polish—and generally with a distinctive Yiddish flavor—was used mainly to communicate with Poles. Only in the homes of a few, those of the local intelligentsia—usually the town's doctor, dentist, veterinarian, or lawyer—was Polish spoken. But whether in small towns or large cities, Yiddish was used not only in the privacy of their homes, but was also heard on the streets, in trolleys, trains, and buses, and in any place where Jews moved and congregated.

Census statistics do exist on the language distribution among Jews but they have to be treated with caution. According to the

*On the streets of Poland, in any city or town, it was still common
to see men, women and children in traditional dress . . .*
WARSAW, 1938 (PHOTO BY R. VISHNIAC. USED BY PERMISSION OF MR.
VISHNIAC.)

1931 Census, only 12 percent of the Jews named Polish as their mother tongue, 79 percent Yiddish, and 8 percent Hebrew. However, we would venture to guess that there was a substantially larger proportion of Jews in Poland whose chief language of communication was Polish. The discriminatory attitude toward the Jews of large portions of the Polish population, and the agitation of the Jewish press before the census, influenced many Jews to abstain from naming Polish as their mother tongue. (The 1921 Census, still guided to some extent by principles of the Minorities Treaty, contained questions on nationality as well as religion. In the 1931 Census a question concerning the mother tongue was substituted for that of nationality.* This change provoked hostile reactions from the minorities, particularly the two largest minorities of Poland, the Ukrainians and Jews.) [35] It might be interesting to note here that, according to the Census data, the Jews resembled the Ukrainians and Belorussians in their adherence to their own native language. Only 14 percent of the Ukrainians and Belorussians named Polish as their mother tongue.

Although no statistical data exist, recollections of that period suggest that the number of Jews who were bilingual far exceeded those whose native tongue was only Polish. The census did not recognize bilingualism, the possibility that two languages could be "native." There were also a substantial number of multilingual individuals who spoke various combinations of Yiddish, Polish, Hebrew, German, Russian, Ukrainian, Belorussian, French, etc. But Poles, even if they were multilingual, almost never spoke or understood Yiddish. This was also true, in those small towns where the Jews formed a numerical majority. Poles were the dominant group and they looked with disdain on Yiddish. Still attached to Yiddish was the nineteenth-century label of "jargon." "The disdainfulness toward Jews reflected itself in the attitude toward their language." [36] According to common expressions among Poles, one

---

* In the instruction manual, it was specified that in response to the question of one's mother tongue (języke ojczysty) "should be listed the language which the person considers closest to him." As quoted in: Stanisław Mauersberg, *Szkolnictwo Powszechne dla Mniejszości Narodowych W Polsce Latach 1918–39*, Wrocław: Ossolineum, 1968, p. 12.

spoke Polish but one jabbered in Yiddish. A few rare Poles spoke Yiddish and they were regarded as great curiosities when encountered by Jews; they were treated with delight.

Jewish Visibility

In the great majority of cases, the Polish spoken by Jews retained some traces of Yiddish antecedence, manifested in intonation, grammatical structure, and in vocabulary and expressions. And apart from the verbal language, there was the distinctive nonverbal language—typical gestures, facial expressions, body movements, etc., different from those of Poles. This raises the fascinating question of Jewish "visibility" in Poland. As Goffman has noted in another connection, the term "perceptibility" would be more accurate than the term "visibility," which has gained wide usage.[37] The central question here is to what extent were the dominant Poles able to perceive whether a stranger was Jewish or not. The answer to this question is clear: in many instances they could easily recognize a Jew. As a matter of fact, Jewish visibility in Poland came close to Negro visibility in the United States. Those holding the widely accepted belief that the situation of blacks is unique because of their visibility may find this statement objectionable. Many have been influenced by Fanon, who wrote: "The Jew is disliked from the moment he is tracked down. . . . But . . . I am overdetermined from without. I am the slave not of the 'idea' that others have of me but of my own appearance."[38] He proves to be wrong when one considers the Jews in interwar Poland. As was Fanon, in most cases Jews were disliked from the moment they were seen (or heard). The Polish majority did not need to brand them or pin Stars of David on them to recognize them. I would not hesitate to estimate that at least 80 percent of the Jews were recognizable to Poles.[39]

The difference between Jewish visibility in Poland and the visibility of blacks in the United States was not so much in its degree as in its basis. The visibility of most blacks is based on their phenotypic—external physical—characteristics. (But there are also

Negroes who are physically indistinguishable from whites.) [40] The basis of Jewish visibility was mostly in sociocultural characteristics, only occasionally in phenotypical traits. Poles generally maintained that they could distinguish a Jew by his external physical traits, and as with stereotypes in general, there was some grain of truth to this statement, although distorted and exaggerated; among Jews was found a greater proportion of phenotypical characteristics that are associated with Mediterranean and Oriental types within the Caucasian race than among the Poles. [41] Nevertheless, the socio-cultural characteristics played a larger part in making them easily distinguishable. The cultural differences that played a major part in the visibility of the Jews were (1) very different religious practices and open engagement in them, in a land which considered itself deeply Catholic; (2) differing names and especially surnames—high proportion of German surnames, contrasting sharply with those of Poles; (3) language—the wide use of Yiddish and the characteristic Polish with its Yiddish-influenced intonation, syntax, and expressions; (4) nonverbal language—dissimilar gestures, facial expressions, body movements and mannerisms; (5) typical dress, especially among the older generation; (6) food habits and foods markedly different from those of Poles, such as the use of sharper ingredients—onions and garlic in cooking. (Poles referred to Jews in a derogatory way as onion-eaters, herring-eaters, and as garlic-smelling); (7) complete absence of religious observance among many of the assimilated and young secularized Jews, whose irreligiousness appeared more obvious than that of secularized Poles.

How strong the religious factor was in Jewish visibility can be illustrated by the childhood reminiscences of the eminent psychiatrist Helene Deutsch, whose Polonized family was completely nonobservant and whose brother converted to Christianity:

> I often saw that same priest on the streets, on his way to administer extreme unction to a dying soul. These encounters, so frequent that they should have become a matter of indifference to me, never failed to move me. The sight has lasted in my memory all my life: the priest in his white lace surplice holding before him the viaticum, followed by a hunch-backed altar boy

carrying the censer and a shrill little bell, which he shook constantly to remind the faithful to kneel down. All the passersby would sink to their knees like wheat stalks in the wind. *I alone, the Jew, would remain standing in solemn silence. I felt marked by a stigma and full of shame.* I did not belong (italics supplied).[42]

Size of Population; its Urban-Rural and Occupational Distributions *

The social factors of the size of the Jewish population and its urban-rural and occupational distributions also contributed to the high visibility of Jews.

According to the census of 1931, there were 3,113,933 Jews in the country. They made up 9.8 of the total population of Poland; this was then the highest percentage of Jews in any land outside of Palestine. Interestingly, it was the same percentage as Jews had formed in the prepartitioned Kingdom of Poland, and about the same as that of blacks in the American population.

Jews formed the second largest ethnic minority in Poland. The Ukrainians (13.9 percent) were the first, and the Belorussians (3.1 percent) the third. However, while the Ukrainians, the Belorussians, and to the small minorities of Germans and Lithuanians, were all concentrated in specific regions (comparable to the Mexican Americans in the American Southwest), the Jews were distributed throughout Poland, albeit unevenly (rather like Negroes in the United States). They were substantially underrepresented in Western Poland, making up only 1.5 percent of the population of Silesia, 2.1 percent of that of Posen and 1.8 percent of that of Pomerania. Still, there were Jewish communities in all seventeen provinces of Poland. In this the Jews differed sharply from the Ukrainians who lived (with minor exceptions) only in four south-

---

* These and the rest of the figures appearing in this chapter are, unless otherwise indicated, from special calculations made on the basis of the official Polish census data of the interwar period. The calculations and analysis appear in: Celia S. Heller, "Populations of Pre-War Poland—An Epitome of Differentiations," University of California, Los Angeles, 1959 (Unpublished).

ern provinces, where the Poles were not in the majority (Tarnopol, Stanisławów, Wołyń, and Polesie).

While the Jews, unlike the Ukrainians, were not concentrated sufficiently in any one province to form its numerical majority, they did concentrate in the cities and towns of predominantly rural Poland. Four out of every ten Jews lived in a city where there were more than 10,000 Jews. Jews constituted between one-third and one-fourth of the total population of each of the five major cities of the country: Warsaw, Łódź, Vilno, Cracow and Lvov. In those five cities almost a quarter of the entire Jewish population was located. There, as in other large cities, they tended to be found in specific Jewish neighborhoods. To give an extreme example, 90 percent of the inhabitants of the Nalewki and Muranów sections of Warsaw were Jewish. As for the small towns, a great number of them were predominantly Jewish in character. The population of some very small towns was almost entirely Jewish, servicing the peasantry in the surrounding areas. In many more, the Jews constituted a majority.

The Jews were a primarily urban population in a country whose dominant group and whose other two major subordinate groups were primarily rural. As many as 76 percent of the Jews but only 27 percent of the Poles, 7 percent of the Ukrainians, and 3 percent of the Belorussians were urban. Constituting one tenth of the country's total population, the Jews formed over a quarter of the urban population and only 3 percent of the rural population.

From the urban-rural comparison, one could deduce that occupationally Jews differed markedly from the Poles, Ukrainians, and Belorussians. The striking characteristic of the occupational distribution of Jews in Poland was that they were primarily concentrated in commerce and handicrafts.[43] As for agricultural occupations, only 4.3 percent of Jewish breadwinners, as compared with 58.8 percent of Polish ones, were found in them.* Nevertheless from another comparative perspective rarely employed, the 4.3

---

* The 1931 Census data on occupation do not lend themselves to a comparison between the Jews and the two large minorities, Ukrainians and Belorussians. However, from their rural concentration, one can deduce that their percentages in agricultural occupations even exceeded that of the Poles.

percent of Jews in agricultural occupations represents a relatively high figure. Both by percentage and numerically, there were more Jews in agricultural occupations in Poland than in any of the Western countries of that time. (The Jewish farmers in Poland were very different from the urban Jews and resembled non-Jewish farmers in some notable ways. Like Polish peasants, a large majority of them were located on small farms.)

As we saw in the preceding chapter, this distinctive urban character and distinctive occupational structure were mainly the product of adaptation to the external environment through the centuries. In Biblical times, the Jews were an agricultural people. In Poland, as was mentioned earlier, business and commercial pursuits were historically the caste function of the Jews. While the

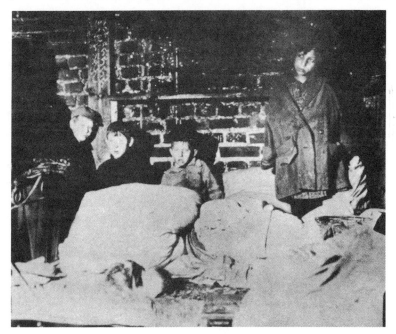

Oppressive poverty was real among large sections of Polish Jewry . . .

CHILDREN OF TWO FAMILIES LIVING IN A CELLAR AFTER BEING EVICTED FROM THEIR HOMES IN THE 1920s. WARSAW (YIVO INSTITUTE FOR JEWISH RESEARCH)

occupational distribution of the Jews will be given more attention
in the next chapter, we want to note here that the above occupational concentration constituted another condition of their potential visibility. To Poles this tended to signify Jewish economic advantages. And since the words commerce and business convey an
image of economic well-being, it is necessary to point out here that
oppressive poverty was real among large sections of Polish Jewry.
True, in the small urban stratum of the very rich—in large business and industry but not in large land estates—Jews and individuals of Jewish origin figured prominently. But the majority of the
Jewish "capitalists" were artisans (whose tiny living quarters doubled as workshops), owners of small businesses or of stalls in markets, or peddlers. As a *New York Times* correspondent noted during that period, often the whole stock in trade of those stall owners
and peddlers was around twenty złoty (then four dollars) and
their daily income one złoty (twenty American cents). He noted
that "these Jewish peddlers who have given the Polish landscape a
characteristic note are pictures of walking misery." [44]

Widespread poverty among the Jews was not alleviated, but
was actually growing progressively worse during the two decades of
Polish independence. But the increasing poverty of the Jews was
not seen as a major problem by the dominant group. On the contrary, this increasing poverty, as we shall soon see, was to a large
measure the result of the so-called solution, championed by the
nationalists and imposed by the government with the approval of
many Poles, to what they defined as Poland's major problem: the
Jews. It is not that there were too many individuals in commerce
and the professions for Poland's size. [45] The fact that many of them
were Jews was interpreted as damaging to Poland. Thus we come
back to the social definition of Jews as a "foreign growth on the
body of Poland." The society's choice of the Jews as the major
problem was tied to the social definition of Jews and was due to
important economic and political factors we shall delineate in the
next chapter.

Once Jews were viewed as the number one problem—a problem to be solved by eliminating them through discrimination or
violence—the fact that they were highly visible was convenient for

the oppressors.* The sociocultural differences of Jews proved as compelling as phenotypic differences elsewhere.

The extremely negative social definition was a subjective factor that intensified the effect of the above objective factors in Jewish visibility. Even where the cultural differences of individual Jews were minimal, they were often perceptible to Poles. This was dramatically but painfully borne out when the Nazis marched into Poland. Frequently, the Nazis could not at first tell some Jews

The majority of the Jewish "capitalists" were artisans whose tiny living quarters doubled as workshops, owners of small businesses or owners of stalls in markets . . .

A MAN AT HOME KNITTING SOCKS ON A MACHINE. GRODZISK MAZO-WIECKI, WARSAW PROVINCE. (YIVO INSTITUTE FOR JEWISH RESEARCH)

* And when in doubt, it was not too difficult to ascertain this "important" fact, since a system of official identification existed in Poland. Each person was obligated to have an official identification with one's photograph on it. In this document the person's religion was clearly marked, in addition to name, age, sex, etc.

apart from Poles. But there was present enough "Polish trash," as the murdered historian Ringelblum expressed it, "and they pointed out who was a *Jude* (the only word in German that the Polish hooligans knew immediately)." [46] And after the Germans introduced and enforced the strict system of identification, including the wearing of the Star of David, such hooligans and other Poles were tempted with payment and rewards to deliver Jews who were passing.

The Poles' perception of Jewish differences was heightened by the tremendous negative importance they attached to such differences, as well as the frequent exposure to them. The predisposition to be concerned with whether the person one encountered or dealt with was a Jew was rooted in the social definition of the Jew. This predisposition, heightened by the economic difficulties from which Poles had suffered in the interwar period, was activated by the anti-Semitic campaign that the Polish nationalists pushed throughout independence and that became especially vicious during the 1930s. It infused the old stigma of Jewishness with new life and new meaning. These differences reinforced prejudice and discrimination in the sense that they were utilized and served to rationalize prejudice and discrimination. To prejudiced Poles the fact that the Jews were different from them in religion, culture, or occupation often constituted proof of the correctness and reasonableness of their attitude toward Jews and the way they treated them.

Thus, the visibility of Jews in Poland, as is visibility in general, was determined not only by the extent of the actual differences but also by the dominant group's subjective interpretation of these differences. The Jews in Poland were in their visibility, as in their caste status, the Negroes of Poland. Their high visibility made them especially vulnerable to the widespread anti-Semitism strongly planted in the Polish nation and flourishing in the interwar period: prejudice, discrimination, and violence.

III
⌊The Pattern of Oppression

The apparent paradox of Jewish existence in independent Poland was that the Jews were culturally less different from Poles and yet more oppressed by them than at any other time in Poland's history. Organized political anti-Semitism, which had come into being before independence, became the dominant force during independence, uniting the Poles and dividing the nation into Poles and Jews. With some fluctuation in its intensity, anti-Semitism continued throughout Polish independence. The brutal attacks against Jews that had greeted independence were repeated with greater force and organization in the 1930s, as anti-Semitism became especially rampant and vicious during the rise of fascism in Europe. In interwar Poland, anti-Semitism was not simply the manifestation of the lunatic fringe; it was respectable and in the forefront of political affairs—a fact one must grasp in order to understand how pervasive Polish anti-Semitism really was.

Inequality of Power

To comprehend how desperate the situation of the Jews was, one must understand their extreme vulnerability, which was rooted in the inequality of power between the Jews and the Poles, an inequality tied to the numerical relation of these two groups: the Poles were the majority and the Jews the minority. The compelling aspect of the power inequality was, however, that the Poles owned or controlled the means of coercion and destruction: the state and its machinery. The actual manifestations of this inequality cannot be completely understood if treated independently from the subjective factors which made the exercise of power against Jews seem right and proper. Without the power, the Poles' anti-Jewish attitudes could not have been translated into effective discrimination and oppression. Without these attitudes, the Poles' power would not have been fully utilized against Jews.

The Poles' exercise of potential power over the Jews was ostensibly curtailed by the Minorities Treaty and the provisions of the Constitution of 1921. But the existence of the Treaty was of little help to the Jews, since enforcement mechanisms by an international body were not set in motion.[1] The League of Nations, under the guarantee of which the Treaty was placed on February 13, 1920, was becoming increasingly impotent. It was incumbent on the League to make the rights of minorities effective through carefully designed ways and means, but the League failed to exercise effective sanctions against the violators of this Treaty as well as other international treaties. This being the case, one cannot help but wonder now whether the Jews of Poland would not have been better off without this Treaty, which was then acclaimed as a great accomplishment by many Jews in Poland and abroad, particularly in America. For the Treaty raised the expectations of the Polish Jews, especially the young. At the same time, the existence of the Treaty only angered the Poles, and there was no way that the Jews, without the force of international sanctions, could make them abide by it. Also violated and frequently circumvented in regard to Jews (and Ukrainians) were the provisions of the Polish Constitution, regarding the equality of all citizens.

In independent Poland after World War I, the Poles exercised their power over the Jews with fewer constraints than ever before in their long history of coexistence. Before, sovereignty over the Jews had been divided between the King and the magnates. Matters that did not fall under explicit jurisdiction of either could be decided by the Jews themselves. This made possible the broad autonomy of the Jewish people, discussed in chapter 1. In contrast, in independent Poland the measure of autonomy derived from the Minorities Treaty became the bone of contention, for the exercise of power over the Jews found rationalization in the prevailing Polish conception of national sovereignty: It was the right of the Poles to rule in their land and for the Jews to be subject to their will. If we ask who gave the Poles that right, the answer is: they had the power and they assumed the right.

At the start of the twentieth century two contrasting political ideas as to the kind of Poland that ought to emerge with independence vied with each other. One was the narrow nationalistic conception, enunciated by Roman Dmowski—the head of the National Democratic Party—and championed by the Polish right. The second was a "federalist" conception, advocated by Józef Piłsudski and his comrades in the Revolutionary Faction of the Polish Socialist Party. It called for Poles to admit other ethnic groups to equality.

After independence was declared various schemes of making the Polish state into a federal union of nationalities were put forth by leading Poles and debated in a number of clubs and associations that sprung up, such as the Association of Polish Federalists.[2] In none of these schemes did Jews figure as one of the *nationalities* to be included in a Polish federal union. (The schemes addressed themselves to the territorial nationalities of the former Commonwealth Kingdom of Poland, such as Belorussians, Ukrainians, and Lithuanians.) Nevertheless, the idea, championed by Jewish nationalists, of Jews as an indigenous nationality might have become acceptable had federalism succeeded. But federalist plans were fought effectively by the National Democratic Party, which attacked them as endangering the cohesivensss and strength of the new Poland. The ideas of Roman Dmowski (one of the two Polish intermediaries at the Peace Conference in Versailles)[3] found support among members and followers of the center parties, as well as other parties of the right, and enthusiastic commitment among the young. As early as 1922, Piłsudski considered federalism a lost cause in Poland as "all hopes of implementing his plan faded away." [4]

But even after the hope for Polish federalism collapsed, Piłsudski and some of the men who fought with him held on to the conception of the primary significance of the state in Poland's reality and destiny (*idea państwowa*). They tended to see the new Polish state as a modernized continuation of the Commonwealth of Poland, which had bound together disparate peoples. In the new state, they emphasized, the tie of citizenship and loyalty to the Polish state of people of different ethnic backgrounds would assure the kind of unity that was necessary for returning Poland to the greatness that was once hers. This conception is symbolized in the continued work and writing of Tadeusz Hołowko, one of the noblest followers of Piłsudski and one of the sincerest exponents of this idea, who strove to win the Poles away from the path of narrow nationalism. His overall goal was for national minorities in Poland to have "equal opportunity for economic development; he did not want to break their national distinctiveness, . . . he only asked one indispensable thing from them: loyalty to the state." [5]

However, it was not this conception that triumphed, but the narrow one, championed by Dmowski, which emphasized the "national" dimension (*idea narodowa*) of the new Polish sovereignty. Dmowski proclaimed the Polish nation, comprised of indigenous Poles only, as the vehicle of Poland's progress. It became the philosophy of the National Democratic Party which Dmowski shaped and whose chief theoretician he remained for a long time. Central to Polish nationalism, as it crystallized before and became dominant during independence, was the idea of the nation state as the organic entity growing out of soil, blood ties, religion, folkways and folk memories. [6]

About one third of the population of independent Poland was composed of non-Polish ethnic groups. The Jews were found throughout Poland. In three of the country's seventeen provinces, the Poles were a minority (14.5 percent of Polesie's population, 16.6 percent of Wołyń's, and 22.4 percent of Stanisławów's). In

another four provinces, the Poles ranged from 49.3 to 59.7 percent
of the total population of each province (Tarnopol, Nowogródek,
Lvov, Vilno).[7] The ethnic minorities in Poland were marked by distinct language, religion, culture and social organization. Thus cultural and social pluralism was a fact in Poland, but a fact that the
dominant group refused to accept. Despite the objective reality
that Poland was a multiethnic state and despite the recognition of
this reality by the Minorities Treaty, the conception that prevailed
in Poland was one of a monoethnic state. It expressed itself in the
slogans: "Poland is composed of a nation, not of nationalities" and
"Poland for Poles only." [8]

The arrogance, the lack of comprehension, and the hostility of
the government and large sections of the Polish people toward cultural and political autonomy of minority groups is pointed up when
we compare interwar Poland with interwar Czechoslovakia.
Czechoslovakia, too, resented its obligation to sign a Minorities
Treaty. But having done so, it did not proceed to violate the Treaty
and turn its resentment against the Jews. On the contrary, it fully
implemented the Treaty. In contrast to Poland, the philosophy of
the new Czechoslovak state was a pluralistic one. More than anyone else, Thomas Masaryk played a decisive role in formulating
the philosophy before independence and in directing the nation
along its paths after independence. Before independence he expressed full sympathy for those Bohemian Jews who demanded
national minority rights in the new state. His sympathy is reflected
in the rhetorical question he asked: "How can the suppressed nations deny the Jews that which they demand for themselves?" [9]
Soon after independence was gained, on June 21, 1919, President
Masaryk declared:

> Today I can only repeat that my attitude toward the Na-
> tional Jews has not changed. I do not see why in our state,
> where a number of nationalities have been dwelling together
> side by side, the Jewish nation alone should be regarded as an
> undesirable factor. I can assure you that, consistent with my
> constitutional powers, I shall put my views into action, also in
> the field of politics. You may always count on me.[10]

No major Polish leader, let alone the president, made such statements. Even Marshal Józef Piłsudski, who was generally regarded by Jews as favorably disposed toward them, never made a statement asserting the rights of Jews as a nationality.[11]

The representative voices in Czechoslovakia were those proclaiming the philosophy of ethnic pluralism, but the strongest voices in nascent Poland were those of narrow, monolithic Polish nationalism. According to the latter, a uniform culture was supposed to correspond to the uniform state. Cultural differences within the country were abhorred as weakening national unity. The possibility that there was anything in the Jewish culture, in Jewish traditions worth incorporating into the culture of Polish society would have been considered preposterous. Insofar as there was cultural diversity in Poland, it was perceived as a condition from which the country suffered and of which it had to rid itself.[12] The traditional Jewish autonomy, which developed under the kings and princes of Poland, was not viewed as a source of national pride but as a historical error. This "error" Polish nationalism aimed to rectify.

Thus, in contrast to Czechoslovakia, where Jews could freely assume all the rights that were theirs under the Treaty, in Poland the assertions of such rights was deeply resented. This resentment is reflected in the differing attitudes toward and treatment of the Jews elected to the parliament and municipal governing bodies in each country. In Czechoslovakia they were regarded as part of the regular political order, as legitimate respresentatives of those Jews who considered themselves members of the Jewish nationality. They were treated the same way as were the representatives of the Czechs and the Slovaks.

But in Poland, the existence of Jewish representatives in the legislative body of Poland was regarded by many as an anomaly. The exercise by Jews of certain rights of political autonomy, derived from the Treaty (such as the election of their own representatives to Parliament and municipal bodies) was often interpreted as Jewish hostility and ingratitude to Poland.[13]

Poles were mostly ignorant of or unable to comprehend the

Poland resented the "imposition" of the Minorities Treaty. The existence of Jewish representatives in the Parliament of Poland was regarded by many Poles as an anomaly . . .
JEWISH MEMBERS OF THE POLISH DIET. (YIVO INSTITUTE FOR JEWISH RESEARCH)

coexistence in Judaism of particularism and universalism—devotion to the Jewish group coupled with loyalty to Poland. The National Democratic Party, which increasingly was becoming the voice of the nation on the question of the Jews, raised the specter of a state within a state. It warned the Jews that if they insisted on cultural and political autonomy, the Polish nation would have to fight them.

The Party of Hate

The rise of the National Democratic Party at the end of the nineteenth century and its increasing anti-Semitic stance prior to independence have already been noted. What I want to emphasize here is the role of this nationalist party (commonly referred to as

Endecja) * as the chief bastion of political anti-Semitism after independence was gained.

Its foremost leader, Roman Dmowski, was not doctrinaire in
the application of the philosophy he preached but was a man of as-
tute political acumen, compromising from time to time in order to
gain leverage for his party. He used anti-Semitism to rally right-
wing opposition to the government and forge it into a major political force. However, a general tactical line was pursued by his party
even after Dmowski gave up his active part in Polish politics.
Crises were seized upon to press the anti-Semitic solution and to
attract attention to it through militant protest and tactics. The
early use of this weapon, when Dmowski was still in the center of
Polish politics, was characterized to his face as "monstrous" by
Louis Marshall, the prominent Jewish-American leader. According
to Marshal, Dmowski replied: "I think that your characterization is
not out of place. In fact I like the word monstrous." Whether or not
Dmowski, the "advocate of European manners and polished
style," [14] said this tongue in cheek, the fact remains that these
"monstrous" policies and tactics yielded results and Poland moved
in the direction that Dmowski and his party set for it (but not so
fast as the radical splinter groups that eventually emerged from
the party desired).

Sociologists have generalized from cross-societal studies that
extreme aggression and discrimination result from two kinds of
circumstances: the first when the dominant group considers discrimination to be an effective way to reduce the ability of the minority to act as a social competitor—especially a competitor for
scarce economic goods; the second when the dominant group de-
fines the minority's different social norms as a form of deviance
that endangers its sacred traditions, values, or norms. [15] Both these
conditions the nationalists proceeded to bring forth. The Endecja
was consistent and persistent in its solution to all Poland's ills: the
freeing of the country from the Jews. This solution followed from
its basic premise that the Jews were a foreign minority that was

* This party changed its official name in 1919 from National Democratic Party to
Populist-National Association, *Związek Ludowo-Narodowy*, and again in 1928 to
National Party.

dominating and exploiting the Polish nation. The Endeks contended that this control by Jews, this manipulation of Poles, permeated all aspects of Polish life: Especially critical was the Jewish domination in the economic and cultural spheres. According to them, Jews in many disguises—from Orthodox to Polonized—were transforming and destroying the lofty indigenous Polish values and ways. They contended that, although Poles had acquiesced to Jewish exploitation by remaining passive for a long time, they had reached with independence a new determination to rid themselves from this foreign domination.

By equating the Jews with foreign domination, the party appealed to the patriotic fervor for which the Poles are world famous. In presenting a simple formula to solve Poland's economic problems by getting rid of the Jews, the Endeks exploited the traditional dislike of Jews. Their formula found easy acceptance in large parts of the Polish population. Well organized Endek propaganda channelled the anti-Jewish predispositions of the Polish people into a general attitude that the Jews constituted the greatest threat to Poland's economy. Thus this party, originally of the Polish middle class (a relatively small and weak class) won a popular base and grew in strength. And its anti-Semitic platform was translated into a national policy as a result of the capitulation of the government to this party and its allies at important junctures, in the early 1920s and late 1930s. Because of the economic difficulties and the political instability of the country, the party succeeded in exercising a tremendous influence on governmental policies toward Jews. Convinced of the popularity of the Endecja's anti-Semitic stance, the government made concessions. These ranged from governmental tolerance of anti-Jewish manifestations, through measures aiming indirectly at Jews, to an official anti-Semitic policy. The concessions varied with who was in the parliamentary majority and with the nature of the government coalition. But the concessions did not succeed in pacifying the militant nationalists from the radical splinter groups; on the contrary they encouraged them to escalate their tactics and demands regarding the elimination of Jews from all spheres of Polish life. Government measures against the Jews were condemned by them as hypocritical half measures. They demonstrated against them and appealed to the Polish people not to be diverted by them. This usually resulted in stronger declarations against Jews by government officials and stronger anti-Jewish measures.

The culmination of this process came in the last years before World War II, when the government announced its official policy of ridding Poland of the Jews, without even providing an assimilatory escape valve. The role that the Polish government played in tolerating or actively pursuing the policy against Jews was especially crucial, since the regulation of ethnic relations was traditionally in Poland—as in Central and Eastern Europe in general—within the domain of the government. The overall trend of the measures, indirectly or directly aimed against Jews, during the interwar period was to make the economic and political status of the Jewish population correspond to its social position of an inferior caste. Consequently, in their social status and in the treatment accorded to them the Jews of Poland came to resemble a conquered population. But the ideological interpretation of the oppression of Jews—disseminated first by the nationalists and eventually also by the government—was that it represented a necessary effort to free Poland from the hegemony of a foreign group, the Jews, who were spread throughout Poland.

Political Instability

A major factor propelling Poland to this pseudo-solution was the political instability of the country. No sooner was an independent Poland declared in 1918, than the country was threatened by civil war. The two great antagonists were Piłsudski, then a leader of the right wing of the Polish Socialist Party and Dmowski, the leader of the rightist National Democratic Party. Fortunately for resurrected Poland, the great Polish patriot and famous pianist, Ignacy Jan Paderewski, was trusted by these two antagonists to head the interim government. Paderewski's appointment avoided a civil war, although political stability did not ensue; in the short period between the recovery of independence in 1918 and the Piłsudski coup of 1926, fourteen governments rose and fell as a result of changing party coalitions. In this period none of the major parties was able to obtain a parliamentary majority. Characteristic of the political scene were the frequent splits, resulting in a plethora of parties; the struggle among them often became an end in itself. In the party rifts personalities tended to play a greater role than programs. The maneuvers of ambitious leaders and their cliques were conducive to bringing about an atmosphere of tension and hate.[16]

Meanwhile the country was faced with tremendous difficulties. Upon its creation, the new state lacked an administration and a treasury, and the boundaries of the country were not yet fixed. Western Poland was still in German hands and the Soviet Army was marching into the eastern territories abandoned by the German army. The Ukrainian nationalists were establishing themselves in the southeastern parts of former Poland. Under such conditions the first Diet of independent Poland was formed in January 1919; neither the left nor right succeeded in obtaining a majority. (They were almost evenly represented, the balance being held by the center.) However, soon after it came into being, the Diet succeeded in issuing declarations concerning Poland's form of government, afterwards known as the "Little Constitution." A two-house Parliament (*Sejm* and *Senat*) was proclaimed as the highest organ of power in the new state. The executive function was to center in the Head of State and the Government formed by him in consultation with the *Sejm*. Józef Piłsudski was confirmed as Head of State. The Diet then proceeded with the task of drafting a full constitution. In 1921, after long debates, the Parliament adopted the Constitution (commonly referred to as the March Constitution), which was very democratic in form. In the wide civil rights it proclaimed, it incorporated, as noted earlier, provisions of the Minorities Treaty. The Constitution established the division of power into the three branches. A two-house Parliament was to be elected by universal suffrage to replace the existing Diet and an elected President was to replace the Head of State.[17]

The first general election under the new Constitution took place in November 1922. The left suffered further losses, but the right did not succeed in obtaining the majority it had expected, although the Endecja obtained a plurality in the new Parliament. (The largest party of the left was the Polish Socialist Party—*PPS*, and of the center, the Polish Peasant Party—*Piast.*) To the consternation of the right—and particularly the Endecja—the National Minorities' Bloc, led by the Jewish politician Yitzhak Gruenbaum, succeeded in electing enough members to hold the balance of power in the presidential election.[18] Indeed, the first President of Poland, Gabriel Narutowicz (the candidate of the left and a good friend of Piłsudski) was elected thanks to the National Minorities' Bloc.

The rightists branded the new President with the epithet "Narutowicz, the President of the Jews." The anti-Semitic attitude of the Endecja, and the right in general, increased greatly. In the election of Narutowicz, they saw the confirmation of their thesis that the Jewish minority was wielding its power and was bent on ruling Poland. And they found the use of anti-Jewish slogans expedient in furthering their influence among the Polish nation. They succeeded in equating socialism with Jewish rule in the minds of many.

Two days after the President entered office, he was killed by a nationalist fanatic, the painter Eligiusz Niewiadomski. In certain parts of Poland, thanksgiving masses were held in churches because "the Jew who had been chosen President of the Polish Republic was killed." As Piłsudski observed, in the eyes of many Poles, Narutowicz, the *szlachcic* (member of the Polish gentry) had instantly become a Jew.[19]

The political situation that followed the assassination was extremely unstable. Increasingly the parties of the center declined and those of the right and the left monopolized the political scene. They concentrated their activities in the Diet and their maneuvers often paralyzed the executive branch. The critics termed the existing state of affairs a "dietocracy." One cabinet followed another in rapid succession while Poland was facing tremendous difficulties. The country had to be reconstructed economically; its finances had to be stabilized; a unified system of law and administration had to be established. The situation was aggravated by the economic crisis and its accompanying catastrophical inflation. Unemployment rose and the country was torn by strikes. A union between the right and the center (so called *Chjeno-Piast*) emerged and manifested itself in various configurations. It excluded the left—which had played a major part in the struggle for independence—from the actual participation in running the country. The once promised reforms were not forthcoming and the rights of minorities were not honored.[20]

The Quest for Stability

It was under such circumstances that Marshal Piłsudski seized power in 1926, opposed by the right and supported by the left. His return to power marked the beginning of the second phase of the interwar period: the rule of the Piłsudski camp—commonly referred to as *Sanacja*—which lasted until the Marshal's death in 1935. Piłsudski had the approval of large portions of the Polish nation, who believed that only this hero of Polish independence could provide the country with the political and economic stability it needed. His advent was greeted with relief by most Jews, who knew that he was not anti-Semitic and that he was appreciative of the role played by the Polonized Jews in the struggle for independence. Indeed, the situation of the Jews improved at first. They were protected by the government against armed attack by the nationalists. And the prime minister, Kazimierz Bartel, promised that the cultural and economic restrictions on Jews would be eased. However, this came to naught. During the Sanacja regime measures were taken that made it harder for Jews to earn a livelihood.

Increasingly the Sanacja regime (composed largely of men who, like Piłsudski himself, were originally from the Polish left) was moving in the direction of the right. By means of a decree, the Piłsudski government modified the Constitution. The president was granted the right to dissolve parliament and to issue degrees with the binding power of laws. The Marshal bypassed existing political parties by forming the Non-party Bloc of Cooperation with the Government (*BBWR*), the motto of which was "strong government and no parties." The Polish Socialist Party and the left in general, which supported his ascendency, became disenchanted with his actions. They mounted an anti-government coalition with the center—the so called *Centrolew*—aimed at reviving the parliamentary system. Piłsudski responded by assuming the post of prime minister and by influencing the then President (Ignacy Mościcki) to dissolve parliament (August 25, 1930).

Thus bitter political strife reappeared with new force after a short period of relative peace. A number of opposition party leaders were arrested and imprisoned in the fortress of Brześć. In the election that was held, the government succeeded in winning a majority on its ticket of the Non-party Bloc of Cooperation with the Government. "The nation was now ready to accept his [Piłsudski's] government *de jure* as well as *de facto*, and, for the rest of his life, democratic institutions in Poland were reduced to an empty form." [21] The rightist wing in the Bloc gained control and filled the key positions in the government and administration ("The Colonels' Regime," 1930–35). This seizure of the administrative apparatus, with its accompanying control over large numbers of civil servants, transformed these former revolutionaries into bureaucrats, concerned with guarding their careers. [22]

These men moved ideologically and in their policies closer and closer to the nationalists, especially on the Jewish issue. While the Marshal abhorred anti-Jewish demagoguery and did not tolerate it as long as he lived, the economic policies harmful to Jews continued under the Colonels' regime and assumed new forms. Also, this regime hosted Goebbels on his visit to Poland in 1934 and signed a ten-year nonaggression pact with Germany in the same year, followed by a trade agreement. Piłsudski was still alive at this time. In 1934 Poland also denounced the Minorities Treaty and declared itself no longer bound by its provisions. During the same year the government maneuvered the passage of a new constitution, designed to give personal government the stamp of legality. Adopted next year, the new constitution (the April Constitution) concentrated the power in the executive and severely limited that of the legislative. However, it formally retained articles 7 and 9, which proclaimed equal rights to all citizens irrespective of religion and national origin. [23]

The "Heirs" of Piłsudski

After the death of Piłsudski, in May 1935, the struggle for succession began among the three cliques of the Sanacja, the Piłsudski camp. Two of them combined—the one headed by President Mościcki and the one by Rydz-Śmigły—and succeeded in replacing the "Colonels' Group." This struggle resulted in the substantial weakening of the Sanacja camp. It was further weakened when the victorious team dissolved the mass organization, the Non-party Bloc of Cooperation with the Government (*BBWR*), in which the Colonels' Group's influences were strong.

The new regime found itself in a difficult situation. Although it proclaimed itself the heir of the Piłsudski regime, it did not enjoy the same wide popularity that it had when the Marshal was alive. Among the men who came to power there was none with either the charismatic quality or the moral authority to hold the nation together. There was a growing dissatisfaction among large sections of the population because of their increasing economic deprivation. Disorders broke out; strikes and protest manifestations by peasants became rampant. As Władysław Sikorski, a moderate, characterized the situation in Poland in October 1936: "The misery in the land is too great and there are too many interested in utilizing it to bring about internal complications, for one not to fear them." [24]

Strong offensives against the government were mounted both by the left and the right. (There was also a united centrist opposition, the so called *Front Morges*.) The nationalists utilized the dissatisfaction among the Polish people to press their anti-Semitic program by organized violence against the Jews. The men at the helm were desperate for a "solution" that would prevent a revolution, which seemed to them imminent, and allow them to continue to guard the destiny of the country, the mission they were convinced they were best fit to perform. To prevent the increasing discontent of the Polish people from being successfully directed against them, they embraced the "solution" of the nationalists, which they judged that the Polish people would respond to. They embarked on an *official*, explicitly enunciated anti-Semitic policy, explaining that: "the effect of these separate political aspirations [of Jews] and the effect of their numbers, plus their major influence over many areas of social and national life, is to make the Jews, in the present state of affairs, an element that weakens the normal development of national and state strength that is currently being achieved in Poland." [25]

The new leaders were mostly Piłsudski's fellow legionnaires of World War I days; some, like he, were former socialists. But their conscience seems to have been satisfied with their perfunctory words against anti-Jewish violence as marring the honor of the "great Polish nation" and projecting a wrong image abroad of its barbarism. They uttered these phrases as they presented their master plan to solve Poland's economic and political problems by getting rid of the Jews. The Polish people, particularly the nationalists, understood such words as encouragment to further violence.

Official, Anti-Semitic Ideology

Having disbanded the mass organization in which the Colonels whom they replaced had been influential, and also lacking a social base, the new rulers set up in 1937 what they intended as a new mass organization, the Camp of National Unity (OZN), open to all citizens who accepted its principles, except of course Jews. Its aims were to mitigate the internal antagonisms in the government and to consolidate the Polish nation behind it. This organization became the focus of national consolidation around the Jewish issue, defined as the just struggle for the economic self sufficiency and cultural purity of the Polish people. Its leaders in a series of declarations clearly enunciated that the only way to lift Poland from its dire economic predicament, as well as to achieve the country's political stability and cultural greatness, was by striking at the Jews. On the occasion of the launching of OZN, in February 1937, its formal Ideological Declaration was presented over the Polish radio by its head, Adam Koc. It was the beginning of an intensive propaganda campaign: numerous announcements, interviews, and articles appeared in the press and radio elaborating on the ideological declaration. Three million copies of the declaration, with its infamous paragraph 9 concerning Jews, were printed.[26]

A few of the prominent members of the Piłsudski camp could not stomach this drastic departure from the principles of their venerated leader. This is conveyed movingly in the diary of Janusz Jędrzejewicz, who served as Minister of Religion and Education. He describes the private meeting at which Adam Koc read the OZN Ideological Declaration before presenting it to the public on radio:

> I cannot recall a more tragic meeting. We were all old friends, bound by the common struggle for independence under the same flag of Piłsudski, to whom we were so devoted. And here one of us, moreover one of the top men, Adam Koc, who was commonly referred to as "noble-minded," presented us with the political organization's policy which departed so drastically from the principles that we had professed for so many years. . . . We were devastated with what we heard from Koc.[27]

It was the end of any influence of the liberal wing of Sanacja. Some men of Piłsudski's followers withdrew from active politics, but many more compromised in varying degrees with the openly anti-Semitic policies of the government. And they were joined by a greater number of new men, "led by considerations of sheer opportunism and ambition for a place for themselves at the table of beneficiaries of power." [28] The leaders of Poland proceeded to the violation of the Constitution's declaration of equality of all citizens, while continuing to pay lip service to it. Even the Premier, General Felicjan Sławoj-Składkowski, made a much talked of declaration in which he proclaimed that the economic battle against Jews was "O.K." (owszem) for Poles to engage in, but violence was not. Thereafter, Jews jokingly referred to the "O.K." government. The domestic policy of this government harmonized with its foreign policy. Poland was enlarging its ties with Nazi Germany as its leaders were hosting high Nazi officials at hunting parties in the rich Polish forests.[29]

Economic Conditions

To understand the mass appeal of the formula that Jews were responsible for Poland's economic difficulties, it is necessary to realize how ubiquitous those difficulties were. Poland, more backward than other European countries before World War I (the partition and foreign rule were important factors in arresting its economic development), was greatly affected by the economic weaknesses that arose in the postwar period. For example, the collapse of the German mark, which affected the currencies of neighboring countries, greatly accelerated the devaluation of Polish currency. And the ensuing policy of financial restriction, practiced throughout Europe, had a particularly disastrous effect on the underdeveloped Polish industry. Throughout the two decades of its independence, Poland remained industrially one of the most backward countries of Europe. As characterized in the much quoted sentence by the several times premier, Kazimierz Bartel, "internally Poland was and is a land of paupers." [30] It was primarily an agricultural country of "industrial islands amid an agrarian ocean." [31]

The peasants constituted the most numerous stratum, for the world of the manor and the gentry was decaying rapidly in the interwar period. But the pressing problems of the peasantry remained unresolved. Large estates, constituting in number only one percent of all agricultural holdings, made up half of all the agricultural land in Poland. In contrast, 65 percent of all agricultural holdings were too small to support a single family. In addition to these peasants with their tiny parcels of land were a large number of landless peasants—over 5 million—about one fourth of the rural population. The misery of the rural population could hardly be alleviated by migration to the cities because of lack of industrial development and the widespread unemployment there. And the government failed to reduce the problem substantially through fundamental agrarian reform.

In this respect the economic policies of the government were largely determined in the interwar period, as in many respects throughout Polish history, by the interests of the land-owning class. True, as early as 1919 the Parliament adopted a resolution calling for agrarian reform. And the following year—when the Bolshevik Army was marching on Warsaw and there was fear that it would find support among the aggrieved peasantry—Parliament hurriedly passed "under the whistle of Bolshevik bombs" [32] an agrarian reform law, embodying the principles of the earlier resolution. But after the Bolsheviks were defeated, the law was not enforced. Five years after its passage, it was modified and the provisions for parcelling of the large estates were curbed. However, even the provisions of the modified law were not fully applied.

When Marshal Piłsudski came to power, there was hope in the country that he would act boldly to implement the agrarian reform. But disappointment set in, especially when an alliance was sealed at the estate of Prince Radziwiłł between the Marshal and the Polish aristocracy at the end of 1926. A month earlier an important landowner had been appointed Minister of Agriculture and another Minister of Justice. Agrarian reform was doomed. The government continued to deal only with a small part of the most acute needs of peasants by confining parcelling to state-owned lands without expropriating large private landholders. The Sanacja regime tried to appease the peasantry by a moratorium on agricultural debts.[33] Some of these peasants, lacking collateral, and unable to obtain loans from banks, had used the traditional Polish channel of borrowing from Jewish money lenders. Therefore, in these cases the moratorium meant that the peasantry had been pacified largely at the cost of individual Jews. Some were financially ruined.

This in a sense exemplifies the Polish government's approach to Poland's economic problems. The Jews, a thoroughly urban population, could have been used as an asset in a rational plan for the modernization of Poland, which would have made possible the absorption of the surplus population from villages by industry. A clue to their tremendous economic potential is found in the disproportionate contribution that Jews made to the initial industrialization of Poland in the nineteenth and beginning of the twentieth century. To point to this Jewish potential, which Poland did not simply fail to utilize but actually proceeded to suppress, is not merely to project contemporary ideas into a different historical era. Far-sighted men of that era recognized it. For example, toward the end of 1920, when the spirit of the Minorities Treaty was being violated through anti-Jewish violence and economic boycott, Louis Marshall appealed to the Polish government to put an end to these demonstrations in order to further Poland's interests. In asking the Secretary of the Polish Legation in Washington to convey his message to the Polish government he emphasized what an asset the Jew would prove if "he were treated in Poland as he is in the United States":

> You . . . know what a valuable asset the Polish and Russian Jews who have come hither have been to the United States. They have become an important factor in our industrial and commercial life. In fact they have created new industries. They are producers, engaged in every form of manufacture, in all the trades, as well as in the professions. In the great majority of instances they arrived here without financial means, and yet, through industry, perseverance, intelligence and strict attention to their duties, they have added to the wealth of the Nation. They have not been drones. They have not become public charges. . . . The Jews who have remained in Poland are of the same flesh and blood. They have the same innate qualities. Their misery and misfortunes have, to outward appearance, made them the objects of ridicule and of repulsion to those who do not know and understand the inner man. All that they require is an opportunity, the advantages of liberty and equality, a friendly word, kindness instead of harshness, and it will inevitably follow that they will do for Poland what those who have come here have done for America. What Poland needs is the establishment of industries, the development of her great resources and of her commerce. Give the Jew half a chance and he will make the present industrial desert blossom as the rose.[34]

And in the 1930s, one of Poland's outstanding men of commerce, the Polonized Jew and Polish patriot A. Gepner, and the organization he headed, the Central Association of Commerce, appealed again and again to the government not to destroy the potential that Jews represented but to harness it to lift Poland from its economic difficulties.[35] When signs appeared that certain European countries were beginning to rise from the Great Depression of 1929, pleas were forthcoming from the same sources for the government to abandon its disastrous policy and allow the industrialization of Poland to proceed, which would solve the crucial problem of unemployment.[36]

But the leaders who came to the helm, former fighters so adept in the struggle for Polish independence, proved to be unsuited to the challenge of reconstruction and modernization. Their *Weltanschaung* and the values by which they lived—as those of the intelligentsia in general to whom they belonged—bore the prominent influences of the gentry, from which many early members of the intelligentsia derived. They had little understanding, as well as no practical knowledge, of the role of business and industry in a modern state.[37] Thus, instead of harnessing the potential for modernization that the Jews represented, their solution to Poland's economic problems was to squeeze Jews out of their occupations to replace them with Poles. The result was a moderate occupational shift of Poles at the cost of further impoverishment of the Jewish population, but virtually no alleviation of the hardships of the Polish peasantry. According to Simon Segal, the 23 million people who constituted the agricultural population of Poland consumed *one-third* as many industrial commodities as the 5.5 million people of that category in neighboring Czechoslovakia.[38]

Fearful of the ferment among the peasantry, egged on by the nationalists, and commended by those Poles who gained or anticipated gain, the government proceeded with economic measures against the Jews, oblivious that they were ruining the country economically. Throughout its independence, Poland failed to make up for the great economic losses suffered during World War I. It also failed to integrate economically the three regions of the country that had been partitioned. Its industrial equipment and production methods remained antiquated. As a result, Poland never succeeded in equaling the highest industrial output it had reached prior to independence.[39]

Anti-Jewish Economic Policies

The target of governmental measures was the Jewish population, which had been suffering tremendous economic hardships to start with. Largely impoverished before the war, its economic position further deteriorated during it. (The wealthy among them suffered as well; their business became curtailed in independent Poland with the disappearance of the large Russian market for industrial goods from Poland.) It would have been difficult enough for the Jewish population to recover economically without government aid. Of course, Jews received quite the opposite of aid. Not only did the government fail to help them, but it actually pursued its aim of solving Poland's economic problems at the cost of the Jews through direct and indirect measures. The rationale was that the Jews through concentration in vital areas of economic live controlled them, and that it was necessary to break this pattern.

The factual ingredient in the rationale behind such policies was the Jews' distinctive occupational distribution to which we alluded in the preceding chapter—they were greatly concentrated in commerce and handicrafts. Of the Jewish breadwinners, 36.6 percent were in business and commercial occupations, mostly of petty trade, as compared with only 3.4 percent of the Poles. There were more than six times as many Poles as Jews in Poland, but six out of every ten people in business and commercial occupations were Jews.[*]

Such facts were easily manipulated in the anti-Jewish rhetoric, which claimed that the Jews were controlling key economic areas. Actually, the concentration of Jews in these occupations generally did not mean they had economic advantages that Poles lacked. Recall that the occupational structure of the Jewish population had evolved largely because of its usefulness to the ruling nobility. But in the economic system of independent Poland the

[*] These and the rest of the figures about the occupational distribution are, unless otherwise indicated, based on the 1931 Census data and pertain to breadwinners. The calculations and analysis appear in: Celia S. Heller, "Populations of Pre-War Poland—an Epitome of Differentiations," University of California, Los Angeles, 1959 (unpublished).

The government pursued its aim of solving Poland's economic problems at the cost of Jews through direct and indirect measures . . .

TAX COLLECTOR AND JEWISH STALLKEEPER, CRACOW, 1938 (PHOTO BY R. VISHNIAC. USED BY PERMISSION OF MR. VISHNIAC.)

large proportions of Jews in certain occupations made them into an easy scapegoat for Poles and above all for the politicians who played on their prejudices. The Jews were treated as if they had been solely responsible for this condition.

In fact, large sections of Polish Jewry, especially the young, wanted a fair plan for the eventual occupational diversification of the Jewish population, what was termed its "normalization." Many of the Jewish petty merchants and artisans would have preferred to work in large industry and in the government industry and bureaucracy than to be self-employed and have to struggle so hard for economic survival. (In crafts and industry 55.5 percent of Jews and 15.7 percent of Poles were self-employed but did not employ others.) [40] The percentage of Jews employed in crafts and industry actually more than doubled within a decade; Jews constituted 9.1 percent of all those employed in these occupations in 1921, and 19.3 percent in 1931. Many more Jews would have taken this path, since industrial employment would have afforded them a substantial economic improvement. But discriminatory practices in hiring, the six-day week (which forced Jews to work on Saturday and precluded the substitution of Sunday), and a shortage of jobs made such a shift impossible for many.

The government was not interested in an occupational transformation of the Jews; it preferred economic strangulation. This is clearly illustrated in connection with its major policy of nationalization. While the government moved slowly and carefully in land reform, it proceeded boldly to nationalize whole branches of commerce and industry that had been pioneered by Jews (tobacco, salt, matches, alchohol) and turn them into government monopolies.

This was in a sense premature nationalization, and it had an adverse effect on the industrial development of the country in general: it excluded private enterprise from the fields entirely controlled by government monopolies. But it had a particularly disastrous effect on Jews.

Hand in hand with nationalization went the discriminatory hiring policy against Jews in nationalized industry, as well as on the railroads and in public transportation run by the government.

In addition to discriminatory hiring, Jews were also being forced from jobs they had held before nationalization and replaced by Polish workers. One of the most effective early indirect measures of eliminating Jews from government-owned industry and commerce was the Compulsory Sunday Rest Law, limiting the work week to 48 hours, which was adopted at the end of 1919. While the implementation of this law represented an improvement for Polish workers, it spelled loss of jobs for many Jews because it made work on Saturday compulsory. For example, in 1924 the Jewish workers of the Szereszewski Tobacco Company of Grodno, formerly owned by Jews, were ordered to report for work on Saturdays or lose their jobs.[41] As a result of such discrimination, by the 1930s very few Jewish workers were left in the tobacco and alcohol industries.[42]

Jews were markedly underrepresented in large-scale industry. Only 3.5 percent of the Jewish workers, contrasted with 37.4 percent of the non-Jewish workers, were employed in the largest enterprises of Poland. Eight out of ten Jewish workers but only four out of ten non-Jewish workers were found in small shops. Almost every second Jew in the occupational category of industry and handicrafts was in the garment industry.[43] Jews thus had minimum representation in the modern sectors of the Polish economy; therefore, poverty was worse and more widespread among the Jews than among urban Poles. (In the 1920s, about 80 percent of the total Jewish population lived in what was then considered poverty.) [44] The standard of living of large parts of the Jewish population was comparable to that of impoverished Polish peasants. It is difficult to convey to the western mind the squalor and misery in which large numbers of Jews lived. The advent of the world economic depression brought a higher rate of unemployment to Jewish than non-Jewish workers, since unemployment was substantially lower in state-owned industry from which Jews were excluded. Moreover, the Jewish unemployed, as former employees of small business, were largely ineligible for government unemployment assistance, which covered enterprises with more than five employees.[45]

Adversely affected by governmental policies and measures

were the petty merchants, craftsmen, and other self-employed, who constituted the bulk of Jewish "businessmen" and "industrialists." One measure aimed at Jews although not mentioning them was the law of 1924 that withdrew all concessions for the distribution of products, which had been granted by the industries before they became government monopolies. It was passed despite the vigorous protest of the Jewish Deputies in the Polish Diet, who argued that it would spell economic ruin for 32,000 Jewish families.[46] These concessions were ordered to be reissued exclusively to veterans of the Polish army, most of whom were Poles. Since many of these veterans had no business experience, some rented the concessions back to the individuals from whom they had been taken away. In this manner "the Jew . . . was actually compelled to support a Gentile, who sometimes had a number of such concessions." [47]

Or take the Compulsory Sunday Rest Law: the petty merchants could not afford to be closed for two days. Since many of them were deeply religious and considered it sinful to violate the Sabbath with work, the choice was often between moral anguish and starvation.[48] Jewish small businesses and shops were also severely hit by the governmental orders to modernize. For example, bakeries were ordered to do so or to be shut down. But modernization required an outlay of capital most small enterprises lacked, and banks discriminated sharply against Jewish businesses when it came to granting of credit. This led to the collapse of many small Jewish businesses.[49] It must be remembered that even without these governmental orders to modernize, many petty Jewish businesses and shops folded because of the competition of the Polish producer and consumer cooperatives that came into being after independence. Many more would have met this fate were it not for the growth of Jewish credit cooperatives. Producer and consumer cooperatives failed to take hold among the Jewish population because of its distinctive economic profile: the predominance of self-employed in petty business and crafts. But the credit cooperatives developed to fill the pressing requirements of these Jewish petty entrepreneurs, in dire need of the minimal capital that would enable them to survive economically. The role of these credit unions

TWO JEWISH BOYS PEDDLING BAGELS AND CANDY. WARSAW, 1920S.
(YIVO INSTITUTE FOR JEWISH RESEARCH)

was the attempt to "protect the widest strata of the Jewish people from economic destruction" and they constituted "in a way perhaps the only protection of the [limited] possessions of the masses of Jews." [50]

One of the most flagrant measures was the decree issued by the Ministry of Commerce in August 1936 ordering that signs on stores and establishments carry the name of the owners (as they appeared on birth certificates).[51] By then the government was openly expressing its approval of the anti-Jewish boycott (recall the declaration of the Premier of Poland in June of the same year), and this measure aimed to strengthen it: It made it easier for customers to avoid Jewish enterprises. Worse, it helped the organizers of picketing and terror to single out Jewish enterprises whose firm labels were Polish.

Thus the government policies had severely negative consequences for the bulk of Jewish businessmen, already in a precarious economic situation. Generally local officials were especially zealous in applying government ordinances when it came to Jews. (Often they also took extra measures within their local jurisdiction to add to Jewish hardships.) This is exemplified in taxation, which was especially oppressive to Jews. The intricate system of taxation in this primarily agricultural land put the main burden on small- and medium-sized private business—largely Jewish—which already had the competition of government monopolies and cooperatives to contend with. Taxation was not on profit alone, but also on turnover. In addition, the local tax offices were noted for their arbitrarily high appraisals of Jews' property, and their zealous enforcement of the laws when dealing with Jews. Those who were unable to pay often had their belongings confiscated. Diaries of young Jews vividly reflect the fear of these officials, entering their houses unexpectedly and removing household goods.[52]

Then there were the governmental measures designed to drive older Jewish artisans from their crafts and to prevent young Jews from entering them. In 1927 a law was passed, imposing a system of licensing on the hitherto free practice of crafts. Although over one-third of Poland's artisans were Jewish, the law required that the examinations be conducted solely in Polish. Furthermore, the examining commissions set up by the craft chambers consisted mostly of Polish artisans, noted for their anti-Jewish prejudices. Since many highly skilled Jewish artisans, especially of the older generation, were literate in Yiddish but not in Polish, the Jewish deputies in the Parliament asked that older craftsmen be exempted from such examinations. This request was only partially granted. Thousands of qualified Jewish craftsmen could not become licensed. Without a license, they were not permitted to use helpers, finishers, and apprentices. As a result, many were left without a livelihood. Those who attempted to circumvent these regulations were subjected to snooping by Polish craftsmen and constant harassment by officials. Also, with the curtailment of op-

Jewish credit cooperatives attempted to "protect the widest strata of the Jewish people from economic destruction. . . ."

THE ORGANIZERS OF AN EXHIBIT ON THE JEWISH COOPERATIVE MOVEMENT. ON THE WALL: PORTRAIT OF MARSHAL PIŁSUDSKI AND MAPS OF THE DISTRIBUTION OF JEWISH CREDIT COOPERATIVES IN THE TARNOPOL PROVINCE. TARNÓW, TARNOPOL PROVINCE 1930S.

portunities for apprenticeship, it became difficult for Jewish youths to learn the more skilled crafts.[53]

While forcing the Jews out of their traditional occupations, the government, at all levels, flagrantly practiced discriminatory hiring not only in nationalized industries and public transportation but also in the civil service, including the public school network. This was explained as an attempt to counterbalance the entrenchment of Jews in the professions. Of course, the percentage of Jews in the professions can be differently assessed depending on the perspective. On one hand, Jews made up 21.5 percent of Poland's professionals, but only 9.8 percent of the total population. On the other hand, the 21.5 percent figure was lower than their proportion in the urban population of the country (27 percent). Still, whether one uses the first or second approach, the fact is indisputable that Jews flocked to free professions, such as medicine and law. And the percentage of Jews in them seemed to increase rather than decrease as a result of the governmental policy: Excluded from civil service and government controlled occupations, they did their utmost to enter these free professions. (The 1931 figures show an extremely low proportion of Jews in public service—1.8 percent— and a high one in the professions of law and medicine—33.5 percent and 56.0 percent respectively.) [54]

In this under-industrialized country, a civil service career was very desirable. To provide the growing number of relatively educated people with the kind of jobs that would allow them to claim the superior status of the intelligentsia, as well as to provide them the means of a livelihood, became an important function of the Polish state. The result was a disproportionately large civil service. Jews were systematically excluded from it.[55] This exclusion explains even more than the increase of Jews in the free professions, the tremendously high rate of unemployment among the Polonized Jewish intelligentsia.

In a speech before the Senate, at the beginning of March 1929, Senator Koerner (a Jew) protested these exclusionary practices:

> We have a Constitution, one of the most democratic, which does not discriminate on national or religious grounds: all citi-

zens are equal before the law. We also have on paper civil
equality and even some nationality rights, derived from the Minorities Treaty. Despite all this, we stand before and knock at
hermetically sealed gates for the right to work. We must break
the barrier of deeply rooted prejudices, blinded to the fact that
among Jews too there are capable and qualified people which
the country could and ought to utilize.[56]

It is indeed ironic that the Jewish people of Poland, from
whom so many illustrious world figures stem, appealed to the Polish government and the Polish people in these terms: "that among
Jews too there are capable and qualified people." Little thought
was given by the government to the possibility that its discriminatory and oppressive policies against Jews were curtailing human
resources, so important for Poland's development. The government
focused in a myopic fashion on the problem of unemployment
among Poles and it deluded itself into believing that it could solve
this by exclusionary practices.

A reflection of the rhetoric that expressed this self-delusion is
found in the parliamentary debate to outlaw on "humanitarian
grounds" the kosher slaughtering of animals, led by the Diet-
member Mrs. Prystor, the wife of one of the closest collaborators of
Piłsudski. It resulted in the restriction of kosher slaughtering in
1936. In 1938 the issue was revived and the Diet passed a law to
ban it altogether by 1942 but war broke out before the bill went to
the Senate. Actually, the whole issue of the "inhumane" slaughtering of animals was a coverup for pushing Jews out of the meat
processing industry.[57]

Among the most devoted champions of the economic campaign against the Jews were members of the developing Polish
middle class. Historically, the Jew had been the man of trade in a
country where trade was a demeaning occupation. At the highest
levels of society custom and honor precluded commercial pursuits.
In partitioned Poland, these attitudes had undergone substantial
transformation in the Prussian part under the influence of German
economic ideas and practices. To some extent they were also
weakened in the other parts, owing to the impact of positivist
ideas, which gained influence in the 1870s. In independent Poland

more Poles were going into business and even more aspired to do so. However, they had to compete with Jewish merchants for whom business was practically hereditary, and who were not easy to best in economic competition.[58] And so self-interest was very much involved in the Polish merchants' support of political programs that would eliminate Jews from competition and in initiation of anti-Jewish programs through their organizations, such as the Association of Polish Merchants and the Association of Christian Restauranteurs. For example, the latter passed resolutions calling on municipal governments to revoke licenses of Jews to operate restaurants and groceries.

Almost two years after economic warfare against the Jews was officially proclaimed by the government, its mouthpiece, *Gazeta Polska*, complained in its leading article that the "noneconomic psychology" of Poles was hampering "Polonization" of the country's economic life. "We must admit," it wrote, "that to this day we are a nation with an extremely noneconomic psyche." But it consoled itself with the anti-Semitism of the younger generation, which it interpreted as an indication that spontaneous processes were operating to develop a new economic sense among young Poles:

> It is highly encouraging that the young generation of Poles is filled with a desire to actively participate in the economic life. The constant strengthening of anti-Semitism in its midst brings it closer to the economic problems of the nation and state. . . . Already the young generation realizes that its emotionalism concerning the Jewish question constitutes only one side, the secondary side. The young Pole understands that the actual direction of the economic life of Poland must rest in the hands of Poles only, that we must bring to an end the old aristocratic prejudices which granted the privileges of individual economic advancement to Jews.[59]

The "privilege" that the Jewish businessman was seeking to maintain was the right to personal safety while pursuing his trade in free competition. The young generation so extolled for its anti-Semitism were those young who engaged in anti-Jewish terror, which was often referred to in the Polish press by the euphemism "emotionalism of the young." And this terror, indirectly encouraged by the government, found much support from Polish businessmen.

The Role of the Church

The Catholic Church was the only force in Poland that might have contained the spread of anti-Semitism. It did just the opposite. There were few other places in the world where the Church possessed such strength and enjoyed such wide allegiance. In the minds of most Poles, patriotism and Catholicism were closely linked together. During the long period of foreign rule, the poetic image of Poland as the Christ of nations became the prevalent conception. It was then that the Catholic Church became an important champion of Polishness and the symbol of resistance to foreign rule.[60] With independence, the Polish government recognized the centrality of the Church by according it a privileged position. Both the constitutions of 1921 and 1935 specified the pre-eminence of the Catholic Church among the other faiths in Poland.[61] Moreover, the actual position of the Church exceeded that of the constitutional provisions. As a study of the Catholic Church in the interwar period notes: "Although the Catholic religion was not formally treated in both constitutions as the state and ruling religion, in fact it did play such a role in pre-World War II Poland." [62] In the same ideological declaration of 1937 in which the government officially proclaimed its anti-Jewish policy, it underlined the privileged position of the Catholic Church:

> The Polish Nation tied itself at the beginning of civilized
> development with the Catholic Church and proved repeatedly its
> attachment to it. . . . The Polish Nation, overwhelmingly Cath-
> olic, is attached to its Church, and that is why the Church
> ought to be treated with special care. In regard to other faiths,
> our stand is that defined in the constitution, rooted in the tradi-
> tion of Polish religious tolerance.[63]

Some of the major privileges of the Church were the result of the Concordat which the Polish government signed with the Vatican. Among these was religious instruction of Catholic children by priests in the private as well as in public primary and secondary schools of Poland. In 1934 attendance in the classes teaching religion was made compulsory.

The church thus continued as the bastion of anti-Semitism, both in its traditional form and in the "modern" form pursued by the nationalists.[64] In the past the persistence of the Jews in their ancient faith had been seen by the Church as a danger to the Catholic faith of the country; now, the growing secularization of Jewish youth in modern Poland was viewed as a new form of the same danger. From the perspective of the Church, the secular tendency among young Jews represented continuity and obstinacy in the Jewish error: rejection of the true faith. (Secularization among Poles was not so perceptible in its external manifestations as that of the Jews. The young generation of Poles appeared less distant from the old ways of the Catholic religion than were the young Jews from Jewish Orthodoxy.)

The Church feared that secularization would grow with the integration of Jews into Polish society. This fear was expressed in sermons and was a predominant theme in the Catholic press. One of the many examples is the response to the anti-Jewish pogroms of 1936 in the Jesuit periodical *Przegląd Powszechny*. It condemned formalistically the use of force but hastened to add:

> One should let the Jews be but eliminate them from the life of Christian society. It is necessary to provide separate schools for Jews so that our children will not be infected with their lower morality.[65]

A resolution was adopted by the Synod of Polish Bishops calling for separation of Jewish children in schools and for prohibiting Jews from teaching Polish children.[66]

If the concern about maintaining the faith figured as a prominent factor in its continuation of traditional anti-Semitism, more mundane factors operated in its endorsement and legitimization of modern political anti-Semitism. The Church was a very large landholder in Poland.[67] Although its lands were legally subject to the

Agrarian Reform Law, the government did not enforce it. Since the Church was a huge landowner in a country of impoverished and landless peasants, the use of the Jews as an economic scapegoat served its interests well.

Catholic organizations and the Catholic press were among the most effective propagandizers of the "justice" of the nationalists' anti-Jewish cause. For example, if one compares the Catholic Action organization in Poland with that of the other countries, "the specifically Polish aspect of its program was its anti-Semitism. Although the organization was also supported by anti-Semitic circles in some other countries, in the Catholic Action in Poland anti-Semitism manifested itself most sharply and most brutally." The same could be said of the Catholic press, which persistently poured out anti-Semitic venom: "In no other country did such a massive 'Catholic' Jew-devouring literature exist as in Poland." [68]

Catholic priests figured prominently among the authors of anti-Semitic literature. One of the most prolific was Józef Kruszyński. Among his numerous books and pamphlets was one entitled *The Talmud, What it Contains and What it Teaches*.[69] It was a compendium of lies and distortions presented as the teachings of the Talmud, which supposedly instructed Jews in wickedness. In the 1930s, the priest Stanisław Trzeciak distinguished himself and became quite influential by spreading the gospel of hate in sermons and writings. He combined religious hate with political anti-Semitism in his work, *The Program of Jewish World Politics— Conspiracy and Deconspiracy*.[70] It was a modernized Polish version of the myth of the Elders of Zion.

The distribution of such books was not very large; their influence stemmed from the fact that their ideas were utilized in newspapers, periodicals, pamphlets, and leaflets. In these, the Talmud figured prominently as the chief source of instruction regarding the evil to be practiced by Jews toward non-Jews. The eminent Polish orientalist Tadeusz Zaderecki (who knew Hebrew) refuted these fabrications in *The Talmud in the Fire*. Mass publications ignored it, and therefore it did not reach many Poles.[71] So influential was the calumny against the Talmud that its very name provoked discomfort in most Poles.

An example of the viciousness of the anti-Semitic literature was a popular calendar, which depicted a devil surrounded by books, one of which was marked "Talmud." The caption of the picture read: "The books of Judah; Satan himself must have written them with the blood and tears of non-Jews." [72]

People were swayed even more by the vehement anti-Semitic preaching of the Polish clergy. Among the first lessons Poles learned in school from the priests was that the Jews had killed Christ. In the autobiographies of young Jews, numerous references appear to the effect of these teachings on Polish children's behavior toward Jewish children. For example, a young woman from a middle class, Polonized home in Southeastern Poland wrote in her autobiography:

> From the fifth grade on I went to school with Christian children. I then began to be aware that I am a Jew. After religious instruction [priests taught the Catholic religion in the public schools] and before Catholic holidays, the stories were revived about ritual murder and about Judas. I personally got along well with Catholic girls. Whenever I brought them some goodies before Purim or Passover, they readily took it, even though the matzah supposedly had "Christian blood" in it. It was no use to try to discuss this matter rationally with them. When they had no argument left, they would conclude "it is nevertheless true that you use Christian blood in the matzah. We were told this." Sometimes they would add, "Jew go to Palestine." [73]

So effective were these teachings that large portions of the Polish population still believed that Jews practiced ritual murder of defenseless Christians, especially children. [74] More yet believed that the Jews had killed their God. And if they could kill God, why should plain Polish folk have doubted that Jews were bleeding resurrected Poland? After all, this was the message they received both from the sermons of priests and educated men in government and political parties.

Eventually this message was pronounced by the head of the Polish Church; it was no longer left to the discretion of individual priests and bishops. In 1936, the Primate of Poland came out

openly in support of the anti-Jewish campaign. Cardinal Hlond, in
a pastoral letter read from the pulpits of most churches, gave his
spiritual blessing to the campaign in the economic and cultural
spheres:

> A Jewish problem exists, and will continue to exist as long
> as the Jews remain Jews. This question varies in its intensity
> and manifestations in different countries. It is especially difficult
> in our country and ought to be the subject of serious consider-
> ation. Here I shall touch briefly on its moral sides in connection
> with the present situation.
>
> It is a fact that the Jews fight against the Catholic Church,
> they are free-thinkers, and constitute the vanguard of atheism,
> of the bolshevik movement and of revolutionary activity. It is a
> fact that Jewish influence upon morals is fatal, and their pub-
> lishers spread pornographic literature. It is true that the Jews
> are committing frauds, practicing usury, and dealing in white
> slavery. It is true that in schools, the influence of the Jewish
> youth upon the Catholic youth is generally evil, from a religious
> and ethical point of view. But—let us be just. Not all Jews are
> like that. . . .
>
> I warn against the fundamental, unconditional anti-Jewish
> principle, imported from abroad [Nazi Germany]. It is con-
> trary to Catholic Ethics. It is permissible to love one's own na-
> tion more; it is not permissible to hate anyone. Not even Jews.
> One does well to prefer his own kind in commercial dealings
> and to avoid Jewish stores and Jewish stalls in the markets, but
> it is not permissible to demolish Jewish businesses, destroy their
> merchandise, break windows, torpedo their houses. One ought
> to fence oneself off against the harmful moral influences of
> Jewry, to separate oneself against its anti-Christian culture, and
> especially to boycott the Jewish press and the demoralizing Jew-
> ish publications. But it is not permissible to assault Jews, to hit,
> maim or blacken them. . . . When divine mercy enlightens a
> Jew, and he accepts sincerely his and our Messiah, let us greet
> him with joy in the Christian midst.[75]

It is important to note that this pastoral letter came from a
churchman who prior to it was considered part of the moderate
wing—in contrast to the bulk of the Polish clergy which was very
nationalist—and who carefully followed the Vatican line. Also to be
recalled is that it was issued a year before the government formally

announced its anti-Semitic policy through the Ideological Declaration of OZN. Significantly, the pastoral letter contained the main themes of modern as well as traditional anti-Semitism. However, it drew a line between Polish anti-Semitism and the Nazi variety (without naming it specifically) by rejecting unconditional racist anti-Semitism and anti-Jewish terror as un-Christian. Recall that the same line was drawn by the government; but official anti-Semitism still led to an increase in violence. Actually, the pastoral letter expressed well how far the Polish nation as a whole had traveled down the anti-Semitic road by the beginning of 1936.

IV
Organized Terror and Abuse

M ost of the governmental measures that were squeezing Jews out of their traditional economic pursuits without providing them with other ways of making a living were preceded by militant anti-Jewish activities, including boycotts and terror. Terror became the chief weapon of the militant anti-Semites, and the success of all other tactics they employed depended on it. Terror was unleashed with a special bravado by the young radical splinter groups from the nationalist *Endecja*. For "integral nationalism easily passed over into racialism," [1] especially among young people devoid of the sentiments found among some members of the older generation who had worked and fought together with Jews for Poland's independence. Their tactics of terror and abuse brought young militants into the center of the national arena: the attention of Poles and the apprehension of Jews was focused on them. There were a number of groups among them: O.N.R. (National Radical Camp), OWP (Camp of Greater Poland), *Falanga*, ABC, ZMN (Association of Young Nationalists), etc. Inspired by the Nazis, their overall goals were to deprive all Jews of Polish citizenship, expropriate their property, and expel them.

The boycott campaign of Jewish stores and enterprises became highly effective because of the terror that accompanied it. Despite their general dislike of Jews, it was not easy to convince

Poles to abstain from patronizing Jewish enterprises. True, there was wide envy and resentment of those Jews who prospered in business; and in addition Poles held the notion that products manufactured by Jews were shoddy.[2] But the Polish masses, especially the poor peasants, could not afford fine products; their chief concern was to obtain the goods they needed as cheaply as possible. And Jewish craftsmen, selling their products from pushcarts and stalls during marketdays, offered the cheapest prices. In the towns and cities, bargains could be found in Jewish stores. Therefore, such signs as *"this is a Christian store,"* catchy slogans such as *"patronize your own,"* and holy pictures of Christ and Mary prominently displayed in the windows of Christian stores could not have prevented Poles from seeking bargains in Jewish stores.

The reign of terror, unleashed by radical nationalist groups accomplished what mere propaganda could not. Students and toughs began picketing Jewish stores, threatening Poles who dared to enter. Also, psychological terror was used to shame the Poles who patronized Jewish enterprises and who sought the services of Jewish doctors, dentists, and lawyers. A much-used technique was to photograph Poles entering such places and then to publish their pictures with derogatory captions in hate sheets and pamphlets. In the shrill propaganda of "de-Judaizing commerce" accompanying the terror, the Jewish stall, the Jewish pushcart, the Jewish shop, became the main economic problem facing Poland and their destruction the chief means of economic liberation. Store windows were smashed, stalls and pushcarts were overturned, merchandise was destroyed, the Jewish owners knifed, beaten, and victimized. In a few large Jewish-owned stores bombs were planted.[3] This organized pattern of terror was widespread throughout Poland.

On the economic front, the greatest cruelty and brutality was displayed by the terrorists against the Jewish poor, while they exploited the sterotype of the wealthy Jew. A glimpse of it is provided in the moving description by the Polish novelists, Wanda Wasilewska, in her protest statement, entitled "Dark current":

> Here fifteen, sixteen people live in one room. Here five people sleep in one bed. . . . Here at a shaky table the meal consists of a tiny slice of bread, garnished with onion. . . .

> Leathersticher. Shoemaker. Barber. They all live this
> way. . . . It is against such people that the scoundrels in stu-
> dent's attire move. . . . Louder and louder shout the young
> throats. . . . The slogan of economic struggle is raised against
> the paupers of the Jewish street. Why look for those responsible
> [for Poland's economic problems elsewhere] when it is so
> easy to find them nearby, in a street of the Jewish quarters?
> Why suppress when it is so easy and so safe to vent one's anger
> in a fight with a bowed porter [Jewish porters who carried
> heavy loads on their backs], with a Jewish boy selling watches,
> with an old Jewish woman [selling bagels]? [4]

In such attacks against the most defenseless and poorest, the
popular slogan "beat up a Jew," resounded. This was the slogan of
a new type of violence, in addition to the sporadic spontaneous violence against the Jews, which had a long history in Poland. It went
beyond the traditional pattern, in which adolescent gangs would

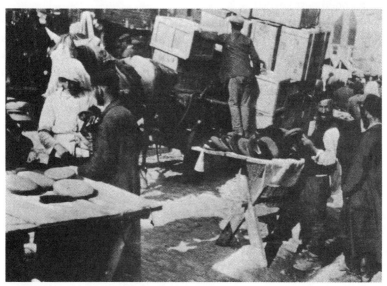

Jewish craftsmen, selling their products directly to the peasants
during marketdays, offered the cheapest prices.
THE BUSY MARKET PLACE. POLISH PEASANT WOMAN BARGAINING.
GARWOLIN, LUBLIN PROVINCE, 1930S.(YIVO INSTITUTE FOR JEWISH
RESEARCH)

attack Jewish children, throw stones at Jewish adults, and set dogs on Jews of all ages. The new violence was highly organized, systematic, and persistent, culminating in pogroms.[5] Przytyk, Mińsk-Mazowiecki, Brześć-Litewski—these were towns in which pogroms took place; they became household words among the Jewish masses who feared that their town might be next on the list. They knew that all Jews in Poland were in danger because killing Jews was contagious in the atmosphere of hate that reigned in the country. Indeed, according to the official figures reported to the Diet by the Premier of Poland, General Sławoj-Składkowski, 21 pogroms and 348 anti-Jewish outbreaks took place in 1936 in the Białystok region alone.[6] Many more pogroms would have occurred in smaller towns had the Jews not organized preventive action and self-defense. By 1938, Jews were also seeking court action, but the perpetrators often went free, or else received short or suspended sentences.[7]

Polish universities became the stage of the most extreme anti-Semitic activities. The strategy of striking at the universities proved effective for a number of reasons. The initial successes were tied to the fact that the city police had no jurisdiction within the university grounds because of the traditional rules of university autonomy. Coupled with this was the fact that the university guards were not equipped to deal promptly with incitement to violence, and certainly not with riots. The initial terror gathered momentum as the majority of faculty and students remained passive. According to Z. Nowicki, then president of the Polish Teachers' Association, and Professor T. Kotarbiński, the head of its University Section (in a memorandum submitted to the Minister of Religious Creeds and Public Education), the militants counted on this passivity.[8] Whether or not they also anticipated the quick concessions from university administrations and their failure to punish the guilty, this is what actually occurred and served as encouragement to further terror. Terror became a most effective way for militants to obtain what they wanted at the university and for attracting attention of the mass media. Interestingly, toward the end of 1937, a Bulletin of the Jewish Congress in New York, discussing what was happening at Polish universities, commented thus:

> The American University man may find it rather incredible that outside groups, led by politicians who are completely out of place in the sphere of education and research, should resort to instigating student fraternities to carry on terroristic extracurricular activities.[9]

If so, then Americans who witnessed campus militancy of the 1960s would find it easier to understand what happened at Polish universities in the 1930s. As a matter of fact, the atmosphere was very similar and so was the behavior of students, administration, and faculty—except that in Poland the Jews were the target of the militants.

The University, the Hotbed of Anti-Semitism

From the very beginning of independence, social anti-Semitism had existed at the Polish universities. The university dormitories were run by fraternities, which excluded Jews. This was a major reason for the decision made in 1922 by concerned Jews to build special dormitories for Jewish students in the university cities of Poland. The festive opening of the Warsaw facility took place in 1926.[10] By then the anti-Jewish political campaign was widespread at the universities. Its focus was on agitation for a Jewish quota. It aimed at bringing back to the universities of independent Poland the exclusionary policies of the Czarist era. The Jewish students who found their way into Polish universities did so on the basis of stringent, impersonal criteria of merit (the *matura* certificate of graduation from high school, which involved difficult comprehensive examinations, and additional difficult qualifying entrance examinations in certain fields, such as medicine and engineering). No special provisions existed for them because of linguistic handicaps, nor were there at that time any special provisions for any underpriviledged groups, including Polish peasants.

Jewish students overcame such handicaps by individual determination and hard work. Their cultural heritage of emphasis on learning and their traditional response of overcoming obstacles that Gentiles placed before them were important social factors in their successful entry to universities. Soon Poles started noticing that the proportion of Jews among the student population was greater than their proportion among the total population. Clearly, this state of affairs was not pleasing to most Poles, in light of the prevalent social definition of Jews as a foreign body and the then common conception of university education as an extraordinary privilege. Such an education was not only the means to high ranking occupations but a "permanent asset" which set an individual apart. It bestowed "a title, a dignity" that was everlasting. To Poles it had an affinity with the bestowal of titles of nobility, the memory of which still played a part in how Poles viewed themselves and others.[11] The solution was provided by the largest opposition party, the nationalist Endecja. It clamored for a Jewish quota (called *numerus clausus*, a closed number). Students otherwise fully qualified were to be excluded from the universities because the fixed ratio of Jews had to be maintained. The idea caught on among the Polish youth, especially the university students. The militants among them pressed for the establishment of such quotas. The first quotas in independent Poland were instituted as early as 1921 at the School of Medicine and the School of Law at the University of Lvov. However, the then Minister of Religious Creeds and Public Education ordered the Rector of the University to discontinue the quota because it violated the Polish constitution.[12]

Despite this reversal, persistent agitation for Jewish quotas continued. At first came "informal" quotas, which were introduced at the beginning of the 1924–25 school year at various institutions of higher learning. Appeals to the government by Jewish representatives in Parliament and by other leaders of the Jewish community met with a standard answer: because of university autonomy, the government could not interfere. The Jewish leaders pleaded in the name of the Polish constitution and argued that university autonomy was not supposed to violate the highest law of the land. Dr. Dawidsohn, a member of the Polish Senate, pointed out that the government was not so mindful of university autonomy when other things than Jewish rights were involved.[13]

Although these arguments testify to Jewish resistance, that resistance nevertheless bore little fruit. The failure of the government to react to unofficial quotas encouraged the student activists from radical rightist organizations and certain fraternities to press for an official quota system. The All-Polish Conference of Students, convening in Vilno in February of 1925, adopted by an overwhelming vote a resolution calling upon the government to draft a parliamentary bill to establish an official Jewish quota at all schools of higher learning. Another resolution demanded that diplomas received by students from universities abroad not be recognized in Poland, in order to limit the number of Jews in the professions.[14]

Apart from resolutions, the universities were disrupted by heated agitation and militant activities, to the day World War II began. From time to time universities were closed by the administrators in the hope that the storm would pass. But the campaign against Jews persisted, well maneuvered by the young Endeks and members of the extreme splinter groups. It became particularly vicious during the 1936–37 school year and continued thus until Poland was invaded. From time to time at various universities a "Jewless day" was proclaimed by the militants; on such days they would force all Jews from school. Eventually the "Jewless day" became the "Jewless week."[15] At all times and at all universities Jewish students were heckled, humiliated, and attacked by some of their Polish fellow students and helpers from anti-Jewish terrorist groups outside the university. A Jewish law student wrote after his graduation:

> I was sick over having to study in Poland. I envied the people who managed to study in France, Belgium, or Palestine. If I had only been able to go abroad. But I did not have the resources.[16]

These words assume special meaning since they came from a person for whom the university attendance represented tremendous achievement. In high school, he had managed to overcome a substantial linguistic handicap; at his home only Yiddish was spoken. But for him, and for Jewish students in general, the fruits of their achievement were made bitter by the hate that dominated the university atmosphere.

Finally, the universities completely abdicated to the sowers of hate. A stringent Jewish quota was openly instituted at all schools of higher learning in order to "bring peace" to the university. But the terror and agitation continued and remained unpunished by the university administrators. By their militant and disruptive tactics, the radical nationalist students succeeded in intimidating the administration and faculty into introducing in October of 1937 such "reforms" as the classroom seating ghettos.[17] An eighteen-year-old Jewish boy, the son of a tailor, who could never have aspired to a university education was nevertheless so touched by this event. He wrote in his diary:

> The newspaper headlines read "At the University a seating ghetto was established." A few words but how much meaning! Separate seats for Jews. Again we are moving backward, to the Middle Ages and their superstitions. Of course, the Endek intellectual level is not above the mentality of the Middle Ages.[18]

The Minister of Religious Creeds and Public Education, Wojciech Świętosławski greeted the seating ghettoes as a wise step taken by the heads of the universities "endeavoring to maintain order." Earlier, in a declaration before the Polish Diet, the same Minister had condemned the attacks on and torture of Jewish students by those who "come to school armed with clubs, knifes and sticks." He had deplored then the passivity of the students in general who "failed to take energetic steps to quell in the bud these excesses" and asserted the following:

> Under such conditions the university administration cannot maintain order despite its best intentions. . . . The masses of citizens—especially the professors, students, and the parents of relatives and students—ought to participate in a campaign to condemn the excesses. The passive attitude of the public would threaten the ethics and morality of the land. . . . I hope that the fact alone of my making known the excesses which took place in the schools of higher learning will meet with a response from all citizens who care about the honor and good name of our university youth.[19]

A minority of brave teachers—conservative as well as liberal—opposed the introduction of seating ghettos. They were often insulted and bodily attacked by militants. Among them were such leading professors as the geophysicist Stanisław Kalinowski, the sociologist Ludwik Krzywicki, the professor of medicine and Senator, Mieczysław Michałowicz. The last, a devout Catholic, appealed to the students and public as "a Senator of the Polish Republic who swore to uphold the Constitution" and as one who in his "conscience wants to remain a faithful Christian": "if God did not hesitate to put the spirit of His Son in a Semite's body, it is not a human matter to decide who is worse or better." [20] But even such appeals did not carry much weight in the climate of opinion that then prevailed.

The administration caved in and introduced seating ghettos, And the Minister Świętosławski approved them. Here then we note a pattern similar to that pursued by the government in the economic sphere. Violence was condemned in words but encouraged in deeds, through concessions granted to the perpetrators of violence at the cost of the victims of violence. Further violence was the result. (To what extent the encouragement was intentional could be argued. In the case of the Minister of Education, I am certain that it was not. There is, however, little room for doubt about the effects of the concessions.) [21]

After the establishment of the seating ghettos, the terror at the universities increased. It aimed at complete exclusion of Jews from higher learning, under the slogan of the militants "the ghetto, the beginning of *numerus nullus.*" Toughs invaded the classrooms and laboratories and forcibly removed Jewish students. But the blame was now put on the Jewish students, whose response to the ghetto had been to stand against the walls rather than to take their assigned seats. Their protest incurred disapproval from various quarters. The university administrators refused to punish the perpetrators of violence, on the grounds that the Jews had provoked them by refusing to sit in the seats assigned to them. In addition, the administrators—and even some instructors—ordered from the classrooms those Jewish students who refused to take their seats.[22] Ironically, among the institutions where such events occurred was the Wawelberg and Rotwand Technological Institute, which had been founded by the Wawelbergs, a wealthy Jewish family, and handed over by its descendents to the Polish state after independence. At the J. Piłsudski University of Warsaw, Jewish students were ordered to appear before the university disciplinary authorities because they refused to sit in the seats assigned to them. Some professors excluded Jews from their seminars by making it a condition for admittance that they sit in the separate seats, which they knew Jewish students would refuse to do.[23]

These concessions resulted in an acceleration of the anti-Semitic campaign. Many more Jewish students were attacked; a few were killed.[24] The bands of student terrorists, elegantly turned out with their university hats tipped at a fashionable angle, armed with canes and knives, did not confine themselves to the university grounds. They took walks in the evening to hunt for Jewish students. If one was Jewish, one tried to avoid the militants; one watched the corners where they congregated, but their fun consisted of surprise attack on Jewish students. A Jewish student newly accepted at the University of Cracow described in his autobiography his first evening in the city. Upon his arrival, he had ventured on a walk in town and was beaten up by an Endek group: "I was so disgusted, that I felt like returning home without unpacking . . . For a long time I felt horrible. I was scared. It seemed as if everybody out there was waiting to attack me." [25]

Occasionally the terrorist acts touched the sensibilities of Poles. Reports came out of Polish male students kicking Jewish female students, which violated the image of the chivalrous Polish male. But the Polish press generally spared their readers such details. It was mostly laconic in its reporting of Jewish students killed by the militants.[26] In contrast, its coverage was extensive when it came to the demonstrations and rhetoric of the young militants. As noted then by a perceptive observer:

> The "Young Generation" is now in style. The reactionary press of all shades does not stop from writing, discussing, reporting about the needs, the aspirations, the "ideals" of the young generation. Also the government officials and university administrators accommodate the young with such things as seating ghettos at universities.[27]

Soon high school students attempted to emulate the university militants. Since it was neither compulsory nor tuition free, high school attendance was considered a mark of privilege, and militant students wanted to deprive young Jews of this privilege. But in this case the Ministry of Religious Creeds and Public Education took a decisive stand. Because secondary schools were under its direct jurisdiction, its intervention could not be charged, in contrast to the universities, with being a violation of school autonomy. Thus the attempt to establish a seating ghetto at a major high school swiftly resulted in its losing the status of a state school.[28] Since such status was of considerable advantage, the loss of it proved to be an effective warning to secondary schools in general.

The Nationalist Intelligentsia, the Fountainhead of Anti-Semitism

While much of the impetus and bravado of the anti-Semitic movement came from the young generation, the molding of the movement was accomplished by the adult intelligentsia. If brute force was the chief anti-Jewish weapon of young students, the pen was the weapon of their elders. The proponents of cultural anti-Semitism waged their war in journals and books. It must be recalled here that before independence Jewish intellectuals and artists were being drawn into Polish cultural life in increasing numbers. A Jewish creative force, narrowly confined for centuries in its own stream, was released in the nineteenth century to nourish Polish arts and sciences, and did so for a long time, even after the bulk of Polish Jewry had been destroyed by the Nazis. Did the Poles—so known for their patriotism—look with favor upon these new sources that were enriching their culture once Poland had become free? Some did, but their voices drowned out by the nationalist intellectuals who sounded the battle cry that Jews, through their prominence in cultural life, were undermining Polish art, literature, and the language. To the nationalist intellectuals, as important as the economic struggle was against the Jews, the stakes on the cultural front were higher, for the Polish soul was being endangered.

Among the most popular anti-Semitic books of the 1930s was *The Fall of Israel*, written by several Endek intellectuals under the pseudonym Henryk Rolicki. Published by National Thought, the organ of the National Party, it was reprinted a number of times. Its appeal lay in its promise that the supposed evil power of the Jews, which had brought down whole nations, was in its last phase and could be destroyed.[29] The message of the anti-Semitic intellectuals fell on fertile ground. In the highest intellectual circles of Poland the absurd notion prevailed that Jews had no culture, no ethics, in contrast to the Poles' European culture and Christian ethics. The educated Poles, to say nothing of the common people, seldom were aware that Warsaw was the center of a modern Yiddish literature, which had both Jewish and non-Jewish admirers in the Western world.[30] In this very religious country there was hardly mention by Polish intellectuals of the common elements in the Judeo-Christian tradition. On the contrary, if anything scholarly writings were used to bolster the argument that the Christian religion had little or nothing in common with Judaism.[31]

As it did in the economic area, in the cultural area anti-Semitism fluctuated in intensity throughout the interwar period. It reached a high point in the early 1920s, and an even higher one in the 1930s. In the 1930s, a racist attack was launched against "Jewish" members of the integrated intelligentsia (including Poles of Jewish descent), from which the most illustrious men of Polish letters and science were not spared. The idea was often expounded in journals, books, and newspapers that no matter how Polish these people appeared to the untrained eye, they were in fact polluting and undermining (Judaizing) Polish culture.[32] Cultural anti-Semitism surpassed former restraints when it was officially proclaimed by the government in 1937 and subsequently reiterated and elaborated by its representatives. For example, Colonel Wenda, as the spokesman of the Camp of National Unity and Vice Marshal of the Polish Diet, went on the radio to explain how "Polish cultural and social life must preserve its independence from Jewish influences, foreign to our spirit." [33]

Both the nature and the fluctuation of cultural anti-Semitism are exemplified by the treatment of the foremost Polish poet of the interwar period, Julian Tuwim.[34] In 1921 it was said that that "Tuwim's writing is not Polish; he merely writes in the Polish language." [35] His Polish being impeccable and beautiful, it would have been incredible had he been accused—as were others—of "corrupting" the Polish language by "infesting" it with Yiddishisms. But he, as well as other Polish poets of Jewish background, was charged by the nationalist literary critic, Zygmunt Wasilewski, with displaying "Semitic" characteristics of "vampirism" and sadistic cruelty. The well-known Polish playwright Karol Hubert Rostworowski, claimed Tuwim was corrupting Polish literature with Jewish characteristics: that Tuwim's poetry contained utilitarian and revolutionary elements, lacked sensitivity to and love of nature, and was full of "sensual fury characteristic of the Eastern Semitic race." It testifies to the atmosphere of that time that this charge was taken seriously enough to warrant systematic refutation.[36]

Attempts to refute the arguments of the anti-Semites did not weaken their influence. Ridiculing them was no help either. For example, Andrzej Stawar, a Pole, asked the anti-Semites how Jews could be Judaizing Polish literature when they supposedly had no culture.[37] But for many Poles the anti-Semitic pronouncements of the intellectuals legitimized their traditional anti-Jewish feelings. They therefore responded to them rather than to their critics. Jacob Lestchinsky captured well the mood and influence of the Polish intelligentsia, which possessed an exaggerated consciousness of its particular role in the nation:

> The Polish intelligentsia more than any other section of the people bore the onus of forging the destiny of the newly created state and therefore sensed most keenly the cruel disillusionment. It felt most tragically the poverty and insignificance of the available material and spiritual forces in comparison with the enormous tasks which history had set before the new Poland. The intelligentsia everywhere plays a role far surpassing its quantitative importance and in Poland they had made greater sacrifices than all other classes and had in consequence assumed the crown of the martyrs and emancipators of the father-

land, gaining vast influence over the fate of the republic. Moreover, regardless of the fact that their ranks included
represenatives of the peasantry and the urban middle classes,
the Polish intellectuals were ideologically the legitimate heirs of
the *szlachta* (gentry), a class noted for its megalomania. This
group had not only infected all others with its chauvinist ideology and megalomania but with its discontent and nervousness
as well as its disguised inferiority complex.[38]

Thus the broad economic and political factors which made
Poland ripe for organized anti-Semitism were operating with special strength in the case of the intelligentsia. Also, their own immediate interests were involved. Among the upper intelligentsia,
many had secured and many more aspired to bureaucratic posts,
and in this way became very dependent on the "ruling clique."
Therefore, "while still claiming its exalted position as an elite" the
intelligentsia "became exposed to political corruption and to servil-
ity and lost much of its dignity and independence."[39] And in the
case of the lower levels of the intelligentsia, whose material situation had deteriorated during independence, exclusionary policies
against Jews held out the promise of wider opportunities for them.
Had posts been filled on the basis of objective criteria alone, many
Jews would have landed in them. But the anti-Semitic ideology
justified keeping individuals out of civil service and teaching jobs
simply because they were Jews. When the government launched
its official anti-Semitic policy and instituted the Camp of National
Unity, white collar workers' organizations, such as the Association
of Social Workers, were among the first to join it. And discriminatory policies were also gaining in the professional associations.
For example, the Association of Lawyers published a directory that
listed the religious affiliation of each lawyer. The association also
demanded that Jews be denied admittance to the bar. In the last
years preceding the war there was movement in many professional
associations to introduce the "Aryan paragraph," modeled on Nazi
Germany's, that would have excluded Jews from membership.[40]

Polish Opposition to Anti-Semitism

One must not lose sight of the fact that there was among Poles some organized and individual opposition to anti-Semitism. On various occasions the Polish Socialist Party (PPS) cooperated with the Jewish socialist parties—mostly with Bund and sometimes with Poale Zion—in their fight against concrete anti-Jewish measures. In the last years before World War II, this party vigorously attacked the government's policy of official anti-Semitism. It charged that a coalition of Sanacja-Endecja was in the making which spelled fascism and a betrayal of everything that Józef Piłsudski stood for.[41] During that period, the Democratic Clubs (founded in 1937), and their successor, the Democratic Party (1938), fought anti-Semitism as part of their struggle to rescue Polish democracy from the fatal assault upon it by the forces of extreme nationalism and by the government itself.

The Democratic Party attracted outstanding individuals of different political shades, as well as some who had formerly been nonpolitical. Among the best-known names connected with this organization—which was popularly known as the "Party of the Progressive Intelligentsia"—and its endeavor to restore democracy in Poland were Colonel January Grzedziński, Professor Marcel Handelsman, and the diplomat Tytus Filipowicz.

Whether as a matter of tactics (to attract Jews to the party) or as a matter of principle, the Communist Party was consistent in its condemnation of anti-Semitism as a tool of the ruling class (among which they included big Jewish capitalists) used to split the natural unity of the working people. As early as June 9, 1923, Stefan Krulikowski, a Communist deputy (a Pole) declared, in a discussion in the Diet: "Everything is permissible in regard to the Jew in Poland: one is allowed to attack him physically, insult him. . . . Everyone observing life today can easily see that the Jew is placed outside the protection of the law. To wrong a Jew, to deprive him of a human designation, has become a matter of principle." As he was speaking a deputy from the seats on the right called out: "Leave it. They will defend themselves without you." [42]

In this exchange is symbolized the attitude of those political parties which were not anti-Semitic but remained silent in the face of it. This attitude is exemplified by the peasant parties (*Piast, Wyzwolenie*) which were originally committed to equal rights for minorities. After 1931, as a united party (*Stronnictwo Ludowe*), they abstained from taking a stand against anti-Semitism, in fear of being branded as the lackeys of Jews. Indeed, they demanded that "middle class functions [should] more and more pass into the hands of Poles" and urged that Jews emigrate. And the political parties that had been mildly anti-Semitic before were by the late 1930s enthusiastic supporters of the official anti-Jewish policy of the government. For instance, the centrist Christian Democratic Party, the party of the lower middle class and craftsmen, adopted in March 1937 a formal resolution calling for the "removal of the harmful influences of Jewry and Masonry which cannot be done without the intervention of the state." It demanded the "de-Jewification of cities, commerce, industry and the professions, as well as the removal of those Jewish influences injurious to Polish culture." [43] In short, the political opposition to the anti-Jewish campaign became increasingly confined to the Polish left, which commanded the allegiance of only a small part of the Polish population.

But among those prominent Poles who courageously continued their associations with Jews and who as individuals spoke out against the "promoters of brutal methods" there were not only leftists but also conservatives, liberals, and some without political identification. In the forefront were the Greek Catholic Bishop Grzegorz Chomszyn, the writer Maria Dąbrowska, and some prominent scholars in addition to the professors previously named, including the sociologist Stefan Czarnowski, the geophysicist and pioneer of higher public education Antoni Dobrowolski, the classicist Tadeusz Ganszyniec, the linguist Henryk Ułaszyn.[44] Among those people who could not be intimidated was also one of the best known novelists in Poland, Maria Kuncewiczowa. In response to an article in the radical nationalist periodical *Prosto z Mostu*, which had attacked her for actively supporting Jews, she wrote:

> Jews today are placed outside the law. In their misery, who will support them? I know that at this moment religious criteria

are not "relevant"; they are becoming completely replaced by nationalist criteria. But the blood of my forefathers spilled for Poland in the Dąbrowski Legion, in prisons and in uprisings, as well as my own conscience, give me the right to want an honorable Poland, chivalrous and Christian. In such a Poland I believe and I shall never betray her.[45]

But the number of such individuals decreased as organized anti-Semitism increased. The circles of "integrated" intelligentsia were thinning, as Polish intellectuals who stood by their "Jewish" friends were insulted, mistreated, and even beaten. They were disparagingly called "Jewish lackeys." A growing number of newspapers and periodicals were vituperative in their "exposés" and attacks on the defenders of Jews. Their true or fabricated Jewish ancestors were dragged out to prove that they were Jews in disguise. How virulent the atmosphere was can be gathered from the fact that the defenders of the Jews often had to disclaim that they had any Jewish ancestors.[46]

Nevertheless, the moral and physical courage of those Poles who were not silenced in their opposition to anti-Semitism inspired and brought solace to many Jews. This applies not only to the nationally known individuals but also to the unknowns who dared to treat Jews with humanity.[47] The Jews generally admired and spoke of them with special affection (the religious Jews called them *tsadikim*, righteous Gentiles). In her diary, a sixteen-year-old girl recalled one such man:

> I came back from the funeral of the principal of the public school. This is the reason I am in a terrible mood. He was such a good and just man. He did not make differences between Jews and Catholics. For him all were equal. . . . At the cemetary, we all cried, young and old alike.[48]

Still, from a sociological perspective, it is important to note that even among those courageous Poles who opposed anti-Semitism there were few who in their thinking could go beyond religious pluralism and admit the validity of cultural pluralism. The same could be said of the Polish Socialist Party. While it consistently opposed anti-Semitism, it refused to recognize Jews as a separate national group and insisted that the full assimilation of

Jews into the Polish nation would take place under democratic socialism.[49] The idea of Jewish cultural distinctiveness, that a separate Jewish nationality could be fostered on Polish soil, was unacceptable to most opponents of anti-Semitism. They were convinced that full Polonization of the Jewish masses would eventually occur in a democratic and tolerant Poland. Anti-Semitism, they were sure, was playing a major role in slowing the process of Polonization and in preventing its taking hold among the Jewish masses. They thought it natural that in a democratic Poland, enlightened Jews would prefer Polish to Jewish ways. By permitting Jews to be Poles without renouncing their religion, Poland would be bestowing a gift that most socialists could not conceive enlightened Jews would refuse. Their personal Jewish friends, usually highly Polonized, were to them the prototypes of the "Poles of Mosaic faith" into whom the great number of Jews would eventually become transformed in a Poland free of anti-Semitism. They were therefore especially aroused when anti-Jewish prejudice and discrimination were directed against the Polonized Jews.[50]

Among the small number of fighters against anti-Semitism whose vision extended beyond religious pluralism alone was the publicist Tadeusz Hołówko, the philosopher Count Dunin-Borkowski, the writer Stanisław Vincenz,[51] and the gifted essayist and reporter Ksawery Pruszyński. The last maintained that the Jewish question was above all a moral question: whether people have the right to determine their own destiny. Pruszyński put forth the advanced idea that the Jews themselves should have the right to decide how much they wished to participate in the larger society. Thus he maintained that assimilationism, Zionism, and Orthodoxy were all equally valid. Accordingly, he urged the Polish government to refrain from taking sides in this matter and leave it completely to the individual Jews to decide which road they wanted to follow.

Pruszyński also perceived with unusual clarity the negative effects of organized anti-Semitism on the country at large. He pointed out, for example, how much more useful it would be to Poland if Jews were allowed to develop its industry instead of being squeezed out of it. Warning against the impoverishment of Polish arts and sciences, he emphasized the tremendous contributions that individuals of Jewish background had made to Polish culture.[52] But the pronouncements of Pruszyński and the other opponents of the anti-Jewish campaign proved to be voices in the wilderness.

Unsubdued Anti-Semitism

The anti-Semitic climate of opinion that cyrstallized in interwar Poland had many ingredients. The basic component was the widespread traditional anti-Semitism, which had persisted for centuries. It was marked by religious beliefs and medieval myths of the evil Jew as the Christ killer, the devil, who used Christian blood. Superimposed upon the traditional beliefs were the nationalistic stereotypes of the Jew as the antithesis of everything Polish: the enemy and corrupter of Polish values, the underminer of Polish nationhood, the Communist. Such beliefs, were especially prominent among white-collar workers, government employees, and students. These stereotypes were consistent with the overall social definition of the Jew as different and foreign. On top of all this was the "modern" notion of the Jew as an economic exploiter.[53] The Polish middle class found this notion especially appealing. Also present were sexual stereotypes of the Jewish man and woman as perverted sensualists, given to overindulgence and immorality, spreaders of pornography and traffickers in prostitution.

In this climate of opinion, the image of the Jew that emerged was that of a monstrous creature with many ugly faces that he skillfully disguised. As the prominent writer Benedykt Hertz remarked, "it suffices to call something Jewish and it becomes odious." [54] With Church, school, and press all fostering such images it was not difficult to turn the frustrations of the Polish people against Jews.

The writer Aleksander Świętochowski can not be counted among the friends of Jews, but he correctly conveyed the reaction of most Poles to the denunciations of anti-Semitism by a few prominent Poles:

> The Jews and their defenders . . . unfold in vivid images
> the monstrosity of their [the anti-Semitic terrorists'] acts; they
> remind the Polish people of a whole catechism of religious com-
> mandments and a whole code of civil duties . . . . most people
> do not care, and if they do, they harbor loud or quiet sympathy
> and recognition for the anti-Semitic perpetrators.[55]

A similar appraisal of the pervasiveness of anti-Jewish feelings
was made during the same year by a man of dissimilar views, Dr.
Jechiel Halpern—a Jew and a socialist:

> We are fully aware that anti-Semitism, in every form and in
> every sector of life, works against the interests of the Polish
> working classes, both urban and rural. Nevertheless, among
> these masses deeply rooted and constantly activated prejudices
> exist which produce in them an indifference and even a silent
> approval of anti-Jewish violence. It consoles us that the Polish
> peasant refuses to be drawn into participating in the organiza-
> tion of pogroms, that the Polish worker sometimes opposes such
> actions, that some sectors of the intelligentsia speak out against
> medieval measures of separating Jews. But the sad fact remains
> that when it comes to "peaceful" removal of Jews from eco-
> nomic posts, to keeping us out of civil service and municipal
> service jobs, to excluding Jewish workers from government
> owned industries, to discriminatory practices against Jewish
> businessmen and artisans, to refusal of credit to Jews—in the
> struggle against all of these measures we are almost completely
> alone.[56]

By the time the Polish government officially proclaimed its
anti-Jewish stand, the Polish nationalists had succeeded in achieving a large degree of consensus among the population concerning
the "Jewish question." However, this consensus was not present in
the issue of the incorporation of racism into anti-Semitism. This
can be seen in the "Puder" affair, which occurred about a year and
a half after the government's first official declaration of its anti-
Jewish stand.

A priest named Puder, a convert from Judaism, was attacked
by a man shouting anti-Jewish invectives at him while he was performing the Sunday service in the Church in Warsaw to which he

had been newly assigned. The announcement of this assignment after the retirement of the old priest, the well known anti-Semite Trzeciak, provoked a flow of racist protest and innuendo in the nationalist and in a large part of the Catholic press. Father Puder was imputed to have declared himself of Jewish nationality and therefore to have denied being a Pole. The priest had promptly denied this.[57]

The unprecedented attack in this Catholic country on a priest dressed in holy vestments and administering Catholic rites came as a shock and caused much consternation. The Jewish press asked whether anti-Semitism were possible without racism; the Polish press asked who was a Jew. The radical nationalist press—reflecting the opinions of the younger generation of the nationalist movement, upon which the Nazi ideology had increasing influence—took a racist position. For example, the paper "Self-Defense of the Nation," the organ of the National Radical Camp (ONR), in discussing Father Puder's assignment dwelt on his racial features: "How will Poles who come to church be able to partake in the service, looking at a priest in whose face nature has written, in a clearer way yet than his public declaration, his Jewish nationality?" The view of less militant rightist circles is exemplified in the unequivocal statement by the well known publicist Stanisław Mackiewicz, editor of the rightist Vilno newspaper Słowo. He noted that "a Jew is anyone who is of Jewish descent."[58]

That part of the press which expressed the government's stand tended to shy away from a racist position. When it did touch on the problem, it rejected racism as a foreign influence, one that is contrary to Polish tradition and the Catholic religion. In the fall of 1938, in the bulletin of the prestigious Association of Polish Legionnaires, the government's view was made unusually clear. Its author, the writer and poet Józef Relidzyński (a former member of Piłsudski's Second Legion), asserted that the government's official anti-Jewish declaration was not of a racist character. He went on to explain why the government could not apply its anti-Jewish policy to Poles of Jewish descent:

> For us legionnaires—who had in the Legion comrades of
> Jewish descent that were both excellent soldiers and upright
> Poles—the so called "Aryan" descent of a person is not and can-
> not be an exclusive proof of his genuine Polishness . . . Our
> soldierly and national conscience cannot accept that a son of
> one of our comrades of Jewish descent—who together with us
> bled on the battlefield or suffered in prison for Poland—that a
> youth, brought up in the purest spirit of Polishness, should be
> exposed to insults at school or elsewhere and be excluded from
> the national community because of his descent.[59]

While the government found racist witchhunts of Poles of Jewish descent distasteful, it considered just and proper to single out those citizens of Poland who were Jews for differential treatment. Having exhausted the arsenal of anti-Jewish measures of that time the government came out for the mass emigration of Jews.[60] The government's call and plans for the mass removal of Jews won enthusiastic support from most Poles. Jewish emigration as a solution to Poland's ills held out the promise of city jobs for poor peasants, the end of exploitation for Polish workers, the command of the business market for the Polish bourgeoisie and the "purification" of Polish culture for the intelligentsia. Much discussion in the Polish parliament revolved around this issue. The rhetoric ranged from rabid anti-Semitism through milder "civilized" expressions to statements "friendly" to Jews that seemingly expressed concern over the fate of the poor Jewish masses who were undergoing economic strangulation. However, irrespective of the tone and motive of the statements the fact remains that one category of Polish citizens, who had resided on Polish soil for many centuries, was defined as a surplus population and singled out for emigration.

But where were Jews to go? The doors of Palestine were closed and a stringent immigration quota prevailed in the United States. The Polish government came up with a grandiose scheme: colonies for Poland. At the annual meeting of the Assembly of the League of Nations, in September 1936, Poland brought up what it considered its major problem, that of the Jews. It also registered before the appropriate committees of the League its interest in the

League's placing colonies under a Polish mandate so as to enable Poland to settle its Jews there. A month later, the Minister of Foreign Affairs, Colonel Beck, made an official declaration that international banks should help Poland finance a mass emigration of Jews. In the same speech to the nation in which he defended the propriety of his voicing at international meetings Poland's interest in colonies, he assured the Poles that Germany was going to abide by a policy "of good neighborliness and nonaggression," stipulated in the German-Polish treaties.[61]

The government remained preoccupied with Jewish emigration until the outbreak of war. At the end of 1938, the government spokesman, General Skwarczyński (then head of OZN) in a speech before the Diet devoted himself to "basic programmatic thoughts," which were to "guide" the government's "parliamentary activities and legislative initiative." During the aftermath of the sacrifice of Czechoslovakia, General Skwarczyński stood before the Polish Diet and declared that "The pressing matter of the international political scene is the more normal division of the Jews among the countries of the world." And according to him, and the government he represented, the Jewish question was one of "the chief and most difficult problems facing the Polish nation." In accordance with the theses OZN had fully elaborated six months earlier, he pointed to "the necessity of freeing the Polish culture from the influence of the foreign Jewish mentality." He asserted "that the solution to the Jewish question has to be achieved most of all by the most conspicuous reduction in the number of Jews." [62]

Of course, the colonies never materialized. Jews were held responsible for this. At about the same time as Colonel Skwarczyński was urging legislative action against Jews, the *Gazeta Polska,* the organ of the Polish government, was using a threatening tone on the matter of colonies. In an article entitled "Let the Matter Be Stated Properly," it accused the Jews of procrastinating and not giving sufficient support to the cause of colonies and hinted that the Poles might resort to pogroms or Nuremburg Laws against them to gain this support.

If we compare the amount of Jewish energy spent in fighting against "emigrationism" with that spent on propaganda for funding colonial territories for emigration, we easily arrive at the conclusion that in this latter matter Jewish opinion is doing virtually nothing. And when it does . . . it is only after such occurrences as the famous Kishinev or Odessa pogroms, or after such decrees as the present German decrees. And this is very dangerous, especially for the Jews themselves.[63]

At the beginning of 1939, Prime Minister Sławoj-Składkowski made an official declaration of the government's position, in a response to a parliamentary question. In it he emphasized that in the view of the government, emigration was "indispensable" for the "solution of the Jewish question in Poland." [64]

Lulled by the overtures the Nazi government was making toward it, the Polish leaders inflated themselves into thinking that Poland was a major power in Europe.[65] And so Poland's attention was focused on its Jews as Nazi Germany was about to invade it. To the very end anti-Jewish terror reigned at the universities. It was the summer of 1939—after Germany had served notice to Poland that the nonaggression pact was being terminated—that the third Jewish student of the University of Lvov was murdered by the radical nationalists.[66] To the very end the Polish press railed against the "Jewish menace." The nationalist journalists and publicists were campaigning loudly for the removal of the books of the great Polish writers of Jewish background—Tuwim, Słonimski, Wittlin—from schools and bookstores.[67] The ideologues of hate shouted that Poles "must not put the Jewish question aside": "Remembering Germany, let us not forget the Jews." [68] And the government seemed to heed this formula: In the spring of 1939, when the Polish government was anxious to get guarantees from Britain in case of a German invasion, it insisted that the agenda of the forthcoming meeting in London contain the question of Jewish emigration from Poland.[69] And in an interview for domestic consumption in May of 1939, General Skwarczyński, as a government spokesman, reiterated that nothing had changed in the government's policy toward Jews: "We aspire to diminish the number of Jews in Poland." [70]

The government thus weakened the country by neglecting its real internal problems and jeopardized it by refusing to recognize the Nazi danger. The men who had weakened the country were fantasizing about a mighty Poland with colonies abroad while the people they led—whose conditions were not improving and were often getting worse—were fantasizing about an easier life in a Poland free of Jews. The slogans "Jew get out of here" and "Jew go to Palestine" resounded from the mouths of children as well as adults and stared from inscriptions on walls. Their message was blunt and clear.

PART II
HOW THE JEWS DEALT
WITH THEIR SITUATION

V
The Jewish Jews:
Orthodox in Faith,
Traditional in Culture

In Poland to a greater extent than anywhere else in interwar Europe, Jews continued to cope with their peculiar situation in the traditional "Jewish way," both in actual numbers and in their proportion to the total Jewish population of the country. Apart from being very old, what distinguished the Jewish traditional way of life, was that it was permeated with both religious orthodoxy and distinctiveness of language and culture. These features were once characteristic of most Polish Jews, but during the nineteenth century they began to be eroded by the twin processes of acculturation and secularization. Both processes reached such a momentum before independence that they were not contained, although acculturation was perhaps slowed by the anti-Jewish atmosphere of independent Poland.

In the interwar period, Jews varied widely in their degree of secularization and Polonization and in the combination of these two. Nevertheless, two polar social types could easily be recognized among them: one type was hardly touched by either process, and I designate such individuals as the Orthodox-traditionalists. They referred to themselves as *Yidishe Yidn*, Jewish Jews, and sometimes labeled the others as *Goishe Yidn*, Gentile Jews. The Orthodox-traditionalists were devoted to the complete conservation without any change of Jewish religious behavior and cultural distinctiveness, in which their Jewish identity was rooted. The other polar type were the assimilationists. They were completely Polonized—identificationally as well as culturally assimilated—and highly secularized.

Before the twentieth century, it seemed to many, and especially to those who embarked upon it, that assimilation represented the future of Polish Jewry, the mode that would replace the traditional pattern. Actually it remained to the very end an extremely deviant pattern, rejected in the interwar Poland by the bulk of Jewry, and followed mostly by those who had become assimilated prior to independence or by their descendants. In contrast, the Orthodox-traditional pattern, branded as the way of the past by many, still commanded in independent Poland the adherence of a substantial part of the entire Jewish population. Probably around a third of the total adult population was Orthodox-traditionalist. (Any estimate of the size of this group must be rough since direct data on the subject are unavailable.) [1] Its proportion was higher in the shtetlekh than in the larger cities, and much higher among the older people than among the young. Adherence to the Orthodox-traditional pattern also varied with class: it persisted most among small-business people and petty traders, considerably less so among the rich bourgeoisie and the proletariat.

Between these two polar types was found the rest of Polish Jewry, containing the large majority of the younger Jews: fragmented, convulsed, shifting from one program to another. On them the two final chapters of the book concentrate. It will help us to understand the goals they set before themselves for coping with their situation, the variety of ways in which they tried to achieve them, and the frustrations they encountered, if we first examine the Orthodox-traditional pattern from which they departed and the assimilationist pattern which they rejected.

High Visibility

The people we are concerned with in this chapter were the most visible among Polish Jewry. As today one cannot help but recog-

nize the "Ultra-Orthodox" Jews of the Williamsburg section in
New York or of the Me'ah She'arim section in Jerusalem, so it was
in interwar Poland. In Poland, however, they were more numerous
and were not concentrated in single cities but composed a substantial portion of almost every Jewish community and of the scat-
tered Jewish rural population. Their dress alone, in the case of
males, signaled unmistakably that they were Jews. This traditional
attire is still found—of course not in Poland, but in Israel and the
United States.

Males did not shave, in literal and strict observance of religious law: "Ye shalt not round the corners of your heads, neither shalt thou mar the corners of the beard" (Leviticus 19:27).
Thus they wore beards at a time when the Poles rarely did. Also
common among them, especially the *hasidim*, were *peyes*, side-
locks. Their clothes were somber: a black caftan worn over the
trousers—known in some parts of the country as *kapote* and in
other parts as *bekishe*—which varied from knee length to ankle
length. (The Poles referred to it as *chaɫat*. One of the pejorative
terms for Jew, *chaɫaciarz*, derived from it.) The quality of the
fabric and the fit of the caftan expressed variations in the class
position of the wearers. For prayer, the caftan was girdled with
a black silk cord. Under the caftan was always worn an *arba'
kanfot:* a white vest, covering the chest and back, with tassels
(*tsitsit*) at the four corners. The tassels often showed, especially
when worn by children below the age when they began dressing
in the caftan. This undergarment was worn in observance of the
rule in Deuteronomy (22:12): "Thou shalt make thee fringes
upon the four quarters of thy vesture, wherewith thou coverest
thyself."

There were regional differences in the type of hat the Orthodox-traditionalists wore but it was everywhere distinctively Jewish. In the central regions—formerly Congress Poland—a black
cap was worn. It was referred to both in Yiddish and in Polish as a
"Jewish cap." In contrast, a soft wide-brimmed felt hat, also black,
was worn in southern Poland, former Galicia. On the Sabbath and
holidays, the rabbis and some men of distinction donned the
shtrayml, a black velvet hat with brown fur trimming. Since males

were supposed to have their heads covered at all times, indoors they wore a skullcap, called *yarmlke* or *kapale*.

The female dress was not so distinctive during the interwar period. By then most of the Orthodox-traditionalist women, except the very old, wore modern dress. They still abided by "modesty" in dress however: sleeveless, short-sleeved and decolleté fashions were taboo among them. Married women wore their hair covered at all times with kerchiefs or wig (*sheytl*). Poorer women wore wigs only on holidays and festive occasions. The well-to-do wore them every day, and especially fine ones on holidays and festivals. The mark of a beautiful *sheytl* was that it looked natural and re-flected the newest hair fashions. Although many Orthodox young married women continued throughout the interwar years to cover their heads, most of them abandoned the once common practice of shaving off their hair upon marriage.

With minor exceptions, Yiddish was the mother tongue of all the Orthodox-traditionalists. Many of them, especially of the older generation, spoke only enough Polish to communicate in business and public encounters with Poles. Not infrequent among the older generations were those who spoke no Polish. In independent Po-land many of the children from Orthodox-traditionalist homes had first been introduced to Polish in school. Many boys of such back-ground—especially in small towns and among those who attended the Orthodox Jewish schools rather than public schools—had no special motivation to master the Polish language. Thus, as a rule, the Orthodox-traditionalists were linguistically very separate from the Poles. Their Polish was the subject of much amusement and ridicule among Poles.

However, one did encounter Orthodox Jews who spoke Polish well. This was especially true in former Galicia, where Polish had been the official language since 1869, rather than in former Congress Poland and other areas where the official language until independence had been Russian. Among the upper and upper-middle class Jewish Jews were found men, extremely observant and traditionally dressed, who had excellent command of the Po-lish language. Even more prominent among the upper strata were women who spoke Polish well. Rare cases even existed of upper-class Orthodox women who could barely communicate in Yiddish but spoke Polish beautifully.

Their extreme visibility made the Jewish Jews quantitatively the most susceptible to anti-Semitic discrimination and attack. In general, the Polish image of the stereotypic Jew was a caricature of the Jewish Jew. Therefore, most Poles, when they encountered a person whose appearance fit this stereotypic image, tended to see in him immediately the negative traits that the stereotype contained. The Orthodox-traditional Jew was often perceived by Poles as laughable: dressed in an outlandish way, worshipping in a ludicrous manner, jabbering strange sounds, and ridiculous in his efforts to speak Polish. He was therefore considered by many Poles, particularly the young, the proper subject of jokes and ridicule. Common was the Polish "fun" of pulling earlocks, especially those of little boys to hear them cry out in pain.

The Traditional Culture in the Interwar Period

Thus the Jewish Jews were almost always aware of impending danger. Consciousness of belonging to a group that had to maintain itself amid a sea of enemies shaped their entire outlook. But their highly developed and well integrated culture provided them with a meaningful interpretation of the surrounding hostility as well as a way of dealing with it in order to survive.[2] One of the most sensitive approaches to the values and "spirit" of this culture, as perhaps to any culture, is to examine its concepts of past, present, and future. And it is particularly fitting for us to review the Jewish traditional concepts of time, since they bear on the central question of this chapter and the rest of the book: how did various categories of Jews in interwar Poland deal with their distinctive situation? But it is also important to state at the outset that the actual behavior of the traditionalists did not always correspond to the beliefs and norms of their culture; sometimes their actions sharply transgressed them.

The Orthodox-traditionalists clung to a double image of the present. On one hand, they regarded it as grim, oppressive, and painful, since they lived in exile, among people for whom it was natural to resent or hate Jews. This image reflected itself in their Yiddish sayings: an object hard to move because of its weight was characterized "as heavy as Jewish *tsores*" (misfortunes). If something that people disliked persisted they referred to its endurance as being "as long as the Jewish exile." On the other hand, the Jewish Jews had the idea the present was a transitional period that would eventuate in a glorious future—a future that would see the Jews' return to their own land, the Holy Land, and would be a continuation of their proud past. Just as that past itself was not too distant and its fruits, such as the Torah, were still enjoyed, so the great future was not too far off. The Messiah might come; the miracle could occur any day: the Jews would be freed from suffering, mankind would be renewed, and brotherhood would reign. Thus the Orthodox-traditionalists had two conceptions of the present: one with respect to life in the Gentile world outside, and one with respect to life among their own. While the first "present" was sharply dissociated from the proud past and glorious future, the latter was regarded as an integral link in time's chain.

Individual life, like time "among one's own" generally, was looked upon as a steady flowing stream with no sharp breaks in it. The age of freedom was not differentiated distinctly from that of responsibility, for responsibility began with childhood and continued after death. (A person who had failed to discharge his obligations while alive was believed to do so after death.) No particular stage of human life was idealized or glorified; each was thought to have its compensations. In childhood one was considered to have freedom from anxiety; in maturity, the joys of building a household; in old age, the respect of others. People looked back with a certain nostalgia on their childhoods, but seldom tried to prolong their youth, or linger with it. Just as there was no sharp break between youth and maturity, so there was no such break between this world and the next; it was widely believed that the dead could return, and did.

This notion of life as a continuous process was reflected in many aspects of traditional culture. Learning was thought of not as a process stopping at a given time but as continuing to the end of life. Similarly, a "dominance-submission" pattern was continuous. One had to submit to one's father, but every father was also a son and had to continue to submit to his own father. Although there were discontinuities the general trend of this culture was to conceive of life as a steady flow without sharp breaks. Even such modes of behavior that were not sustained permanently—like the demonstrative affection parents showed their small children—did not come to an abrupt stop. Children who "regressed," who though beyond the age of demonstrative affection still craved it, were seldom rejected. Parents continued to bestow demonstrative affection on such a child, and what disapproval they showed tended to be mild and expressed only in words.

The fact that there were few "rites of passage," or initiation, and that even these were not greatly emphasized, fitted with the traditional view of life as continuum. (For example, much less was made of Bar Mitzvahs among these Orthodox people than is nowadays among non-Orthodox Jews in America.) According to religious law, a child was not supposed to be responsible for his sins until his Bar Mitzvah, but in practice such responsibility began earlier.

The Orthodox-traditionalists strongly adhered to the principle that it was a Jew's obligation to do all that was possible to survive in the Gentile present. At the same time everybody had an obligation to do his utmost to live among his own a life permeated with Jewish faith and Jewish ethics. In living thus, Jews would testify to the existence of the God of truth and righteousness. Also, such a way of life would afford them purpose and joy in the present, redress the sins that had brought the Jewish people into exile, and bring about Israel's redemption. Jewish life had to have well-founded goals, which would motivate all activities. Only life with a purpose, *takhles*, was meaningful; life without it was wanton. The things that were thought to give purpose to life were the same as those that brought esteem. They were vividly symbolized in the blessing of the new-born male baby at the circumcision ceremony: "May he be raised for the Torah, the wedding, and good deeds." One's duties were threefold: toward God, toward family, and toward the community. And it was considered imperative that they be fulfilled in strict conformance with the prescriptions of the *Ha-lakhah*, the legal part of the sacred literature. Therefore, religion was not regarded as a separate area but as inseparable from all aspects of Jewish life. Indeed, among the Orthodox almost every detail of daily life had a sacred significance. And much of that life and activity revolved around prayer, celebration of the Sabbath and holidays, learning, the family, and good deeds toward others.

Direct duties to God involved prayer, and Jewish males were supposed to pray three times a day. A network of synagogues and houses of prayer were spread throughout Poland. Wherever Jewish Jews lived, it was very likely that there would be a synagogue or prayer group within walking distance. The behavior in the synagogue or house of prayer reflected the lack of separation between the sacred and the profane. Between prayers, people felt free to engage in conversation about all kinds of matters. There was also constant movement in and out of the synagogue. People who arrived after the prayers started would catch up by whispering the missed prayers at tremendous speed. A person who ended a certain set of prayers earlier than the congregation did often stepped out for some fresh air. Unquestionably, the synagogues were generally noisier than the churches. This was perceived by Poles as one more expression of Jewish inferiority. But for the Jewish Jew the conversing, the moving in and out were not signs of disrespect. In the house of his Father the traditional Jew felt at home. It was incomprehensible to him that he should not move freely and speak freely between prayers.

Jewish Jews distinguished, not between the sacred and the profane, but between the everyday and the holiday, between the Gentile and the Jewish.[3] Experiences and likeable things were called *yontevdik, shabesdik,* holiday-like, Sabbath-like; they had "Jewish charm." In their everyday life, temperance and sobriety were obligatory. Excessive laughter was avoided, and discouraged from childhood on as a sign of stupidity. "Why do you laugh so much? Is stupidity egging you on?" a mother would say to her children. A similar attitude was preferred toward eating and drinking. It was considered repulsive and un-Jewish for a man to get drunk. Of anyone who did, it was said, "He drinks like a Gentile."

Eating was considered to be important because it maintained life and Jewish mothers who had enough food were persistent in urging their children to eat more. But an adult was not supposed to "plunge his whole head into food." The term reserved for animals was used when talking of a person who ate too heartily or too much: "He doesn't eat, *er frest*," was a common way of describing such a person. Another frequent expression was, "He eats like a coarse Gentile," it being implied that a man of refinement and learning would not eat with gusto on an ordinary day.

Thus in his everyday life the Jewish Jew was supposed to reject experiences that were extreme or cost the individual his self-awareness and self-control. He tended to be in a state of readiness to cope with the hostile environment and the burdens of everyday life in order to survive. On holidays, however, spontaneity and self-indulgence were not simply permitted but actually encouraged; one could behave in ways set apart from daily life. On the Sabbath one could dwell upon the goodness of food; men of refinement, scholars, and everybody else would smack their lips and exclaim over the fish and the other holiday dishes—"it has every flavor," or, "it has a real holiday taste." On holidays one could drink, and even the "beautiful Jews," men of eminence, learning, and bearing, did so. To drink a glass too much on a holiday was to express one's joy in it, and in the Torah. For a grown-up Jewish Jew to dance on an ordinary day was to incur the suspicion of insanity, but on a holiday he could dance ecstatically with full social approval. (Hasidim were especially exuberant.) At weddings and circumcisions, holiday behavior was called for. It was a sign of great friendship if a guest who was a "beautiful Jew" forgot his decorum and drank, danced, and jested. The holidays, and those events during which holiday behavior was in order, were looked forward to as times of joy and renewal. (Remember that the Orthodox-traditionalists as a rule did not participate in forms of recreation that were popular among other Jews as well as urban Poles: movies, sports, theater, etc.) Every week the "Sabbath Queen" was ushered in with love and let go with regret. Perhaps the centrality of the Sabbath and holidays in Jewish traditional life was best captured by Ahad Ha-am's famous saying that more than the Jewish people keeping the Sabbath, the Sabbath has kept the Jewish people alive.

Some of the joy in celebrating holidays, as well as in the other ways of living a Jewish life, was the imprint that the hasidic movement had left on traditional Judaism. In the words of Abraham Joshua Heschel, it "uncovered the ineffable delight of being a Jew." [4] During the interwar period, Poland was the center of Hasidism. The heads of various hasidic dynasties, the rebes, continued to command the allegiance of large numbers of men. Some still maintained huge households, entertaining hundreds of visitors, especially on holidays. Such were the Gerer (Góra Kalwarja) and Alexander (Aleksandrów) rebes; both were from former Congress Poland. The rebe of Belz (from former Galicia), and the Ḥofets Hayim (from former Lithuania) also had a tremendous following. The rebe or tsadik was a charismatic figure, and he played a number of roles. Foremost among them was that of *melits yosher*, an attorney pleading before God for those Jews who came to him with their troubles. In that capacity the rebe helped to cure them and to free them from problems over which they had no control. But the rebe also performed the role of *guter Yid*, a "good Jew," to whom Jews could pour forth troubles that were capable of resolution and receive the best advice. [5]

It is most important to understand that the exultation in the observance of the Sabbath and holidays, so prominent not only among hasidim but also among the Orthodox-traditionalists in general, was a way of transcending the misery and degradation of everyday life by a people strangulated by poverty and subjected to hate and oppression. So was the study of the Torah, prescribed to all males in accordance with their capacity. "Laborers, peasants, porters, artisans, they were all partners in the Torah." [6] In most Orthodox-traditional homes, no matter how humble, there were a few sacred volumes in addition to the prayer books. The Torah was thought to be the source of joy as well as wisdom. Its study was to continue throughout one's life. "The Torah has no bottom" went the saying. The concept of learning as an unending process is reflected in the terms applied to a scholar. It would not be said of him that he was a "learned man"—rather that "he knows how to

study," or "he is a great learner." One's learning was never complete enough to justify the attribute "learned." (The expression "he
is an educated man" applied to secular education.)

Sacred scholarship was still venerated in the interwar period.
The word *iluy*, precious and beloved, designated the young prod-
igy in Torah. "Where there is Torah, there is wisdom," was the
Jewish saying. Torah learning was considered so valuable that it
needed no validation by good deeds. To be sure, a man who shared
his learning with others received additional esteem, but the fact
that "he knew how to learn" was enough to assure him status.
Thus, even if he did not share his learning or give to charity, he
was never "coarse" or a "pig"—terms that applied to a man of
wealth who did not spend part of his wealth on the needy and the
community. It was easily conceivable that a man could have much
wealth and yet lack refinement, but it was unimaginable that a
man of learning could behave improperly. Learning was equated
with refinement, and the term *eydele Yid* ("refined Jew") meant a
man of much learning. The rich man, even if he were charitable
and did good deeds but had no learning, did not reach his max-
imum status until he married his children into a prestigious family. A man of learning needed only to be greatly learned to reach
highest status.

Sacred learning was stressed as a channel of mobility, open to
all. Theoretically, higher status could be achieved by every Jew. A
boy from the lower class who was talented and ambitious could
become a "learner," and if he had luck he could become well-to-do.
However, a man who rose from the lower class, unless he were a
learner, was on shaky ground. For lineage, *yikhes* was much emphasized as a source of prestige. The people who were considered
to be of great yikhes were those whose families traced themselves
to revered rabbis, great scholars, and very rich men who were
learned and community conscious. To merit prestige, a newly rich
man had to begin to behave in a "respectable manner." But even if
he were charitable and tried to behave respectably, every
misstep—no matter how trivial—caused people to refer to his lowly
origin. In contrast to the newly rich, the position of a learned man
who came from the lower class was not different from that of other

learned men. That his father was a laborer was mentioned only to point to his great personal worth, that in spite of such an obstacle he managed to become a learner. Thus, the learner created his own yikhes (*atsmo*) which did not need ancestral support.

Just as learning did not require validation in terms of other things, so it was considered preferable that it not be used as a means of obtaining material benefits. Sacred learning was a value in itself, and one was supposed to pursue it with love and joy. Among the Jewish Jews there were scholars who devoted all their time to learning. They were not looked down on for not occupying themselves with making a living; on the contrary, they were treated with great respect. (Other men who were not trying to make a living were considered idlers.) Usually the wife was the economic provider, and she was highly esteemed for being married to a man who was devoting his life to learning. (In-laws often supported such a learner and his family.) Men who engaged in business or worked but devoted their spare time to learning were also talked about with reverence. "He cannot tear himself away from learning," went the saying. Others would turn to both kinds of men of learning for personal advice and opinions about community and world affairs. Such men would also lead others in the study of the sacred literature on Saturday and holidays: posing questions, answering difficult questions, and interpreting the text. Children were sent to a man of learning to be tested on their progress.[7]

Traditional Jewish Education

As learning occupied such a central position, every town, no matter how tiny, had at least one ḥeder or Talmud Torah.* These traditional elementary schools for boys continued to function in interwar Poland in the same manner as before. There was little state control over them, since Polish authorities conceded that they were purely religious in character. And no reliable statistics were

---

* Originally Talmud Torah designated a school for poor children. During the interwar period this distinction mostly disappeared, and both were used depending on the locality, to designate the traditional elementary school.

All traditionalist parents—with the exception of those who could
afford a private tutor—sent their children to a ḥeder . . .
A ḤEDER CLASS (TRADITIONAL ELEMENTARY SCHOOL) IN WARSAW,
1930S. NOTE THE "JEWISH CAP," WORN BY BOTH TEACHER AND PUPILS.
(YIVO INSTITUTE FOR JEWISH RESEARCH ABRAMOVITCH COLLECTION)

ever compiled on how many hundreds of them existed. All traditionalist parents—with the exception of those who could afford a
private tutor—sent their children to a ḥeder. Many ḥadarim, especially those in the small towns and serving poor children, were
crowded and unhygienic places, often located in the home of the
melamed, teacher. "In the ḥeder in which I started there was not
even a floor," related one informant from a small town in central
Poland. Another described the ḥeder he attended thus: "the glass
in the windows was broken and pillows and rags were pushed into
the frame to protect the room from cold and wind. Into this single
room were crowded more than twenty children." Much has been
written about the inadequacies of these schools and the lack of
pedagogic training of their teachers.[8] Still, the malamed used some
effective traditional techniques in addition to the proverbial rod,
such as, for example, the picturesque way of teaching the difficult
Hebrew alphabet. For instance, he compared the letter *bet* to a

room with an open wall, the letter *gimel* to a soldier who put his foot
forward to march. Since the hadarim were regarded by secularized
Jews as dens of medieval backwardness, it should be noted that
very few, if any, children with reading problems seem to have
come out of them. This is especially noteworthy because they were
learning to read in Hebrew, a language they did not understand.
The beginning of learning the meaning of the Hebrew text came
only when the child mastered reading. Then he was ready to com-
mence with the study of the Pentateuch.

In the interwar period, a new type of *ḥeder* emerged, which
was highly regarded among the Orthodox-traditionalists. It was
founded by the most influential organization among them, the
Agudat Israel, (commonly referred to as *Agudah*) through its educational arm, *Khorev*.* The new type, incorporated some secular
subjects into its curriculum and also cautiously utilized selected
modern pedagogical methods. The Agudah developed these
schools as a response to compulsory primary school education in
independent Poland: it feared the impact of compulsory education
on Jewish children. For reasons that will become clearer later, the
Agudah's relations with the Polish authorities were for a long
while considerably better than that of the other Jewish organizations involved with running schools. Thus in 1922 the Ministry of
Religious Creeds and Public Education recognized the Khorev ḥadarim that incorporated secular subjects into their curriculum by
exempting their students from attending public elementary
schools.[9] The secular subjects were generally taught in Polish, and
this too was a factor in winning such official recognition. However,
the education in this new type of ḥeder still revolved mainly
around the Torah, and the secular subjects were regarded as
purely utilitarian in character. Each week 18 to 38 hours (depending on the grade) were devoted to traditional learning and 14 to
secular topics. It was an eight-year school, attended by boys aged
six to fourteen.[10] In contrast to the secular Jewish schools, the

---

* The schools of the Mizrachi religious Zionists, are not discussed here, although
they gave serious attention to Torah learning, because they represented a substantial departure from the traditional pattern of education. They will be dealt with in
the context of modern Jewish education (chapter 7).

authorities were quite lenient in interpreting the law when it came to these Orthodox schools. However, after the 1932–33 Polish school reform, and particularly beginning with the 1935–36 school year, stricter controls were put on these schools, as far as the instruction of Polish or secular subjects was concerned.[11]

Statistical data about the Khorev schools are far from uniform; different figures appear in different publications. Considerably higher figures in the number of schools and students for 1934–35 are given in the official Polish publication than those released by Khorev for 1937. According to the former there were 557 hadarim and Talmud Torahs attended by 61,328 children; according to the latter there were 360 such schools with 53,000 children.[12] Although inexact, these figures are indicative of the tremendous decline of the Khorev schools in the last few years. This decline was in turn a product of the marked deterioration in the situation of the Jews in general, and the Orthodox in particular, after the death of Piłsudski. On one hand, the further economic crisis, due to the boycott and terror, made it more difficult than ever to finance these schools. On the other hand, more rigorous control of those schools that entitled their students to be exempted from public school attendance made it harder for such schools to exist.

It must be emphasized here that the above figures refer not only to Khorev's new type schools but also include the older hadarim, confined solely to Torah subjects, whose students were not exempt from public school. However, one post World War II study (tracing its information to a letter) states that in 1937, 107 of the schools, including 15,106 children, were of the new type.[13] Anyway, my interviews suggest that many more children from Orthodox-traditional homes attended public elementary schools in the morning and a heder in the afternoon. (The Khorev afternoon schools were usually superior, in terms of facilities and methods of instruction to other hadarim and Talmud Torahs.) And almost all such children, prior to entry into public school at the age of seven, had attended heder since they were four or five—sometimes three.[14]

Supplementary afternoon traditional education was also made available by Khorev to girls, and this represented a tremendous breakthrough during the interwar period. Finally facing up to the fact that the extreme neglect of traditional education for females (because it was not required of them to study the Torah) facilitated a more rapid departure from Jewish patterns of behavior by young women than by young men, the Agudah founded the Beth Jacob schools for girls. As the journal of the Beth Jacob association wrote in 1924: "To this day you can encounter in many a Jewish home the strange combination of boys devoting themselves to sacred study, in the manner of past generations, while the girls—knowing nothing about Judaism—are being raised in the bosom of a foreign culture." [15] And the President of the Agudah, Yitzhak Meyer Lewin, reporting the accomplishments of the Beth Jacob schools at the Agudah national convention of 1928, prefaced them with the remark: "Everyone knows how sadly among us the education of daughters had been neglected. They learned everything and knew everything, except Jewishness" (Yidishkeyt). [16]

According to the Khorev statistics, there were 250 Beth Jacob schools for girls in 1937 with 38,000 students. Only 14 of them had full curricula exempting the students from attending primary public schools; the rest were afternoon schools. [17] In both only female teachers were acceptable. Since there was a great shortage of women teachers qualified to teach Judaic subjects, in 1931 Khorev opened the Beth Jacob Teachers' Seminary and Boarding School in Cracow. [18]

Although the Beth Jacob schools for girls constituted a substantial innovation in the Orthodox-traditional pattern of culture, the predominant emphasis nevertheless continued to be on the proper education of boys. In addition to the ḥadarim and Talmud Torahs, which provided the indispensable primary education that enabled every male to fulfill his religious obligations, there was a large network of secondary schools devoted to the study of the Torah, the so called "small yeshivot." There were also the "grand yeshivot," many world famous and some centuries' old. These were the schools of higher sacred learning, comparable to secular universities. Among the most celebrated were the ones of Mir, Baranowicze, Bobów, Vilno, Grodno and Lublin. The first, Mir, was established in 1817; the last, Yeshivat Hakhme Lublin,

opened in 1930. Its modern buildings and facilities made the latter
unique. (The money had been raised by its first dean, the great tal-
mudist and Agudah leader, Rabbi Meyer Shapira.) It set its traditional scholastic standards extremely high, to attract the very elite.
Candidates for admittance to the Lublin yeshiva had to know by
heart 200 Talmud folios (400 pages).[19] The grand yeshivot were
attended by future rabbis, judges of religious courts, directors of
the small yeshivot, etc. But most of their students had no other
purpose than to study the Torah. This was the culmination of their
early home socialization in the value of learning as a goal in itself—from the cradle on mothers sang the popular lullaby, "The
Torah Is the Highest Good."

Sense of Community

The Torah, which the Orthodox-traditionalists revered and loved
so much, put great emphasis on the relation of man to man; its
basic precepts governing such relations were part of the common
knowledge and belief in the traditional community. One often
heard it said that on Yom Kippur God forgives sins against himself
but not against men. Much cited was Hillel's famous saying that
the fundamental principle of the Torah is "Do not do unto thy
neighbor what thou wouldst not like to have done to thyself. The
rest is commentary." Even more was demanded, however, than
the literal reading of Hillel's Golden Rule would indicate; there
was as much stress on doing good as on not doing harm. Jews
were supposed to show mercy, compassion, and justice to one
another. They regarded themselves as *"bney rakhmones,"* children
of pity, and saw tender-heartedness as one of the most characteristic of their positive traits. One's obligation to the family came
first, but the community was an extension and counterpart of the
family. When a person was moved to act harshly towards another
Jew he was supposed to check himself by recalling that, after all, it
was a *yidish kind,* "a Jewish child," that would be the object of his
harshness. Adults as well as children were "Jewish children"—all
being children of God. This notion carried much meaning among

the traditionalists and it was not easy for them to fail to respond to the plea of a person stressing that he was a "Jewish child." As such he was entitled to justice.[20]

Indeed, justice, *tsdokeh*, was the term used for charity. Giving to the needy was an act of justice. Among the most complementary descriptions of a person was that he was a *bal-tsdokeh*—a man of great charity. Among the other good deeds stressed was performing a *gmiles-khesed*, act of loving kindness—lending money to people in need without charging interest or demanding notes and securities. Aiding a sick person is another example. The phrase "to save a Jewish soul" was used without additional elaboration. Some well-to-do women sent the best food and delicacies to poor people who were sick and to destitute mothers who had just given birth. It was a good deed to visit the sick and people in mourning. The greater the social distance, the higher the deed ranked. Bringing peace to the community or to a divided family also ranked very high, and a man who was known as a peacemaker earned much esteem. Moreover, an individual who did a good deed for an orphan received greater credit than if he had performed a similar deed for any other person in the community.[21]

The one who performed good deeds for the needy overcame his initial human failing of not being able to project himself into the position of the needy. "The well-fed does not believe the hungry one," went the saying. His returns for doing good deeds were, therefore, very high. The belief was prevalent that, when a man died and was called before God to be judged, his good deeds came forth to testify for him. Orthodox men at funeral processions chanted, "Charity prevents death."

But to act conceited because one lived up to the ideal ways of fulfilling one's duties to God, family, and community was considered highly improper. Such a person would be described by the Hebrew expression *bal gayve*, conceited man, or in Yiddish, *er blozt fun zikh*, he puffs himself up. However, it was more than fitting to engage in activities and place oneself in situations that brought prestige and resulted in praise from others. Although prestige and recognition were not supposed to be the mainspring of one's actions, there was ample awareness that they constituted, despite ever-repeated warnings, a main incentive. What the culture did emphasize, apart from the importance of fulfilling its goals as sacred duties, was the enjoyment to be gained in simply pursuing the goals it set. People were expected to take pleasure in learning, to rejoice in their children, and to delight in performing good deeds. To a great extent, they did do so despite severe economic difficulties and the depressing reality outside, and Jewish traditional life did contain a large element of joy and satisfaction. This was expressed when the completion of the writing of a new Torah was celebrated, when one's children said something clever, or when the master of the house tried to "beautify" a poor beggar and make him feel at home at a Friday night meal.

With all this, it becomes easier to understand the strong element of compensating personal security felt by the traditional Jews despite the vicious persecution to which they were exposed. The outside world was hostile, but within his family and among his own kind the Orthodox-traditional Jew felt safe. Any Jewish Jew who came to a new town, even if he had no relatives there, would find that he could enter almost any traditional home he chose. "Among Jews you cannot get lost," was a frequent saying.

But pointing out that group consciousness, a sense of solidarity with all other Jews, was a striking feature of traditional Jewish life is not to imply that the traditional Jewish community was one of constant inner harmony or that all lived up to its ideals. This was far from so. Especially in the interwar period, when that community and its way of life were being sharply attacked by Gentiles and by Jews, there was much disagreement and conflict. The everyday reality had its seamy and shabby sides, some of which we shall soon encounter in the discussion of the political maneuvering on the local community and national levels. Others will become more apparent in the final chapters of this book.

Informal relations, too, were marred by friction, though the traditional norms required solidarity, helpfulness, and a kind heart. There were some marked deviations from these norms and they were often of an economic nature. Remember, the bulk of the Jewish-Jews were petty traders and craftsmen struggling against ensnaring poverty. A consciousness existed in the traditional community of widespread jealousy towards those well off. The often repeated dictum, "You must not gouge people's eyes," also meant that one should be careful not to give others the opportunity to be jealous. Actually some of the conflict erupted as part of the competition among traders and craftsmen selling their wares in a limited market. And so they clashed over "unfair" competition, and also over such matters as loans refused, debts and rents unpaid, and evictions from stores and homes.

No matter how serious the quarrel, the norm among the Orthodox-traditionalists proscribed taking it to court or reporting the opponent's misdeeds to a government agency. Although there was wide conformity, nevertheless there were, of course, individuals who reported economic violations, real or fabricated, of their competitors. Outwardly Orthodox, such individuals severely departed in their behavior from the ethical code they professed.

Much more frequent were the purely personal squabbles which were endemic, despite frequent admonitions and strong condemnation of quarreling. This type of bickering, I am convinced, reflected to some extent the Jews' suppressed hostility toward their outside persecutors. Traditional Jews could not express the resentment they felt toward Gentiles for fear of brutal retaliation, and they did not have a scapegoat handy, so they vented their hostility in petty quarreling among themselves. An indication of the validity of this interpretation can be found in the fact that not infrequently in these quarrels people avoided mentioning things that would really hurt their opponents. In these instances one accused another of many things and abused him, but one refrained from touching his sorest spot (such as apostasy or insanity in the family).

Formal Community Organization: the Kehilla

As we move toward the discussion of the formal community organizations, the *kehillot*, which seem to have been plagued during the interwar period by constant quarrels, we ought to keep in mind the psychological factor of displaced hostility as a partial explanation. After independence, the legitimacy of the kehillot as religious communal organizations was recognized and their rights outlined in an executive decree issued by Marshal Piłsudski on February 9, 1919. However, it was binding only in central Poland, the former Congress Poland. In other parts of the country, the old laws of the partitioning powers still applied. There was considerable dissatisfaction among the Orthodox-traditionalists with the lack of legal uniformity and the resulting confusion. The Agudah held that the confusion increased the possibility that secular political parties would gain control of specific kehillot operating in each town and city. It must be remembered that soon after independence the Zionists and Bundists began vigorous efforts to "democratize" the kehillot, to change their religious character and transform them into organs of national autonomy.[22] The Agudat Israel saw in these efforts a dangerous organized drive to undermine the traditional institutions of Polish Jewry, to pave the way for its de-Judaization. And it was determined to defend the traditional structure of the kehilla, especially its Torah underpinnings. The kehilla thus became the arena of bitter political struggles by Jewish political parties and factions, each charging the other with using illegitimate means to keep or win control over it.[23]

If we recall, the Poles in general found the ideas of Jewish national autonomy on Polish soil highly offensive. In contrast, Jewish religious autonomy was more palatable; the government could justify its existence as the continuation of Poland's tradition of religious tolerance. (Nevertheless, the extreme Polish nationalists attacked the existence of the kehillot, which they depicted as mysterious associations where dark Jewish plots were being hatched.) Thus, after Marshal Piłsudski returned to power, he accommodated the Agudat Israel, his staunchest supporters among Jews. In 1927, the government enacted a uniform code regulating "Jewish *religious* communities" in the entire country. As many as 599 kehillot fell under its jurisdiction. The Agudah won large majorities in the kehilla elections of that year, thanks to this law. According to the report given the following year by its president, at the Agudah's fourth national convention, about 2,300 men had been elected as officers of the kehillot. Approximately 1,700 of them were Orthodox Jews, of whom 1,500 were members of the Agu-dah.[24]

According to the 1927 law, the kehillot were to be run only by a board in towns with less than 5,000 Jewish inhabitants, and by board plus an additional council in towns with a larger Jewish population. (The local rabbi was to be the ex-officio member of the board.) All of these officials were to be elected by Jewish males, over twenty-five years of age, in secret ballot, according to the principle of proportional representation. Candidates had to be over the age of thirty. The age limit alone biased the results in the direction of overrepresentation of Orthodox-traditionalists in the kehillot.

This law gave the Jewish population the legal status of a religious association, composed of local communities. Each community council, as well as their central organization (the Religious Council of Jewish Communities, consisting of 17 rabbis and 34 laymen) had the legal status of corporations. (The Central Council never actually met.) [25] The law of 1927 was the government's concession to Jewish autonomy. The law specifically limited Jewish autonomy to religious matters: maintenance of rabbis, synagogues, ritual baths, cemeteries, religious education, and control over ritual slaughter of animals for kosher meat; it also permitted the kehillot to provide welfare for poor Jews and to administer foundations for such purposes. However, even in such matters, the law granted the government extensive rights of supervision over the boards and councils; the government retained the right to veto elected officers and to replace them with its own appointees under certain circumstances, and the right to control any item in the community budget.

Here is an illustration of the process of budget supervision in a shtetl in central Poland. One year the kehilla board had submitted its proposed budget to the appropriate Polish official, the *starosta* (county head), but he rejected it on the ground that the rabbi's salary was too high. After the board had resubmitted the budget without any change, the *starosta* fined all its members; a delegation of the board, headed by the rabbi, tried to convince him to withdraw the fines.

*Under Marshal Piłsudski, the Polish government in 1927 enacted
a uniform code regulating religious communities . . .*
MEMBERS OF THE KEHILLA BOARD, INCLUDING RABBI YITZHAK RUBIN-
STEIN, MEMBER OF THE POLISH SENATE, VILNO, 1920S.

"Rabbi, it is too much. I do not earn more," said the Polish official to the rabbi. "Please, pardon me for being so bold," inter-
ceded a member of the delegation," but our rabbi has not exerted
himself mentally less than you have, sir, in order to reach his position." This and other cases suggest that the kehilla boards and
councils did not cave in under government supervision.[26]

Clearly such supervision did not exist in the case of the Catholic church, even though the government subsidized the church.
The analyzed allotments from 1927–39, show that the Jews received less than one percent of the total sums spent in support of
religious institutions, (while the Jews constituted a tenth of the
total population).[27] At the same time, the Jewish population turned
out to be more heavily taxed by the Polish government, as was
shown earlier.

To enable the kehillot to maintain the religious and welfare
services, the law granted to them the right to levy a surtax (*etat*)
on the local Jewish population. The board of each kehilla decided

on the amount to be paid by every family, in accordance with its financial capacity. But as the Jewish population was becoming increasingly impoverished, it was unable to support double taxation. For example, the Lódź kehilla's statistics (they are among the best communal records of that period) show that in 1929 half of the Jewish families—too poor to pay anything—were exempted even from a minimal levy. Such minimal fees (5 to 25 złoty per year, then 60 cents to 3 dollars) were paid by 33 percent of the families. Only 13 percent were considered able to bear moderate fees. A considerable portion of the total amounts raised through the kehilla surtax, in small as well as large cities, was contributed by the rich.[28] However, these amounts were pitifully inadequate to meet the needs of a population growing poorer daily.

Another source of income was fees from ritual slaughtering of cattle and fowl under the kehilla's supervision, but this income was considerably curtailed in January 1937, when the government passed a law limiting the production of kosher meat. As for overseas aid, it seems that in the 1930s only 12 to 14 percent of the total expenditures of the kehillot were provided by American and other Jewish agencies from abroad. (American and world Jewry's concern was then concentrated on the German Jews.) [29]

Nevertheless, the local kehillot struggled to provide some help for the most needy, as well as to maintain religious facilities and services for the entire community. Provision of relief for the "declasé and impoverished, at least the most basic necessities for existence" was a "cardinal task" and became a frantic preoccupation.[30] Each kehilla had to have a *moes-khitim*, a fund to provide for the holiday needs of the poorest families. It was considered a disgrace for the whole community if there were people left in town with no special holiday food. In addition, they tried hard to continue with a fund for *gmiles-khesed* (acts of loving kindness), which provided small loans to people in emergency situations. Also, the kehillot usually did their best to scrape up some money to pay the tuition for the religious instruction of children whose parents were too poor to do so themselves.

To provide these services, which traditional Jews considered minimal, the kehillot incurred debts and had great difficulties discharging them. This sharpened the factional antagonisms and mutual accusations of wrongdoing within the kehilla organization. And in turn, it provided occasions for government intervention.[31]

In the 1930s the government authorities were increasingly exploiting their right of supervision, taking advantage of the intrigues and backstage maneuvering of the various factions. It was not uncommon occurrence for the government to invalidate the council's election of its president. Also, the authorities frequently disapproved of the composition of election committees.[32] In some instances, particularly in large cities, they dissolved the community councils, and appointed commissions in their place. Some of this interference seems to have occurred at the invitation of members of the Agudah, who were attempting to counteract the efforts of the secular political parties to run the kehillot. Unfortunately, to this day there is no objective study of these manifestations. Each side accused the other of terrible wrongdoings. Tentatively, I surmise that there was some truth and also much exaggeration in these accusations. But without such a study it is hard to draw the line between the two. As we shall see in the final chapter, the socialist Bund was mounting a concentrated drive to wrest control of the kehillot from the hands of the religious Jews, whom they considered backward "fanatics." In turn, the Agudah did not shrink from taking advantage of its relatively good relations with the Piłsudski government to strengthen its position. As a result of its initiative, a ruling was issued by the Minister of Religious Creeds and Public Education on October 24, 1930, granting the kehilla election commissions the authority to remove from the list of legitimate voters those individuals "who took public stands against the Judaic religion." [33] This ruling evoked special consternation among Bundists and other antireligious elements. However, even some very religious individuals found it unpalatable. Eventually, the Agudah's close cooperation with the *Sanacja* regime, which did little to alleviate the lot of Polish Jewry, repelled even some Jews who preferred that the kehillot not become secularized.[34]

Before examining how this close cooperation with this regime evolved, it would serve us well to review the basic attitudes of the

Orthodox-traditionalists which made it possible. First of all, Jewish Jews tended not to challenge the Poles' right to dominate and tried to accommodate themselves to their domination. For the Orthodox invoked the Talmudic principle that the law of the land is the law. They relied on persuasion and cooperation with existing Polish authorities to alleviate their conditions. Thus when it was necessary to deal with Jews, the Poles in authority generally tended to feel more comfortable with Jewish Jews than with the "modern" ones who insisted on being treated as equals.

The Traditional Pattern of Accommodation

In independent Poland, the Orthodox-traditionalists responded to their caste situation as Polish Jews had for long generations: conformity and docility in outward form but defiance in essence. They defied their Gentile oppressors by leading a Jewish life, despite all the obstacles, They did not resent and therefore did not challenge the social segregation of Jews. The Poles' reason for excluding Jews, "Jewish inferiority," was simply ridiculous tò the Jewish Jews. But they themselves tended to self-segregation because of the double danger they saw in the proximity to Gentiles. First, Gentile influences would disrupt the Jewish way of life. Therefore the Jew was supposed to build a hedge around it, to protect it. Second, most Gentiles—with the exception of the righteous ones— hated Jews, and this hate was likely to manifest itself when least expected. (It was said that no matter how a Jew tried to please a Gentile he could never succeed for long.) Therefore, self-segregation was a way of reducing the chances that hate would erupt. Those who departed from the traditional community branded it as a ghetto and its beliefs and ways as religious orthodoxy. But for those within, it was not a ghetto but a Jewish life among Gentiles, not orthodox religion but true Judaism. Judaism relieved, illuminated, and hallowed for them what the outsiders perceived solely as the squalor, staleness, and vulgarity of the ghetto.

The Orthodox-traditionalists accommodated themselves to the caste rules and assumed the posture of inferiority knowing very well that they were not inferior as human beings to their oppressors. In sheer force, but in no other way, did they feel inferior to the dominant Poles. Therefore, their concern was mostly with physical and economic survival in the face of oppression, and not so much with psychological pain.[35] For the Jewish Jew was sealed off by his faith and tradition from the psychological effects of his lower caste position. His conception of himself remained unaffected by the majority group's stereotypes. His Jewish identity was firm and intact; he traced it to Abraham's Convenant with God, and he was Abraham's descendant. The Jewish system of honor, markedly different in its essence from the Polish system, protected Jewish Jews psychologically: It shielded them from the mindless fun made of them and their sacred customs as well as from willful attempts by Poles to humiliate them. Derisions or torments by Poles did not touch their Jewish honor or pride, their *koved*, but testified to the inferiority of the perpetrators. The fact that traditional Jewish honor was immune to the actions of Gentiles was incomprehensible to acculturated Jews and especially to the assimilationists. They were embarrassed to witness Jewish Jews bowing and literally dancing when ordered to do so by Poles who found it amusing. Having absorbed the standards of Polish honor, they lost the understanding that the traditional Jews did not feel demeaned when they succumbed to power and force of gentiles, or their "goish" sense of fun.

In his relations with fellow Jews, the Jewish Jew saw himself as very susceptible to shame. This susceptibility, like tender heartedness, was held to be a distinctive Jewish characteristic. It was therefore considered evil to do anything, whether obvious or subtle, that would shame a fellow Jew. The norms dictated that one was not to point to a person's lowly occupation, state of deprivation, bad health, or misfits in the family. As one informant from a traditional home related:

> As a child I had a friend from that family in which there was a *shmadke* [woman who converted to Christianity]. My mother warned me that I should never mention the word "convert" or anything similar in her presence so as not to hurt her.

In a sense, "no one is a 'victim' who assumes responsibility for himself and his responses, even when he does not have the power to control the consequences for his situation." [36] This feeling of responsibility was a source of Jewish strength, and the traditional Jew's sense of responsibility was supposed to extend beyond himself—to the family and the Jewish community. At the center of his beliefs was that all Jews are mutually accountable to each other. The rabbinic saying that the destiny of every Jew is interwined with the destiny of every other Jew was often quoted. The Talmudic story that illustrated this moral was also cited. This story tells of men who were traveling in a boat. One of them started to bore a hole in the bottom. When the others protested, he replied that he was only boring it under his own seat. "Yes," said the others, "but when the sea rushes in we shall all be drowned together with you. So it is with Israel. Its weal and its woe are in the hands of every individual Israelite."

For the Orthodox-traditionalists, Jewish "strength" lay in surviving in face of brutal force without becoming brutalized. This was possible, they believed, because they had the Torah, which was a source of light and nobility. It was therefore essential for Jews to hold on to a way of life based on it, for the traditional Jews were very much aware of the faults as well as the good qualities that made them "different from all other nations." On the positive side they considered themselves distinct in their "Jewish charm," "Jewish heart," and "Jewish head"; on the negative in being quarrelsome, contentious, difficult, overwary, and fearful. "If Moses, our teacher, could not get along with the Jews, how can a plain Jew?" was often asked. The recognition of their own wariness and timidity found expression in sayings such as "A Jew is afraid of his own shadow."

The imaginary dangers and fears preying on them—such as the "evil eye" or even ghosts—often served to mask the very real dangers and fears arising from their actual situation as a persecuted minority. They were a projection of the suppressed fear of violence and of abuse, rooted both in childhood experiences with anti-Semitic violence and in the historical memory of Jews. There was much fear in the atmosphere, but its real sources were seldom identified. The traditional people tended to talk about persecution or violence only when it actually broke out somewhere. Otherwise, it was better not to dwell on the possibility of such things. And so one tried to forget. However, danger was not to be banished by attempts to forget it, and fear continued to infect the air. Only it was often attached to unreal dangers such as ghosts. After all, there were methods of dealing with ghosts: many old-fashioned Jews, who did not know how to handle a Polish urchin who threw stones at them, knew that spirits could be driven away by reciting the *Shema'*: "Hear O Israel, the Lord our God, the Lord is One!" [37]

The Orthodox were very confident of the long-term survival of the Jewish people. The words of the Hagadah recited at Seder— "More than one man has risen up against us, and in every generation there rise up against us those who seek to destroy us, but the Holy One, blessed be He, delivers us from their hand"—expressed a belief very much alive among the Jewish-Jews. What troubled them more was the immediate situation, "the present hour of life" (*haye sha'ah*). And here the challenge was to outlive (*iberlebn*) Gentiles' acts of hostility and violence. This was not likely to be achieved through force, they thought, since the Poles could employ more force. Force would therefore only inflame anti-Semitism and increase Jewish suffering. The deep conviction that Jews must not use force was also tied to the belief that force could not be controlled. The popular tale of the great rabbi who created the Golem from clay and gave him life illustrated this. The Golem had been designed to punish those who injured Jews, but he was soon striking indiscriminately. The rabbi himself could not control him and finally had to destroy him.

One method the Orthodox-traditionalists advocated and practiced was avoidance: to go out of one's way if necessary in order not to face hostility. However, since some contact was required— especially in the economic sphere—it was held that one had to use one's wits to get around the hostile Pole. Much of the Jewish humor had to do with this. Putting on the mask of a clownish inferior, was one way of disarming a Pole's hostility. When it came to dealing with government officials, the Orthodox-traditionalists clung to the old institution of the *shtadlan*, the intermediary, literally, the "one who exerts himself" for others. This custom dated back to the time of the court-Jew, who would intervene on behalf of other Jews and the community at large, before the kings and princes of Poland.[38] Since it was commonly believed that most Poles who disliked or even hated Jews nevertheless had a favorite Jew,* a *Moszek*, such a favorite of a powerful Pole could get some relief for other Jews.[39] However, the task was considered far from easy, and therefore individuals who succeeded commanded much respect. (Of course, it was easier when the person in authority was a righteous Gentile, but such luck was the kind of blessing one could not count on, traditional Jews would say.)

This then was not acceptance of or resignation to hostility, but ways of coping that involved ingenuity and wit. However, these ways, proven effective in Polish society with its traditional anti-Semitism, showed themselves to be increasingly less effective in the nationalist, independent Poland with its modern forms of anti-Semitism. Avoiding the hostility of anti-Semites by remaining in their own neighborhoods was becoming less feasible, as organized nationalist youth bands invaded them, seeking excitement and thrills in terrorizing the most peaceful and fearful Jews. It was next to impossible to get around the anti-Semitic militants, who were trained to be conscious of such "Jewish ways." And effective intercession with Polish officials was becoming increasingly rare. Powerful Poles were fearful of endangering their power, for they risked being exposed as "accommodators of Jews" by the extreme nationalist organizations.

As a result of the diminishing efficacy of the traditional mechanisms of coping with their oppressive situation, politicization began making inroads among the Orthodox-traditionalists. This is exemplified in the changes that were occurring in the Agudah. It had come into being in 1912, with the purpose of preserving the traditional way of life, and it defined itself as a nonpolitical association. It competed directly with the *Mizrachi*, the religious wing of

---

* Individual Orthodox-traditionalists who experienced such favoritism from a given Pole usually did not tend to minimize his anti-Semitism but would instead say, "He hates Jews but he likes me." To be so inconsistent was regarded as a Gentile quirk, and it too figured prominently in Jewish humor.

Zionism, which had originated a decade earlier and combined Orthodox Judaism with modern Zionism. The Agudah saw in Zionism the profanation of the belief in the coming of the Messiah. From its very inception, Mizrachi represented a new phenomenon: a political orientation by Orthodox-traditionalists, at least in regard to the recovery of Palestine: Its motto was "the Land of Israel for the People of Israel on the basis of the Torah." [40] After Polish independence was won, Mizrachi also took a political stand in regard to the status of Jews in Poland: It followed, and persisted in, the general Zionist line of seeking national autonomy for the Jews. In contrast, the Agudah could and did adjust to the state's definition of the Jews as solely a religious group. The Agudat Israel, despite its accommodation to the Poles' rule and point of view, was becoming politicized by the objective circumstances of the Jewish situation. The politicization of the Agudah was occurring irrespective of its continued formal endorsement of the traditional ways of dealing with Polish hostility and irrespective of its continued claims of being nonpolitical.

Agudat Israel—from Accommodation to Politicization

Considering itself not a political organization but rather an association for preserving the faith and the Jewish way of life based on it, the Agudat Israel placed great stress on the maintenance of religious facilities, its educational function, and its welfare work. The main pillars of the organization were the heads of the influential hasidic dynasties, foremost among them the rebe of Ger, Abraham Mordechai Alter. However, the head of one of the great hasidic dynasties, the Alexander rebe, refused to endorse the Agudah and allowed his followers the choice of whether to support it or the Mizrachi. [41] (Generally, the Mizrachi attracted non-hasidic Orthodox-traditionalists, many of them *mitnagdim.*) In line with its nonpolitical self-definition, the supreme authority of the Agudah was not vested in its central committee but in a Council of Sages: a group of rebes who had to approve all major decisions.

The "nonpolitical" Agudah nevertheless decided to be represented in the Polish Parliament when Jewish political organizations (with Zionists in the lead) entered the arena of Polish politics right after independence. Its leader did not want to leave the representation of Jews in this august body of Poland to these parties, whose aims were at odds with Jewish tradition. Upon entry into the provisional Parliament, the Agudah's representatives expressed joy over the resurrection of Poland and confidence in the just rule by Poles.[42]

If the entry into the provisional Parliament represented a departure from its nonpolitical stance, then its behavior during the 1922 election certainly was a drastic deviation from its basic philosophy of accommodation to the Polish majority: the Agudah joined the National Minorities' Bloc, championed by the Zionists of former Congress Poland. Taking this step, the Agudah emphasized, did not mean that it approved of the Minorities' Bloc as a stable feature of Polish politics. Rather, it argued, that it was joining in order not to disturb Jewish political unity in fact of the great anti-Jewish hostility that the Polish–Bolshevik war had triggered. Also, it justified this step as a necessary electoral tactic for that particular time: preventing a split in the Jewish vote and thereby achieving a representation in Parliament proportional to the numbers of Jews in the total population.[43] Indeed, this goal was reached in the election; and 6 Agudah members were among the 35 Jewish candidates who won seats in the Diet.

Before the election, however, within Agudah itself there seems to have been some opposition to this tactic. One of its leading figures, Meshulem Kaminer, warned that in exchange for a few Jewish deputies a number of Jewish livelihoods would disappear and a new wave of persecution against Jews would begin.[44] This prediction came true. Despite the fact that the Agudah never again supported the National Minorities' Bloc—on the contrary, it fought it staunchly and consistently—the participation of it and of other Jewish organizations in that bloc during the fateful election unleashed a hostility from Poles that could not be reversed.

Once elected, the Agudah men tried to resume their policy of "understanding" they had instituted in the provisional Parliament: accommodation to the Poles' will concerning Poland's political system and conciliation with the government in power. They rejected the militant politics of the Zionists within Parliament and the Bundists outside it as irresponsible and in the long run inimical to Jewish coexistence with Poles. They felt it was poor judgment for Jewish parties to form alliances with either the Polish rightist or leftist opposition. As expressed early in its official publication, the right "seeks to destroy the life and existence of every Jew as an individual" while the left "seeks to destroy the Jewish people as a people." [45] (The same idea was voiced by Sartre after World War II in his *Anti-semite and Jew*.) [46]

Thus, the Agudah's representatives voted on issues rather than party lines. Their general aim was to work within the existing political framework of Polish society in a manner to protect Jewish life and Jewish rights. This, in their estimation, meant acting with great caution, avoiding "doctrinaire approaches." It is reflected in the Agudah's eventual accommodation to the government's definition of Jews as a religious rather than a nationality group. In the provisional Diet, mirroring the atmosphere generated by the Minorities Treaty, the representative of the Agudah, the venerable Rabbi Perlmutter, declared clearly that the Orthodox considered Jews also to be a nationality and stood for the religio-national autonomy.[47] The Orthodox-traditionalists' fundamental conception of the character of the Jewish people was one of indivisibility between religion and nationality, and yet the Agudah did not continue to insist that Poles must accept this, but compromised instead.[48] Wherever possible, the Agudah leaders avoided a challenge to the existing government; instead, they tried to improve the treatment of Jews by personal contact with government leaders.

Thus, the typical Agudah representative in Parliament still defined himself, and was defined by the organization, according to the traditional concept of the Jewish intermediary, the shtadlan.[49] He was the outstanding Jew who, because of his extraordinary qualities, could plead the Jews' case before powerful Gentiles. The Agudah men in parliament—Deputies Rabbi Moshe Elihu Halpern, Rabbi Aaron Lewin, Elihu Kirschbraun, Senator Osher Mendelsohn and others—were depicted in the Agudah publications as the embodiments of the ideal traditional Jewish virtues: learning, refinement, freedom from personal vanity, deep concern about fellow human beings and about the welfare of the Jewish community. Indeed, these men behaved with great dignity in the Polish Parliament. An early example is that of Rabbi Halpern in the provisional Diet: Dressed in traditional garb like the other Agudah representatives, he was impressive in his mastery and elegance of the Polish language and in the manner he defended Jews without offending the Poles' sense of honor. On February 28, 1919, he managed to cool the heated atmosphere generated by a Jewish representative (Noah Pryłucki) who had challenged the honor of a Polish representative. The following year he rose to answer a Polish deputy's attack on the Talmud as a source of Jewish evil; he calmly refuted the arguments and concluded that never again would he grace with an answer such base attacks on the Jewish faith, which violated both Poland's tradition of religious tolerance and the dignity of her parliament. Rabbi Halpern's behavior symbolized "the attitude of Agudat Israel for many years and perhaps the entire period of independent Poland." [50] Also in dealing with the heads of various ministries and high rank government personnel, the Agudah representatives tended to approximate the ideal image of the shtadlan. This is indicated by no special admirer of traditionalism or Orthodoxy, M. A. Hartglas, of assimilationist background and a Zionist representative in the Diet, who wrote about the period following the 1928 election, when Zionists and Bundists were attacking Agudah for having sold out to Piłsudski:

> Kirschbraun [the Agudah representative] behaved toward the Polish Ministers with such dignity and Jewish pride, spoke so courageously to them, that I would have never expected this from a member of the Agudah. . . . Unfortunately not all our Jewish representatives were able to behave with such courage when dealing with non-Jews. Yes, they managed to be very brave and very extremist when they spoke in the Jewish Caucus, they managed to speak sharply and even aggressively in the Diet when they spoke for the benefit of the press. But person to person with a "Goy" they became so subservient that it was simply impossible to recognize them. [51]

To comprehend fully the special relation of the Agudah with the Sanacja regime, it is important to recall that the Agudah was greatly frustrated in its policy of "understanding" prior to Piłsudski's coup: Political and economic anti-Semitism in the aftermath of the 1922 national election made it extremely difficult for the Agudah representatives to practice restraint and to achieve anything by the method of intercession in dealing with men for whom "anti-Semitism was a profession." Increasingly Agudah representatives took the government to task for failing to act against violations of the Jews' rights. It was therefore with relief that they greeted Marshal Piłsudski's return to power in 1926. The Prime Minister of the new government, Professor Kazimierz Bartel, clearly enunciated a positive change toward the Jewish minority. His declaration specifically stated that the government would proceed from "the assumption that economic anti-semitism is harmful to the state." [52]

The Agudah thought that Józef Piłsudski "the founder of independent Poland," was the man who could and would lead the Poles away from the narrow path of anti-Semitism upon which they were drawn by the nationalists. They gave their enthusiastic support to him and his government. At the end of 1927, when the hasidic rebes convened in Tarnów, they issued a statement reminding all Jews that as "loyal citizens" it was "their duty to conduct politics, which correspond to the interests of the government and the state." [53] In accordance with this call, the Agudah worked hard to persuade the Zionists and other Jewish political groups not to enter the National Minorities' Bloc in the forthcoming election of 1928, since this path "would be dangerous for Polish Jewry." Instead, it urged them to join Agudah in a bloc of Jewish unity aimed at guarding Jewish interests. It failed in this; only two small groups, the Folkist Party and the Association of Merchants, joined it. Nevertheless, this Jewish bloc polled a large number of votes (171,987) in the 1928 election, but because of the split in the Jewish vote none of its candidates was elected. [54] In addition to this Jewish bloc, the Agudah (and its partners) also participated in Piłsudski's Non-Party Bloc of Cooperation with the government (BBWR). On this ticket, one Agudah representative, Elihu Kirschbraun, was elected to the new Diet. Thus, among the fifteen representatives from Jewish parties, the Agudah was underrepresented when compared with the preceding Sejm to which its delegates were elected on the Minorities' Bloc ticket (6 out of 35 were then Agudah members). Nevertheless, the Agudah followed the same line in the 1930 election, both running their own ticket and joining the government BBWR ticket. On the first, one Agudah representative was elected to the Sejm; on the latter, one to the Sejm and one to the Senate. (The two Agudah men elected on the government ticket were now members of the BBWR parliamentary club in the Polish Parliament.) [55]

Evidently the Agudah was no longer much concerned by the size of its representation. By then it seems to have been willing to consider something that the Zionists never did—that it might have been a big mistake for the Jewish groups to have run their own candidates for Parliament. It is noteworthy that the Agudah president, Yitzhak Meyer Lewin, in discussing at the third convention of the organization the fact that not a single candidate had been elected on its own ticket in the 1928 election, reminded the Agudah leaders that "we see that in these countries where no separate Jewish politics are engaged in, the position of Jews is much better." [56]

By its policy and behavior the Agudah clearly indicated to the Sanacja regime that it rejected the alternative of opposition. But the Agudah also made clear, contrary to the accusations heaped on it by Zionists and Bundists, that it "was entitled to and would continue with its right to pursue an independent policy when it came to guarding Jewish interests." [57] The result of its policy were the earlier discussed favors and concessions in the realm of traditional education and kehilla organization granted to it by that Piłsudski regime. Perhaps these could be considered minor in the context of the regime's economic measures, which adversely affected the Jews, but from the perspective of the Agudah's values, these concessions appeared important. For as the President of the Agudah said to its leaders at the 1928 convention, after reviewing the "catastrophic" economic conditions of Polish Jewry and turning to its "spiritual" state: "Our sons and daughters are being lost to us." Having said that he moved on to lay stress on the Agudah's accomplishments in the field of education, and in preserving the religious character of the kehillot. Since the Zionists had outmaneuvered them in the parliamentary elections of 1928, they decided not to allow the same to happen to them in the kehillot. The Agudah was also concerned with the terrible economic situation of Polish Jewry, which was a constant theme in the activities of the organization as well as the pronouncement of its leaders. It is exemplified in the above report by the President of the Agudah who declared:

> In the last five years we have seen three million Polish Jews facing complete economic ruin. Numerous factors account for it, . . . and one does not see a way out. The greatest part of [Polish] Jewry is impoverished. Hunger is spreading and taking terrible forms. . . . This burden that weighs on suffering Jewry gets heavier and heavier from day to day, from year to year.[58]

In 1928, when this declaration was made, the Agudah leaders had great faith that Piłsudski would find a way out. Under him Poland would reach the political and economic stability that would make possible a reversal of economic measures adversely affecting Jews. By 1934 it was clear that the government was not moving in this direction, and yet the Agudah continued to support the Sanacja regime. Its president wrote in its widely read Yiddish daily:

> No matter how many demands we have of the present regime, which has not fulfilled our just demands—it remains obvious that any other regime consisting of the present opposition would be incomparably worse for the Jews and for the country in general . . . We remain firm in our belief that the present regime, which maintains order in the country with a strong hand, strongly and firmly protects the security of the Jewish population and prohibits all antisemitic outbursts.[59]

With the example of Germany next door, the Agudah was fearful that worse things would happen if the Sanacja regime were replaced. That regime meant to them the influence of Piłsudski.

And indeed a worsening did occur, and violence against Jews was unleashed, but not because the opposition came to power; Piłsudski died and with him the main restraining force against the Sanacja's use of anti-Semitism as a political weapon.

The decisive event in the collapse of the Agudah's policy of "understanding" with the government was the legislation against the kosher slaughter of animals (at the beginning of 1936). To the Agudah, the rhetoric of the sponsors of the bill (posing as humanitarians and depicting this Jewish religious practice as barbaric) was a direct attack on the Jewish faith. It saw in this measure a dangerous violation of religious freedom and an open attempt to undermine the possibilities for leading a Jewish life in Poland.[60] Thus it opposed the government more on this than on any previous measure.

Soon after, in March of the same year, the Agudah came out in support of the half-day general strike against the Przytyk pogrom, a protest led by its arch-opponent, the anti-religious socialist Bund. Indeed, "the path which led from the Agudah's joining the government list in 1928 to its joining a Bundist demonstration was a long and tragic one." [61]

The collapse of its faith that Jews could go on coexisting with Poles was also reflected in the profound change in its attitude toward a Jewish national home in Palestine. The Agudat Israel had pursued an anti-Zionist policy since independence, rejecting the Zionist idea of mass departure from Poland. It was dramatically expressed when the Agudah representative, Rabbi Perlmutter, dressed in traditional garb, rose in the Diet on May 27, 1919, and recounted how on his way to the chamber he had been jeered at with shouts of "Go to Palestine instead of to the Sejm." He explained that the time had not arrived yet; one day the Messiah would come and the Jews would go there. "But now we must live here where our forefathers have lived and are buried. . . . we shall remain in Poland as long as it takes, until Providence calls us forth to the Land of Israel." [62]

⋅ In the last few years before World War II, however, the Agudah leaders favored the creation of a Jewish state in Palestine. Thus in practice the Agudah was moving closer to the very Jewish parties whose influences it had been created to oppose. It now proclaimed that only through unity could Jews gain some strength.[63] This represented quite a departure from its activities during the Piłsudski period, when the Agudah, in the interest of preserving the traditional mode of life, had not hesitated to accept government support to limit the influence of the secular Jewish parties.

Conclusion

The traditional mode of coping, developed during centuries of oppression, proved impotent under the conditions of modern anti-Semitism. Nevertheless numerous Jewish-Jews could not shed it, since it had become deeply imprinted in their psyche and inextricably intertwined with their religious Orthodoxy and traditional culture. But among the young, the movement away from both was strong, and in the 1930s it even swept the shtetlekh, the last forts of traditionalism. These small towns, especially in former Congress Poland, which in the past had been least touched by outside waves of change, now were engulfed by them. Although rapid change characterized all social strata, it was particularly pronounced among the workers and poor. The traditional mechanisms for checking deviancy broke down. In the past one of the most effective sanctions was for the community to shun the deviant; but now the deviant was withdrawing from the traditional community.[64]

Young people were increasingly unable to draw psychological sustenance from the traditional culture and traditional communal life. This was especially true of those with marked intellectual predispositions, of whom there were many. Having broken away from Orthodoxy, they no longer viewed themselves as bearers of a fate that was full of pain but also contained the indestructible seed of Redemption in the future. More and more, the young saw themselves as victims of political forces operating among Poles and in the world at large. From this position of victims they aimed to liberate themselves by political action. They regarded the traditional method of dealing with the Poles as weak, spineless, and undignified.

However, viewed from a socio-historical perspective, the highly integrated traditional culture provided Jews with a meaningful interpretation of the surrounding hostility. Also from such a perspective, the pattern that the Jews developed of coping with hostility, under the conditions of traditional anti-Semitism, represented accommodation in form only and nonviolent resistance in essence. The Jews, a relatively powerless group, who inevitably would have been overcome in an open.contest of force, survived and at times improved their situation through this form of "resistance." But under modern conditions of organized political anti-Semitism, the same behavior stopped being functional: it no longer facilitated survival, let alone improvement in conditions. Thus a mechanism that once had functionally signified nonviolent resistance became transformed into one of passive surrender. And many of the younger generation, sensing the present impotence of such behavior, rejected it with disgust, unable to remember that this mode of behavior had been functional as well as proper in the past.

VI
Assimilationists:
Poles in Culture
and Self-Identity

The existence in Poland of assimilated Jews who regarded themselves as Poles was little known among world Jewry, let alone among non-Jewish people: Jewish assimilation was associated with Germany and other Western countries. And yet conscious assimilation in Poland dates back to the nineteenth century. Its actual and spiritual descendants constituted in interwar Poland a type at the opposite pole from the Orthodox-traditionalists; they were fully Polonized and had at most a minimal Jewish self-identity. They seldom referred to themselves as Jews. When it was necessary or appropriate to indicate their religion or background they mostly used the designation "Poles of Mosaic faith" or "Poles of Jewish descent," but Jews in general tended to refer to them as "assimilated or "assimilators."

Although they represented a very small portion of the total Jewish population, the very fact of the existence of the assimilationists * as a social type in Poland is of historical and sociological

An earlier version of this chapter can be found in Celia Stopnicka Heller, "Assimilation: A Deviant Pattern Among the Jews of Inter-War Poland," *Jewish Journal of Sociology*, 15, no. 2 (December 1973): 221–37. This chapter incorporates the results of additional research.

* I call them "assimilationists" instead of "assimilated" to give cognizance not only to the results of the process but also to the fact that originally assimilation was for them both a conscious program and a method of solving the Jewish problem.

significance. Poles in general were of a strong conviction that the Polish Jews were unassimilable, and yet here was a group fully acculturated, which persisted in their self-identification as Poles until the very end.

Assimilationist Ideology vs. Jewish Ethnic Consciousness

It can truly be said of them that they bore the deep marks of their origin and their past on their brow. [1] Despite the anti-Semitic outbreaks that greeted independence, they clung to assimilation * when independence was ushered in and still thought that they would become fully integrated in Poland. These outbreaks they interpreted as a temporary setback, for which Jewish nationalism, no less than Polish nationalism, bore responsibility. As Israel Cohen, who came to Poland on a mission from Britain (at the time of the anti-Jewish violence preceding the signing of the Minorities Treaty) wrote in his diary (entry, January 7, 1919) after his conference with Professor Władysław Natanson, the scion of one of the most distinguished assimilationist families: "Discussed pogroms: he said Jews were to blame as much as Poles . . . He argued that Jews had all rights" as citizens. But Professor Natanson also made clear that he "could not understand how anybody could claim rights in Poland who didn't declare himself [of] Polish nationality." [2]

The rights alluded to above were those proclaimed by the first

---

* Acculturation and assimilation are used in this and in the following chapter as two distinct concepts, although they are related in concrete phenomena. The term "acculturation," according to an authoritative definition, includes "those phenomena which result when groups of individuals having different cultures, come into continuous firsthand contact, with subsequent changes in the original cultural patterns of either or both groups." Robert Redfield, Ralph Linton, and Melville J. Herskovits, "Memorandum for the Study of Acculturation," *American Anthropologist,* 38, no. 1, (January–March, 1936): 149. By assimilation is meant "the adoption by a person or group of the culture of another social group to such a complete extent that the person or group no longer has any characteristics identifying him with his former culture and no longer has any particular loyalties to his former culture." Arnold M. Rose, *Sociology: The Study of Human Relations,* (New York: Alfred Knopf, 1956), pp. 557–58.

Polish Diet in its declarations concerning Poland's form of government (afterward known as the "Little Constitution"): civil rights to all citizens of Poland, irrespective of religion and national background. This is what the assimilationists had aimed at before independence and were therefore grateful that independent Poland had promptly proclaimed itself a democracy with equality in citizenship. To the assimilationists, the major obstacle to the full implementation of these rights—and to the acceptance of Jews by Poles—was Jewish cultural distinctiveness. They were determined to correct this, imbued as they were with the nineteenth-century belief that the antagonism toward the Jews would disappear with the disappearance of Jewish cultural differences. As early as May 1919, a national convention of the "Association of Poles of Mosaic Faith," was held in Warsaw. The main speakers emphasized that since Poland was now free, the chance to eliminate Jewish cultural distinctiveness was finally presenting itself. In the words of one of the most prominent delegates, "the Jewish masses [were] culturally backward and fossilized through centuries by religio-racial separation." A concentrated educational effort would be required to make them culturally Polish. (The United States was used as an example to show how quickly Jews assimilate in a society free of persecution.) But a new stumbling block was presenting itself in the form of Jewish nationalism which, according to them, could wreck Polish Jewry's great chance. The delegates at the convention condemned Jewish nationalism vigorously, speaking out sharply against the activities of the Zionists (in the international arena) on behalf of a Minorities Treaty. They thought such activities to be irresponsible and dangerous to their goal of normalizing the relations between the "Christian and Jewish population" and achieving "the unification of the Jews with the Polish nation." Despite the long history of Jewish autonomy in Poland, the bylaws of the Association of Poles of Mosaic Faith pledged it to act "against cultural and national autonomy but [for] equality in citizenship and full political and social rights of the population of Mosaic faith, as well as other citizens." [3]

After the signing of the Minorities Treaty (December 25, 1919), one Diet member after another, representing the various political parties of Polish Jewry, rose in the provisional Polish Diet: each proclaimed that Jews, who were loyal and patriotic citizens of Poland, claimed the rights of national minorities guaranteed by the Treaty. The single dissonant voice was that of Deputy Lowenstein, one of the leaders of the Association of Poles of Mosaic Faith; in their name he declared that Poles of Mosaic faith admit "sincerely and steadfastly to Polish nationality" only, and did not consider themselves of Jewish nationality.[4])

This was an event of utmost importance in the relation between the assimilationists and the rest of the Polish Jewry; on the most basic issue that was dividing Poles and Jews at the beginning of independence, the assimilationists were unequivocally lining up with Poles. That the event took place in the highest chamber of Poland imbued it with special symbolic significance. It marked the end of the nineteenth-century pattern, in which some prominent assimilationists acted as intermediaries between the Jews and Poles and were accepted as such by Jews. Then, the assimilationists had occupied leading positions in the Jewish community organizations of major cities and were initiators or sponsors of many communal institutions. Although this pattern was on the decline at the beginning of the twentieth century, it only came to an end during independence, with the growth of Jewish nationalism. Assimilationists were no longer regarded by Jews as fit to lead them or represent them. Throughout the interwar period, the Jews tended to view them as taking the side of the dominant group against them. Thus assimilationists were rarely elected to political office by Jews. When they held such office, it was usually because they had been appointed by Polish central or local government authorities.[5] In the 1927 elections to the kehillot, the assimilationists suffered an unprecedented defeat: they were eliminated from the boards and councils of most, even in the cities where they formerly dominated.[6]

By then the ideology of assimilation could no longer move or inspire even young Jews, including those who spoke Polish only, to enter the ranks of professed assimilationists. The anti-Semitism of its first decade spelled the end of this ideology in Poland. However, most of those who had embraced the ideology of assimilation before independence or were born to assimilationist families, continued to hold on to it. Except among them, neither the professed program nor method of assimilation gained ground among any part of Polish Jewry. This is demonstrated by the almost complete failure of a small group of youths from assimilationist families to revive, in the late 1920s and early 1930s, the initial missionary zeal of assimilationism. These "neo-assimilationists," as they were termed by an old ideologue of assimilation, were concentrated in the Association of Academic Youth for Unity. (They referred to it as ZAMS, its Polish initials, or simply Unity).

Interestingly, when, with Piłsudski's return to power, the Agudat Israel saw new opportunities for itself, so did Unity, which had lain dormant for almost a decade. Unity characterized the past decade in its monthly organ:

> The [Polish] nationalist madness grasped the minds of people to such an extent that it was a test of endurance to maintain ourselves on the surface of social life. Long and dark for our cause were the first ten years of [resurrected] Polish statehood. Under the influence of the *Endecja*, the overwhelming majority of the Polish people were against Jews.[7]

With the advent of Piłsudski, the time was judged propitious to act and Unity revitalized itself. (The organization of the older assimilationists, the Association of Poles of Mosaic Faith, remained largely dormant.) At Unity's national convention in 1928, it proclaimed the goal of spreading assimilation among the Jewish masses: it rejected both Zionism and any form of Jewish autonomy in Poland as a "state within a state." Thus it disapproved of the Piłsudski government's granting of juridical status to the kehillot, and it called for their abolition. (This contrasted sharply with the position of all the other secular Jewish organizations which aimed at the transformation or broadening of the kehillot.)

While most Jews were objecting that assimilation was not a solution in Poland even for those Jews who desired it, since Polish society was proving unwilling or incapable of accepting Jews as equals, these neo-assimilationists were optimistic during the early days of the Piłsudski regime. According to them the number of

Poles sympathetic to assimilation as a solution to the Jewish problem was rising; even the prevenient anti-Semitic outbreaks at the
universities did not deter these young people.

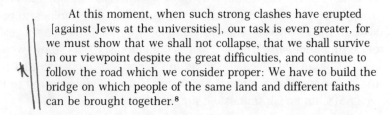

> At this moment, when such strong clashes have erupted
> [against Jews at the universities], our task is even greater, for
> we must show that we shall not collapse, that we shall survive
> in our viewpoint despite the great difficulties, and continue to
> follow the road which we consider proper: We have to build the
> bridge on which people of the same land and different faiths
> can be brought together.[8]

But as far as Polish Jewry in general was concerned, the ideology of assimilation had died for them at the beginning of independence and could not be revived. In the words of the well
known Polish writer Benedykt Hertz: "Assimilation. Today this
movement is generally considered ineffectual, bankrupt. And in
some measure rightly so." [9] Anti-Semitism aborted the growth of
identificational assimilation even among those who were becoming
highly acculturated. This explains why the proportion of the
assimilationists in the total Jewish population seems to have remained more or less constant during the interwar period.

No exact figures exist, but one can estimate the proportion of
the assimilationists from certain census data. Thus, I have arrived
at the estimate that the assimilationists constituted one-ninth to
one-tenth of the Jewish population, which numbered over 3 million (270,000-300,000 assimilationists).[10] However, this figure has
been considered too high by a few historians whom I consulted;
they think that it was between 150,000 and 200,000. I emphasize
again that there is no way of arriving at an exact figure.

Estimates of what proportion the assimilationists constituted
among the various strata of the Jewish population are even looser
than the above, for no census or other figures exist for a base. Assimilationists were especially prominent among artists and the
leading Jewish intellectuals; the latter were among the most prominent intellectuals of Poland.[11] On the basis of the interviews I
conducted, I should estimate that as many as 90 percent of them
were assimilationists. Another stratum in which they were propor-

tionally overrepresented was that of the very wealthy Jews. I should guess that about half of them were assimilationists. But assimilationists were virtually non-existent among the workers,[12] the small traders and the poor, who were minimally acculturated. Thus the great distance between the assimilationists and the bulk of the Jewish people was one both of class and of culture.

Cultural and Identificational Assimilation

This distance found its ultimate expression in identificational assimilation. This group differed from the rest of the Jewish population not only in their degree of acculturation (Polonization) and in their advocacy of assimilation, but also in their conscious self-identification as Poles. Identificational assimilation was the decisive factor in the break between the assimilationists and the rest of Polish Jewry.[13] The assimilationists were little conscious of an interdependence, in terms of a common destiny, with the Jews. On the contrary, many of them strove, in the words of a Polish historian, "to break the thread that connected them with the Jewish community." [14] The assimilationists emphasized their deep bonds to the Polish nation and their distinctness from the rest of the Jews. In their own eyes they were Poles to whom the label Żyd, Jew, had been wrongly affixed, although it was appropriate for most of the rest to whom it was applied. From their perspective, the only thing that made them different from the rest of the Polish people is that they were non-Catholic. Note: I did not say they were Jewish in their religion, for most of them in practice were far removed from it. Reform Judaism had not become institutionalized in Poland.[15] Most assimilationists were nominally of the "Mosaic faith" because they lived in a society where everyone was expected to have a religious designation (especially after 1934, when religious instruction became compulsory for all students in primary and secondary schools). Here Kallen's definition of a Jew comes to mind: "Anybody is a Jew who of his own free will calls himself by the name." [16] By this definition most assimilationists, in sharp contrast to the overwhelming majority of the Jews, were not Jews.

It could perhaps be argued that this did not hold to the same degree for the small group of young assimilationists of Unity, since in contrast to other assimilationists they began to refer to themselves sometimes as Jews-Poles. However, if we probe further into their rhetoric, we find that this self-designation did not go much beyond asserting that one is of Jewish descent, at a time when young people at the universities, who tried to forget or hide this, were being cruelly reminded of it. Criticized by the Jewish press as "worse than the old assimilationists" because nothing bound them to Jewry, they addressed themselves to this issue in their monthly organ, in an article which began thus: "From all sides we hear comments: 'Assimilation is bankrupt,' 'how can one nowadays, after all that has happened be an assimilator?' 'Are you at all Jews and what links you to Jewry?' " The response to these questions began forthrightly: "One could answer, mostly religion. But let us be sincere, the great majority of us are nonreligious people. Therefore what do we have in common?" And here lies the problem— there was nothing that they could point to except common descent. This common descent, they explained, accounted for the difficult task they had taken upon themselves to try to bring about the complete assimilation of the Jews in Poland.[17] A year later we find a further elaboration on their attitude toward Jewish descent: in contrast to other young assimilationists, "for a member of 'Unity,' Jewish descent is not a heavy load, a drag that one would like to rid himself of as soon as possible in life's competition, or something that one would very much like to hide." But again there was nothing said there of a pride in the struggle of Jews to survive as a people or of a link with Jewish culture. There was, however, a typical assimilationist expression of the deep bond with Polish culture: "Polish culture is for a member of 'Unity' . . . the very air he breathes and without which he cannot live." [18]

One must not forget that by the time Poland had become independent, the members of this special small group, as well as the younger assimilationists in general, were fully de-Judaized and Polonized. In independent Poland, the assimilationists were at least the second generation of assimilation, and many of the youths and adolescents were third or even fourth generation. Alek-

sander Hertz has noted that the nineteenth-century assimilationist
movement was not an attempt to abolish the caste system but to
escape it, without conversion to Catholicism, by means of Polonization. (Of course, the assimilators hoped that eventually the caste
system would disappear as more and more Jews became assimilated.) The first generation embarked upon this method of escape,
often conscious that they would not entirely succeed—since the
marks of lower caste status were too deeply ingrained in them—
but with faith that their children and grandchildren would. They
consciously pursued the goals of de-Judaization and Polonization
by systematically abandoning Jewish patterns of behavior and
changing their style of life into a Polish one. This expressed itself
in the sharp linguistic shift from Yiddish to Polish in their primary
as well as secondary relations. But their children and grandchildren were socialized from birth in the Polish culture, often
with the help of a Polish maid or governess.* Thus, during the interwar period, some of the older people still had Jewish cultural
characteristics, but by then most of the assimilationists were
thoroughly acculturated.

Socialized as Poles, the assimilationists—especially the
younger ones—like Poles in general, largely proceeded on the assumption that Jewish culture (which they seldom graced with the
name culture) was inferior to the Polish one. Interestingly, that
was much less the case with the generation that had originally embarked upon assimilation. True, their ideologues had openly put
forth the idea of Jewish cultural inferiority,[19] but the rich men of
commerce and the industrialists of the nineteenth century pursued de-Judaization and Polonization as a means to an end. They
were practical men; they did not necessarily think Jewish culture
inferior, even if they found the Jewish community too small and
stifling for their talents and ambitions. However, their sons and
daughters, whether intellectuals or rich bourgeois, saw little or
nothing of value in the Jewish heritage.[20] They held that, as descendents of Jews, they had nothing valuable to contribute to the

---

* The close ties and influence of these are reflected in the interviews I conducted,
in the memoirs of assimilationists, and in Yiddish novels. The maids and governesses were important agents of acculturation.

Polish nation; but they had much to contribute as individuals and as Poles. Any positive Jewish values, such as the special emphasis on education and intellect, that they may have retained they generally did not recognize as Jewish but as universal. Many of the other values which they celebrated they marked as Polish: a romantic patriotism, love of land and nature, "ancient" hospitality, the knightly values of honor and bravery, chivalrous dignity, gallantry, and so on.

Through my interviews, I have collected some material about home socialization. I would like to quote from one such interview, conducted in English, with an intellectual, in whose family "the break with the Jewish tradition" was initiated by his grandfather, "probably at the beginning of the nineteenth century."

    I Do you recall from your early childhood if your parents ever referred to Jewishness or what it meant?

    HE It is a rather difficult question. I am trying to go back, you know, to my tender years. No, it was nothing very serious. I don't recall any striking incident. No, of course, you know, there was realization that you are Jewish but don't forget that the attitude in my environment toward Orthodox Jewry was a hundred percent negative. Well, the Jew with his long caftan was seen as something very primitive, dirty in the physical sense, and rather undignified. In addition, the idea of Jewish nationalism at that time, when I was a young boy, was very, very weak. So Jewish meant religion, lack of culture, something very primitive, dirty, noisy, rather repulsive.

    I If that was your image, did your parents in any way point out how you as a Jew were different from these people?

    HE Yes, absolutely different because we were Polish and all our ideas and ideals were Polish. Our culture was Polish and the goal set forth was to become Polish. In short, there was no sphere of contact between this assimilated group [and the rest of the Jews] unless some people [were] especially interested in promoting this cultural assimilation and playing part of protectors, of cultural protectors, sponsors. It was rather a patronizing attitude with regard to the broad masses of the ghetto. I am referring to people like the mother of———, well people, sort of apostles of Polish culture and active in this respect, organizing, for instance, Jewish schools, high schools for Jewish girls—very Polish—and try-

ing to assimilate the girls from the Orthodox environment to
the Polish culture.

The general outlook of the assimilationists on things Polish
and Jewish is reflected in their contrasting attitudes towards the
Polish and Yiddish languages. They tended to perceive the first as
beautiful and were often rhapsodic about its graces, while the latter they experienced as ugly. Its sounds were considered guttural,
its intonation ridiculous. It is noteworthy, that often the same people delighted in some of the harsh consonants of Polish, which
were a challenge to the tongue. This attitude comes through even
in Korczak's children's book, *Mośki, Joski, i Srule,* whose protago-
nists are Jewish children. The author (later a heroic figure during
World War II) was lyrical in his description of the Polish speech of
the peasants: "Polish phrases like Polish field flowers arrange
themselves into happy fields or rise clearly and burst into rays like
the sun." But Yiddish is generally "the screaming and ordinary
jargon of quarreling and name calling." [21]

The assimilationists refused to recognize Yiddish as a language and referred to it as the jargon,[22] using the same deprecia-
tory references to it as the Poles did. Yiddish to them was the
badge of shame, the mark of low caste and low culture, and they
took special pride in their failure to speak it and to understand it.
And yet Yiddish, as was shown earlier, was the main language of
the majority of the Jews in Poland and often the only language of
the lower strata. This linguistic separation is indicative of the social distance between the assimilationists and the rest of the Jews,
especially those of the lower strata.

Large portions of the Jewish population still adhered to a Jewish way of life, markedly different from that of the Poles. The assimilationists saw this as an expression of their ignorance and
superstition; the overall image they had of Jews and Jewishness
was the same image that the Poles had—an overwhelmingly negative one. They felt that a huge social divide existed. This comes
out vividly in the memoirs of M.A. Hartglas, a member of the
Polish Diet. A young lawyer, after being converted to Zionism, he
attempted to bridge this social distance and mix socially with Jews:

> I was surrounded by people who were not stupid; they were
> intelligent, nice and good people, but I was offended by their lack
> of European culture, lack of social graces. . . . A sheet of glass
> separated me from them: I was a willing and sympathetically
> disposed observer, but I could not live with them. I suffered with
> them, loved them, was able to sacrifice myself for them, but in
> everyday social life, I was aloof. . . . I went to social gatherings—
> but after a few ineffective attempts I could no more. The sheet of
> glass appeared and divided us. . . . after a few visits to their homes,
> I left with a bad taste in my mouth. I was brought up in a certain
> manner and in a certain culture, and there was the negation of all of
> it.[23]

The cultural and identification assimilation of the "Poles of Jewish
background" expressed itself throughout the interwar period in their
romantic patriotism which sometimes bordered on chauvinism. They
sang praises to the Polish land, to the valor of Poles, to the heights of
Polish culture, art, and music. This celebration of things Polish is
prominently displayed in the writings of Polish novelists, poets, and
writers of Jewish background—Leśmian, Tuwim, Wittlin, Slonimski.
Jews—let alone Jewish themes—hardly figure in their creations, only
fleetingly if at all.

The extent of identificational assimilation also came through vividly in my interviews. Most of the informants referred with great pride
to ancestors who had fought in or had financially supported the Polish
uprisings for indepedence.[24] Let me illustrate with an excerpt from such
an interview with a former member of a wealthy bourgeois family, who
was in his twenties when World War II broke out. To my question "In
your memory of childhood, can you recall anything distinctively Jewish
in your family?" he answered:

> Well, my grandfather did not speak Yiddish. . . . He was a Polish
> patriot and anti-German. I remember that when the Germans reached
> Warsaw, he stood on the balcony and cried. Well, already his father was a
> patriot. It is said that he was involved in the uprising of 1831. . . . I
> understand that he financially supported the uprising. . . . My grandfather
> had a beautiful library of Polish books. And of course his house was not
> kosher. . . . But I do remember him praying at home and putting on

tephilin [phylacteries]. I was a small boy when he died. I
don't know whether he went to synagogue on high holidays or
not. He was interested in everything Polish. As for me, I was
never Bar Mitzvah.

Mobility through Conversion

And yet often their Polishness did not exempt them from the dominant social definition in Poland of being Jews essentially no different from other Jews, even if in appearance they seemed Polish.
To the assimilationists, the situation in which they were placed
seemed flagrantly unjust and especially onerous. They were defined Jewish, and so treated, when in fact they were Poles with a
sense of peoplehood based exclusively on the Polish fatherland.
The assimilationists fought to the very end this social definition,
which did not distinguish between them and the rest of the Jews.
But they did not even succeed in being recognized by the majority
as having intermediate status as Poles of Jewish descent, comparable to the mulattoes in Brazil, the Cape Coloured of South Africa,
or the Eurasians of India under British rule.[25] As in the case of descendants of Negroes in the United States, prominence and acculturation did not exempt them from their caste stigma. The fact
that some of them made outstanding contributions to Polish literature, humanities, law, science, and mathematics was often interpreted as a threat to Polish culture, which was seen as being
undermined (Judaized) by their presence.[26] With the advent of official anti-Semitism the assimilationists, like the Jews in general,
were excluded from the ruling Camp of National Unity, which
came into power in February of 1937. Thus, in the final analysis
no set of achieved criteria of distinction was sufficient to release
the assimilationists from the Jewish caste and to elevate them to
the status of Poles. "To be Polish is to be Catholic," was the prevailing conception among the dominant group.

Historically conversion to Christianity was in Poland the only
avenue of escape from the inferior caste. When we examine conversion among the assimilationists of the nineteenth and the twen-

tieth centuries, we find that among the rich bourgeoisie it was often a two-generational process. The captains of commerce and industry consciously embarked upon acculturation, socializing their children exclusively in the dominant culture. Their children, thus socialized, often became converted when they reached adulthood. This can be illustrated historically with actual cases of prominent families.[27] To most assimilationists, conversion was no disaster. Even those who looked down on religion in general as superstition, a survival from another age, generally did not view Christian observance with the same disdain they had for the Jewish religion.[28] For the young adults, conversion was often the logical conclusion of a process that had begun in their childhood. Most had pleasant and warm memories of church attendance with governesses or maids, even if it was sometimes clandestine because parents were firm agnostics or atheists.

The total number of conversions per year was estimated by Dr. Tartakower to have been between' 2,000 to 2,500 in the late 1920s and early 1930s.[29] No statistics are available as to what percentage of the total conversions were by assimilationists. However, on the basis of my interviews, I gather that this was the case of most conversions. That being so, the above figures would support the impression gained from reports in Jewish newspapers that rate of conversion was very high among the assimilationists but very low among the Jewish population in general.[30] As a rule, Jews, even the highly acculturated or secularized, tended to recoil from conversion, regarding it as apostasy.

Most of the conversions in the interwar period can be divided into two categories: (a) pragmatic; the conversion enabled one or one's children to enter into positions otherwise closed to them (or one thought that it would); and (b) assimilatory; the conversion represented a final step in the process of Polonization, otherwise completed. Of course, there were cases of conversion on purely religious grounds, both among the assimilationists and Jews in general; however, they were extremely rare among the Jews as a whole but more frequent among the assimilationists. The spiritual emptiness common among the assimilated and completely secularized rich bourgeois families seemed to have resulted in a mystic yearning in some of their young. An assimilationist described these "mystic" conversions to Catholicism in the way they were usually pictured at that time in assimilationist circles by sympathetic individuals:

> Their [the converts'] upbringing and their external conditions of life have estranged them completely from the Jewish religious tradition. It became for them something completely dead and not understandable. . . . Their life in the society surrounding them brings them close to the Christian practices and mystique. On the soul yearning for spiritual nourishment falls a ray of mystic "grace." The symbolism of Catholic worship, its concreteness and sincerity, in affecting the esthetic sensibilities conquers the soul, especially the female soul.[31]

Still, the "mystic" conversations constituted only a small proportion of the total conversions among the assimilationists.[*]

Aleksander Hertz, who knew the assimilationist circles well, reports that in many cases the rationalization for conversion was: "I am converting for the sake of my children. I would never do it for myself." [32] In other instances conversions occurred when individuals married Christians, especially because civil marriage did not exist in Poland. But conversion also became a common occurrence among the young unmarried assimilationists, as reflected in the persistent allusions to it and direct discussion of it in Unity's periodical. Its articles debating whether or not converts should be allowed in the organization convey the impression that the greatest number of conversions were pragmatic ones.[33] My interviews suggest the same. To cite from an interview with a man from a rich bourgeois family who was a university student in the nineteen thirties:

> We, the assimilated Jews, with the rising anti-Semitism before the war, had to face up [to the question of] whether to remain Jews. One always had the alternative of conversion. A few of my family converted. Everyone in the family knew that they did it for convenience. We were discussing these ques-

---

[*] That this was so, was generally agreed upon by Jews, Poles, and even by assimilationists, but tended to be differently interpreted by each.

tions, the various alternatives. . . . we were discussing this in
our organization of university students [Unity] . . . Some of
them eventually converted but most did not.

On the other hand, the prominent and gifted essayist and reporter, Ksawery Pruszyński, a noted philosemite, wrote in 1937 in
a prestigious literary journal about the great number of assimilatory conversions:

> I regret that many Jews consider assimilation to Polishness
> inseparable from a change to Christianity. And not being con-
> vinced on grounds of faith, they see it as one more tie to Polish-
> ness. Adhering to an old faith or admitting the lack of any is
> worth much more than the superficiality, which is in the final
> analysis hurtful. Of course, the cause of this is the situation,
> wherein the christened Jew is "more highly regarded" than the
> one of Mosaic faith.[34]

What Pruszyński perhaps missed is that although they may not
have been religious in the strictest sense, some converts nevertheless saw in their conversion a mystic link to the Polish nation. I am
reminded of a well known intellectual couple who, when Poland
was attacked by the Germans, decided to convert to Christianity,
so as to bind themselves inextricably with the suffering Polish nation, to be indistinguishable from the rest of the Poles.[35]

Anyway, if we probe further, we discover that the two categories of conversion—pragmatic and assimilatory—represent pure
types, and actual cases had features of both. Moreover, the rationale behind the two types is not so different. As was shown earlier,
the assimilationists were not only culturally but identificationally
assimilated. Most of them had no desire to transmit a separate
Jewish identity to their children. On the contrary, they hoped that
their children or grandchildren would merge completely into the
Polish nation. (Many of them favored intermarriage with Poles
much more than with people who were culturally and identificationally Jewish.) As they were already culturally and identificationally assimilated, those who chose conversion for pragmatic reasons did not understand why they had to continue as nominal
Jews and see their ambitions frustrated. By means of a perfunctory

ceremony, they could achieve the position they desired equally well. Similarly, if all that was needed to prove themselves Poles was a ceremony, why not go through it? After all, religiously they were just as removed from the Jews as from the Catholics, and perhaps even more so; culturally they were like the rest of the Poles and far different from the Jews. Why then not be nominally of Catholic rather than nominally of "Mosaic religion"?

Moreover, most assimilationists had relatives (with whom they often maintained close contact) who were converts or children of converts. The appropriate question now becomes not why so many assimilationists were converted but rather why more did not convert. Among the older assimilationists, there were those who felt that precisely because of the rising anti-Semitism, it would be unconscionable or undignified to convert. In one of my interviews, I was told by a woman about her old father-in-law, a *powstaniec* (veteran of the Polish insurrection, who was completely assimilated and in whose family there were many Christians) whom she had once asked why he did not convert: "He answered that he wanted to be buried as a Jew, especially because of the anti-Semitism. He wanted to show that they are Poles of Mosaic faith who fought for Polish independence."

Among younger assimilationists, there were those in the socialist and communist movements who would have considered it unthinkable to compromise in this manner with their ideology.[36] Then, too, because Poles were their reference group, many assimilationists grasped that more was required of them in becoming Catholic than a ceremonial step. And among them were those who considered it immoral to embrace a faith in which one did not believe. This was the position of Unity, which in its Ideological Declaration, adopted at the beginning of independence, condemned "opportunistic conversions" as "morally corrupting." [37] Confirmed when the organization resurfaced in 1928, this point of view was continuously promoted in its monthly, *Unity*.

Another factor inhibiting conversions was the conscious recognition among some that the stigma of Jewishness was not thereby removed and that conversion led to deceit. Poles often discovered attempts to hide one's Jewish birth, and found such attempts laughable or contemptuous. How strong the stigmatic quality of Jewish background was can be seen in the "unmasking" of Jewish ancestry of political opponents, which was a frequent device on both left and right.[38] The madness of these charges and countercharges is epitomized when they finally landed on the heads of those who hurled them with impunity against others. A few leading Jew haters of the extreme nationalist organizations were shown to have "Jewish blood in their veins." Libel suits resulted from a few of these cases.[39] Under the influence of Nazi ideology, the mere fact that one had Jewish ancestors constituted an increasing obstacle to complete acceptance. In the Catholic press numerous articles appeared, charging that most conversions had been contrived for self-interest. An extreme example, because it advocated the exclusion even of "sincere" converts from the community of Poles, is one that appeared in the Lvov *Church Gazette:*

> For every sincere Jewish convert we should have respect, for the deceitful, calculating neophyte—scorn. The fact remains that the majority of Jewish conversions arouse suspicion, but there are single cases of individuals genuinely converted and Catholic. These individuals we ought to receive in a brotherly fashion into Christian society. But this does not mean that we have to accept them to Polish society. Conversion can make a Christian of one who was of Judaic faith *but cannot make a Jew into a Pole* (italics supplied).[40]

Commenting on similar articles, in connection with the "Puder affair," discussed in chapter 4, the author of a column in the influential Jewish daily *Nasz Przegląd* explained that Polish nationalism (and not only in its extreme brand, "for when it comes to converts the front is much broader") finds no room for converts in Polish society. Addressing himself to the "tragedy" of the converts during the 1930s, he concluded:

> The Jews withdraw from the converts, as from individuals who have broken with Jewry, and do not want to have anything to do with them. And so converts are not Jews, and cannot be Poles. Although they do everything in order to please the [Poli-

sh] people to whom they are attracted, and even if they often
come out against Jews, wanting to prove their devotion, . . . it
does not help them at all. Polish racism has arrived to the point
of "not recognizing converts as Poles, ". . . despite their contributions, despite their knowledge, despite their talents, and
even despite their "neophyte devotion" [in form of anti-Jewish
statements]. Is this a tragedy? For certain individuals yes. For
the Jewish people it is of little significance.[41]

The above attitudes toward new converts make us understand
why the personal relations of neophytes were to a large measure
confined to other neophytes, recent descendants of converts, and
to the assimilationists from whom they derived. This was true even
to a greater degree of the assimilationists who chose not to convert.

The Assimilationist Community

The assimilationists were not allowed to integrate fully into Polish
society, to which they felt culturally and identificationally akin.
They were increasingly excluded both from its public realm and
from its wide range of primary social relations. The entrance of
those who remained non-Christian into cliques, clubs, and institutions of the dominant group, on a primary level—which had begun
in the nineteenth century and levelled off at the beginning of the
twentieth—was substantially blocked after independence. If we
follow Gordon's definition that such large entrance constitutes
structural assimilation, then we can conclude that the group under
discussion was culturally and identificationally but not structurally
assimilated.[42] And it is in this sense that they were marginal. However, to some degree the leading intellectuals, writers, and artists
were able to maintain their friendships and some other primary
contacts with members of the Polish intellectual and artistic community, even if they were increasingly being attacked in the press
and discriminated against in formal organizations.[43]

The assimilationists formed an exclusive community, the
center of primary contact for a group of families—often related by
kinship—where "Polishness," "European manners," and "civilized

behavior," were greatly valued. In contrast to their assimilationist fathers and grandfathers (many of whom were concerned about not becoming completely estranged from Jews, whom they hoped eventually to Polonize) most of them were estranged and accepted this estrangement. "Unity" was in this respect an exception: it was reclaiming the original goal of trying to assimilate the Jewish masses. Many more, however, faced up to the social reality, recognizing that it was futile for them to continue to preach the gospel of assimilation to the Jews of Poland under the conditions of anti-Semitism that prevailed. In regard to their own social situation, however, the fully Polonized Jewish bourgeoisie, as viewed from the outside, lived in a make-believe world of their own construction. In some of its specific features it may have been different from the one depicted by Franklin Frazier in his *Black Bourgeoisie*, but it was equally removed from reality. If "social life" or "society" was a main prop of the American black bourgeoisie's world of make-believe, *polskość*, Polishness, was a main prop of the assimilationists' world. They adored it, they flaunted it, and vied with one another in displaying it. In their own circles, they could express their Polishness without being accused of masquerading. In the outside world, both among Poles and Jews, their Polishness tended to be at least suspect.

Within their own community, the assimilationists, it seems, sought escape from the social deprivation, the psychological derogation, and the humiliation resulting from their ascribed status in the larger society. Among their own, they felt most at home and most at ease; they did not have to hide who they were and could take pride in their family history and accomplishments. Further, they managed to a considerable degree to shut out the reality that their Jewishness was an ever-present fact of the larger Polish society. In their own community the assimilationists went to great lengths to shelter their children from that reality. That they were "of Jewish descent" was gently broken to them, not too early, but at a time when it became necessary for them to learn that painful truth.

Considering that they were living in a society permeated with anti-Semitism, it is noteworthy that the surviving assimilationists claim to have had no (or very little) personal experience of it, especially in their childhood. After much probing, they do recall some incidents, but they are interpreted as not significant. For example, an intellectual responded thus to my probing about his adolescence:

> When I was 14 or so, I was very popular and I was elected to represent my school at a convention of all secondary schools. But then I was not allowed to serve [being Jewish]. As a matter of fact, ———— [he mentioned a now-prominent Pole] was a friend of mine and he told me that he was against my representing our school. I thought it rather decent that he was frank with me.

The reports of the assimilationists probably reflect their psychological suppression of experiences of prejudice and discrimination as well as the insulation by the assimilationist community provided to its members. Professor Ludwik Hirszfeld—who only retrospectively became conscious of it while passing as an Aryan during World War II, in writing about the interwar period noted: "Poland was sick on this subject. . . . [But] I did not understand the anti-Semitism in all its depth because I derived from an assimilated family. . . ." [44]

It is true that the low visibility of assimilationists, in contrast to the high visibility of Jews in general, made them quantitatively the least prone to anti-Semitic prejudice, discrimination, and attack—especially in fleeting encounters where their identity was not known.

Often their great wealth protected them from the pressures of economic anti-Semitism, which choked the masses of Jews. [45] It is ironic that economic anti-Semitism, which subsumed all Jews under the stereotype of "rich Jew," hit hardest and affected the poor Jews most. Nevertheless, the outside reality was increasingly intruding as anti-Semitism intensified. As is characteristic of militant ideologies, militant anti-Semitism could not be contained and had no room for exceptions. A growing number of newspapers and periodicals were vituperative in their "exposés" and attacks on prominent assimilationists because they were Jewish. Similarly, they accused defenders of Jews of being Jews in disguise. Discriminatory policies were gaining in professional organizations, and the assimilationists were not spared. As shown before, the ranks of "integrated" intelligentsia were thinning, as Polish intellectuals who stood by their "Jewish" friends were insulted, mistreated, and even beaten.

The assimilationists were hit hardest through their children, who suffered at schools and universities. The Jewish quota applied to the assimilationists as well as to the rest of the Jews, and so did the university seating ghettos. They were not exempted from the heckling of and bodily attack by Polish students and their helpers. In this connection it is important to note that Unity became one of the most active organizations in the resistance to the anti-Semitic terror at the universities, and perhaps the most successful in the attempt to mobilize friendly Poles to protest.

If the assimilationists, as asserted earlier, were less vulnerable to anti-Semitic discrimination and terror because of their low visibility, in a sense they were psychologically more vulnerable than most Jews, and particularly more so than the Orthodox-traditionalists. As was shown in the preceding chapter, these last were sealed off in their faith and tradition from the psychological effects of lower caste status. The assimilationists, however, were psychologically wounded in their unsuccessful attempts to escape from their inferior caste status and deeply humiliated when personally subjected to prejudice, discrimination, and terror. As one of my informants explained:

> People have strange ideas about the Polish assimilationists. We suffered most. We were Poles, we loved Poland and it was hard for us because of the increasing anti-Semitism. We were violently anti-Zionist. Poland was our country and we did not see why we should pick ourselves up and go far away. At that time Zionism seemed a preposterous idea to us.

Self-Hatred

How did the assimilationists respond psychologically to the dilemma of being culturally and self-identificationally Polish and yet being defined as Jews and treated as such? They looked at Jews and one another with the eyes of Poles, who constituted their reference group. They perceived the cultural characteristics of Jews as stigmas that disqualified those who had them from full social acceptance. In referring to them, they tended to use among themselves (but not so often in front of Poles) the standard negative terminology for Jew and Jewish characteristics.[46] The remnants of such characteristics in themselves and other assimilationists they regarded as stigma symbols, which called attention to "a debasing identity," breaking up what would otherwise be a coherent picture of Polishness, "with a consequent reduction in . . . [the] valuation of the individual." [47] These remaining traits constituted their "negative identity," the identity fragments they submerged in themselves as undesirable or irreconcilable with their "positive" Polish identity.[48] They followed the common pattern among stigmatized people and made attempts to correct what they saw as the objective basis of their failings. Their home socialization was bent on eradicating such traits. Mothers would pounce upon such "traits of Jewishness" in their children and try hard to correct the blemishes. "Do not talk with your hands" was a common admonition.

The assimilationists were so obsessed with Jewish traits as discrediting symbols that discovering the traits became a game in which they tried to outdo one another. Much of the gossip among them revolved around the Jewish signs that reappeared in others in unguarded moments, and around their discovery in people who had been hitherto successful in not revealing them. Although mostly private, the anti-Jewish sentiments of the assimilationists occasionally became public manifestations. One that attracted considerable attention, because it came from the pen of one of the most prominent Polish writers, was the article by the young Antoni Słonimski, "About the touchiness of Jews," which appeared in a much respected literary periodical. Provoked by the attack of some Jewish nationalist critics on his friend Julian Tuwim's new poems as containing anti-Semitic stereotypes of Jews,[49] he unleashed a vitriolic tirade against Jews. It contained most of the major themes about the faults of Jews, which were part and parcel of Polish anti-Semitism.[50]

Among the top political anti-Semites, among the leaders of extreme nationalist groups, were sons or grandsons of Jewish assimilationists. Whether or not this was an extreme example of the phenomenon of self-hatred,* it was so interpreted by both Poles and Jews. The presence of such anti-Semites of Jewish ancestry lent itself to sensationalism, gossip, and numerous anecdotes. An example is the story about a well-known Pole who as a young man was becoming a militant anti-Semite. Once when he returned home from a physical attack on defenseless Jews (*bojówka*), his father asked him where he had been. After he had told of the fun his group had fighting Jews, the father said: "Do you still have that cane with which you broke the Jews' heads? Go and use it on your mother." In this case, the revelation supposedly cured the son of anti-Semitism. But in other well known instances such revelations were not a deterrent. Often, the sons' or grandsons' anti-Semitic efforts would be redoubled as proof of "selfless" Polish patriotism and devotion to the militant nationalist ideology. Two of my informants, members of assimilationist families, admitted to having relatives who were rabid anti-Semitic leaders. One related: -

> Imagine, we had a fascist youth leader in our own family. My father's sister's son converted. And his son was a leader of fascist youth. But this was something shameful which was not talked about in the family. As a matter of fact, when one came in contact with the converts or their children in our family, this subject was not discussed. We got along well, with the exception of course of the fascist. Of course, we had converts but most of the family did not convert.

It would be more proper for a psychologist than for me to speculate as to whether the self-hatred of the assimilationists represented a loathing of things that stood in the way of their aspira-

* Such negative attitudes toward the ethnic group from which one derives, as described above, have been analyzed by social scientists as the phenomenon of self-hatred. I do not mean to imply that any attempt to disaffiliate from the Jewish people is necessarily an expression of self-hatred. See Kurt Lewin, "Self-Hatred among Jews," *Contemporary Jewish Record*, 4 (June 1941); Everett C. Hughes, "Social Change and Status Protest: An Essay on the Marginal Man," *Phylon*, 10 (1949): 58–65.

tion to be Polish or a displacement of hostility toward the dominant group for not accepting them as Poles.[51] Whatever the case, there is no doubt that the assimilationists in Poland were subject to much frustration. Many of them tore out their Jewish "soul" to use Memmi's image, that soul which Poles thought "irremediably bad."[52] All that remained was their Jewish descent, and that most Poles proved incapable of forgetting completely, seeing in it the irreversible stamp of Jewishness. This was the personal tragedy of the assimilationists as their hopes, nurtured through a few generations before independence, turned to naught. The goal of integration to which they aspired—being accepted as Poles and being judged as individuals, irrespective of their ethnic descent—mostly failed to materialize. The case of the assimilationists in Poland illustrates the sociological principle that in ethnic relations the crucial factor is not the degree of cultural difference of the subordinate group but the degree of emphasis on ascription in the society.

Return to Jewishness

Did the anti-Semitism, which in its crescendo affected even him and his children, bring the assimilationist back to a Jewish self-identity? Did it cause him to "choose" himself as a Jew, if not in pride then in humiliation?[53] (After all, Jewish history abounds in cases of turning and returning.) In most instances it did not.[54] Among young assimilationists, more often anti-Semitism led to radicalization, and they flocked to the Polish Socialist Party and the Communist Party, which held out the promise of full integration in a socialist Poland. But the negative reactions to Jewishness described above were evident among members and sympathizers of these parties, no less than they were among the assimilationists of other political persuasion, conservatives or liberals.

While anti-Semitism strengthened nationalist sentiments among Jews in general, not many of the assimilationists found their way into Jewish political movements, which offered nationalist solutions to their problem of integration or marginality. None found their way to Orthodox-traditionalism, which would have meant giving up not only their Polishness but the modernity of which they were so proud. The near impossibility of such a move comes through in the response of Unity to a call by an Orthodox leader that Jewish youth return to its roots. This call was dismissed as an "Echo from the other world":

> An element [Orthodoxy], strangely persistent but nevertheless dying and *destined to disappear, a tragic anachronism,* raises its *weird head* to prevent the natural and inevitable process of the breakdown of the walls of the physical and spiritual ghetto (italics supplied).[55]

Joining a Jewish nationalist group was more conceivable, but it was a hard choice to make and even more difficult to implement. The assimilationists' spontaneous reactions to Jews and to their behavior were often those of repulsion and distaste, and the Jewish masses were not eager to receive them. Still there are a few records of turning back to the Jewish people, culture, and identity that have the quality of religious conversion.

One example is that of Jakub Apenszlak, who as a young man reclaimed his Jewish identity. Eventually he became editor of the influential pro-Zionist Jewish daily, *Nasz Przegląd*.[56] Indeed, a few assimilationists went so far as to seek the solution to their marginality, as well as to the Jewish problem in general, in Zionism.[57] Among the most prominent was Hartglas, a member of the Polish Diet, who was quoted earlier. I want to quote him once more in order to illustrate with his tragic confession the fact that Jewish nationalism as a personal solution to marginality had little chance of being successful or personally rewarding to Polish assimilationists. He wrote:

> I personally found myself on the border of two worlds: Jewish and Polish. . . . throughout almost my entire life two factors collided: a Polish education and childhood, attachment to the Polish nation, to its culture and land. And spontaneously there arose in me a love for my martyred Jewish people, its sufferings and its rebirth in its own homeland. This was the reason that I suffered during my entire life from a splitting complex, because

there is no power which can melt together these two different spirits. . . . As a Jew, I could not forget the injustices which my people experienced in Poland (I personally did not experience them), and as one assimilated into Polishness . . . I had to share the resentments toward Jews, which even the best of Poles harbor. And this spiritual split, which tormented me all my life, poisoned the best moments of my life.[58]

Conclusion

Nevertheless, I dare to speculate that had there been more time, the return of assimilationists to the Jewish people, would have evolved into a social movement. Perhaps a sign of it could be detected in the speech of Senator Zdzisław Zmigryder-Konopka (1897–1939). He was from an assimilationist family, a classicist, highly decorated with Polish military orders for bravery; he was appointed to the Senate by the President of Poland to represent Polish Jewry. In November 1938, at a celebration of the twentieth anniversary of Poland's independence, organized by assimilationists that had fought for it, he stated:

> At this moment I want to look at the situation with the eyes of a Pole of Mosaic faith and I declare that *we Jews* assimilated for generations *now detect in Zionism . . . national honor.* This, however, does not cancel out our own position. . . . (italics supplied)[59]

Yes, in the time that remained, most clung to their assimilationist position. They saw the illusions of assimilationism die, but they could not let go of its basic premises. To the end many assimilationists persisted, even more desperately, in an attempt at a psychological escape from their situation. Their response fits Sartre's concept of inauthentic: "What characterizes the inauthentic Jews," he has said, "is that they deal with their situation by running away from it; they have chosen to deny it, or to deny their responsibilities, or to deny their isolation, which appears intolerable to them."[60]

VII
Between Tradition and Assimilation

The interwar period, which was marked by the collapse of assimilationism in Poland, was nevertheless a time of large-scale abandonment of the traditional pattern of life, especially by the young. What had been predicted earlier by the pioneers of assimilation, as well as by the traditional leaders, did not come to be. Both, after all, foretold (unaware of any common element in their views because of the extreme difference in context and rhetoric) that, once the Jews of Poland began to depart from the traditional pattern, they would eventually lose their distinctive identity. The assimilationists were inspired by the vision of a future when Jews would be Poles (albeit some of Mosaic faith); the traditionalists were frightened by the specter of a future worse yet than the present, when Jews would become *Goyim*, Gentiles.

What was a dream for the former and a nightmare for the latter did not materialize. The anti-Semitic outbreaks marking independence fully discredited assimilation. The conditions imposed on them by the Polish majority in independent Poland proved to most Jews that assimilation was not the solution to their situation.

Although the avenue of flight from their situation by claiming identity of Poles showed itself to be illusory, the traditional Jewish way was no longer acceptable to many people. On the contrary, a great number of the young categorically rejected the traditional pattern of life as narrow, rigid, backward, and unsuited to modern times: a source of weakness and shame. They perceived it as draining Jews of life and energy, of making them impotent to deal with the grim realities of Polish oppression and hate. For those of the older generation who departed from the traditional way of life before independence, the break had required such conviction and effort that few could conceive of returning to it.

Although I have spoken of the culture of Jews in interwar Poland, in the broad sense as a way of life, it must be realized that Jewish culture had lost its homogeneity. I emphasize this because of the nostalgic tendency of today to equate that way of life with a post-Holocaust romanticized image of "shtetl culture." [1] Actually, there was much variety in the culture of the Polish Jews. Some of it was the consequence of the partitions of Poland. More of it was due to European social currents that reached the Polish Jews in the nineteenth century, gathered momentum at the end of that century and the beginning of the new one, and grew in strength in independent Poland. Between the two world wars the Jewish community suffered from rapid and massive change. The distance between the generations was of the dimension that precedes and accompanies revolutionary movements. [2] The Jewish family, so often stereotyped as the bastion of unity, was torn by sharply conflicting views of life, by clashing values, by ways of behavior that were glaring in contrast. The generational gap among the Jews in interwar Poland is epitomized by the not-uncommon occurrence of Orthodox fathers in medieval dress, steeped in the Talmud, and revolutionary sons and daughters engaged in underground political action.

The two important kinds of change that I want to concentrate on in this chapter are (1) the process of *acculturation*—individuals moving away from the traditional Jewish culture and toward the culture of the larger society; (2) the process of *secularization*—individuals moving away from an orientation and behavior governed and sanctified by religion and toward an orientation and behavior which they saw as governed by reason and tested by empirical reality, and which they called "modern." My focus will be on the larger first generation of acculturation and secularization (Jews among whom these processes became manifest only during the interwar period) rather than the smaller second generation. Acculturation and secularization differed among different social categories of Jews. Between the two crystallized patterns of "Jewish Jews" and "Poles of Jewish descent," stretched a wide range of degrees and combinations of acculturation and secularization.

Acculturation-Polonization

The acculturation of the Jews in independent Poland was almost exclusively that of Polonization. (The move toward Russian, German, and Austrian culture stopped and was even reversed.) It is

Young people broke the strong ties of long-fixed traditional codes of thought and behavior . . .
WEDDING PICTURE OF AUTHOR'S PARENTS, EMANUEL AND IDA HELLER, STRYJ, 1923. HER FATHER, A TALMUDIC SCHOLAR, AND HIS PARENTS, LANDOWNERS, WORE TRADITIONAL DRESS AND SPOKE YIDDISH ONLY AT HOME. EMANUEL AND IDA DECIDED THAT THEY WOULD SPEAK POLISH TO THEIR CHILDREN, NOT YIDDISH.

noteworthy, however, that Polonization was weakest in the Vilno and Eastern border areas, inhabited by the territorial minorities—Lithuanian, Ukrainian, Belorussian—which resisted and fought Polish influences. Another distinctive feature of the interwar period, sometimes difficult to discern, was that the ultimate goal of cultural assimilation among the Jews was no longer identificational assimilation.[3] Thus in independent Poland there were some Jews—mostly upper middle class and professionals—who in their culture were as Polish as the members of the assimilationist community. They did not, however, consider themselves to be Poles; their Jewish self-identification remained as the last vestige of their Jewish ethnicity. The typical pattern at the height of the assimilationist movement was—complete cultural assimilation that lead to claiming the identity of Poles. But the anti-Semitism of the interwar period finally aborted this development in many. Most of them recognized that the option of becoming Poles did not exist for them in resurrected Poland (except in the form of "passing"). Therefore, the more characteristic pattern of independent Poland was that of Polonization (shifting toward the direction of Polish culture) without identificational assimilation (considering oneself a Pole).

This is exemplified in the contrast between Warsaw Polish-language dailies owned by Jews and aimed at Jewish readers before and after independence. The pre-independence, *Nowa Gazeta,* was—as the eminent Polish-Jewish historian, M. Bałaban claimed—an "assimilationist" newspaper "which followed such a conception of assimilation that it completely ignored Jewish interests." [4] Contrariwise, the *Nasz Przegląd,* founded in 1923 (it was to become one of the best newspapers in Poland), was consciously on guard to satisfy and protect Jewish interests.

The tremendous growth of a Polish-language Jewish press during the interwar period testifies to the fact that Polonization was proceeding rapidly. There were three large Jewish daily newspapers in the Polish language—the above mentioned Warsaw *Nasz Przegląd,* the Lvov *Chwila* and the Cracow *Nowy Dziennik*—each financially solvent and with many readers. In addition, there were a great number of periodicals in the Polish language, both geared to the general Jewish public and to specific audiences. Unquestionably the combined Yiddish and Hebrew press was much larger than the one in the Polish language, but the best years of the Hebrew press were just before independence. And what was unique to the interwar period was the growth of a large and vibrant Jewish press in the Polish language.[5]

Rapid acculturation was occurring in the sphere of language and was proceeding in the direction of complete linguistic assimilation among a large part of the middle class. There was some awareness of this by those intellectuals who opposed cultural assimilation.[6] The significance of the linguistic change ought to be appraised in light of the fact that the distinctiveness in the culture of the Jews in Poland was epitomized by their separate language, Yiddish, and by its tenacity throughout centuries of Jewish existence in that country. The mother-tongue of almost all Jews in Poland up to the end of the eighteenth century and most Jews up to World War I was Yiddish, albeit a Yiddish influenced by the Polish language and full of Polish expressions. With the advent of Polish independence, the break in the linguistic homogeneity of the Jews, which had begun in the nineteenth century, became marked, especially among the young.

Although the Jews had lived on Polish soil for long centuries, the overall language pattern of Jewish children and youth in interwar Poland could be compared with that of second-generation Americans. I cannot help but be impressed by the similarity between the rapidity of Polonization among them and that of Americanization among children of European immigrants in the United States. In many middle class families, the parents spoke Yiddish, particularly to one another, but the children spoke Polish. In some middle class families, consciously concerned about the advancement of their children, the parents chose to expose them to Polish at home before they went to school, so as not to handicap them linguistically. In such cases the parents addressed the children in Polish only and, in more rare instances, even resorted to banishing Yiddish from the home (some did this in spite of their own broken Polish).

Regrettably one cannot present adequate figures about the

language distribution among different age groups and social classes. And even the figures for the Jewish population at large are far from adequate, but it should again be noted that linguistic assimilation was greater than indicated by the 1931 census data. In that census, 12 percent of the Jewish population listed Polish as their mother tongue. But even if that 12 percent figure were valid, it would still be inadequate as an indicator of the linguistic trend among the Jews; we do not know the proportions of Polish as the mother tongue among the different age groups and classes. And we know from observation, supported by limited statistical data, that it was much more prominent among the young middle class Jews. A large part of middle class children and youth, especially in the larger cities, could not speak Yiddish at all. In contrast, among the lower strata, the young as well as the old spoke among themselves only in Yiddish. According to a study which appeared in 1939, about half of the Jewish high school students declared Polish as their mother tongue.[7] An earlier official study (1929–30 school year) showed that almost the same proportion of all Jewish students at Warsaw's schools of higher learning had listed Polish as their language at home.[8] Moreover, figures concerning mother tongue or language spoken at home can be used at best as indicators of *complete* linguistic assimilation, not of linguistic acculturation, which was much more extensive. The latter was proceeding on a large scale even among lower class children. Unlike many of their parents, most children from the lower strata could communicate in Polish. Many of such children had not been able to speak Polish when they entered public primary school, but did so by the time they graduated.

In addition to language, one of the most obvious forms of acculturation was the Polonization of proper names (a subject completely neglected in the study of Polish Jewry). The practice of Polonizing first names became very widespread, particularly among the younger middle class people. But as was the case with language, it varied greatly in degrees. Very prominent were Polonized versions of the original Jewish names. Because often they were those Old Testament names which were absent or rarely encountered among Poles, they continued in the Polonized version to give the bearer away as Jewish. As an example, the name *Mojżesz* (Moses) or its diminutive and endearing form, *Moniek*, replaced *Moishe* and *Moishele*. Adults born into very acculturated families, as well as the assimilationists, usually did not give their children such names. They chose names that were used by Poles, which they considered esthetically superior to Jewish names, both the original and the Polonized renditions. Thus, to continue with the same example, the distinctively Polish name *Mieczysław* and its diminutive *Mietek* replaced the Polonized versions of Moses. These name changes figured prominently in the jokes of acculturated Jews about their own foibles.

Changes in names, in dress (discussed earlier), and in language were the more obvious forms of acculturation, which were at the same time symbolic of the less perceptible forms. While the above "obvious" changes were occurring faster, there was also a substantial shift in the direction of Polish values and norms, especially esthetic ones. It might be fitting to place this phenomenon in a historical perspective before elaborating on it further. Just as the Jews in their centuries' long contact with Poles inadvertently absorbed Polish words into Yiddish, they also unconsciously absorbed other Polish cultural traits and fit them into the context of Jewish culture (as exemplified in Jewish folk music and tales). I am referring to the nonpurposive acculturation—a slow and long lasting process that occurred among all strata of the Jewish population. As is almost always true when two cultures meet, this acculturation was not one-sided; Jewish cultural traits were also absorbed by the Polish culture.[9] But the acculturation of a minority in the direction of the majority culture is usually stronger than the reverse, and in our case is exemplified in much fewer Yiddish words, or expressions, in the Polish vernacular than Polish ones in Yiddish. Apart from language or food, neither the Poles nor the Jews generally recognized the similarities in their cultures (especially in the nonmaterial aspects), which were products of centuries of contact. The borrowed cognitive, emotional, and behavioral traits became embedded in a different cultural context and their origin was often not perceived.

Contrasted with this slow process of nonpurposive acculturation, what occurred in the interwar period was a pronounced shift in the direction of the Polish language and culture, of which Jews were generally conscious. (Conversely, as has been noted in the first part of this book, the Poles' perception was distorted in the direction of minimizing their awareness of Jews becoming Polonized and maximizing their consciousness of existing cultural differences between Jews and Poles.) The sizable shift was to some extent the result of "forced assimilation," the Polish government's educational policies, soon to be discussed, and the economic policies, discussed earlier. But it was also to a certain degree "voluntary," even if the idea of Polonization no longer held out the promise of equality in Polish citizenship. One could hardly say of the Jewish intelligentsia who pursued Polonization in independent Poland that they "became Polish with heart and soul," the way their predecessors were described in a Warsaw Yiddish paper in 1896.[10] If anything, their Polishness was accompanied by a heavy heart and troubled soul. But the enthusiasm of the earlier generation was crucial in bringing about the "take-off stage" in the process of purposive acculturation among the Jews, which the anti-Semitism in independent Poland failed to reverse. Acculturation continued to be tied to the mobility aspirations of Jews. It is noteworthy that many of the Jews who were already on the road to Polonization when independence came, or who entered it during the years that followed, continued to employ some of the rationalizations that had evolved earlier. They interpreted their move as a departure from a fossilized culture toward a living one, from a primitive to a sophisticated way of life, from an inferior "Oriental" pattern to a civilized "European" one.

The above was particularly true of the intelligentsia and those who aspired to join it. Their models and inspiration were top figures of Polish culture—writers, poets, scientists, professors—who came out of Polish Jewry and achieved recognition before independence, and who could not be dislodged from prominence even by anti-Semitism. True, the above interpretations of Polonization were profoundly disturbed by Polish organized anti-Semitism of the thirties and the rise of Nazism in Germany. How those who had traveled far on the road of Polonization attempted to deal with the cracks in their ideological justification caused by the above events will be dealt in the next chapter.

Space does not permit an extensive treatment of the heroic efforts of Polish Jewry to further their own culture, despite poverty and despite oppression by Poles. Still, it is important to clarify here a seeming contradiction which may hamper the understanding of the phenomenon of acculturation in independent Poland. It is widely known that during the interwar period, in Poland Jewish culture was more alive, and functioning on a larger scale than anywhere else in the world. The strength of religious schools, the number of secular schools and of students in them, the size of the Jewish press and periodicals, the number of books published in Yiddish and Hebrew, the network of Jewish libraries and cultural clubs were unmatched elsewhere during that time. If so, is it erroneous to speak of rapid and substantial Polonization, in the sense of acculturation? No, I am convinced that it is not. Both of these phenomena were present and characterized Polish Jewry during that period.

This dialectical feature of the Jewish reality in Poland was alluded to by the pioneer of sociological study of Polish Jewry, Arieh Tartakower, in his article "The Jewish Culture in Poland between the Two World Wars." Jewish political organizations made a great effort to counteract "assimilatory" (in the sense of language and culture) trends: "It is definitely no exaggeration to say that both in their programs and in the daily activities of all Jewish political parties, cultural matters occupied a very prominent place and in many instances even the first place." [11] But if their goal of counteracting "assimilatory" trends and fostering Jewish culture was the same, there was much division and much conflict among the organizations concerning what forms the distinctive Jewish culture in Poland should take. It expressed itself in the bitter *Kulturkampf* between Hebrew and Yiddish and in the competition between the different school systems run by the different Jewish organizations. This tie to competing political organizations imbued the cultural field with dynamism, excitement, and special significance. But the tie also had its negative consequences. The energy spent in internal strife weakened the realization of the overall goal of counteracting the strong "assimilatory" influences on young Jews.

The Public School as an Agent of Polonization

The chief agent of Polonization was the public school system of Poland. The Polish government failed to bring into being the special public schools—with Yiddish or Hebrew as the language of instruction—that Jewish nationalists had demanded on the basis of the Minorities Treaty.[12] Article 9 of the Treaty stipulated that Poland would provide public primary schools where instruction would be in the language of the minority "in towns and districts in which a considerable proportion" of the population were "of other than Polish speech." It also provided that "an equitable share" of public funds be granted to the minorities for educational purposes (see chapter 2). Neither of these provisions were fulfilled in regard to the Jews. The granting of government and municipal subsidies for Jewish education, called for in the Treaty, and the size of these subsidies was a constant bone of contention. Once the grants had been established, the municipalities began their tactics of reducing or withdrawing them.[13] Public schools with instruction in the minority's language were established for the territorial minorities, but not for Jews. "We constitute the unhappy exception among the minorities," declared Rabbi Yitzhak Rubinstein, a member of the Polish Senate, during the parliamentary budgetary discussions of 1929.[14]

The refusal by the Polish government and the Polish majority to recognize the rights of Jews as one of the nationalities in Poland has been thoroughly discussed. However, one must also admit that had the Polish government followed a policy of implementing for Jews the Treaty's provision of public schools in the minority's language, its task would have been far from easy. There was bitter strife among the Jews over the language of instruction (Yiddish or Hebrew), and over the general orientation (traditional or secular). Each side tried to press on the Polish government its own conception of Jewish schools, after the Minorities Treaty was signed.

Recognizing the Jews as a religious group, the government provided religious instruction in the Polish language for Jewish children in the public schools. In the early years after independence, it also established some special primary schools which were closed on Saturdays, the so-called Sabbath schools, *szabasówki*. (School in Poland was attended six days a week.) The beginning of the process of phasing out these schools was noted in 1928 and by 1938 there were only about sixty of them left.[15]

In the period preceding the Polish government's official anti-Semitic program, Jewish national leaders and Jewish representatives in the Parliament accused the government of intentionally using the public schools as weapons of assimilation. For example, during the 1928 discussion in the Diet of the educational budget for the forthcoming year, the militant Zionist politician, Yitzhak Gruenbaum, charged that the goal of the government's policy was to "bring about the assimilation of the Jews": "The schools that serve our children have as their aim to divest our children of their national identity, to tear our children away from their Jewish roots." At the same time another representative in the *Sejm*, the Zionist Dr. Yakov Wygodzki, pleaded for government subsidies for the schools that Jewish communities and organizations had founded and were struggling desperately to maintain (he referred to them as "national schools"):

> The Ministry of Education has made the public school not only into a center of combatting illiteracy, . . . but also into a tool of *forced assimilation*.[16]

The persistence of Jewish schools throughout independence, despite the poverty of the Jewish population and despite the lack of adequate subsidies, is a testimony to the importance that Jews attached to education in general and to Jewish education in particular. The task of providing a network large enough to serve the bulk of children of primary school age (for whom school was compulsory) was beyond their means. Unquestionably, it was impossible for them to establish a Jewish school in every small town of Poland where Jews constituted a substantial part of the population. But in some towns where it was possible, the dissension among the various Jewish political groups prevented a single Jewish primary school from coming into being.

Thus we begin to encounter some of the painful facts about Jewish organizations and their politics. They were so fractious and filled with controversy that they could not achieve a sufficient consensus to form a unified Jewish school system. The then-burning issues which fanned the conflict concerning the proper nature of Jewish education were (1) the role of religion in education and the relations between it and secular instruction, (2) the question of Yiddish versus Hebrew, (3) the problem of ideological and political orientation in education.

Jewish primary and secondary schools included a number of antagonistic systems that lined up differently on those issues. The Orthodox-traditional, run by *Khorev*, the educational arm of *Agudat Israel*, was discussed earlier. Of the secular systems the two largest were *Tarbut* schools—Zionist oriented, with Hebrew as the language of instruction and an emphasis on Hebrew culture— and CYSHO (Central Yiddish School Organization)—anti-Zionist, manifestly secular, and socialist in orientation, with Yiddish as the language of instruction and with purposive disregard of Hebrew. In addition, there was the *Yavne* school system, which represented a synthesis between religious and secular education, stressing the importance of both. (It was founded by the Mizrachi, the religious Zionist organization.) Many of its schools were bilingual: general subjects were taught in Polish, the Judaic subjects in Hebrew.[17]

Except for the large cities, not all of the Jewish organizations were able to establish their distinctive primary schools in each city. Faced with the alternative of sending their children to a Jewish school with an orientation opposite to their own, some parents settled for the public school. Where a choice existed, other parents were so disgusted with the tenor of the arguments between the sponsors of the various schools, or so unable to untangle their arguments, that they also became reconciled to the Polish public school.[18] Then, too, certain parents—particularly middle class ones, who were to some extent Polonized or who wanted careers for their children—preferred a Polish school. But the most compelling factor in the Jewish masses' resorting to the public schools was that they were tuition-free. Their poverty often left them with no other way to meet the requirement of compulsory primary school attendance.

There is room for debate concerning the weight of each of the above factors, since no exact studies or data exist. But the indisputable fact remains that around 80 percent of the Jewish children attending primary schools were in Polish public schools. Of course, this could also be viewed from the opposite angle: around 20 percent of Jewish children were in private primary schools as compared with 1.3 percent of non-Jewish children.[19] Anyway, the great majority of Jewish children who were attending public school were socialized there in Polish values as well as in the Polish language. As for the nonpublic Jewish primary schools, they were becoming increasingly bilingual in instruction: Polish-Hebrew or Polish-Yiddish.[20]

To judge from the autobiographies and diaries of young Jews and from the interviews I conducted, many children experienced great difficulties because of the language handicap. But these sources also indicate that the same children often treated this handicap as a challenge which could be met through hard study. Generally the children brought with them from home a thirst for knowledge and a respect for the teachers as conveyers of knowledge, even if the latter appeared to dislike Jews.

In their autobiographies, many young Jews refer to the primary school years as the happiest years of their lives. Particularly lower class and lower middle class youth, for whom the economic struggle to survive proved so oppressive at home, refer to school in glowing terms as "my second home." In addition to the relief from home, the school might have been especially attractive to many male pupils because of its contrast to the ḥeder (elementary religious school where small children were taught the alphabet, reading, and prayer). Before entry into the public school at the age of seven, the great majority of them attended the ḥeder which began when they were four or five. Once in public school, many of them continued with the heder during after-school hours. In the YIVO autobiographies, young Jews were quite critical of their experiences in these schools. Often located in the home of the *melamed* (teacher) these schools were as a rule overcrowded and unhygienic; their hours were long—from morning until dark; their materials of instruction were tattered prayer books; their mode of discipline was the whip.[21] Compared with these dingy places, the public schools were advanced, and appeared to these children as light, spacious, and luxurious; the illustrated books used in classes kindled their interest. Perhaps this helps us to comprehend the favorable recollections of these schools, despite the anti-Semitism with which they were infested. Hopefully, further insight into this paradox will soon be gained as we untangle the attractions of school.

To understand both these attractions and the profound Polonizing influence of the public school, one has to realize how very Polish it was and how very enthusiastic it was in its Polishness. Recall the patriotic fervor for which the Poles are known. Put into this context the fact that for the first time in Polish history there were Polish public schools in that large part of Poland formerly under Russian rule. Unlike partition times, teachers were able to instruct their children in Polishness without fear. In fact, they were encouraged by the government to shape a generation of free and patriotic Poles. It can truly be said that in the public schools Polishness was celebrated: Polish valor, nobility, greatness and beauty.* The lessons in Polish history projected figures of shining Polish heroes. Children were taught to see the Polish land as exceptionally beautiful through the images of the romantic Polish poets. They were continuously fed the idea that the Polish language was the quintessence of beauty. Is it surprising that Jewish children were stirred, in varying degrees, by this patriotic fantasy?

---

* There was an attempt under the aegis of the Minister of Education in the Piłsudski regime, Janusz Jędrzejewicz—a high-minded and generous Pole who took great pride in the multinational heritage of the Polish state—to add civic education to the public school program and to infuse it with a broader conception of patriotism that included respect for the history and culture of the minorities in Poland. However, it did not meet with much success. Some particulars about this can be found in Stanisław Mauersberg, *Szkolnictwo Powszechne dla Miniejszości Narodowych w Polsce w Latach 1918–1939* (Wrocław: Ossolineum, 1968), pp. 208–10.

The exalted world of Polishness unfolded to Jewish children like a magic castle: to glance at, to admire but seldom, if ever, to enter fully. It would be difficult, for instance, to convey the feelings of not belonging, of regret that the little Jewish children experienced as they listened to the prideful recitation by their Polish classmates of the Polish children's credo, which was not for them to utter:

> Who are you? A little Pole.
> What is your sign? The white eagle.[22]

Jewish children were exposed to the crass anti-Semitism of their Polish classmates and the more obtuse anti-Semitism of their teachers. The pains of disenchantment when an admired teacher failed to rise to their defense and the subsequent fantasies about transferring to a Jewish school, where one would be spared such humiliation, often figure in the autobiographies of young Jews. For instance a twenty-year-old youth recollected in 1934 his feeling as a child when in the first grade a Jewish classmate was beaten in school by a group of Polish children who screamed anti-Semitic slurs and yelled "Icek (kike) go to Palestine":

> Why didn't the teacher punish the guilty? . . . I walked Srulek [name of classmate] home. Tears of pain and shame were dropping on his face. For a long time he said nothing. . . . This incident gave me no peace. "*Icek, Żyd*" [kike, Jew], this expression stayed in my mind. School took on a different aspect; the enemy was everywhere. . . . I started thinking of transferring to a Hebrew school. . . . Years later my older brother was the first to throw some light on anti-Semitism, which was at first so hard for me to comprehend. He explained that all people ought to be brothers, help each other and work together. He used wise words like friendship, unity, culture, progress, ideals.[23]

Derogatory names for Jew were frequently heard in school. Another device used by Polish youngsters to taunt their Jewish classmates was to address them by imagined Jewish names instead of their proper Polonized ones. In the autobiographies of young Jews one finds numerous references to such experiences in

school. To cite one example, a girl recollected her first day in a
new school, when she was placed next to a Polish girl:

> "What?" yelled my neighbor. "It's impossible that this is
> your name. Your real Jewish name must be Tsipa or Dvoyra
> (common Jewish names). It's impossible for a Jewish girl to
> have the same name as a Polish girl." This was the greeting I
> received. . . .

And yet the same girl came to admire Polish culture and Polish characteristics and, conversely, to see Jewish traits in a negative light:

> It is quite possible that had I attended a Jewish school, I
> would be less critically disposed toward Jewish things. Only
> now do I realize that the Polish school environment has had a
> depraving effect on us. But then, all Jewish things made me
> nervous and I wasn't interested in them.[24]

Lower and lower-middle class parents were so preoccupied
with providing subsistence for their families, so exhausted by trying to make ends meet while coping with the anti-Jewish harassment, that they often failed to realize what was happening to their
children in the Polish public schools. Looking back at the time
spent in a Polish public primary school, a fifteen-year-old student
of a private Hebrew high school explained:

> As a child I heard little about Palestine. . . . It wasn't be-
> cause my parents were so assimilated that they forgot their an-
> cestral homeland. On the contrary, my parents—and even more,
> my grandmother—were very religious. But they had so many
> economic worries, that they had no time for such things. No
> wonder that I did not know the Jewish heroes, that I did not
> know much about Palestine. I loved my native town, Poland's
> landscape, towns and cities, its kings and heroes: I loved all that
> was Polish. This love grew during my six years in public school
> when I came under the influence of a patriotic woman teacher.
> Since I have been attending the Jewish *gimnazjum* [high
> school] I have felt disillusioned more than once upon learning
> that some of the very kings of Poland that I admired so much
> were bad to the Jews. In gimnazjum I am learning the history
> of the Jews and about their heroism.[25]

Gimnazjum—the Aspiration of Middle Class Jews

Exemplified above is the effectiveness of the public primary school as agent of acculturation. It partly explains the fact that the Polonization of Jews increased throughout independence, despite the growing anti-Semitism. The public school accounts to a great extent for the beginning of Polonization among large numbers of children of workers, craftsmen, peddlers, and petty traders who had remained nearly untouched by it before independence. However, almost all of these school children came from homes that were devoid of Polish influences.

Conversely, for a substantial proportion of middle class children, Polonization either began at home or, if started in school, found some encouragement at home, especially from mothers. Even before independence, in the traditional middle class family the study of the Polish language, as well as secular subjects, was much more acceptable for female children than for males (since women were not required to study the Torah).[26] After independence, those girls became Jewish middle class mothers who instilled in their children the love of the Polish language and culture, frequently accompanied by the feeling that they were superior to the Jewish language and culture.*

Thus, among middle class children, there was more consistency and continuity between the Polish socialization in the public primary school and the socialization at home. Also, with them the process of systematic Polonization was much more likely to continue beyond the primary school. The strategic point of entry to the status of the "educated," to the stratum of the intelligentsia, was at that time not the university but the high school (*gimnazjum*). High school education was neither compulsory or free. Poles and Jews alike considered it not as a mass but as an elitist institution. And yet, because of their cultural emphasis on education and because they were an urban population, a larger proportion of Jews than Poles aspired to a gimnazjum education. But the fact that they were Jewish, limited their admission to the public high schools (operated by the central and local government). Although

---

* See the allusion to his mother in the previously cited letter of Julian Tuwim as an illustration of this. (See chapter 4, note 35.)

the most prestigious elitist schools were private, the public high schools generally ranked above the various types of nonpublic schools, designated collectively as "private" high schools. In an attempt to fulfill their aspirations toward a high school education, Jewish students were willing to settle for such private schools. But these required much higher tuition, which many of the Jewish middle class parents could hardly afford. At the same time, because of the pressing economic difficulties, the Jewish communities were unable to sufficiently subsidize private secondary schools on the scale needed to allow reduced tuition for all those who needed it. The limited municipal subsidies given to schools operated by Jewish organizations were constantly threatened, often reduced, and sometimes withdrawn.[27] Despite all this, a gimnazjum education was pursued with passion and zeal by middle class Jewish parents for their youngsters and by the youngsters themselves as an entry to higher status and modernity. As a Cracow youth—whose family's economic conditions were deteriorating to the point of making it virtually impossible to muster the necessary tuition—reminisced about his ambitions during the last year of primary school:

> There were various reasons for my wanting to go to gimnazjum. Although I did like to study and find out new things, I would be lying if I said that my only motive was the thirst for knowledge. Some classmates were going to attend gimnazjum and join the intelligentsia. And I who was equally capable was to become a craftsman. I could not accept that.[28]

The sacrifices made by parents for their children's education were truly great. They are described with much pathos, and some feelings of guilt, by young Jews, even by those who placed their parents in the category of "making a living" (having *parnose*). Such placement frequently denoted no more than the ability of parents to provide simple food three times a day. To give children a secondary education when one had hardly enough for feeding and dressing them was a Herculean task. And yet once parents had accumulated enough money to get their children into a high school, they rarely withdrew them—as indicated in the biographies of

young Jews. Only in cases of extreme poverty or death of the
breadwinner was a Jewish youngster withdrawn. To do so was
considered a tragedy among middle class people. The desperate
struggle of middle class Jewish parents to get their children into a
gimnazjum and to keep them there, despite the economic strangulation and national oppression from which they suffered, was part
of that heroism of Polish Jewry which was invisible to Poles.

In light of the above, the statistics concerning Jewish youngsters in high schools assume special significance. The total
number of Jewish high school students dropped sharply from the
beginning to the end of the interbellum period: In the 1936–37
school year there were 33,212 Jewish high school students as compared with 48,849 in 1921–22. This also represented a substantial
decline in the percentage of Jews among the total high school

*The strategic point of entry to the status of the "educated," to the
stratum of the intelligentsia was . . . the high school (gimnazjum) . . .*

A GROUP OF FRIENDS FROM THE JEWISH FEMALE GIMNAZJUM MEET-
ING ON SATURDAY. KIELCE, 1938. (PRIVATE COLLECTION)

student population of Poland: from 23.7 percent in 1921–22 to 16.5 percent in 1936–37.[29]

While these figures reflect the deterioration in the situation of the Jews in Poland, they also point to the special forms of resistance by Polish Jews. Despite the growing impoverishment of their parents and despite the severe discrimination which awaited them upon graduation (in employment or at the university), the proportion of Jews among high school students continued to the very end to be higher than their proportion among the total population, which was 10 percent. This testifies to the great commitment of Jews to education, especially since most of the Jewish high school students (73 percent in 1936–37) were attending private schools whose tuition fees were much higher than those of the public schools. (In contrast, two-thirds of the non-Jewish students were in public high schools.) [30]

Many of the private schools, patronized by Jewish students because of the exclusionary policies of the public gimnazja, were Polish rather than Jewish schools. Of all the Jewish students attending private high schools in 1925–26, 41 percent were in Polish schools and 59 percent in Jewish ones. However, by 1934–35 there was a substantial drop to 28 percent in Polish schools. A number of factors accounted for this decrease. With the growing anti-Semitism, there was more discrimination in the acceptance of Jewish students. Then, too, the Jewish youth became more nationalistic in its orientation as a response to the increasing anti-Semitism, and also tried to avoid direct encounters with anti-Semitism by attending Jewish schools.[31] In those cases where Jews kept out or were kept out from Polish schools because of anti-Semitism, they often landed in the kind of "Jewish" gimnazja which differed little from the Polish high schools. Sine the full high school, with its *matura* certificate, was primarily seen as necessary to a professional career, parents were concerned with having their children attend a school with full accreditation (category A) which would make them eligible for entry into a university or professional school. To secure such accreditation, the curriculum in such schools conformed to that in public high schools and the instruction was in Polish. Thus the stress on the Polish language and Polish culture in these private "Jewish" schools equalled that in the Polish schools. However, in addition to the standard curriculum, they offered Judaic subjects. In some of these private schools, Judaic subjects, taught in Hebrew, were treated seriously and tended to be of the same caliber as the general subjects taught in Polish. But in many private "Jewish" schools, the "Judaic" subjects were minimal, received least attention, and were often manned by teachers of lesser caliber. Only in the last few years before Poland fell did a Jewish orientation begin to surface in such schools as a response to the anti-Semitism.[32]

As for the schools in which Hebrew or Yiddish (or both) was the language of instruction, the government placed increasing obstacles in their way. Only few were given the kind of accreditation that would make its graduates eligible for entry into Polish universities and schools of higher learning. This was one of the main reasons that the schools with a pronounced Jewish character encompassed less than a third of the Jewish student body. Twenty-two percent of all Jewish students in secondary schools—7,437 out of a total of 33,212—Polish-Hebrew schools in 1936–37, and barely 2,242 (7 percent) were in schools where the language of instruction was either Hebrew or Yiddish.[33] Furthermore, the latter Hebrew and Yiddish high schools were concentrated in Vilno and the Eastern border areas, inhabited by the territorial minorities, where Jews tended to be least Polonized.[34]

Thus Polonization, which swept the upper stratum in the nineteenth century and moved to the middle strata at the beginning of the twentieth century, became the dominant trend among the middle class youth in independent Poland. Among some of them, this process continued during the time spent in schools of higher learning. The result was that most young professionals, artists, and intellectuals were assimilated, completely or nearly so, both linguistically and culturally. They also often shared the assimilationists' extremely negative attitudes toward Yiddish and toward Jewish culture.

Such attitudes very seldom manifested themselves among members of the lower class. Its young people were less Polonized, and therefore culturally less marginal, than those of the middle

class. Their homes were hardly touched by the process of acculturation. Also, very few of them found their way into the gimnazja.
What was distinctive about the lower class youth is that the secularization—which had begun in that class at the end of the nineteenth century—proceeded among them faster than Polonization.
The overall pattern of change in the Jewish lower class of independent Poland can be characterized as substantial secularization
with minimal Polonization (mostly in the form of Polish as the second language). There one encountered a sharp turn away from
religion and from those traditional values that were considered
backward, but a continued adherence to folk elements of the Jewish culture, as well as to Yiddish, and the turn toward the modern
Yiddish literature by the many who aspired to learning and
"higher" culture. The move away from religion and toward "modernity" found its external expression in and was symbolized by
the earlier discussed massive abandonment of the traditional dress,
beards by men and wigs by women.

Secularization

The interwar period was the time of the extensive breakdown of
the traditional order largely governed by religious values. Many
Jewish families that had proved impervious to secularizing currents before independence now became engulfed by them. Young
people broke the strong ties of the long-fixed traditional codes of
thought and behavior. These ties, which had given their parents
the psychological strength to endure with hope, were now perceived as a constraining harness that had to be broken—no matter
how much pain it involved for oneself and others.

There were some major factors in the loosening of the traditional ties in the lower class. First among them was mass migration: the young were leaving their home towns to search desperately for work in larger cities. Although it was difficult to find
work, it was a bit easier for those who were ready to work on Saturday. Also they came in contact with "big-city" ways and "enlightened" workers whom they emulated. They in turn were emu-

lated when they came back home to the smaller towns. There was much movement back and forth from home; as younger Jews might frequently be unable to find jobs in the larger cities or might lose the ones they had.

In addition, certain aspects of the structure of traditional Jewish society and culture were conducive to the rapid growth of secularization among the young of the lower strata, once its seeds had been planted.[35] Much less was expected of them, and their deviation from traditional norms did not elicit the same indignation. They were plain (*prost*), and as the Yiddish saying went, "what can you expect from a plain person?" Implied in this was that he did not know the deeper meaning of the religious tradition and could easily be led astray. But when a middle class youth—from respectable background (*balebatish*)—deviated, it resulted in greater disapproval of the culprit and pity for the parents. The traditionalists tended to view it as an expression of the general calamity of the impeding breakdown of Jewishness.

Then, too, the traditional structure did not contain so many possibilities of gratification for the lower strata as it did for the higher. The three intrinsic sources of prestige and self-esteem were family background, charity and good deeds, and learning. Ostensibly the access to the last two was open to all Jews, but actually it was greatly restricted for members of the lower class. Even though the avenues of traditional higher education were open to the lower strata, in the sense that poorer youths who were capable and devoted to learning could gain free admittance to a yeshiva, they seldom took advantage of this opportunity. Their families could not afford to give up the little money that they would bring home from work. As for the good deeds that brought prestige, they required generous giving to the poor which the lower class could not afford. True, people of the lower strata also abided by the principle of charity and would, for example, try not to allow a beggar to leave their home empty-handed. But this kind of charity, though it satisfied the donor's conscience, did not bring him any recognition in the community, even if this donation may have required more self-sacrifice than the larger donations of the well-to-do. The people of the lower class were not apt to receive recognition, and much more than others they were subject to shame. Although giving brought prestige, taking when in need was shameful. Lower class persons were often helped by the well-to-do when in need, but the price they had to pay in shame was tremendous.

That the poor person's rewards in the culture were recognized to be far below those of the well-to-do is evidenced in the old Yiddish folk sayings. One example is, "A poor person has neither this world nor the next one." The road to the world after death was through charity and good deeds, of which the poor were financially incapable. The young went way beyond that kind of recognition to challenge the very existence of an afterworld, and many saw in the present world of their traditional parents a confirmation of the Marxist dictum that religion is the opium of the people. The large-scale departure from the old pattern of life by the young of the lower strata was often inextricably connected with their politicization, to be discussed in the next chapter. Many were convinced that in political organization they would find the strength to change both their ethnic and class situation, instead of following their parents' futile path of escape through religion.

If the secularization of the lower class was tied to political awakening, the secularization of the middle class youth was connected on one hand to their mobility aspirations and acculturation, and on the other to the virtual absence of Reform Judaism. Those who were trying to advance educationally and occupationally found Orthodox Judaism too restrictive. And to the acculturated young Jews the typical Orthodox religious service seemed devoid of "European" dignity. The usual absence of decorum in the synagogues or houses of prayer repelled the young, who viewed it with acculturated eyes. Then, too, they tended to associate religion with the distinctive dress and hair style and considered both as backward and fossilized forms. This is not to deny that there were in Poland some Jews of the elder generations who individually succeeded in combining "modernization" in attire, manner, and speech with a practice of the ancient faith. However, this mode never became institutionalized as it had in Germany or in the United States. In the large cities of Warsaw, Lvov, Cracow, Lódź, and a few smaller ones—Częstochowa, Piotrków, Bielsk—there

were even single non-Orthodox synagogues, referred to as "progressive" or "German." They emphasized decorum, and the sermons were preached in Polish or German. However, they were the
rare exception and apart for the very rich and assimilated, the
young Jews of Poland were hardly cognizant of their existence. As
a matter of fact, even the educated young were by and large ignorant that such a thing as Reform Judaism existed anywhere in the
world. This widespread ignorance is exemplified by the erroneous
statement in the diary of a nineteen-year-old who lost his beliefs
while in a gimnazjum and became in his words a "hundred-per-
cent free thinker":

> Apart from nationalism, the question that gives me no
> peace is that of religion. I have been thinking much about it. It
> seems strange that our religion has not yet been exposed to re-
> form. I understand that the Zionists cannot pay attention to this
> problem at this time because there are more important tasks,
> like the rebuilding of our homeland. . . . After all, the Christian
> world went through various reform currents like humanism and
> rationalism. Scholasticism has disappeared from their world but
> it is still rampant in ours. . . . If a Luther does not appear
> among us . . . eventually we shall all become assimilated.[36]

Jewish secularization took extreme forms in Poland and contained a strong anti-religious bias. The frequent immoderation was
related to the fact, noted earlier, that in the Jewish traditional pattern religion was not differentiated as a separate dimension from
the cultural or national dimension. All these were inextricably
bound together in Judaism. To tear out the religious element, to
separate out that which was hitherto inseparable, seemed to
require radical surgery. Anyway, socialist and communist activists
considered it part of their technique of enlightenment and con-
sciousness-raising to break the firmness of faith, which was the
strongest element that had kept the Jews glued to the traditional
pattern. They worked hard and with enthusiasm to turn young
Jews from traditional homes into atheists or agnostics. Also, antireligious militancy attracted the best minds among youths from
traditional homes and sometimes manifested itself in places least
expected: among the brightest students of the yeshivot. From the

devout came some of the most irreligious individuals. These converts to secularism showed the typical zeal of converts to sow the newly found "truth," to "open the eyes" of those "blinded," but in this case by religion.

Religion was a very important issue to the Jewish youth of interwar Poland. The existence of God was a frequent subject of debate, sometimes argued with greater fervor by those who denied Him than those who affirmed Him. Both the secularists and the traditionalists lacked the measure of tolerance that comes easily when the issue is not considered vital. The secularists generally regarded it as a humanitarian task to "liberate" young people from the shackles of tradition. To win them away from religion was to open their eyes to the existence of the wide world outside, their minds to the superiority of rationalism, and their hearts to the cause of "progressive humanity." To leave them be was to allow them to waste away in blindness and to suffocate in a closet. In turn, the traditionalists regarded the secularists as sinners, disrupters of the unity of the Jewish people whose center of gravity was God and His Torah. Dramatic encounters with a certain individual—sometimes an elder sibling—who assaulted their faith during adolescence figure in the biographies of young Jews. For example, a middle class youth recalled how during a summer vacation a Jewish lawyer tried unsuccessfully to convince him that there was no God: "I continued to believe in God because I could not betray the faith that my father instilled in me. But I always felt a resentment against this lawyer because he wanted to persuade me otherwise." [37]

If in some the belief in God could not be completely dislodged, the separation between sacred and profane—nonexistent in the traditional pattern and so essential for secularization—was proceeding rapidly in the young generation. It was not diminished by Jewish religious instruction provided in the primary and secondary schools of Poland, even when attendance was made compulsory. Such religious instruction often proved very ineffective. While the priests teaching the Catholic pupils were able to command authority and were generally accorded respect, the Jewish teachers of religion were as a rule unable to maintain order and were often subjected to ridicule and pranks. In the recollections of school days, both in my interviews and in the autobiographies, the theme is repeated again and again that of all the classes "the greatest disorder was during the lesson of religion." [38] According to Tartakower, this disorder was frequently due to the lack of qualifications of individuals hired to teach the Jewish religion: "such teachers of religion did more harm than good, since they degraded in the eyes of the children the meaning of the Jewish religion and Jewishness in general." [39] However, there were some outstanding scholars and instructors who taught religion in public schools.

With secularization and acculturation came a widespread rejection by the young of the traditional ways of coping with the Jewish situation. Many scorned the old attitudes and behavior of accommodation and nonviolent individual resistance that the Jews had developed through their centuries' long existence in Poland. They looked at such accommodation through the prism of Polish values or radical ideological concepts and failed to see its peculiar heroic qualities. Brought up in the primary schools on stories of Polish armed resistance during partitions as the greatest measure of heroism, they were unable to perceive that there was a distinctive heroism in the very fact of continuing to lead a Jewish life in face of persecution and derision. The bent back—a frequent mark of the traditional Jew—did not manifest to them so much the will of the Jew to go on despite the weight of oppression as it did the "typical Jewish" posture of submission. The ideal image nurtured in school was the image of the brave Pole who stood up straight, met his enemy in combat, and proved fearless even if defeated by superior forces. The traditional Jewish distrust and fear of force was experienced by the acculturated and secularized Jews as shameful, for they perceived it as cowardly acquiescence to persecution. Large numbers of young middle class Jews—those belonging to the intelligentsia or aspiring to it—had internalized the Polish ideals of manhood. They judged themselves and their peers, as well as their fathers, by the extent that they came close to or departed from the ideal image of man—in essence the idealized version of the Polish nobleman: brave, graceful, tactful and perfectly polite. Among the young of the lower strata, the conscious emphasis was more on being modern, and they evaluated themselves and others in terms of how close they came to or departed from their ideal images of modernity.

Generational Conflict

The distance between the sacred and "modern" conception of life, as well as the cultural distance, displayed itself dramatically within the family. The Jewish family in interwar Poland, often romanticized by survivors as idyllic, was wrenched by a fierce conflict of generations. This conflict resembled in many aspects the one that had occurred at the turn of the century, especially of the part of Poland under Russian rule.[40] But it was now on a larger scale than ever before.[41]

The revolt of children, which is universally experienced by parents as painful, was especially devastating for parents steeped in the Jewish tradition. The traditional culture made the parents psychologically very dependent on children, while at the same time it stressed the authority of the parents. "A person alone is alone like a stone," went the Yiddish saying: Such a person missed one of the few great rewards of life, *nakhes:* joy from the good qualities, accomplishments, and good fortune of their children.[42] Also the standing of the parents in the traditional community was very dependent on the behavior of their children. Deviant behavior of children brought shame to parents and, as we have seen, the traditional Jewish culture made its members very susceptible to shame. Moreover, their afterlife was believed to be affected by the behavior of their children. And children's responsibilities to deceased parents were a continuation of their responsibilities to living parents. They owed them, above everything else, *derekherets,* honor and respect. They were, therefore, not supposed to do anything that would have been very painful to their parents when alive. A person who markedly violated this rule of behavior was spoken of as "not having respect for his dead parents."

The commandment "honor thy father and mother" was greatly emphasized in the home socialization of children. From early childhood, the child who failed to accord proper respect to his parents and elders was admonished not to be an *azes-ponim* (brazen faced). The older children, however, increasingly could not be brought back to the "respectful" modes of behavior through traditional means. One of the most effective in the past had been the parent's temporary psychological withdrawal from the child. Then the silent "look" from the father was often enough to check the offending offspring. If the "look" alone did not succeed, the father resorted to not talking to the child. When the family unit was close and bound by common values and norms, children could not long endure the prolonged emotional distancing by the father. But now that the children differed so markedly in values and norms, they felt distant from their parents, whom they measured against the new standards.

They saw themselves separated from their parents by centuries: they regarded the parents who abided by tradition as fixed in the middle ages; they saw themselves as twentieth-century people. The Polish standards and those of "modernity" applied by the young to their fathers diminished them in their eyes and enlarged the distance between them. As a nineteen-year-old working class youth wrote in his autobiography (which he mailed to YIVO in 1939):

> An obstacle to the harmony of our family life is that I and my father are worlds apart. And apart from his fatherly sentiment, nothing binds us. He does not comprehend me and that is why he does not understand me and does not know anything about me. Our conversation consists of nothing intimate, nothing that would bring us together. I cannot share my thoughts with him or ask his advice. He never had a real conversation with me, and when we exchange words, it's about work or family. If he weren't my father, nothing would bind us.[43]

The fathers became de-authorized in the eyes of their sons and daughters. In the middle class, both the distance and the weakening of the elders' authority were often exacerbated, as well as symbolized by the generational difference in language; parents spoke Yiddish or a deficient Polish and children spoke a Polish in which they took great pride. The difference in language not only affected the flow of communication but also its nature. Traditional Yiddish-speaking Jews tended to respond to Polish as the language of authority and force, a fact generally perceived, even if not clearly articulated, by Polonized professionals and other Jews who were concerned with their position of authority vis-à-vis the Yiddish-speaking masses. To illustrate with materials from my interviews, a woman dentist from Warsaw established an office in a small town, heavily populated by Jews. Since many older people had difficulty expressing themselves in Polish and she knew Yiddish, at first she used Yiddish with them. But she soon discovered that this caused her patients to become familiar, to impose on her, and to bargain vehemently about the fees she asked. Consequently she decided to speak only Polish, after which she succeeded in establishing the distance of authority she considered proper. The well-known Warsaw journalist Bernard Singer, who during the interwar period wrote under the pseudonym of Regnis, relates in his recollections of life in the Jewish section of Warsaw a similar case of an esteemed doctor: "Our family doctor even spoke to certain clients in Yiddish, but not too much, because he feared that the distance would disappear and they would not respect him." [44]

Superimpose on this common association of Yiddish with familiarity and Polish with authority the fact that the parents were more likely to use the first and the children the second, and you get the linguistic manifestation of weakened authority. Add to this that the father might have worn traditional garb, which was regarded by the children as backward and sometimes as ridiculous. One finally begins to comprehend how very superior these youths felt toward their fathers and how they no longer saw in them a figure of authority.

In the lower strata, as suggested in the autobiographies of young Jews, the breakdown of the father's authority was more often connected with his economic failure and inability to support his family. The problem of gnawing hunger, of sheer physical survival in face of the difficult economic circumstances of the country in general and the anti-Jewish economic policies in particular, made it impossible for many Jewish men of the lower strata to fulfill their role of breadwinner for the family.[45] The resentment by the children of their fathers' failure found expression in the numerous references by young Jews, in their autobiographies and diaries, to the weakness of their fathers: their lack of initiative, persistence, energy, or practical sense. The father is not infrequently referred to by those from poor or impoverished homes as a *luft-mensh,* "a man of air." Without the firm ground of a definite occupation, he lives on hope that his next petty venture will bring economic relief to the family, but most of his ventures disappear into the air. For example, a young boy whose father was a proverbial melamed, teaching children elementary sacred Hebrew (in traditional society such an occupation was regarded as among the last resorts), and whose mother was a dressmaker related how distant he and his brothers felt from their father. He also told of his father's helplessness in the face of his older son's quitting the yeshiva, adopting European dress, and generally defying his father:

> As the Jewish saying goes, who has money, commands.
> . . . I became sorry for my father for the first time when my
> brother, during a party he made at home, said to one of the girls
> that she should not enter the next room because "there sits my
> crazy father." [46]

Importance of the Mother's Role

Such pre-World War II sources contradict the postwar nostalgic portrayals of the Jewish family in Poland as unified and the authority of the father as undisturbed. The Jewish family, long the stronghold of unity, frequently saw conflict not only between fathers and children but also among siblings with different degrees of secularization or Polonization, or with antagonistic political allegiances.[47] The role least disturbed in the family was that of the mother. Since in the traditional family the main center of authority was the father, the diminished authority of the mother that resulted from cultural distance, did not prove so disruptive. On the contrary, in the family marred by cultural, religio-secular, and ideological conflict, the affective and integrative role of the mother was in some respects strengthened. She is often depicted in the autobiographies and diaries of young Jews as the unifier in the family. For example, an eighteen-year-old high school senior wrote about sibling rivalry in his home:

> It suffices for mother to intervene, peace returns, and we shake hands. The quiet request by mother, or her tears, change us and we pledge not to fight any more, not to upset the dearest person. But it starts all over again.[48]

With the decline of the father's authority the affective side of the mother's role became even more important as a cementing force in the family. In contrast to the father, the mother is almost never presented in a negative light in these documents. Significantly, the acculturated and secularized young still project a positive image of her, which comes close to the traditional idea of the "yidishe mame": the incarnation of goodness and self-sacrifice.

There are a number of reasons why the ties to the mother were less likely to give way under the impact of acculturation and secularization. First of all, these ties were forged during infancy and early childhood. It was entirely the mother's duty to attend to the infant: the father very seldom, if ever, fed the infant, bathed it, or put it to sleep. As the boys in the family grew, their father took a more active part in their religious socialization and instruction. But middle class fathers were at home less often than the mothers. (Poorer mothers, often helped to make a living.) More continuous exposure to the mother tended to bind the child closer, especially since the mother did not use severe forms of discipline. As the youth quoted above noted:

> My mother, a delicate and very sensitive woman, devoted herself to my upbringing. . . . My father was at home less often because he was busy in business. He gave me much less attention. This accounts for the fact that to this day I feel nearer to my mother than my father.

Throughout childhood, severe discipline was usually left to the father. Corporal punishment was considered the most effective method, and that was almost never administered by the mother.

Rather, in such instances the mother would frequently intercede to urge moderation: "do not hit her so hard," do not hit him on the head," etc. Often she placed herself in front of the child to shield him from the blows of the father.

The mother's traditional function of intermediary became enhanced as the cultural conflict between fathers and sons sharpened. The middle class mother was particularly suited for this since she was often more Polonized than the father. Women had a minimal function in religious matters, and received a minimal religious education; this was an important factor in the tendency of mothers of all classes to be more accepting of changes in their children than the fathers were. Husbands often blamed their wives for their children's transgressions. One informant, for example, noted that "when my brother had a European suit made for himself, my father blamed my mother." Another mentions that his Orthodox father had once caught him at a Zionist meeting, and had blamed his mother for his attendance at it.

The autobiographies and diaries testify that the mother's affective role was not only undiminished by economic crises, but that she often proved more able to deal with the economic realities as well. In instances where the father is referred to as a failure, the mother is usually depicted as an energetic, courageous, and practical person. For example:

> My father belonged to the category of *luftmensh* and could not support his family. He was mild, passive and did not aspire to anything. Mother was the opposite: energetic, active, always trying to make ends meet. No wonder that she was nervous and angry at her fate and always fought with him. She accused him of not caring that she worked so hard. As far back as my memory goes, there were these fights. What curses—name calling and yelling! [49]

Or, as a 21-year-old female teacher—from a rural family that had lost its land, and whose mother made ends meet by peddling soap, matches, and kerosene in nearby villages—reminisced:

> My mother never gave up; she always found a way to make life easier for the children, to make our life sweeter. When there

was a food shortage, she told us stories and gave us hope for a
better future. My mother is a plain woman but she possesses
native intelligence and common sense. She acted in a way that
aroused our love and respect. . . . Father was a drifter but she
did not despair. . . . Mother never kissed me, never fondled me,
but the way she looked at me was a caress and a reward.[50]

Disturbed Identity—the Quest for a Solution

The emotional ties to the mother often made it hard for children to
make that complete break with the family which some of the
causes that called them demanded. And yet the causes had a special attraction for youths experiencing an identity crisis: [51] the
many whose traditional Jewish identity was in varying degrees disturbed or demolished by acculturation or secularization. Such a
crisis did manifest itself among extremely secularized lower class
youth but tended not to be so traumatic as among highly Polonized
middle class youth. For among them the Yiddish language and
the folk elements of the Jewish culture were hardly disturbed.
Thus, even without religious belief and observance, they were left
with a core of Jewish culture to which their Jewish self-identity
could attach itself. But in case of the highly Polonized middle class
youth, their cultural Polishness, coupled with the fact that the society denied them the option of being Poles, contained the seeds of
the ambivalence with which they were plagued. The stigma that
the majority pinned to their Jewish identity attached itself to their
minds and hearts and undermined their self-esteem. They were
vulnerable to the insults of Poles, were shamed by them, and had a
hard time recovering from them. Uprooted from traditional Judaism, humiliated and shamed by Poles whom they resembled culturally, often under the stimulus of a strong critical intelligence or
imagination which they possessed, they tended to be very self-
conscious about their disturbed identity.[52] But that critical intelligence prevented them from claiming the traditional identity
which was at times still so much alive in Poland—more than anywhere else in the Western world. The traditional culture did not

have to be reconstructed, did not have to be sought out; it was right there before their eyes. But despite the spatial proximity, and in a sense because of it, there was a tremendous division that made a return rarely desired or possible. Isaac Deutscher, the son of Orthodox parents (who reports having worn traditional dress and earlocks until the age of seventeen), provides in his autography some insight into the impossibility of return for those who emerged from Orthodoxy:

> We knew the Talmud, we had been steeped in Khassidism. All its idealizations were for us nothing but dust thrown into our eyes. We had grown up in that Jewish past. We had the eleventh, and the thirteenth and sixteenth centuries of Jewish history living next door to us and under our very roof; and we wanted to escape it and live in the twentieth century. Through all the thick gilt and varnish of romanticists like Martin Buber, we could see, and smell, the obscurantism of our archaic religion and a way of life unchanged since the middle ages. To someone of my background the fashionable longing of the Western Jew for a return to the sixteenth century, a return which is supposed to help him in recovering, or, re-discovering, his Jewish cultural identity, seems unreal and Kafkaesque.[53]

But important needs that the traditional culture filled were pressing those whose identity was disturbed: the need for hope in a better tomorrow, for transcendental meaning of everyday suffering, and for self-esteem and self-respect. These needs became accentuated, especially among the youth, in face of the economic strangulation, terror, and massive humiliation brought about by organized anti-Semitism. As a twenty-year old high school graduate wrote in 1938 in the preface to her autobiography:

> Jewish youth is engaged in a life struggle. In a way this is true of every human being. But Jewish youth finds itself in specific circumstances which lead to deep tragedy. In such a time, YIVO . . . announced the collection of autobiographies of Jewish youth, thus giving a voice to our spirits in revolt.

And in the autobiography she gives a personal rendition of the same:

> At home there were no prospects for the future. Business
> was bad. I did not see any prospects for a future after I finished
> school. And at home I was being threatened with an interrup-
> tion of school. And even in this tragic situation, despite no pros-
> pects for the future, I wanted to finish school. . . . If anyone
> asked me then what I would do after finishing school, I would
> not have known how to answer. *In this terrible situation I took
> to Zionism like a drowning person to a board* (italics sup-
> plied).[54]

Hope, faith, and meaning were not always sought or found in
Zionism. Some looked for it or encountered it in socialism or communism, others in synthesized ideologies and movements which
combined Jewish nationalism with socialism. Those whose
identity was disturbed by secularization or depleted through Polonization did not have to invent new solutions during the interwar
period. Various ideologies that had sprung up in the nineteenth
century were there, beckoning them and competing for them.
What made this period different is that so many Polish Jews were
faced with the pain and anxiety of a choice about something their
parents or grandparents were not self-conscious about. For the
parents and grandparents, all was present in Judaism: the basis of
their meaningful identity, the source of dignity and hope for the
future, and the ultimate solution to Jewish suffering. But for the
young, there were a number of competing ideologies, each with a
philosophical credo and a world-view transcending the existing
social order. In every one of these, the possibility of a meaningful
self-identity, of hope, and of self-esteem appeared.[55]

The passion with which they embraced these ideologies and
threw themselves into political movements testifies to this. But the
question of which to choose and adhere to was far from easy, as
each ideology (and the yet more numerous political organizations
professing to be the only correct embodiment of each) claimed
exclusivity for itself, not on the sacred grounds that Judaism did
but on objective and rational grounds. For these ideologies did not
present themselves as creeds, which to a large degree they were,
but as rationally justifiable systems of ideas, containing the correct
solutions to basic social and economic problems. In light of this,

the great preoccupation with which of these ideologies to adopt and adhere to, the heating discussions surrounding and accompanying these decisions, as well as the frequent shifts from one organization to another begin to be understandable. The young were preoccupied with the growing question as to which of them in fact provided the most rational and effective solution to the deteriorating situation of Jews.

Distanced from the father but linked to the family through the mother, distanced from Judaism but linked to the Jewish people by a common fate, the young generation struggled under different banners, and against formidable odds, to reach goals with common denominators. They strove to find a new Jewish identity, to fill the voids of collapsed faith, to free themselves from the inferior caste status that their native land assigned them, and to change the political and economic conditions that oppressed them.

VIII
Jewish Resistance to Oppression

The penultimate period of Jewish existence in Poland presents the story of an ancient people coping persistently with an oppressive present, clinging to old hopes or seeking anew for a better future, unaware of the perverse and monstrous fate that lay ahead of them. But our terrible knowledge of the Holocaust hampers us, in a sense, from perceiving the responses of the Polish Jews during the interwar period in the true dimensions of that time, for their actions appear dwarfed and futile, against the monstrous dimensions and completeness of their destruction. It is, therefore, essential for us to remind ourselves, again and again: the Polish Jews did not know and could not know what awaited them.

To grasp the complexity and meaning of the responses, it is important to note two striking dialectical features of the social phenomenon of Jews in interwar Poland: the growing heterogeneity of the Jewish people and a concurrent sharpening of the tendency among Poles to disregard the differences, to rigidify the social definition so that Jewish descent defined a person more significantly than anything else, and to treat all the different Jewish groups and categories as essentially the same—and therefore unwanted. Thus, what was a common subjective factor among Poles became a common objective condition for Jews. The rigid definition with its accompanying anti-Jewish feelings and attitudes, which constituted a cohesive force among Poles, became objectivized into the Jewish common situation: that of discrimination and oppression.

How did this varied population, subject to categorical treatment as Jews, respond? The responses varied greatly along age, class, shtetl versus city, and regional lines, although some, when more closely examined, prove to be variations on the same theme. The primary response was to resist oppression and dehumanization, even if often with kinds of behavior not usually recognized as resistance. Generally, the term resistance is reserved for politically inspired or oriented behavior but for Jews in the Polish atmosphere of hatred merely carrying on day after day as if things were normal and planning for tomorrow, in a deeper sense, constituted resistance. Daily life for Jews required them to ward off oppressive conditions imposed on them by the Polish majority.

We shall, however, consider principally the political forms of resistance. Beginning with Poland's independence, there was a growing politicization among Jews that finally engulfed even the most traditional and Orthodox. A conviction took hold among many Jews that their situation could be changed through massive organization to bring about a social and political structure that would do away with discrimination and persecution and would remove the stigma of being a Jew. The large measure of consensus on these goals was overshadowed by extreme fragmentation of views concerning appropriate means, specific solutions, and tactics. A wide spectrum of Jewish political parties, each in turn subdivided into factions, vied and fought with one another. This was true, incidentally, not only among Jews; the Polish system of proportional representation resulted in a glut of political parties among the Poles and the Ukrainians as well.

Proper classification of Jewish political parties is a challenge because they varied in a number of important ways. It might suffice, however, to divide them here simply into non-Zionist and Zionist parties. The two largest non-Zionist parties were the influential religious party of the Orthodox Jews, the *Aguadat Israel,* and the socialist Bund, aggressively anti-Zionist and antireligious on ideological grounds. A third was the declining secularist Folkist

Party, which was neither socialist nor Zionist. These three antago-
niśtic parties, sharply divided concerning socialism and religion,
nevertheless had certain similarities, objectively viewed, in addition to their anti-Zionism: a goal of Jewish cultural self-determination in Poland and an emphasis on Yiddish as the living language
of Polish Jews. The Zionist movement, which they opposed, became the strongest political movement of interwar Polish Jewry,
but it was divided into a number of differing parties that repre-

*In the Polish atmosphere of hatred, carrying on day after day as if
things were normal, in a deeper sense constitute resistance . . .*
MIDDLE CLASS JEWS PROMENADING IN A MOUNTAIN RESORT, ZAKO-
PANE, 1936. (PRIVATE COLLECTION)

sented a patchwork of positions on some basic issues around which Jewish politics of that period revolved.

In the Jewish politics of independent Poland, one set of issues continued to center upon the ultimate solution to the Jewish problem: Zionism versus Socialism. This debate was complicated by the fact that some Zionists were socialists, too. Then the matter boiled down to whether Jews ought to work for a national home in Palestine, even if they aimed at a socialist society there. Other issues which continued from pre-independence times were that of the role of religion in Jewish culture and whether Yiddish or Hebrew was the proper vehicle of that culture. A new issue arising with Poland's independence was whether or not and how to participate in Polish electoral politics. Here the question of proper tactics was paramount, and much fighting revolved around it. It is debatable today which dominated the Jewish political scene more—the conflict over ideological issues or over tactics. What is certain is that the debates on and bickering about both spilled over into nonpolitical associations, such as educational, cultural, and welfare organizations, splintering a once-unified community. A process that began in the nineteenth century swelled and no longer could be contained: What had been for a very long time a highly integrated set of institutions was being replaced by a multiplicity of competing political or politicized organizations. And yet an important theme can be discerned cutting through the maze of political parties and politicized organizations—Jewish nationalism in several variations. Nationalism became the main force during the interwar period, exceeding the two opposite forces that had once seemed the only alternatives for the Jews in Poland: the Orthodox-traditionalist versus the assimilationist.

Jewish political parties by and large clung to the same positions on the issues we outlined throughout the interwar period. However, certain crucial events at the end of the 1920s and during the 1930s constituted watersheds, so that the sentiments of the Jewish public in the 1920s have to be distinguished from those of the following decade; and those of the early 1930s from the period after 1935. These included internal events—such as the death of Piłsudski, pogroms, the proclamation of official anti-Semitism by the Polish government—and external ones such as the Arab riots in Palestine, Britain's White Papers (of 1931, 1937, and 1939), limiting Jewish immigration and the sale of land to Jews, and the rise of Hitler. Certainly, there is a sharp difference between the Jews' relative confidence, in the early 1920s, that they could affect the government's policies (which expressed itself in their wide support of the moderate Jewish parties), and their desperation in the late 1930s (which expressed itself in their turning away from these parties and toward the radical Jewish parties).

The Appeal of Polish Leftist Parties

Throughout the period of independence the Jewish radical parties had to contend with the competition over membership of two leftist Polish parties: the Communist Party of Poland * (KPP) and the Polish Socialist Party (PPS). The Communist Party was especially mindful of and ready in its drive for membership to exploit the peculiar situation of the Jews, which made them more open to radical ideologies even than disadvantaged groups among the Polish majority.

Although Poland bordered on the Soviet Union, that border was so tightly closed that information about the true nature of Soviet society was as murky there as it was in the West. And Communist propaganda projected the great myth of the Soviet Union as the society that had brought an end to national oppression and was the embodiment of social justice. In addition, there was a specific myth aimed at Jews: Russia, the land of hate and pogroms, was now free from anti-Semitism. If Communism could bring this about in dark Russia, think what it could do in "European" Poland, in which the historical stream of tolerance had not yet dried up completely. It seemed particularly convincing because, among the

---

* This became its official name in 1925; prior to that time it bore the name of the Communist Workers' Party of Poland, which came into being at the end of 1918 as a result of the merger of the Social Democratic Party of the Kingdom of Poland and Lithuania (SDKPL) and part of the Left Wing of the Polish Socialist Party (PPS-Lewica).

numerous Polish political parties, the Communist Party was the only one, beside the Polish Socialist Party, to take a decisive and continuous stand against anti-Semitism. Whether as a matter of principle or a matter of tactics to attract Jews to it, the Polish Communist Party from its very inception to its end vigorously condemned anti-Semitism as a tool of the ruling class (including big Jewish capitalists) to split the proletariat.[1]

On one hand the party had the potential of attracting many of the radicalized Jews, insofar as it was consistently vocal against anti-Semitism (against the "national oppression" of Jews) and held out the promise of a society free from it. But on the other, its being illegal and clandestine in Poland might have precluded it from becoming the mass party it aimed to be. Actually, it had a very small Jewish as well as Polish membership, even though individuals of Jewish background were substantially over-represented in it. Only a few sporadic figures are available but they are worth citing. According to official communist sources, the total membership of the Communist Party of Poland in 1933 was 9,200.* Although the proportion of Jews for that year is not given, the same kind of sources estimate it to have been 35 percent in 1930 and 24 percent in 1932.[2]

That the number of Communists in the Jewish population was small needs to be emphasized, because their substantial over-representation in the Communist Party, and especially in its elite, composed the "factual" ingredient in the stereotype of the "Jew-communist," which had originated before independence. And this was the basis of the apparent credibility of the fabricated story, and the popular slogans connected with it, of a "Jewish-communist conspiracy" (żydokomuna): its base was in Russia and the Polish Jews, being part of it, constituted Poland's enemy from within. This theme, advanced by Polish nationalists, was especially effective in Poland, since it combined the traditional Polish fear of Russia, rooted in historical experience, with the distrust of the Jews.[3] It sounded so convincing because Jews had earlier figured in the

---

* This number did not include the members in Eastern Poland who made up the Communist Party of Western Ukraine and the Communist Party of Western Belorussia, which were established in 1925 as a result of the Comintern's decision.

leadership of the Communist takeover in Russia, and in the interwar period in press reports of Communists rounded up by the Polish police or of anti-Communist trials in Poland.

That Polish anti-Semitism was the main cause of over-representation of people of Jewish origin in the Communist Party of Poland was overlooked, as was the truth—that the Jewish population was overwhelmingly non-Communist and predominantly anti-Communist.[4] Thus the effect of anti-Semitism was successfully turned into a cause of increased anti-Semitism. Because the stereotype "Jew-communist" was so effectively used by Polish nationalists in consolidating the Polish people around a program of anti-Semitism, I devote more attention to the Jewish membership in the Communist Party than mere numbers would merit.

Among the factors accounting for the failure of the party to attract more members and to gain a greater base among Polish Jews was the fierce opposition of many Orthodox Jews. In the small towns, where the traditional pattern was still dominant, the people often feared and abhorred the tiny bands of Communists, who defied community standards. Communist use of violence and intimidation within the community made them in the eyes of traditionalists "worse than gentiles" because they departed from the Jewish way of peace. For openly flaunting their violations of the religious mores and the folkways, they were regarded as true sinners. (The religious held it more serious; when a person sinned privately, he was responsible only for himself; when he sinned publicly he induced others to follow his example.) [5]

The party also encountered great difficulties among the more secularized workers and the poor, whom it considered fertile ground for its operations. In addition to its unyielding anti-Zionist stance, its wavering position over the issue of Jews as a nationality and the fact that many of its leaders were assimilationists hindered its efforts. Throughout its existence, there were some internal disputes in the Communist Party of Poland about the proper organizational form that its activities among Jews should take. Nevertheless, when it created autonomous parties among the territorial minorities in 1925—the Communist Party of Western Ukraine and the Communist Party of Western Belorussia—it did not establish such an autonomous structure for the Jewish minority. Similarly, at the time when the Communist Party of Poland was advocating not only cultural but also territorial autonomy for the Belorussians and Ukrainians in Poland (a position that coincided with the interests of the Soviet Union), it condemned the goal of cultural autonomy for Jews as a reactionary manifestation of Jewish separatism that was attempting to build a "Chinese wall" between the Jewish and Polish workers. The KPP thus followed the Soviet Communist Party line in regard to Jews.[6]

The Communists had a hard time competing with genuine Jewish organizations on "the Jewish street" (an expression very often used by Communists). They frequently emphasized the same immediate issues as the Jewish Bund and the socialist Zionist groups did—excessive taxation, landlords evictions, lack of Jewish schools in the public school system, etc.—and yet they vocally attacked the organizations that pointed to these issues. This tended to boomerang against the Communists.[7]

The party—because it was very disciplined and because its leadership was highly trained in tactics of infiltration—was able to exert more power than its numbers would indicate. Its activists were experts in the tactics of disruption of Zionist and Bund meetings and of boring within Jewish trade unions, where the Bund influences generally predominated. These trade unions, as Communist documents show, were their "main base of operation" for gaining control over Jewish workers by building "red cells."[8] Nevertheless, they encountered increasing organized opposition in the 1930s. Growth of anti-Semitism at home, and the advent of Hitler abroad, strengthened nationalist and pro-Zionist sentiments among Jews. In 1933, the Secretariat of the KPP admitted in its report: "Our vitality on the Jewish terrain has diminished while the activities of the Zionists and the Bund have increased."[9] This shift away from Communist influences among the Jewish workers and poor can be illustrated with the following excerpt from the autobiography of a nineteen-year-old male of working class background, a former Communist:

> I didn't want to be a Jew. I became alienated from Jewishness. I didn't like myself as a Jew. . . . Poland regards me as a

Jew, doesn't want me here, and treats me as a stranger. In this situation, in this sad situation, we see our life more clearly. I see that I am a Jew. Somebody said to me rightly when I was an internationalist that I worried about all humanity, about all nations but forgot my own nation's misfortunes. But today . . . I look around and see that Poland's independence is not my independence . . . because they don't want me here, because I am despised and I am in danger. Any Polish ignoramus, who does not have my knowledge of Polish culture, can with pleasure and without fear of punishment attack me, my honor and dignity, with words and fist because he is a Pole and therefore a "defender of Polish culture." But I am a Jew and therefore not human. Try to defend yourself verbally and you're accused of insulting the Polish nation.* But you can be insulted and called a mangy Jew. Because these are not our courts; these are not our prisons. . . . I am becoming interested in Zionism.[10]

But then in 1934–35 the party line changed. The former open, ruthless warfare against Jewish socialist parties (whose leaders were branded as "social-fascists") was replaced by a concerted effort to get them and the Polish socialists and liberals to join with the Communists in a united front against fascism. Although the Bund, as well as the Polish Socialist Party, rejected the initiatives of the Polish Communist Party to set up such a front (fearing infiltration and Communist takeover for the purpose of furthering Soviet aims), the party did enlarge its influence both among Jewish workers and students and among the PPS youth.[11] The "Popular Front" slogans of the struggle against fascism proved to be more powerful in winning over Jews than the party's former policies.

Still, if one regards the interwar period as a whole, one finds that proportionally the party was more successful in attracting and keeping the allegiance of young people from the Polonized intelligentsia than from the lower strata. To them it held out the twin promises of full integration and socialism. Most of the Communists fell into two broad categories: those with and those without Jewish self-identity (or the nonassimilationists and the assimilationists). The native tongue of the first was mostly Yiddish, and many of

---

* In 1938 and 1939 the Jewish press often reported cases of Jews who had been charged in court with insulting the Polish nation, an offense according to Polish law.

them considered themselves culturally Jewish. They clung to the official Soviet version of its benign treatment of nationalities and had difficulty adjusting to the changing Communist line concerning Jews as a nationality.

But with those alienated from Jewish culture, the party did not need to twist and turn to the extent it did in the case of the unacculturated but secularized Jewish workers and poor. Its leaders could invoke Lenin's argument: Once Jews were emancipated from their caste position, the "progressive" solution for them was to assimilate.[12] The assimilationist position, inherited from its predecessor, the Social Democratic Party (SDKPL), prevailed in the Polish Communist Party, in regard to its Jewish middle class recruits, until the party was quietly dissolved in 1938 by the Comintern (making it "one of the last major victims of the great purges").[13]

Members of the prominent assimilationist families and the highly acculturated circles of the upper middle class were overrepresented among these recruits. The Communism of both originated largely in their contempt for the philistine and money-oriented world of their parents.[14] The latter, as well as the rest of the middle class recruits, tended to complete their process of assimilation within the Polish Communist Party. (Some of them defected from the Zionist left organization, *Poale Zion*, within which they seem not to have found an adequate solution to their identity problem.)[15] Cut off from their Jewish roots, they found in the party the conviction that they were not rootless, "for they had the deepest roots in the intellectual tradition and in the noblest aspirations of their time."[16] Culturally estranged from the Jewish masses, those bent on assimilation generally preferred to carry on their activities among the Poles. After all, the Poles were the majority, and if Communism was to be brought to Poland it was more important to win them over. Most took on Polish pseudonyms and tried not to draw attention to their Jewish background. Actually, they were most successful in recruiting and influencing Jewish youth with backgrounds similar to their own, among the university students and among high school students in the upper grades. The combination of an advanced education and no prospects for suitable work, was a strong factor in the radicalization of those students.[17]

For those whose Polish self-identity was nurtured at home—those who hailed from the assimilationist community—the Communist Party offered a solution to their deeply felt stigma: They believed that the stigma of their Jewish background would finally be erased, for Communist society would be without religion and in it religious descent would be wholly irrelevant. They therefore threw themselves with enthusiasm into underground work to bring about such a society. Their enthusiasm and devotion, combined with high education and culture, accounts to a large extent for their rapid rise to elite status within the party.[18] Another important factor in this rise was that they often could "pass" as Poles in their underground activities. And for work with Poles, the anti-Jewish prejudices that characterized assimilationists were not a liability but an asset. Also, these prejudices made it easier for them to swallow the "camouflaged antisemitism"[19] of the Soviet party whose line they mostly toed.

In their indifference to Jewish suffering and contempt for things Jewish, these radical children of bourgeois assimilationist families saw no contradiction to their revolutionary or internationalist position. They also had their revolutionary heroes who in this respect set precedents for them and with whom they could identify. Foremost among them was Rosa Luxemburg, from Poland and assimilated, who made clear that she had no room in her heart for the special sufferings of the ghetto.[20]

Assimilationists were also overrepresented in the Polish Socialist Party and its elite, and largely for the same reasons as in the KPP. (This is suggested by biographical evidence and by persons whom I interviewed, since the PPS, unlike the KPP, did not keep any statistics on the Jewish origin of its members; it considered such information irrelevant and its gathering contrary to socialist ethics.) In preindependent Poland, the PPS proved to be an effective assimilatory agent for Jewish youths from partially acculturated families, and even for some from traditional homes.[21] However, this became less true with the growth of the Bund and Zionism, and ceased almost completely during independence. The

PPS was unable to compete with the Bund among the Jewish workers and poor. The main reason was that both were proponents of a similar brand of socialism, but the PPS advocated the Polonization of Jews while the Bund was devoted to their linguistic and cultural rights as a distinct nationality in Poland.[22]

Since the workers and poor spoke Yiddish and were minimally acculturated, those of them who were attracted to socialism flocked to the Bund, with the exception of those who embraced Zionist socialism. Thus, during the interwar period, the young "Jews" in the PPS were mainly members of the intelligentsia, and they derived from assimilationist families who considered themselves Poles or from highly acculturated middle class homes. Other actual or aspiring members of the acculturated intelligentsia became Jewish nationalists (mainly Zionist although some also landed in the Bund). But their nationalism differed from that of the secularized workers and poor in being more imitative: largely a response to Polish nationalism from which they had been excluded. In the lower strata, nationalism was to a great extent a continuation of the sense of peoplehood that Jews had possessed before, except that its religious elements were replaced by ideological ones.

The Radicalized Poor and the Bund

The General Jewish Labor Bund (commonly referred to as "Bund") held a special attraction for the radicalized workers and poor because of its consistently respectful attitude and behavior toward the language and culture of the Jewish masses. Prominent among the early leaders of the Bund were assimilated socialist intellectuals on whom it dawned that Yiddish ought not to be dismissed as a jargon. Some of them tried hard to learn it. These socialist intellectuals first thought of Yiddish as a means to reach the masses and to spread culture and education among them.[23] But many of them also came to love and appreciate Yiddish as the living language of the people and important elements of their way of life as folk culture. The Bund played a major role in the beginning of the

Yiddishist movement, which raised the lowly "jargon" into a language of literature and art. This movement also used Yiddish as a vehicle for forging a secular Jewish culture, freed from supernatural and fidelistic presuppositions.[24]

The Bund continued to advance this kind of culture among the secularized youth of the lower strata during the interwar period. The reminiscences of Isaac Deutscher provide an insight into the enthusiasm with which workers responded to Yiddish literature:

> I myself wrote Yiddish, and in Yiddish I addressed large meetings of workers—not always political meetings. I still see before me the masses of young and old, workers, artisans and paupers, who flocked in the evenings to listen to the readings of poetry and drama. . . . Nowhere in the world . . . were people so thrilled by listening to their writers and poets as were the Jewish workers of Warsaw and of the Polish-Lithuanian provinces. Here something like a new Jewish cultural consciousness was forming itself, and it was doing so through a sharp break with the religious consciousness.[25]

A similar attempt among the middle class to further a secular Jewish consciousness with Yiddish as its keystone had been pursued by the Folkist party before independence; the effort largely collapsed after independence, as the younger middle class generation was becoming increasingly acculturated. The great exception was Vilno, called by Jews the Jerusalem of Lithuania. Once the city of rabbinical learning, it was now the center of secular "Yiddish" culture (as was Warsaw). In Vilno, the effort to transform that culture from a lower-class into a cross-class phenomenon met with considerable success.[26] It is eminently exemplified in the creation of the YIVO, the Jewish Scientific Institute, with its seat in Vilno. YIVO concentrated and nurtured scholars who produced high-quality works in Yiddish.

It is thought-provoking that during most of the interwar period the greatest successes of the Bund, a supremely political organization, were in the cultural and educational matters, as well as in the trade union area, and not in the strictly political realm. The popularity of the Bund among the Jews in partitioned Poland has been noted, but its political strength in independent Poland up to 1935 was not commensurate with its impressive beginning, despite the increasing class consciousness of the Jewish workers and poor and the radicalization of their young.

Apart from class exploitation and anti-Semitism, an important factor in this radicalization was the behavior of Jewish industrialists and capitalists who frequently, to protect their own economic interests, tolerated or practiced discrimination in hiring. At a time when the Jewish population was being pauperized by the depression and the anti-Jewish practices of the Polish government, and when unemployment was higher among Jews than Poles, large industries, in which rich Jews had invested heavily, excluded Jews from jobs to a similar extent as had state-owned industries. The well known sociologist of that period, Dr. Arieh Tartakower, has written of discriminatory hiring as a common practice of rich assimilationists:

> The foul attitude of the assimilationists to whom "religion makes no difference" but who actually shut the doors before the starving Jewish worker . . . creates a phenomenon incomprehensible to healthy human logic—the boycott of Jewish labor in Jewish industrial establishments.[27]

Actually, not only the assimilationists but also other Jewish capitalists and industrialists did not resist, and sometimes practiced, discrimination by failing to employ Jewish workers. Often they did this under pressure of the Polish unions, who threatened to strike if Jews were hired.[28] In other instances, particularly because of the Compulsory Sunday Rest Law, Jews who refused to work on Saturday were discriminated against. In addition, some enterprises owned by Orthodox Jews did not hire Jewish workers who were willing to work on Saturday; the owners maintained that religious law did not permit them to hire Jews to work on the Sabbath. Then, too, Polish workers were generally preferred because they were considered less troublesome and less class conscious.[29]

Such experiences made Jewish workers ready for socialist ideas. And indeed, the major following and support of the Bund came from them. But the Bund, except for the last few years, was not able to gain political strength among the impoverished lower middle class, which was so numerous. The reason is that even though the Bund championed cultural autonomy for Jews, its main political preoccupation was to advance socialism in Poland.[30] (Like the PPS, it insisted that the Jewish problem would be solved with the advent of socialism.) With the exception of its approach to Yiddish, the Bund failed to respond to the sentiments of the Jewish people concerning important issues, and in critical moments went against them (except in the last few years before the war, when it unexpectedly emerged as a larger force).

This was to some extent due to its doctrinaire anticlericalism. In resurrected Poland, the Bund considered one of its main principles and tasks to be the fight against "the aims of clericalism to dominate Jewish social life." [31] Thus, as early as 1919, the Bund came out in support of the Compulsory Sunday Rest Law, without modifications that would have allowed Jews to substitute Saturday as a day of rest. It lined up on this issue with the Polish Socialist Party (PPS) which, in the interest of Polish workers, insisted that the rest day be confined to Sunday, so as to prevent circumvention of the law. (The Zionist socialist party, Poale Zion, accused the PPS of nationalistic bias and demanded that Jews be allowed to observe the sabbath on Saturday.) And for two decades, the Bund's struggle against Jewish "clericalism" took the form of fighting to transform the kehillot, whose functions were mostly religious or charitable, into secular organs of Jewish cultural autonomy. It aimed to "bore from within" by trying to get its own people elected to these religious councils. Although it did succeed in taking over a few kehillot, its overall design was to a great extent frustrated by the Jewish public, who tended to view the kehillot as religious institutions that ought to remain such. (The votes for Orthodox delegates far exceeded those for Zionists, let alone Bundists.) [32]

But the major obstacle to the Bund's political strength was its unyielding hostility to Zionism while the Jewish population was becoming increasingly sympathetic to Zionist ideas, as it was increasingly made to feel unwanted in Poland. Although the Bund from its very inception opposed Zionism as reactionary chauvinism and a tool of capitalism, it nevertheless shocked Jewish sensibil-

ities when in 1929 it refused to join the general outcry of Polish
Jewry against Arab attacks upon peaceful Jewish settlements in
Palestine. It irritated them further by proclaiming loudly, in order
to justify itself, that the Zionists and the British shared equal responsibility with the Arabs for the massacres of Jews.

In the final analysis, the unpopular stand taken by the Bund
followed rigidly an ideologically narrow class line and on a number
of issues placed the long range interests of socialism above the
current interests of the Jewish people. Often fiercely at odds with
the Communist Party, it nevertheless shared with Communists a
readiness to sacrifice Jews for the sake of a future utopia. The
Bund's top leaders, who made the important decisions about the
party's policies, clearly articulated this subordination of the Jewish
cause to the cause of socialism. Wiktor Alter, one of its most prominent leaders (who together with Henryk Ehrlich was executed
during the war by Stalin on preposterous charges of having committed espionage for the Nazis) wrote: "The hierarchy of my basic
feelings and reactions in social matters is more or less the following: first a human being, next a socialist, and then a Jew." He said
this at the peak of Polish anti-Semitism, when the whole country
was raging with it and added, *"I cannot look at anti-Semitism
from a specifically Jewish point of view."* [33]

But for the Jewish people as a whole, anti-Semitism was a
very specific experience: they suffered from it, while the rest of the
population did not. Therefore, insofar as the leaders of the Bund
could not, or thought they ought not, respond to Jewish suffering
in a specific way, they built a barrier between themselves and the
Jewish community. The various factions of the Bund differed and
argued over socialist ideology and proper tactics,[34] but in its quest
for socialism, the Bund categorically rejected compromise. Being
preoccupied with the question of always taking a "correct socialist
stand," the Bund often found itself left behind, as large portions of
the Jewish population moved toward particular solutions to their
particular problems. And so, whenever the Bund participated in
the national parliamentary elections, it failed to secure the election
of even a single candidate. In 1922, forty-seven Jewish representatives and senators were elected to the Polish Parliament from

other Jewish parties but none from the Bund (which ran its own candiates, refusing to join the National Minorities' Bloc). The same happened in 1928. During the 1930 parliamentary election, out of the 710,191 votes cast for Jewish parties, only 10 percent went to the Bund (compared with 65 percent for the Zionists and 21 percent for the Agudat Israel).[35] As a rule, they also did poorly in municipal elections.

Ironically, the Bund's preoccupation with the purity of its socialist line not only alienated many Jews but also thwarted full cooperation with the Polish Socialist Party, its natural political ally. At the same time, the PPS could not bend too much to the Bund's demands for fear of being branded as Jewish dominated, and thus destroying the chances it might have had to become a major force in Polish politics. Thus, from the very beginning these two socialist parties, whose ideology was so similar in many respects, were not able to arrive at a joint strategy. Later when democracy, according to both of these parties, was betrayed by Marshal Piłsudski, it seemed they would finally unite (1926–30). But the Bund continued to insist upon "Socialist unity on its own terms or none at all." [36] It refused to join the coalition of Polish parties (*Centrolew*), which was formed to fight autocracy in Poland, because it included parties of the center. Instead, the Bund continued to guard the purity of its ideological class line and of its socialist ideals. Earlier much energy had been spent on endless debates concerning proper international affiliation; now these debates were over the proper line the Bund was to champion at international socialist meetings.

The Appeal of Zionism

Zionism took anti-Semitism much more seriously than the Bund ideology did. One of its basic tenets was that anti-Semitism would not disappear in Europe, and particularly in Poland, as long as the Jews remained there. Thus Zionism insisted on a territorial solution: the Jews could solve their peculiar problem only by regaining their ancient homeland.[37] This is the fundamental way in which it differed from the other modern ideologies that attracted Jews, especially the socialist ones. And it is this unique feature which brought great numbers of Poland's Jews to Zionism. To more and more of Jews it appeared that the only solution left was to get out of there. During the interwar period, Poland provided the bulk of immigration to Palestine.

When independence arrived, Zionism had not yet penetrated deeply into the small towns, but it soon swept the young of the most traditional shtetlekh. It also attracted many of the acculturated middle class Jews. Since Zionism stressed that the return to the Land of Israel meant a return to the original sources of Jewish life and Jewish creativity, symbolized by the Hebrew language, it enabled Polonized Jews to sublimate their negative attitudes toward Jewish "ghetto" traits and toward Yiddish. Actually, Zionism became the strongest political movement because it appealed to heterogenous categories of Jews, in small towns and large cities, varying in degree of acculturation, in class background, and along the dimension of conservatism-radicalism. But this heterogeneity also accounts to a considerable degree for the numerous splits and for the number of different parties within the Zionist movement.

Strongest at the beginning of independence, particularly in terms of influence among voters, were the General Zionists and the Mizrachi, both centrist parties in orientation. (The majority of the Jewish members of the Polish Parliament were elected on their tickets.) The General Zionists constituted the party of democratic liberalism, geared toward the interests of the large Jewish middle class that was becoming pauperized in Poland. They defined themselves as placing the interests of the Jewish people and *Eretz Israel* (the Land of Israel) above class interests and as being neutral on the issue of religion. The Mizrachi was in the center among Jewish parties, but was the most conservative among the Zionist ones. It was the only party to combine Orthodox Judaism with modern Zionism.

Considered as the Zionist right (what now would be termed the radical right) was the Revisionist Party, which in 1935 finally split from the Zionist Organization. It advocated self-defense through paramilitary organization and the mass "evacuation" of

Jews from Poland to Palestine, by any means necessary. To the left of the Zionist center was the Labor Zionist movement. To it belonged the non-Marxist labor groups (for whom Zionism took precedence over socialism), associated in the *Hitahadut* (United Zionist Labor Party).[38] The activities of Hitahadut centered on pioneering efforts in Palestine, and it attracted many of the youths preparing for immigration to Palestine. It championed the revival of Hebrew, in contrast to other Jewish socialist groups which favored the retention of Yiddish. Farther to the left within the Labor Zionist movement was the socialist party, *Poale Zion*, which in 1920 split into right and left. In Poland the left Poale Zion became the stronger of the two. It opposed the cooperation with "bourgeois" Zionist parties, and did not participate in Zionist congresses. However, it cooperated with the Bund in the cultural field, favoring Yiddish over Hebrew, and sometimes with the Communists on political issues. A minor party, it was weak among the workers and poor, and a bit stronger among the intelligentsia.[39]

Each of these Zionist parties had its youth organizations, as did the non-Zionist Jewish political parties and the radical Polish parties to which some Jews belonged. In the interwar period, there was hardly a person outside the traditional Jewish community who during adolescence or young adulthood had not been a member of a youth organization. Most popular were the Zionist ones, which in addition to the party youth organizations also included independent youth movements, such as the left socialist *Hashomer Hatzair*. This organization attracted educated, Polonized middle class youth, many of them high school students. But being Marxist in orientation, it also made a concentrated effort to recruit working class youth.[40] The combined membership of the Zionist youth organizations and movements far outranked in numbers the youth of any non-Zionist party.

Once in them, the youths became imbued with the idea of the regeneration of the Jewish people in their ancient homeland. Numerous cultural activities of the Zionist youth organizations revolved around this goal, the study of Hebrew being among the foremost. Small study groups met periodically, under the guidance of a senior member, to discuss ideological and social issues. The reminiscences of a young woman about her early days in Ha-shomer Hatzair, as a high school student, allow us to glimpse into the activities of the Zionist youth organizations:

> The organization which I joined early, as well as school, had a decisive effect on my life. The older members succeeded in binding us so to the organization that it became precious to us. There was not a day, when I did not spend a few hours there. Our guides organized lectures and discussions on varied subjects and instilled a way of independent thinking and healthy criticism.[41]

And paradoxically the very qualities developed in the organization they first joined—critical thinking and a political approach to problems—often resulted in their leaving this organization for another one. As they were approaching young adulthood, there was the gnawing feeling that the organization in which they had been so happy when they were "young" and "naive" did not really have the correct answers for bettering their own and Jewry's deteriorating situation. There was much shifting from one organization to another, within one camp—such as the Zionist one—or across political camps. Here is the example of a young locksmith, who was first recruited into the Hashomer Hatzair by his fellow apprentices, who after a while came to join the organization's direct opposite within the Zionist camp, the *Betar* (the youth organization of the Revisionists whose membership was much larger than that of its parent body):

> Socialism in theory had no value for me. I always look at the practice. And the practice was in contradiction to the theory. Instead of love and fraternal feelings, I saw hate for brother Jews—because they thought differently, because they had different political views, because they belonged to another party. . . . I stopped believing in Marxist socialism. I became convinced that socialism would not solve the Jewish problem, a solution for which I longed and continue longing. I joined the opposition; the Revisionist Party, the Betar, to work for the good of our people, for the creation of a Jewish state.[42]

Preparation for Immigration to Eretz

At the outset of Polish independence many young Jews who were shocked and disillusioned by the anti-Semitic violence found a new shining hope in the idea of the return to *Eretz*, the Land (of Israel). During the first years after the Balfour Declaration of 1917, the road to a national home for Jews looked clear. Seemingly, the nations were ready to recognize Jewish rights to their own land, and it was up to the Jews themselves to transform the dream into a reality.

Many younger people were determined to transform that dream into reality. Needed were Jews who would leave their families and go to Palestine, to revive the land that for so long had been left fallow. Often, in deciding on an occupation, the question of

Often, in deciding on an occupation, the question of which would be useful in Palestine became important . . .

JEWISH STUDENTS AND INSTRUCTORS IN THE ORT TECHNICAL SCHOOL WORKSHOP, VILNO. (YIVO INSTITUTE FOR JEWISH RESEARCH)

which would be useful in Palestine became important. A common pattern among middle class girls was to learn a trade, which represented a departure from that class's traditional disdain of physical labor. Both boys and girls threw themselves with great enthusiasm into special programs of preparation for *aliyah* (ascent to Eretz). In October 1918 the first groups began their long journey from Poland to Palestine, arriving in April or May of 1919. As early as May 1919, a national conference was held of representatives of the *Hehalutz* organizations throughout the country. This conference reiterated the nonpartisan character of the Hehalutz: to continue as an organization open to all youths who wanted to engage in "productive" labor and prepare for settlement in Eretz. It was to be the "work reserve of Palestine" whose task it was "to build Palestine for the Jewish people through work." Soon it developed into a program of training for physical labor (on land and in the city), and it attracted many middle class youths who aspired to become working class in their own land.[43] This was not defined as "downward" social mobility, but rather was ennobled by the significance of its mission: to reclaim the land that was still desert and swamp and regenerate the Jewish people.

The *hahshara*, a period of training for service in Palestine, was provided on model farms and workshops set up in Poland for that purpose. The volunteers left home and lived for a year or two on *kibbutzim*, collectives (modeled on the ones in Palestine). Many parents objected to this departure of their children and tried various means and tricks to bring them back.[44] But the youngsters were determined and persisted, for in the hahshara they found meaning and hope. But this hope was disturbed by unexpected events. In 1929 the Jews of Poland were shocked by news from Palestine of Jews being killed and wounded by Arabs who had attacked peaceful communities. The news especially startled the young, most of whom were convinced that they would reclaim their ancient land with work and sweat, not with blood. The pathos of the rude awakening comes through the entries in the diaries of young Jews. A seventeen-year-old girl wrote in 1929:

> Dear God . . . I pray for your mercy. . . . Redeem us and
> bring us to our homeland. . . . terrible things have happened in

Eretz which tear our hearts. The Arabs began to fight the Jews: attacked them and tortured them. . . . These happenings moved us here to organize protest demonstrations. . . . How I would like to see my homeland. . . . When I think about it, the words of Yehuda Halevi come to me. "If I were an eagle, I would fly to you." [45]

A severe blow to the Zionist hope arrived in the form of the White Paper, issued by Britain in 1931, for the first time limiting Jewish immigration into Palestine. The disillusionment that resulted from this is reflected poignantly in the diaries and autobiographies. For example, here are the words of one youth:

We had our great hopes that we would win our beloved land . . . that we would leave the horrible Diaspora in which

A period of training for service in Palestine was provided on model farms and workshops . . .

MEMBERS OF A STONE CUTTERS' KIBBUTZ PREPARING FOR PIONEER-ING WORK IN THE LAND OF ISRAEL. VILLAGE OF KLESÓW, NEAR SARNY, VOŁYŃ PROVINCE.

we have been so long mistreated. But these hopes turned into
nothing. . . . Jews are prohibited from entering Palestine. It is
hard to accept but England, on which we counted and in which
we trusted, has betrayed us.[46]

The White Paper had a devastating effect on the young, especially because of the ensuing economic depression in Poland.
There were no jobs in sight. It was particularly difficult for those
who completed the hahshara, because many of them had to return
home instead of proceeding to Palestine. After the active life in the
kibbutz hanging around the house without prospects of an occupation, waiting for the Certificate of immigration, which was not very
likely to come, proved oppressive. This is conveyed at the end of
the autobiography of a high-school educated twenty-year-old girl
from a Polonized middle class home:

> In the organization they had advised me that if I finished
> hahshara I would be able to go to Palestine. I went to hahshara.
> I worked hard and willingly all year long. I planted beets, har-
> vested potatoes, milked cows. . . . Then I worked in a laundry.
> A year elapsed. I finished hahshara, returned home, and then I
> did not know what to do with myself. . . . For the first time in
> my life I became desperate. . . . Now, the thought that I, a
> grown girl, sit around with my unemployed parents and depend
> on them, together with the other children, to feed me, was terri-
> ble to face. I couldn't stand it. After two weeks at home, I bor-
> rowed some money and lied to my parents that a friend in Lvov
> had found a job for me. I went to Lvov. Only a person who has
> tried to find work in a strange city can comprehend what I lived
> through. I went from office to office, from store to store, looking
> for work. Everyday I studied the want adds in the newspapers.
> . . . . I no longer looked for appropriate work. I no longer
> cared: any work would do. Finally I found work as a nanny.
> Full board and twenty *złoty* [four dollars] per month. It is not
> much but for me it is a treasure.[47]

The Disappointment with Jewish Politics
in the Polish Parliament

The White Paper of 1931 was the kind of startling occurrence that
marks a threshold in a people's view of itself.[48] From then on not

many Jews in Poland could avoid the feeling of being trapped in a pit filled with hostility, as the possibility of even a difficult escape was vanishing. A period of despair began, against which Jews struggled, while fierce political and economic anti-Semitism was engulfing them; and the struggle was made more difficult by the people's increasing disillusionment with the parliamentary politics of the moderate Jewish parties to whom they had earlier given their mandate. Jews came to realize that having representatives in the Polish Parliament was not doing them any good. Disappointment was especially great, because they had allowed themselves, in the early 1920s, to believe what the General Zionist leaders had proclaimed—that representation was an important step toward improving their status.

Inspired by the ideas of Jewish nationalism, encouraged by its successes in the international arena (the Minorities Treaty and the Balfour Declaration), the people had greeted with wide approval decisions of the Jewish political parties, especially the Zionist ones, to run their own candidates for Polish Parliament. To have representatives, sitting in the highest legislative body of Poland seemed then the height of Jewish achievement. In the first general election (1922) a larger number of Jewish representatives was elected to the Sejm than in any of the subsequent elections (35 Jewish representatives in the 444-member Diet; in the last Sejm—1938–39 —there were only five Jewish representatives; in the respective 111-member Senates, there were 12 and 2 Jewish senators). The number of Jews voting in national elections declined progressively and fewer Jewish parties participated.[49]

The great majority of representatives and senators sent to the first regular Parliament (called the Second because the one proceeding it had been a provisional one) were from what was then regarded as the political center; none was from the extreme left.* Almost a third of them belonged to the two religious parties. This

* In the 1922–27 Sejm, when the Jewish representation was the largest, the party distribution of the Jewish delegates was: *Zionist parties*—General Zionists, 15; Mizrachi 5; Hitahadut 4. *Non-Zionist*—Agudat Israel, 6; Folkist Party, 1; Association of Merchants, 1; Independent, 2. The respective figures in the Senate were: 5, 1, 1, 3, 0, 2, 0. A. Haftka, "Zycie Parlamentarne Zydów w Polsce Odrodzonej," in I. Schiper, A. Tartakower, A. Haftka, eds. *Zydzi w Polsce Odrodzonej* (Warsaw, 1935), vol. 2, p. 293.

suggests moderation, which one might mistakenly interpret as a development that the Poles looked upon with favor. The opposite was true, because almost half of the representatives and two-thirds of the senators were elected on the joint ticket of the National Minorities' Bloc. As has been noted earlier, the fact that Jews had joined the territorial minorities was highly offensive to the Poles.

The General Zionists of Galicia had objected to joining the National Minorities' Bloc and had run their own candidates, a number of whom were elected to the Sejm.* Here then was one of the main issues in the split of the General Zionists within the Sejm (between the "Galicians" and the Gruenbaum faction) that began earlier in the Provisional Diet and deepened during the election. This split affected the activities of the entire Jewish Parliamentary Caucus (*Koło*) since the General Zionists were the largest group among the Jewish representatives and senators.

The Gruenbaum faction of the General Zionists consisted mainly of men from former Russian Poland. Schooled in the revolutionary atmosphere of Czarist times, they approached the Jewish question in Poland from the perspective of a theory of nationalities, and pressed for overall solutions for the Polish minorities rather than specific solutions for Polish Jews. Their leader, Yitzhak Gruenbaum, was obstinate and doctrinaire in these views. He was convinced that the Polish government would only fulfill its obligations toward the minorities if pressed into it by parliamentary power. Thus he had worked hard to persuade the Jewish parties to join the National Minorities' Bloc in order to forge such power. The representatives from his faction (elected on the joint National Minorities' ticket) conceived their role in the Polish parliament to be that of an opposition. This in itself antagonized most of the Polish representatives, who failed to be convinced by the Jews' frequent assertions that they constituted a loyal opposition.

Markedly different in views and style were the "Galician" General Zionists, led by Leon Reich and Oziasz (Isaiah) Thon. They

---

* In the 1922 elections, the Bund, Poale Zion and the Folkist Party also refused to join the National Minorities' Bloc and ran on separate tickets. However, they got few votes and of the three parties only one Folkist candidate was elected to the Sejm.

had opposed Gruenbaum's idea of joining the National Minorities' Bloc, pointing to the fact that the Jews were not a territorial minority striving for independence but an indigenous population in all parts of Poland. As such their interests coincided more with the Poles than with the Ukrainians or Belorussians. The Galicians emphasized that the Poles were less anti-Semitic than the Ukrainians and Belorussians, who lacked the Polish tradition of tolerance. And when the Galicians refused to support the joint ticket in the 1922 election, they warned that Jewish participation in the National Minorities' Bloc would cause hostility among the Polish majority and produce a reaction against Jews.[50]

Since such a reaction did indeed occur, the Galicians elected to the Sejm on their own ticket now spoke with a new authority in the Jewish Parliamentary Caucus. Tempered by their experience in Austrian parliamentary politics,[51] they preferred to cooperate with Poles in ways that would strengthen Polish democracy and thus assure a proper climate for the eventual solution of the complex Jewish problem. The Galicians favored a "realistic" perspective of dealing with specific issues and solving concrete problems, without a fixed commitment to the Polish right, left, or center. They believed that many Jewish concerns could be worked out through the direct negotiations of the Jewish representatives with the government in power, instead of Jews' being automatically in the opposition.[52]

In 1925 it seemed more than before that the policy of the Galicians was the right one. The Polish government took the initiative in proposing negotiations with the Jewish Parliamentary Caucus on matters of concern to Jews (particularly the increasing poverty of Jews). But what marked it as peculiar was that this overture was made by a coalition government, in which the anti-Semitic Endecja figured prominently. True, the initial proposal was made by Count Aleksander Skrzyński, Minister of Foreign Affairs and the most liberal member of the Polish cabinet. But after the Jewish Caucus responded favorably (the Galicians had the upper hand at that time), it found that one of the chief negotiators for the government was the Premier, Stanisław Grabski, a leader of the Endecja. This being the case, many Jews doubted that any good would come out of this enterprise. The Jewish Parliamentary Caucus was severely attacked by the Bund, which saw in this rightist government's initiative a clever tactic to squelch the opposition by American Jews to loans from the United States, because Poland had not lived up to the Minorities Treaty. Nevertheless, the negotiations continued and resulted in an agreement, formally signed by the Premier and by the President of the Jewish Parliamentary Caucus, Leon Reich.[53]

But the government did not live up to its provisions and soon resumed economic policies harmful to Jews. The predictions of Gruenbaum, the sharp opponent of these negotiations, had come true. Soon Jews began to refer sarcastically to the government's disregard of the *ugoda* (agreement) as *zagłada* (economic extermination).

Thus the two main approaches to Jewish participation in Poland's parliamentary politics failed to yield positive results for the Jewish population. And, as was shown earlier, so did the most conciliatory approach of the representatives of the Agudat Israel who championed the politics of accommodation with the Polish government. Since much has been said about the internal squabbles of the Jewish representatives,* one ought to note that it is highly questionable that they could have improved the situation of the Jews in Poland, even if they had united. The coalition of the minorities could not have been sustained in the face of conflicting interests and mutual hostility. Alone, the Jewish representatives had only a small vote in the entire Diet. Even when united on specific issues, they could not find enough allies among the Polish representatives. From the very first, when Jewish representatives in Polish Parliament raised the issues of the Jews' national minority rights, they soon proved to be impotent. As indicated earlier, they found little sympathy among the Polish representatives. The most democratic of them insisted that the status of Jews in Poland

* The 47 Jewish representatives and senators of the first regularly elected parliament (1922–27) were divided into five political "clubs." Four of these clubs entered the Jewish Caucus, but the fifth (consisting of one individual!) stayed out. A. Haftka, "Działalność Parlamentarna i Polityczna Posłów i Senatorów w Polsce Odrodzonej," in I. Schiper, A. Tartakower, A. Haftka, eds. *Żydzi w Polsce Odrodzonej* (Warsaw, 1935), vol. 2, p. 321.

should be like that of the democratic West: equality in citizenship, not cultural or political autonomy. When the Jewish representatives tried to protect the Jewish population from economic strangulation, they were mostly alone. Those representatives of the Polish left who were not anti-Semitic found the Jewish members, bent on guarding the "middle class" interests of Jews (mostly in petty trade, small business, and small shops) too conservative.[54]

The complete failure of Jewish parliamentary politics was already admitted in 1929 by the prominent Zionist deputy, Yakov Wygodzki in a speech in the Sejm:

> If we ask ourselves what we Jews have gotten after a decade of our loyal opposition in the Sejm and outside of it, I must answer: the concrete results of this struggle amount to zero.
> . . . It is therefore understandable that feelings of disappointment and desperation are increasing among our masses and those voices are multiplying which assert that we can attain absolutely nothing in Poland by means of loyal opposition.[55]

Reduced in number, the Jewish representatives persisted, in the name of broader, common principles with the Polish nation, to register protests in the Polish Parliament, but they mostly fell on deaf ears. They were subjected to repeated humiliation. As Senator Józef Dawidsohn expressed it, "The government points its finger: with this one of the Jewish Parliamentary Caucus I will talk, but with that one I refuse to talk."[56] The Jewish speakers were often drowned out by the rightists and nationalists, and when they were not, most Polish members looked with disdain on those intruders whose repetitive phrases they became tired of. But as long as they remained in the legislature, what other way was there for the Jewish representatives than to continue to protest? Rabbi Rubinstein, a senator, noted, rather sadly, in 1929:

> In the discussion, it is a most unpleasant moment for us to have to repeat the same complaints . . . year after year. . . .
> But since the attitude to our needs and postulates remains, with minor exceptions, unchanged, the criticism must in the nature of things revolve in this one and the same plane.[57]

Still, at that time and throughout the Piłsudski regime, the representatives of the Agudah, as we have seen, held on to their position that their cooperation with the government would eventually bring beneficial results. But after 1936, even they admitted the futility of parliamentary politics. At the end of the following year the Agudah representative L. Mintsberg, in a speech before the Sejm, made a confession that would have been unimaginable while Piłsudski was alive: "Truly, what sort of goal does the Jewish parliamentarian have in carrying out his tragic mission, which consists in being a helpless and powerless witness to Jewish sorrows." [58]

But he, as well as some Galician Zionists, continued to sit in the Polish Parliament and condemn, to the very end of Polish independence, the injustices committed against Jews. For example, the caucus issued a condemnation of official anti-Semitism in May 1938. This note of protest ended with the assertion that the Jewish population was confident that the government's anti-Semitic theses and program "would not take in the broad strata of the Polish Nation." [59] Whether this was merely a perfunctory remark or an expression of the representatives' hopes, the Jewish population had no such confidence. We have noted how the proportion of Jews participating in the national election declined. And by the time of official anti-Semitism, the Jewish representatives who continued to sit in the Polish parliament were regarded by many Jews as opportunists or fools legitimizing a dictatorial regime. As M. A. Hartglas, a member of the Diet, wrote later in his memoirs: "the sympathy of the Jewish people, turned away from us." [60]

Emigration to Palestine

While Jews were turning from the domestic politics of the General Zionists, they were increasingly turning toward the basic goal of Zionism—the return to Zion. In a sense, the emphasis on pursuing politics aimed at changing the situation of Jews in Poland was a departure from the basic tenets of Zionism. [61] At any rate, the Labor Zionists gradually withdrew from Polish politics and concentrated

Jews continued to sit in the Polish Parliament and condemn to the very end the injustices committed against Jews . . .

DR. EMIL SOMMERSTEIN (1883–1957), GALICIAN ZIONIST, MEMBER OF THE POLISH DIET FROM 1922 TO 1939. ARRESTED IN LVOV AT THE END OF SEPTEMBER 1939, HE SPENT THE WAR YEARS IN SOVIET PRISON. HE RETURNED TO POLAND AFTER THE WAR, AND BECAME ONE OF THE FOUNDERS AND THE PRESIDENT OF THE CENTRAL COMMITTEE OF POLISH JEWRY. (YIVO INSTITUTE FOR JEWISH RESEARCH) on activities connected with emigration. In the 1933 elections to the Eighteenth Zionist Congress, the Labor Zionists, who prepared people for such emigration to Palestine, won 38 seats; the Revisionists, who were vocal about its urgency, won 20; the General Zionists, who were disparagingly referred to as "*Sejm*-Zionists," won only 12.[62] These figures reflect the change in mood and attitudes of the Jewish people.

In the anti-Semitic atmosphere of Poland, in the midst of a Europe menaced by Hitler, the vision of the return to Zion contained a promise that quenched despair. That vision, that mystic Messianic hope which "secular" Zionism retained, was now claiming more secularized Jews than ever before. A nineteen-year-old boy noted in his diary: "What a mass mania. The Jewish youth is dominated by a Palestine mania." [63] But only a small part could get there since immigration to Palestine was severely limited.*

The despair of Polish Jews, and particularly the youth, is symbolized in the quixotic plan and attempt to march by foot to Palestine, in total disregard of passport and visa regulations. The plan, which envisioned tens of thousands but actually involved only around a thousand, received wide coverage and criticism in the Jewish press. It ended of course in failure: the marchers had barely reached the outskirts of Warsaw before the police took them on.[64] But the knowledge of it may remind us how much the Jews of Poland wanted to leave in the last few years before their final entrapment. For this happened in 1937, at the time when Arab terror against Jews was raging in Palestine. (These, called by the British "Palestine disturbances," lasted from 1936 to the beginning of World War II.)

In order to exploit fully the very limited possibilities for Jewish emigration to other countries, as well as Palestine, a Central Jewish Emigration Agency was founded, with branches in the major cities. It helped individuals to trace close relatives abroad, to obtain necessary documents and clearance for leaving, and to arrange

---

* And in the niggardly number permitted to enter Palestine—as compared to the millions of Jews trapped—preference had to be given, in the late 1930s, to German Jews, who then seemed in greater immediate danger than the Jews of Poland. V.D. Segre, *Israel—A Society in Transition* (London: Oxford University Press, 1971), pp. 60–62.

transportation. Instruction was also provided in the languages of the New World.

Wealthier Jews had better chances to enter the United States, if they could demonstrate that they would not become a burden to the state. They also had received preferential treatment for Palestine, under the capitalist-visa arrangement. But these, too, were frustrated by the Polish government's stringent rulings and controls against the transfer of wealth abroad. Nevertheless, the Jews were highly overrepresented in the total emigration from Poland and overwhelmingly so in the emigration to non-European countries. A total of 395,223 Jews emigrated between 1921 and 1937, their proportion in the total emigration from Poland being more than twice as large (21.7 percent) as their proportion (ca. 10 percent) in the total Polish population. Regarding the emigration to non-European countries, as many as 64 percent of all emigrants from Poland during the 1931–38 period were Jews.[65] The latest specific figures available show that 19,026 Jews emigrated from Poland in 1934 and 30,703 in 1935.[66]

As high as these figures were, they were far from the numbers that would have left had the doors of Palestine, America, and the world at large not been closed to the Jews. Undermined economically, constantly reminded by the government and the Polish press that there was no room for them in Poland, prodded by slogans of "Jew go to Palestine," not many Jews continued to believe in the 1930s that there was a future for them in the land they had inhabited for centuries. This is reflected in the diaries and autobiographies of young people. Here is one by an eighteen-year-old boy:

> There is only one way out from our situation, to emigrate abroad. This is easier said than done. . . . So what are we to do? We will continue wandering around the streets of Warsaw, Łódź, Cracow and other cities [in search of work]. Often I ask myself: perhaps I am not needed; why do I live? [67]

The Politics of Despair [68]

Such feelings of despair played a part in the increase in the numbers of people, especially youths, who joined the Revisionists. Some transferred their allegiance to them from the Zionist organizations. Growth continued despite concentrated attacks on Revisionists by Zionist organizations and the Jewish press who accused them of being fascists.[69] The paramilitary character of their youth organization, the Betar, and its ideological emphasis on armed struggle (even if its battle sights were directed primarily at Britain) were compatible with Jewish youth's new posture of resisting the victimization of Jews. But what particularly attracted people to the Revisionists is the urgency with which they called for the mass "evacuation" of Jews from Poland and Europe. This made much sense to increasing numbers of Polish Jews who saw the walls of hate closing in on them.

In contrast to the growth of the Revisionists, which was consistent with the growing sentiments of Polish Jewry to leave Poland, the great gains of the Jewish Bund during the last five years before World War II, represent a seeming paradox. For the Jewish Bund persistently rejected the idea of Jewish exodus from their centuries-old "fatherland," whose "sons" they wished to be considered. In 1937, in its Congress Manifesto, the Bund reaffirmed its position: "Today, as always our slogan is still true: right here [in Poland] and not elsewhere—in a relentless fight for freedom, arm in arm with the working masses of Poland—lies our salvation." [70]

It responded to the Polish campaign for Jewish emigration with its own strong propaganda. "Anti-emigrationism" constituted one of its chief arguments against Zionism. And yet this very position helps to explain why the Jewish voters elected more Bund candidates than they ever had before in the kehilla elections of 1936 (in Warsaw, Lublin, Vilno), and in the municipal elections of December 1938 and January 1939 (in Warsaw and Lódź).[71] In a sense, the vote for the Bund represented an answer to the Polish government's and the Polish political parties' persistent and humiliating assertion that there was no room for Jews in Poland, that they must emigrate. The Bund's strong line about the right of the Jews to stay in Poland served as an anchor for many, even if they did not share its ideological premises. By voting for the Bund it seems that numerous Jews, with no other country to go to, affirmed their right to continue to live in Poland. To the Bund's credit, it did not interpret its stunning and unexpected electoral successes as expressions of wide acceptance of its socialist ideology. Rather, it recognized its triumph as a protest vote.[72]

Lack of prospects for leaving Poland, coupled with the bankruptcy of Jewish parliamentary politics, influenced the Jews to shift their attention to local politics. Stuck in Poland, they saw a chance to affect decisions that would govern their everyday life, if they elected strong men in the municipal elections. And the Bund symbolized for them strength in general, and physical strength in particular. The manual laborers in its ranks, seasoned in trade unions and strikes, projected an image of the kind of strength that was needed to protect Jews from violence.

After 1935, it no longer seemed to matter who organized protest or who organized defense, but rather who was most effective in doing it. At this time of acute crisis, the Jewish people as a whole were ahead of their leaders and ahead of their organizations, which continued to be divided, engaging in shrill ideological monologues and accusing the others of grave error or betrayal. Regret for the lack of unity can be found in various articles in the Jewish newspapers and periodicals of that time.[73] A number of articles in leading Jewish newspapers directly addressed the problem. Dr. I. Schwarzbart, a prominent Zionist leader, attempted to analyze objectively why the few initiatives taken toward organizational unity had failed, despite widespread recognition among the Jewish public that it was necessary. And he asked a momentous question a year before the physical destruction of Polish Jewry began:

> Can one state, therefore, that Polish Jewry—faced with the overbearing and adamant threats to its collective life—is stricken with a constitutional societal ailment which does not permit it to lift itself from division to unity, or least to cooperation, despite the unquestionable necessity to join its forces to a common denominator?

The author ended with the warning that the joining of forces had to take place right then "because the arms of the clock of history today move very fast." [74]

Part of the answer to Dr. Schwarzbart's question could be found in the same newspaper six months later in an inconspicuously placed comment: "The Jewish people are not at fault here but its leaders who quarrel about differences that are too subtle and magnified for most people to understand." [75] And the rest of the answer might well have been that the people would have soon bypassed their leaders in forging certain forms of unity, had the "clock of history" not raced so fast, had the Holocaust not come so rapidly.

As far as formal unity of Jewish political organizations around common goals of resistance is concerned, leaders of the Bund were certainly no less and probably more to blame for blocking it than the leaders of the other parties. Significantly, in the last few years they were more intransigent in their position than the "clericalists," the traditionalist Orthodox—Agudat Israel. When as late as the autumn of 1937 a few prominent Jews set out to forge unity by organizing an emergency Congress of Polish Jews, the Bund did not simply refuse to support it, but actually attacked the organizers strongly, both ideologically and *ad hominem*. In the leading article of the Bund's theoretical organ in Polish, they were dismissed as "Six Zionists" who represented the "consolidation of the Jewish bourgeoisie" that is "foreign to the Jewish working masses." The article underlined that as "true" Jewish socialists the Bundists would have nothing to do with this venture:

> Not only because socialism cannot be reconciled with Zionism. But above all because Jewish socialism is the Bund. *And the Bund has rejected and continues to reject categorically any conception of Jewish national unity.* [76]

And yet not only Bundists and their sympathizers but thousands of Jews who favored a Jewish national home in Palestine joined the Bund in the protest actions it organized. For the Bund's "slogans, appeals, and tactics had a clearing of noncompromising struggle against anti-Semitism." [77] Time for compromise and moderation had passed as anti-Jewish violence and humiliation rose. Mass protest from 1936 on involved multitudes who never protested before and many who were previously apolitical. Numerous spontaneous Jewish demonstrations sprung up on the streets of Poland and the police promptly broke them up. Harder to suppress was organized protest. (That it came off so impressively may be partially due to the fact that the Communists were no longer undermining or disrupting such efforts by the Bund but, on the contrary, were active in such protest during the period of the "United Front.") On March 17, 1936, a half-day general strike, originally called by the Bund to protest against the Przytyk pogrom, turned into an impressive mass Jewish demonstration against organized Polish violence. The Jews seemed to have been heartened by this demonstration and particularly by the fact that some Polish workers, mostly socialists, joined them in protest. A year later, after the Brześć pogrom, a number of Jewish parties called for a demonstration to protest the government's failure to punish the incite-

Police broke up spontaneous Jewish demonstrations. Harder to suppress was organized protest . . .
A MASS DEMONSTRATION IN WARSAW DURING THE 1930S. (YIVO INSTITUTE FOR JEWISH RESEARCH)

ment to violence against Jews. Again the turnout was massive. In the fall of the same year (October 19, 1937), a mass protest was held in Warsaw against the seating ghettos and the terror at the universities. A Jewish high school youth wrote in his diary about this protest:

> The whole Jewish community chose to protest against this injustice. . . . We know well that after the university ghetto will come ghettos in other aspects of life. . . . I got up early. Despite the warning of the school director, I found many schoolmates in front of the school ready to join the march. It did not materialize because of the division among the delegates [of the different parties]. . . . But the streets were filled with Jews[protesting]. Jewish stores were closed. The whole community showed its solidarity. . . . nobody forgot this day. It stayed in our minds as one of the important Jewish days.[78]

And so it went to the very end. On April 28, 1939, Hitler renounced the German-Polish nonaggression treaty, which foreshadowed the horrible events soon to come. A few weeks later Polish Jews learned of the new White Paper that the British had issued which closed the doors of Palestine even tighter. (Order 6019 limited Jewish immigration to a final 75,000 in five years.) [79] Again the Jews protested. May 22, 1939, was proclaimed as a day of fast, and all work stopped for a few hours as a symbol of protest.

Self-defense

The Jews of Poland also took to both spontaneous and organized self-defense against violence and humiliation. Some of it was in the form of legal defense. It began in 1936 with the Przytyk trial, when Jewish victims of the pogrom were treated as if they were the guilty. As reported then by one who covered the trial, it reflected the tragic situation of a people "who day in and day out are attacked, who are supposed to be protected by the police and are not, but to whom it is forbidden to defend themselves, especially to organize themselves for self-defense." [80] By 1938 more cases of anti-Jewish violence came to court. The perpetrators often went free or if convicted received short suspended sentences. In addition, legal defense was provided by the Jewish community for poor Jews whom anti-Semitic nationalists dragged to court on trumped up charges of insulting the Polish nation. Usually these were instances of Jews returning in kind the anti-Semitic insults heaped at them by Poles. If the Jew at whom the derision "mangy Jew go to Palestine" was hurled threw back the common retort "Polish pig," he risked being charged with insulting the Polish nation.[81]

The saga is yet to be written of the peculiar heroism of plain Jews, often without a political ideology, sometimes deeply traditional, who responded quickly to danger and whose acumen frustrated some plans of those Poles who wanted more Jewish blood shed. How many pogroms, how much violence was prevented by humble men in the small towns of Poland will unfortunately never be known. Indirectly I stumbled on a few cases during my interviews. And some information is available about the tiny town of Przytyk because of the infamous pogrom of 1936. An earlier pogrom, planned for a certain Friday in September 1935, had been thwarted because some of the town's young Jews had learned that the local Jew-hater was recruiting out-of-town militants for that day. About twenty young Jews organized themselves for self-defense; they assembled sticks, iron bars, and a few revolvers. They were helped in their efforts by a few Poles, liberals and PPS members. Having learned of this, the anti-Semitic planners did not go through with their action.[82]

The 1930s were also a time of the beginnings of organized self-defense on part of Jewish political organizations. A study of this is needed. Written documents are rare, for Jewish self-defense was *de-facto* illegal and was treated as defiance of authority. Those involved in organized self-defense had to be careful not to give the authorities evidence for prosecution. Considering the political situation in Poland after 1935, "it would have been suicidal to write, document, or report about organized self-defense."[83]

In the first two-decades of the century, socialist-Zionists as well as the Bundists were in the forefront of the pioneering efforts for organized self-defense.[84] After independence, however, a much greater role apparently was played by the Bundists. Their ideological opposites, the Revisionist youths of the Betar organization, also engaged in self-defense, which grew out of their basic ideological credo that Jews can stop bearing the brunt of violence only by mobilizing to fight it. However, the degree to which the young Revisionists translated their fiery rhetoric into defense action in Poland has unfortunately not yet been researched. But an important beginning has been made in the study of the Bund's accomplishments, which seem to have been impressive.[85]

The Jewish Bund had two organized militias that spearheaded defense, the *Ordener-grupe* and the *Tsukunft-shturem*. The former was organized in 1920–21 to provide protection to the Bund (to its members, officers, headquarters, etc.) from armed attack by nationalists and Communists. The latter were the militia of its youth organization. The Bund's militias were very much confined to this function until the 1930's. As Poland's internal politics became dominated by anti-Semitism and as violence, proclaimed under the slogans of patriotism, became unleashed against defenseless Jews, the function of the Bund's militias shifted to that of defending Jews: "their livelihood, dignity, honor, and often their very lives." [86]

This transition was not difficult for it to make, since it did not confront the Bund with ideological contradictions and therefore did not require ideological compromise, which the Bund abhorred. According to the Bund's socialist ideology (as well as that of the Polish Socialist Party and the Communist Party), anti-Semitism was a class phenomenon: it was a weapon used by the ruling class to divide and weaken the proletariat. Therefore, to fight anti-Semitism was to fight against the ruling class and for socialism. (Contrast this with the question of unity with other Jewish political parties. The Bund, which regarded these parties as bourgeois, was concerned that such unity would signify its own betrayal of socialism.) The Bund's intentions in regard to anti-Semitic violence were most clearly articulated by one of its top leaders, Z. Arthur, at the 1937 protest rally against pogroms:

> Today the Jewish working class is saying to the fascist and
> anti-semitic hooligans: the time has passed when Jews could be

The saga is yet to be written of the peculiar heroism of plain Jews . . .

AN OLD MAN WOUNDED IN A SMALL SHTETL POGROM OF THE 1930'S. TERESPOL, LUBLIN PROVINCE (YIVO INSTITUTE FOR JEWISH RESEARCH)

subjected to pogroms with impunity. There exists a mass of
workers raised in the Bund tradition of struggle and self-
defense. With them one can wage war, but not pogroms that
remain unpunished.[87]

The Bund's militia groups would promptly move into trouble
spots and situations where Jews were apt to be harassed, intimidated, and beaten up. Often they dispersed nationalists who were
picketing Jewish stores and preventing Polish customers from entering. They patrolled parks and streets where Jews were being attacked by the nationalist hooligans. When terror reached the universities, members of youth militia waited nearby to teach the
hooligans a lesson.

Professor Leonard Rowe has distinguished four major patterns
in the Bund's program of defense.[88] First, much attention was
given to preventive action: to be present in sufficient force in
places where trouble was expected. Such a show of force often
resulted in an abandonment by the would-be attackers of their
original plans. This happened, for example, in the towns of Ot-
wock and Myszków, where pogroms had been planned but where
in each case, a contingent of defenders showed up (Jews from
Bund and Poale Zion and Poles from the PPS and KPP).[89] Second,
when unexpected assaults took place, the strategy was to get there
quickly and to give battle. Third, in order to teach the Polish terrorists that Jews were not easy targets of terror, "it was at times necessary to entrap them into areas and situations where this could be
done." Fourth, infrequently but dramatically, retaliation was meted
out, as in the case following the 1937 attack by ONR nationalists
on the Bund headquarters in Warsaw. Subsequently the ONR
headquarters were stormed and smashed.

Such dramatic and effective retaliation against the fiercest
anti-Semitic perpetrators of violence were quick antidotes to feelings of despair and helplessness among Jews that their objective
situation gave rise to. Jews were also encouraged by the participation of some Poles, mostly members of the Polish Socialist Party
in defense actions. Whether or not numerous enough to affect the
outcome, the very fact that Poles joined them was of considerable
symbolic significance.[90]

The effectiveness of the Bund's defense program was tied to the fact that a large part of its membership consisted of manual workers who "had a lot of muscle power" as well as revolutionary zeal. And, when needed, it could mobilize more Jewish workers from the Jewish trade unions in which the Bund influences predominated: freight porters, slaughterhouse workers, etc. (whose work required physical strength). But it must be added here that the personal ties of the Bund's leaders to Polish socialists greatly facilitated the Bund's defense operations.[91] Also, in the last two years before the war broke out, cooperation between the Bund and the PPS was greater than ever before. Through the Polish Socialist Party, the Bund frequently received reliable information about violence planned by anti-Semitic groups, which some Polish workers reported to their Party.[92] Thus, the Bund's militia groups were able to surprise the anti-Semitic hooligans, who expected free reign. having picked Jews least able to defend themselves.

Apart from curtailing the escalation of anti-Semitic violence in Poland, Jewish self-defense played a tremendous part in sustaining the morale of the Jewish people at a time when hate at home and abroad was so threateningly focused on them. And this morale expressed itself in a continued effort to prevent the collapse of special services for the needy, despite the increasing poverty of the Jewish population and harassment by local government authorities. In most cities and towns of Poland one or more traditional Jewish welfare organizations existed. Impressive modern welfare institutions were maintained in the larger cities, with the aid of foreign Jewish relief funds.[93]

The special generosity the Jewish community displayed toward the thousands of Jews whom the Nazis expelled to Poland deserves notice here. On October 28, 1938, Polish-born Jews were aroused from their sleep by the Nazis and driven across the border to the Polish town of Zbąszyn. Polish Jewry rallied to offer hospitality and relief to these victims of Nazism. Reports in the Jewish newspapers of that time bear testimony to the extraordinary effort made by Polish Jews. Jewish university students opened their dormitories to the German refugees. In his autobiography, a Cracow University student who lived in a student dormitory described his experience:

One night we were waked to give our beds and bedding to the refugees from Germany. At first I thought it was a new form of hazing but soon learned otherwise. The refugees presented a horrible sight, hard to describe. We put two hundred people in the gymnasium. . . . Some refugees were afraid to enter the building, thinking that it was a prison. . . . The number grew. New transports were coming. . . . Like many others, I did everything possible for the refugees.[94]

We now know that the refugees described above represented a modest preview of what was to become the fate of Polish Jewry a year later. But how could Polish Jews have admitted to themselves that their doom was at hand? How could they have imagined the concrete forms it would take? Even today, our minds cannot en-

Jewish morale expressed itself in continued effort to prevent the collapse of special services for the needy . . .

A SUMMER CAMP FOR JEWISH CHILDREN IN POŚPIESZKA, OUTSIDE OF VILNO, 1930S.

compass them, although we know they took place. In the last two years before the Nazis invaded Poland, a phantomlike fear permeated the atmosphere of the Jewish community. As a nineteen-year-old Jewish worker wrote in his diary on the last day of the year 1938—that crucial year of the Munich Pact when the civilized world sought to pacify the Nazis by sacrificing Czechoslovakia:

> Today is the last day of the year. It has been a year full of injustice and suffering, a dark year. There has been not a ray of hope in the darkness of 1938 . . . And how will the future be? . . . What are the reasons for young people to rejoice on New Year's Eve? Why forget that 1938 was also greeted with joy and brought only misery, the worsening of our situation? Dark and hostile forces surround us, as 1939 approaches. . . . Can one appeal to the conscience of the world and people? Will quick help come forth when it will become necessary to fight? [95]

But most Jews tried to fight such feelings, to shake the specter of despair and carry on from day to day. Jews frequently repeated in a humorous vein that the Hitler program could not be realized in Poland because every Pole had his Jew (*swego Moszka*) whom he would save. And since there were over 20 million Poles and only 3 million Jews, the Jews would unquestionably survive. The Nazi period proved this story to be what it was: Jewish laughter through tears. In their martyrdom, they were mostly without Polish help, both physical and moral.

Epilogue:
The Jewish Remnant
in Post-War Poland*

Polish soil became soaked with the blood of Jews and shrouded with their ashes during the German occupation. As there was mostly no help for daily survival, so there was little help given to the armed uprisings in the Jewish ghettos. Of the three million, only about 50,000 Jews survived on Polish soil.[1] The fact that they outlasted the Nazi hell is foremost a testimony to their indestructible will to live.

However, indispensable to that survival in many cases was the supreme humanity of exceptional Poles. Their individual deeds were very compassionate and truly heroic. In aiding Jews these Poles often risked their own lives and those of spouses and children.[2] The Jewish people have recognized the debt they owe to these wonderful Poles by planting trees in their memory in Jerusalem's Yad Vashem and by bestowing upon them the honored title of "Righteous Among the Nations." By doing so they have not

*I began writing this updated and enlarged version of the original epilogue on April 19, 1993—that grevious day when Jews and their Christian friends commenced to commemorate the 50th Anniversary of the Warsaw Ghetto uprising which symbolizes the ruthless destruction of Polish Jewry.

absolved in any measure Poles who could and did not help, the numerous who gloated over the misery of Jews, the fewer who from naked hate or for private gain denounced hiding Jews and turned them over to the enemy.

When the survivors on Polish soil came out of hiding and returned to their home towns, they were mostly greeted with hostility or violence. The Nazis had been defeated, and now Poles were killing Jews that the Nazis had failed to kill. Individual Jews were murdered when they came to ask for the return of homes, workshops, or belongings they had left with Poles. Neighbors' hostility toward their Polish protectors was also not all uncommon.[3] The larger number of men, women and children (about 200,000) —who survived imprisonment, sisyphean labor, and hunger in the camps of Siberia and in the Far Eastern republics of the Soviet Union—were transported by the newly installed, Communist-dominated Polish government to Western Silesia (the German territory ceded to Poland in compensation of the Polish Ukrainian and Lithuanian territories annexed by the Soviet Union). When the Jews crossed the Polish border, they were often accosted with such exclamations by Poles as "the rats have come out of hiding" or "I thought you were dead, what are you doing in Poland?"[4]

And yet, in the moral wilderness of post-Nazi Poland, there were a few amazing Poles who were deeply concerned about the gruesome truth that anti-Semitism did not decrease in Poland despite the fact that the bulk of its Jewish population perished in such a monstrous way. Some of these solicitous Poles formed the All-Polish League for the Fight Against Racism (*Ogólnopolska Liga do Walki z Rasizmem*). But their work was "neutralized." The country was run by Stalinists—among them, it must be admitted with sad regret, were men who were born Jews, such as Jakub Berman and Hilary Minc. They had abandoned their Jewish identity and with it any concern over the continuity of Jewish existence. The Communist leaders were cynical in their pacification and even manipulation of anti-Semitism in order to ingratiate themselves with the Polish people and thus gain power over them.[5]

And so rumored pogroms were not prevented: they were organized in a number of towns (Cracow, Chelm, Rzeszów and others), of which the one in Kielce became best known. About 200 Jews returned to Kielce, and they attempted to reconstruct a community, even if undersized, on the ashes of the prewar one that consisted of around 18,000 members out of a total population of 60,000. When attacked, they could not defend themselves because the few defensive weapons they possessed were confiscated by the police a day before the pogrom took place on July 4, 1946. As a result, 42 Jews were killed and some wounded. Like those in prewar times, this pogrom—as well as all others—started from the blood libel. The "tortured and murdered" boy of Kielce was hidden by the organizers of the pogrom and later found alive.[6] Think of it: after rivers of blood of hundreds of thousands of Jews soaked Polish soil (prior to and during the gassing of millions), the blood accusation was raised again, against the Jews! The pogroms were not officially condemned by the Catholic Church, which, despite its persecution in Communist Poland, remained the bastion of Polishness.[7] But the Catholic intellectual weekly, *Tygodnik Powszechny*, did protest and appeal to Poles to stop the carnage of the Jewish remnant.[8]

News of the pogroms prompted many of the Jewish survivors to flee *illegally*, at the risk of their lives, for refugee camps in Austria and Germany (former German concentration camps) in the hope of eventually being able to go to Palestine (Israel did not exist yet).[9] But about 85,000 continued in Poland, many lured by the promises of a just, socialist society. Foremost among them were returnees from the Soviet Union, those prewar Communists and their sympathizers with a definite Jewish self-identity, whose native tongue was mostly Yiddish and who were mainly settled in Western Silesia. There were also some who did not leave Poland because they considered it their moral duty to try to reconstruct Jewish life, even on a tiny scale, in the country where a Jewish community had existed for almost a millennium. They were the moral guides and provided inspiration to those Jews who did not leave because they were too old, too sick, or too tired to embark on a new journey. More who stayed on were those who considered themselves Poles, not only of Polish citizenship but of Polish nationality. They were linguistically and culturally Polish and identified themselves as Poles. Some were married to Poles, others assumed Polish names during or after the war. Many had been Communists or their sympathizers before World War II.

The efforts of those bent on reconstructing Jewish life in Poland were thwarted once the Communists became entrenched. At first, the new Polish government, installed with the help of the Soviet Union in liberated Poland, for its own political reasons favored the reestablishment of a Jewish community (mainly to win sympathy, which would help secure its recognition by the United States and other Western countries). The immediate postwar period can be characterized as one of hostility toward the remaining Jews on the part of the Polish population at large but of government protection of the Jewish organizations and institutions (which came into being with the financial aid of American Jewish organizations). The price of this government protection was Communist control of the Polish Jewish organizations and institutions. That control, which at first was hidden, became open once the Communist government was more firmly established in Poland. In 1947, the government began imposing restrictions and in 1949 assumed overt control, forcing Jewish organizations to break their connection with Jewish organizations abroad. (The representatives from the American Joint Distribution Committee were expelled.)

This form of Jewish existence continued until the "Polish October," October 1956, when de-Stalinization began. Consistent with the pattern of modern Polish history, whereby major societal or political changes were accompanied by anti-Semitic manifestations, the beginning of de-Stalinization was marked by strong anti-Jewish excesses. Jews were branded as Stalinists or their lackeys and incited to get out of Poland. It is then that most of the thriving model cooperatives and Jewish schools in Western Silesia— established by Jews with a Jewish self-identity who returned from the Soviet Union—folded. As a result of all these experiences, when the new head of government, Władysław Gomułka, allowed Jews to go to Israel, over half of Poland's Jews left. Most of those who remained did so because they regarded themselves as Poles and continued to have faith in the new "socialist" Poland. Also, many found it expedient to hold on, often under changed Polish surnames, to the high or middle positions they had achieved in the government and its bureaucracy, in the ruling party, in the army, in the intelligentsia, and in the academic or other professions. Nevertheless, they too, ultimately became victims of anti-Semitism in the "socialist" Poland they had helped to create.

The end of liberalization in Poland, like its beginning, was accompanied by anti-Semitism. During March of 1968, an organized "anti-Zionist" (a euphemism for anti-Jewish) campaign was launched against those self-defined Poles whom Polish society as a whole tended to regard as nothing but Jews. It turned into one of the most extensive witchhunts in the history of that country. The harassment began with an attack on and purge of a few people in top positions in the party, in the government, in the army, and in public life, but soon it broadened to include individuals of Jewish origin in all walks of life. They were pressured to provide proof of loyalty to the state and party, proof which, when given, failed to exonerate them.[10] Anti-Semitic insults were hurled at individuals of Jewish descent. The students protesting peacefully against the end of liberalization and the tightening of controls in Poland were alleged to be misled into insurrection and counter-revolution by clever, traitorous Zionist plotters. They were mercilessly suppressed. When interrogated by the police, arrested students of Jewish or mixed parentage were repeatedly asked to state their nationality, and their response "Polish" was rejected as not true. Others who were "real Poles" were asked, "why did you tie yourself to these filthy Jews?" (*z plugawymi Żydami*) or, "why did you allow yourself to be used by these kikes?" (*Mośki*)[11] Their "Zionist" leaders were arrested and put on trial. The parents of these students—sometimes prominent Communists—were removed from their jobs, as were other individuals of Jewish origin. All these were urged to leave Poland, but permission to do so was given to them only if they renounced Polish citizenship and applied for exit to Israel. (Many who did so, changed course in Vienna.)

Of special interest to social scientists and historians may be the fact that the anti-Jewish drive was essentially not the manifestation of an ethnic problem. In contrast to the prewar years, in 1968 Poland had a tiny percentage of Jews (even if one uses the Polish social definition, which includes under that label crypto-Jews and Poles of Jewish descent).[12] Actually, the anti-Jewish occurrences were manifestations of the struggle of various factions within the Polish political elite, operating in the context of Poland's position in the Soviet orbit.[13] They also differed from the earlier ones in Communist Poland in that they were part of an official "anti-Zionist" policy, openly proclaimed at party and mass meetings, as well as in the mass media (rather than secret machinations of powerful Communists).

The fact that the campaign was given a different name, that of "anti-Zionism," did not prevent the Polish people from recognizing it as anti-Semitism. The following saying was circulating in Poland:

> Question: What is the difference between present and prewar anti-Semitism? Answer: Before the war it was not compulsory.

And indeed my content analysis of the Polish Communist daily paper, *Trybuna Ludu*, bore out the above saying. The 1968 "anti-Zionist" propaganda contained all the major themes of the organized prewar anti-Semitic campaign in Poland.[14]

Because it recognized the "anti-Zionist" campaign for what it was, anti-Semitism by another name, does not mean that the Polish public disapproved of it. On the contrary, there was little sympathy for the "Jews" who had constituted a sizable proportion of Poland's Communist elite. One of the strongest convictions, quite widespread in all strata of the Polish population—even the intelligentsia—was that these "Jews" were responsible for the difficulties that the Polish nation was facing: the "Jews" in high positions in Warsaw. Therefore, they tended to see the March 1968 campaign as a successful attempt to transform their country into "the Poland of Poles."[15] There was (and still is) a collective ignorance among the Poles of the fact that what accounted for the oppressive activities of the "Jews"—as in the case of the "real Poles" who were part of the Communist elite—was not their origin or the religion to which they were born but their Communist ideology and Communist indoctrination. In both instances, human vanity to hold on to elevated positions with their tremendous advantages—in contrast to the austere conditions of the people at large—as well as gripping fear of Communist vengeance, if one did not conform to the party line, were determining factors. The "Jews" among them mostly came to Communism as Polonized young idealists in prewar Poland; after the war, when Communism was established in the country with their assistance, some of them turned into villains trapped in their own devices in an insidious system.

Most of those who were victims of the March 1968 "anti-Zionist" campaign left Poland and went abroad into what they termed exile. And so many who tried very hard to dissociate themselves from the Jewish fate were marked as Jews—and marked for that fate by their "indigenous" Polish Communist Comrades, acting with the approval of Soviet authorities.

During a large part of Communist rule in Poland, the subject of Jewish history, culture, and consciousness were largely taboo. Almost eradicated was the memory of the Jewish struggle and of Jewish martyrdom during the Nazi period. The Polish government, like the Soviet one to whom it owed its existence, decreed that Jews must not be cited as particular victims of the Nazis, in writings about that period or in monuments to it. The special nature of the Warsaw Ghetto uprising of 1943 was not to be mentioned; the uprising had to be seen as part of "the national Polish struggle against the forces of racism and fascism."[16] Even the captions of the exhibits in the former Auschwitz (Oświęcim) concentration camp had to conform to this rule; the term *Jew* hardly figured in them.

Also silenced in Communist Poland was the story of those exceptional Poles who risked their lives to help Jews. No honors were bestowed on them; on the contrary, they were excluded from the Veterans Organization, *ZBoWiD*. Individual efforts by former members of the Underground Council to Aid Jews—commonly referred to as *Żegota*—to join the Veterans Organization, on the ground of having fought against the Nazi occupiers, met with no success. (*Żegota* was established in Poland at the end of 1942 and beginning of 1943 by the Polish Government in exile, known as the London Government.) Those former members of *Żegota* who had won any decorations after the war ended received them only from Israel as "Righteous Among the Nations"! Commenting on these occurrences in his memoirs published toward the end of Communist rule in Poland, Stanisław W. Dobrowolski, the head of the Cracow chapter of *Żegota*, sadly asked this rhetorical question: "Is this just? Does a Pole who during four years risked his life to protect Jewish fellow citizens deserve recognition as a fighter against the Hitlerite occupation or does he not?"

The neglect of Polish heroes who aided Jews was part of a larger design determined by Moscow, among them the fulfillment of its anti-Jewish line pursued in the Soviet Union and in its satellites. But even when Moscow's grip was strongest, there were single Poles who decried the disappearance of the Jewish community in Poland. Among the best known, especially in the United States and Israel, for his writings about the Holocaust and the annihilation of Poland's Jews, is Władyslaw Bartoszewski, the former head of the Warsaw *Żegota* and former inmate of Auschwitz. Sometimes tolerated because of his fame abroad, he was nevertheless ultimately arrested in the Communist dictatorship.[17]

A voice that the government tried hard but could not silence was that of the poet Jerzy Ficowski, who refused to "neutralize" his memory of the Jewish tragedy he witnessed as a youth. He was "frequently and generously endowed with bans" and since 1976 could get nothing published in Poland, except in the underground press. Ficowski continued to gaze at the "ashes" and to give "artistically convincing shape to what cannot be embraced by words . . ." His poems convey how this Pole misses the Jews who had been so much a part of the Polish landscape and Poland's life:

> and I wander round cemeteries
> which are not there
> I look for words
> which are not there . . .
> to rescue after the event[18]

If the words of a poet among a people who honor their poets could not pierce their tendencies to demonize and hate Jews, what could? Some optimistic persons in Poland and abroad thought that this was going to come about when in January of 1987—toward the end of Communist rule—Jan Błoński, a "real Pole," a devout Catholic, a distinguished professor of literature at the illustrious Jagiellonian University, dared to call on the Polish people to reclaim their memory of its Jews "whose blood remained in the walls, seeped into the soil" of Poland. In an article entitled "A Poor Pole Looks at the Ghetto," which he published in the esteemed Catholic intellectual weekly, *Tygodnik Powszechny*, he pleaded for Poles to face the question of responsibility "in a totally sincere and honest way." They must, he said, admit their failure during the Nazi period to "fulfill their duties of brotherhood and compassion." And Błoński went on to instruct his fellow Poles how to expiate for this sin:

> We must say first of all . . . Yes we are guilty . . . when we lost our home, and when within that home, the invaders set to murdering Jews, did we show solidarity toward the Jews? How many of us decided that it was none of our business? I repeat, instead of haggling and justifying ourselves, we should consider our own faults and weaknesses . . . It is only this that can gradually cleanse our desecrated soil . . .[19]

This article resulted in a heated controversy in the same weekly as to whether, in fact, the Poles bore any responsibility for the vast deaths of their Jewish fellow citizens during the Nazi occupation. Some articles by prominent authors criticized and others approved Błoński's position.[20] Its editors also received numerous letters expressing the readers' outrage at the "anti-Polish libels" which, they charged, Professor Błoński resorted to in his article. In turn, the editors informed the readers that a great number of their letters because of "their emotional language and tone do not deserve publication." They also added that, contrary to their common assertions, their "very letters testify that anti-Semitism continues to exist in the country, even though today there are practically no Jews left in Poland."[21]

How correct the editors of the intellectual Catholic weekly were in their judgment of Poland's reality is clearly mirrored in the anti-Semitic manifestations that followed the victory of Solidarity and the collapse of Communism. Very supportive of Solidarity were some of the sons and daughters of the former "Jewish" members of the Communist elite. As for the non-Communist Jews who still remained in Poland, the best known among them, the cardiologist Marek Edelman—one of the few surviving fighters of the Warsaw Ghetto uprising—took an active and visible part in the Solidarity movement. He was a member of its Citizens' Committee and was arrested during the declared state of emergency in Poland.[22]

And yet twenty years after the disgraceful Communist "anti-Zionist" campaign—when "Jews" were purged from the Communist Party as well as from the ruling elite—in post-Communist Poland, with its program of democratization, anti-Jewish hate erupted again, contrary to what many in the West expected. The Jews are being blamed for the post-Communist economic and social problems, as well as the brutal Communist past. The concept of the "real Pole of pure blood," as contrasted with the "secret Jew" or the individual in whose veins "bad Jewish blood" flows, echoes widely in conversations and even in the press. The arrival of the free press and free speech heralded anti-Jewish expressions and slogans. Anti-Semitic graffiti has been staring from Polish buildings: "Jews go to Israel," "Jews to the gas," and the Nazi German catchwords, *Juden raus*.

One can try to imagine how Jews felt when their eyes met such signs. A friend who lives in America since 1969 told me with restraint that during his visit to Poland in October of 1990 he kept seeing for weeks on the very wall of Warsaw's *Umschlagplatz* the motto in Polish: "The only good Jew is a dead Jew." This was the loading place from where people were herded in cattle cars for the final journey to Treblinka. He recalled the *Umschlagplatz* from the time he was four years old: he was there, to be taken with the other Jewish children, but his mother succeeded in saving him.

I shall not cite from the shocked reactions of Jews from America and Israel who confronted the new anti-Semitism with its obscene expressions during their travels in Poland after Communism was defeated. Instead, I shall quote from the response of a prominent Pole, Bolesław Wierzbiański, the editor of the New York Polish language daily, *Nowy Dziennik* (*The Polish Daily News*). Upon his return from a visit in Poland, he wrote in the 1–16 December 1990 issue: "For a Pole living in the heterogenous American society or in the liberal Western European countries the phenomenon of anti-Semitism and the placing of responsibility for Polish tragedies and inefficiency on Jews is incredible, embarrassing and harmful." He concluded that if anti-Semitism in Poland is "artificially" promoted, then it must be "eradicated"; if it is a sickness, then it must be "treated."[23]

Wierzbiański expressed himself thus in discussing the first free election in post-Communist Poland. In that presidential election, the anti-Semitic weapon was used prominently and very effectively against the former Prime Minister, Tadeusz Mazowiecki. It may well be that his speaking up for Jews was not the sole factor which cost him the presidency, but it certainly accounts for the very small vote he received. After he publicly condemned the new anti-Semitism, the rumor spread that he, a devout Catholic and the former editor of a Catholic paper, was a covert Jew. His supposed Jewishness was proclaimed in signs on walls decorated with the Star of David and in vicious campaign leaflets. I even heard some Poles—employed in New York but having the right to participate in Polish elections—proclaim with strong conviction that it was out of the question for them to vote for the *Żyd* (Jew) Mazowiecki.

In the same election (in which for the first time in the country's history a worker was elected President) Lech Wałęsa—that worker—referred to himself as a "100 percent Pole" and demanded that the "Jews" in Polish politics not hide their Jewishness but identify themselves as such. In these remarks, he seemed not to hesitate to mention that even Adam Michnik only "whispered" about his Jewishness. Parenthetically, Michnik—a prominent leader in Solidarity—had chosen Wałęsa as the godfather at his son's baptism.

Not surprisingly, Polish crypto-Jews—wounded by this statement by the head of *Solidarity*—denounced it as an anti-Semitic ploy. Significantly, a few years later, during this visit to Washington as the first official guest to the partially completed structure of the United States Holocaust Memorial Museum, President Wałęsa admitted: "I myself stepped on the anti-Semitic landmine." He spoke then about the "moral obligation of Poles to fight anti-Semitism and xenophobia" and pledged that "As long as I have anything to say in Poland, I will oppose anti-Semitism."[24] Moreover, he then announced the creation in Poland of a Council for Polish-Jewish Relations to combat anti-Semitism.

It must not be omitted here that a few months later President Wałęsa made a historic trip to Israel, where he received an invitation, rarely given to foreign statesmen, to address the *Knesset*, Parliament. And in a highly emotional utterance, he apologized for the wrong done to the Jewish people and made a moving appeal for forgiveness: "There were among us those who did evil, those who perpetuated evil. Here in Israel, in the cradle of your culture and renaissance, I ask for forgiveness."[25] That act was subject to much criticism in Poland by the many who maintain with impunity that Poles have no reason to ask Jews for forgiveness. After all, they argue, Poland has been historically the land of tolerance . . .

The above state visit was reciprocated by the Israeli President Chaim Herzog's official visit in Poland. Both were expressions of good diplomatic relations being forged between Israel and Poland, in contrast to the years when Poland was Communist.[26]

The improved relations translated themselves into a joint project of the two governments: the commemoration of the 50th anniversary of the Ghetto Uprising in Warsaw. On the evening of April 19, 1993, a celebration was mounted: a sound-and-light show staged by a Polish director at the 36-foot high Warsaw Ghetto Monument. Theatrical smoke arose from the back and enveloped the monument to simulate the destruction of the ghetto by fire. The noise of a train was supposed to symbolize the cattle cars that took the Jews of the Warsaw Ghetto to the death camp of Treblinka. But a Cantor did intone mournfully the traditional *El*

Moleh Rachamim, the prayer commonly chanted at Jewish funerals. All this was unfortunately preceded by quarreling as to who was fit to represent the ghetto fighters. And representatives of some American Jewish organizations had threatened that they would boycott the celebration unless the Carmelite sisters vacated Auschwitz. At the ceremony that nevertheless materialized, President Wałęsa gallantly motioned Marek Edelman, the surviving Warsaw Ghetto fighter and a party to the above quarrel, to accompany him in laying a wreath at the monument. Prime Minister Rabin also placed a wreath and waxed enthusiastic, even if solemn: "We have opened a new chapter in our relations with the Polish people and government."[27]

Some Polish public figures, inspired especially by Prime Minister Rabin's behavior, thought that this "impressive" celebration in Warsaw would lead to positive changes in Jewish attitudes toward Poles. For example, Jan Nowak-Jeziorański, a prominent figure in Poland, thought that, indeed, the celebration of the Warsaw Ghetto Uprising in itself constituted a "decisive step in Poland's relations with the whole Jewish Diaspora." (Nowak-Jeziorański, like Jan Karski, served during World War II as a courier for the London Government.) He emphasized that "perhaps even the Polish public fails to realize what a great impression this celebration made and how it improved the image of Poland in the Western world."[28] The Polish media reported extensively and movingly the commemoration. One very striking occurrence was the one minute of silence on national television. Nevertheless, there is some indication that the Poles in general were not very pleased with the tremendous attention given to the Warsaw Ghetto Uprising. To them the significant event is the 1944 Warsaw uprising of the soldiers of the Polish Home Army (directed by the London Government in exile), which was crushed by the Nazis as the advancing Soviet Army failed to come to their aid. Then, too, one heard Poles complain in exasperation that "every other day [there] is an important commemoration of this or that . . . People are simply fed up."[29]

There are those Jews outside Poland who see this "show" and other efforts by the Polish government to improve its relations with Jews as chiefly economic maneuvers or attempts to improve the image of Poland abroad. Among them are the extreme pessimists who hold to the view that "the entanglement of Jews with Poles will never be ended and never be healed."[30]

We know how very risky it is for social scientists or historians to predict the future. It is impossible to say when and if the Jewish question will cease to loom so large in Polish consciousness. What can and ought to be said, however, is that today Polish anti-Semitism is not a major Jewish problem. It is a Polish problem for Poles to solve. There are few Jews in Poland. To reiterate, there are only 6 to 10 thousand people in Poland—mostly aged—who openly identify as Jews in a population of 38 million inhabitants. Even if the crypto-Jews are added, in the high estimate of 50,000 to 100,000, Poland's Jews constitute at most a meager one-third of a percent of its total population.

With such a tiny percentage of Jews in that country, it is hard, especially for outsiders, to fathom why the Jewish question continues to preoccupy so many Poles under democratization. In the West this is viewed as a dramatic case of the paradoxical manifestation of "anti-Semitism without Jews." Crucial insight into this puzzling dilemma is gained when one remembers that a high proportion of Poles are convinced that hundreds of thousands— some even think millions—of Jews are present in Poland, but hiding their Jewishness. And so the murdered Jews still live in their consciousness and haunt them as internal enemies to be feared even more because they appear in "the disguise of Poles." In addition, many Poles believe that those Jews whom the Communist government, created by Żydokomuna (Jew-Communism), allowed to go abroad when "real Poles" were not permitted to leave have been spreading falsehoods about them and their beloved fatherland. Poland, the country of tolerance, is viciously depicted by them as anti-Semitic. And what is particularly galling to Poles with such beliefs is that those "terrible" Jews are now coming to Poland as visiting tourists and sometimes as foreign investors, and they perceive them as mockingly displaying their prosperity. Indeed, more Jews born in Poland are visiting, sometimes out of nostalgia for the Polish landscapes—the meadows, the rivers, the

forests celebrated in verses of beloved poems learned in childhood. Their children and grandchildren are arriving in search of
their roots and to learn "first-hand" about the Holocaust. They often leave with images of Auschwitz and of those Jewish cemeteries
still to be found in some of the shtetls which their ancestors left
and which they were drawn to visit. But some also recall that "the
headstones that had been lovingly cut and carved were losing any
sign that human hands had wrought them. They were becoming a
geological layer—a landscape."[31]

As for the Jews who continue to live in Poland—the old
who are too tired and worn to leave and the younger ones who despite everything love Poland or for other reasons choose to remain
there—they know that, if push comes to shove, there is a place to
escape to: Israel. This contrasts with the large number of Jews in
interwar Poland who were harassed to "get out" but had nowhere
to go.

No, Polish anti-Semitism today is not the major problem
that faced the Jews before the war. Still, Jews all over the world,
and particularly in Israel and in America, are—and ought to be—
interested in any efforts on the part of Poles to deal with the
ancient malady of anti-Semitism that continues to inflict their
country. Thus many of them welcome President Wałęsa's and the
Polish government's attempts to eliminate anti-Semitism and appreciate their symbolic gestures of treating Jews with human dignity. Some Jews also tend to regard with hope, mixed with caution, the new moves by the Pope and the Catholic Church to
remove the religious sources and underpinnings of Polish anti-
Semitism. A noteworthy example is the unprecedented event
which took place in Poland on January 20, 1991: during mass in
all Roman Catholic churches of the land, a pastoral letter was read
informing the Poles of the Jewishness of Jesus and Mary (a fact
largely unknown among the masses of Poles) and condemning
anti-Semitism as "contrary to the spirit of the Gospel" and
"opposed to the Christian vision of human dignity."[32]

Of course, as many Jews realize, one reading of a pastoral
letter, as commendable as it may be, will not eradicate the poison
of anti-Semitism lodged in the Polish nation. True, the Church,

more than any other institution or organization in Poland, could play a decisive role in erasing the widespread prejudice and the hate of Jews. But to do so, it would have to conduct continuous and concentrated pastoral work and reshape its religious instruction in the schools. (Since the collapse of Communism, compulsory religious teaching and prayers, characteristic of prewar Poland, have been reestablished in public schools.)

It would be particularly fitting for the Church to embark upon such an influential program because it was the initiator of anti-Jewish activities at the beginning of the Jews' presence in Poland (as was shown in the first chapter of this book). It was also the bastion of hate against Jews throughout their centuries-long existence in Poland. In promoting such an unprecedented drive against anti-Semitism the Church could utilize not only religious sources but also the writing and the legacy of the philosemites— cited throughout this book—who left an alternative Polish tradition for Poles to turn to.

Perhaps it is time for Jewish organizations in the United States and other places to ease up on their preoccupations with Polish anti-Semitism. For the fact is, as the "Righteous Pole," Stanisław W. Dobrowolski, stated in his memoirs: "The history of the Jews in Poland is definitely a closed chapter today." This is so even when recently some few younger people in Poland, mostly of mixed Catholic-Jewish parentage, are returning to a Jewish identity. (Certain American Jewish organizations are giving material and other attention to this occurrence.)

And yet, the link to the past Jewish community of Poland continues to exist, to some limited extent in the Poland of today but much more in Israel and also in the Jewish communities of the Western world, where numerous descendants of Polish Jews live. That link is and will be as strong as the numbers of them who cling to a Jewish self-identity and to a proud, if sad, memory of the Polish community that once was. For that community is now an integral part of past Jewish history for all Jews to share in, as is the Jewish community of Spain whose final tragedy it was destined to eclipse.

Notes

I. Historical Perspective: Tolerance and Hate

1. This chapter is based on numerous historical works in Polish, Yiddish and English. Among the pre-World War II authors of books and articles in Polish, the distinguished historians Maier Bałaban, Szymon Askenazy, Emanuel Ringelblum, and Ignacy Schipper deserve special mention. I would also like to draw attention to the post-World War II book by Artur Eisenbach: *Kwestia Równouprawnienia Zydów w Królestwie Polskim* (Warsaw: Książka i Wiedza, 1972). In Yiddish, the prolific works of Jacob Shatzky and Raphael Mahler are important sources for the history of Jews in Poland. As for materials available in English, apart from the well known scholarly works of S. M. Dubnow and Salo W. Baron, the book that would be of special interest to the general reader is the one by Lucy Dawidowicz: *The Golden Tradition* (New York: Holt, Rinehart, 1964). In writing this chapter, I found the following article very useful: Adam Vetulani, "The Jews in Medieval Poland," *Jewish Journal of Sociology*, 4 (December, 1962): 274–94. And even though I wrote the chapter before the release of Professor Bernard Dov Weinryb's book, I did check it against that important work: *The Jews of Poland—a Social and Economic History of the Jewish Community in Poland, 1100–1800* (Philadelphia: Jewish Publication Society of America, 1973).

II. The Social Definition of the Jews

1. This was expressed by Sir Stuart Samuel in his report on the mission to Poland he headed, on behalf of the British Government, to investigate

The goal of the Polish government and large portions of the Polish nation in the 1930s—a Poland free of Jews—became a reality . . .
TOMBSTONES IN AN OLD JEWISH CEMETERY. NOTICE THE ENGRAVED POLISH EAGLE. (YIVO INSTITUTE FOR JEWISH RESEARCH)

the massacres and ill treatment of Jews. The mission arrived in Poland September 18, 1919, and stayed until December 6, 1920. See: *Report by Sir Stuart Samuel on his Mission to Poland, Presented to Parliament, Miscellaneous No.* 10 (London: His Majesty's Stationery Office, 1920), p. 14. Fifty years later Adam Ciołkosz, a former leader of the Polish Socialist Party and a former member of the Polish Diet, pointed to those figures, among other things, to support his thesis that the extent of Polish anti-Semitism is exaggerated in current treatments of that period by Jewish writers. What he fails to take cognizance of, is the effect that the anti-Jewish excesses had on the Jewish population in general. See: Adam Ciołkosz, "Dzielnica Żydowska Obozu w Jabłonnie," *Zeszyty Historyczne*, no. 20 (1971): 178–99. Also consult the response by a Jewish historian: Yeshaye Trunk, "Di Poylishe Demokratye un Der Heymisher Antisemitizm—(An Entfer Adam Ciołkosz)," *Tsukunft* (May–June, 1973): 226–30.

2. Biography, No. 3834, YIVO Archives.

3. Israel Cohen, "Documents—My Mission to Poland (1918–19)," *Jewish Social Studies*, 13 (April 1951): 149–72.

4. Diary, No. 3580, YIVO Archives.

5. "Der Lager in Yablone," *Der Moment*, July 20, 1920, p. 6. In September 1920, a Jewish soldier, Jakób Klotz—a volunteer in the Polish Army—was tried for desertion because he refused to go to the detention camp. See "Kazimierz Sterling," *Zjednoczenie*, 3, no. 5 (May 1933): 2. See also: Adam Ciołkosz, "Dzielnica Żydowska Obozu w Jabłonnie," *Zeszyty Historyczne*, no. 20 (1971): 178–99. The author, a Pole, regrets this event "for which there is no justification" but argues from a Polish perspective that it was an "episode of small significance." But for the Jews of that time it was an event of much importance, part of a constellation of events that symbolized their precarious position in the newly independent Poland. For how the Polish Jews viewed it then, see the following article to which Ciołkosz refers although he fails to grasp its projection of the subjective side: "A Permanent Pogrom," *Jewish Chronicle*, October, 1920. This side also comes through in: M. A. Hartglas, *Na Pograniczu Dwóch Światów, Pamiętniki*, 1952 (unpublished).

6. "Di Onteyl fun di Yidn in Farteydikn fun Lomze," *Der Tog*, August 9, 1920, p. 7. "Der Oyfruf fun der Yidisher Akademisher Heym," *Der Tog*, July 13, 1920, p. 3; "Fun Yidishn Komitet far Milkhome Farteydikung," *Der Monat*, July 23, 1920, p. 7. See also, Azriel Shohat, "Pinsk Ben Ukrainim, Bolshevikim, Ve-polanim," *Gal-Ed*, 2 (1975): 209–36.

7. For example, the influential weekly, *Myśl Niepodległa*, whose editor was Andrzej Niemojewski. See also, "Di Bashuldikung fun Bolshevizm," *Der Tog*, August 6, 1920, p. 3.

8. He continues: "When the Jewish civil population shot clandestinely from windows and roofs of their houses and threw from them hand grenades." See: "List do Ignacego Paderewskiego," in Józef Piłsudski, *Pisma Zbiorowe*, 5 (1937): 81. It is interesting that Piłsudski cites the prevailing rumors as facts, especially since in the same letter he reported that the Jews and Belorussians agreed to participate in the municipal government he set up but the Lithuanians refused. The Lithuanians were "more shocked by Piłsudski's coup than they had been by the Communist occupation. They protested and continued to denounce the Poles as invaders and imperialists." M. K. Dziewanowski, *Joseph Piłsudski—A European Federalist, 1918–1922* (Stanford, California: Hoover Institution Press, 1969), p. 139. Note that Piłsudski did not raise the possibility that the acts against the Polish soldiers were committed by Lithuanians but ascribed them solely to Jews. Ciołkosz, in discussing similar events in Lvov, mentions that shots were fired at the Polish soldiers from rooftops: "I imagine that the perpetrators were free Ukrainian riflemen, but it was easy to put a rumor into circulation that Jews were shooting." Ciołkosz, "Dzielnica Żydowska Obozu w Jabłonnie," *Zeszyty Historyczne*, no. 20 (1971): 191; For an article on the pogrom in Pińsk which took place under similar circumstances, see Azriel Shohat, "Parashat Hapogrom Be-Pinsk, Ba-hamishah Be-april, 1919," *Gal-Ed*, 1 (1973): 135–73.

9. "Bafel fun Krigs-Minister Vegn Di Eksesn Mitsad Soldatn Oyf Yidn," *Der Tog*, April 30, 1920, p. 11; On reports of attacks in trains: *Der Tog*, June 14, 1920, p. 3; June 30, p. 3; July 15, p. 3; July 30, p. 7.

10. *Tephilin*, are two small leather cases containing slips inscribed with quotations from the Pentateuch: one is fastened with leather thongs to the forehead and one to the left arm during morning prayer. For facts about Rabbi Schapiro's execution, see Eliyahu Eisenberg, ed.: *Plotsk—Toldot Kehilah* (Tel-Aviv, Hamenorah, 1967), pp. 193, 399. All attempts at posthumous rehabilitation, in which the widow was represented by H. A. Hartglas, failed. "Der Toyt Urtl Ibern Rebe Khaim Shapiro in Hekhstn Gerikht," *Der Moment*, December 5, 1920, p. 5.

11. Diary, No. 3580, YIVO Archives.

12. Simon Segal, *The New Poland and the Jews* (New York: Lee Furman, Inc., 1938), p. 202.

13. W. F. Reddaway, "The Peace Conference, 1919," in: Reddaway *et al*, eds., *The Cambridge History of Poland—From August II to Pilsudski* (Cambridge: At the University Press, 1951), p. 499.

14. League of Nations, *Protection of Linguistic, Racial and Religious Minorities by the League of Nations*, Geneva, 1927 (C.L. 110. 127. 1. Annexe.), pp. 42–45.

15. "Traktat z Polską," and "Konstytucja Rzeczypospolitej Polskiej—Ustawa z Dnia 17 Marca 1921 Roku," in Kazimierz Kumaniecki, *Odbudowa Państwowości Polskiej—Najważniejsze Dokumenty 1912–Styczeń 1924* (Warsaw: Czernicki, 1924), pp. 238, 507–29.

16. On behalf of the Supreme Council of the Principal and Associated Allies, Clemenceau wrote in the covering letter, addressed to Ignacy Jan Paderewski and presented to Poland with the Minorities Treaty: "I should desire, moreover, to point out to you that provision has been inserted in the Treaty by which disputes arising out of its provisions may be brought before the Court of the League of Nations. In this way differences which might arise will be removed from the political sphere and placed in the hands of a judicial court, and it is hoped that thereby an impartial decision will be facilitated, while at the same time any danger of political interference by the Powers in the internal affairs of Poland will be avoided." From the letter reproduced in Oscar I. Janowsky, *Nationalities and National Minorities* (New York: Macmillan, 1945), p. 182. Also: "List p. Clemenceau do p. Paderewskiego," in Kumaniecki, *Odbudowa Państwowości Polskiej*, p. 235.

17. See Joseph S. Roucek, *The Working of the Minorities System under the League of Nations* (Prague: Orbis Publishing Co., 1929), pp. 30–38; *Memorials Submitted to President Wilson Concerning the Status of Jews of Eastern Europe, and in Palestine, by Representatives of the American Jewish Congress, on March 2, 1919* (New York: American Jewish Congress, 1919); Letters of Louis Marshall to President Wilson and to Mr. Paderewski, in *Louis Marshall, Champion of Liberty—Selected Papers and Addresses*, ed. Charles Reznikoff (Philadelphia: Jewish Publication Society, 1957), 2: 583–85; 593–95. Joseph Tenenbaum, who was delegated at the end of 1918 to represent Polish Jewry among the representatives of Jewish organizations active at the Peace Conference in Paris, recollected later the concerted effort of these organizations to bring about the passage of the Minorities Treaty. See Joseph Tenenbaum, *In Search of a Lost People—the Old and the New Poland* (New York: Beachhurst Press, 1948), pp. 176–77.

18. An example of this was the excitement produced—according to the Jewish Telegraphic Agency report on July 5, 1924—when the newly elected Board of the Warsaw Jewish Community, which was to meet on July 7, was ordered by the government to conduct its proceedings in Polish and to exclude the public and the press. The Jewish Parliamentary Caucus protested, since the government order violated the Minorities Treaty.

19. "To Leon Berenson," in *Louis Marshall, Champion of Liberty*, vol. 2, p. 630.

20. Aleksander Hertz, "The Case of an Eastern European Intelligentsia," *Journal of Central European Affairs* (Jan.–April 1951): 10–26; Jan Szczepański, Les Classes Sociales de la Societé Polonaise Contemporaine, *Cahiers Internationaux de Sociologie* (1963): 205–11; Aleksander Hertz, "O Małości Pana Zagłoby," *Wiadomości Literackie*, no. 1226, September 28, 1969, pp. 3–4.

21. "Now, a caste is doubtlessly a closed status group. For all the obligations and barriers that membership in a status group entails also exist in a caste, in which they are intensified to the utmost degree." In *From Max Weber: Essays in Sociology*, eds. H. H. Gerth and C. Wright Mills (New York: Oxford University Press, 1958), p. 405.

22. Aleksander Hertz, "Kasta," in *Żydzi w Kulturze Polskiej* (Paris: Instytut Literacki, 1961), pp. 74–104.

23. For a review of this controversy, see Gerald D. Berreman, "Caste in India and the United States," in *Structured Social Inequality*, ed. Celia S. Heller (New York: Macmillan, 1969), pp. 74–81. My use of the term accords with the broad definition given by Berreman of caste as "a hierarchy of endogamous divisions in which membership is hereditary and permanent." Harold A. Gould has written a penetrating criticism of scholars who insist that caste is a social structure confined to the Pan-Indian cultural world: "their error arises from a failure to make better use of social history, an insufficient appreciation of the conceptual tools that empirical archeology has made available for studying evolution of social organization, and a tendency to ignore the principle of saliency in data collection." Harold A. Gould, "Caste and Class: A Comparative View," Addison-Wesley Modular Publication, no. 11 (1971), p. 4; See also: Marvin Harris, "Caste, Class and Minority," *Social Forces*, March 1959, pp. 248–54.

24. V. I. Lenin, *Critical Remarks on the National Question and the Right of Nations to Self-Determination* (Moscow: Progress Publishers, Scientific Socialism Series, 1971), p. 13.

25. I share this conviction with Aleksander Hertz, one of the most penetrating analysts of Poland's social structure. See: Hertz, "Kasta," pp. 74–104; Also: Gunnar Myrdal, *An American Dilemma: The Negro Problem and Modern Democracy*, 2 vols. (New York: Harper and Row, 1944); John Dollard, *Caste and Class in a Southern Town* (New Haven: Yale University Press, 1937).

26. For an example of such a case, see: Madeline G. Levine, "Julian Tuwim: 'We, the Polish Jews,'" *The Polish Review*, Autumn 1972, pp. 82–89.

27. Erving Goffman, *Stigma: Notes on the Management of Spoiled Identity* (Englewood Cliffs, N.J.: Prentice Hall, 1963), p. 49.

28. And yet, it must be noted that in some instances converts or their descendants did not change their surnames. No sociological study was conducted in the interwar period that will allow us to compare and generalize about those who changed their names and those who did not.

29. I am grateful to Dr. Chone Shmeruk of the Hebrew University, Jerusalem, for calling my attention to these letters. See: Stanisław Witkiewicz, *Listy do Syna*, eds. Bożena Danek Wojkowska and Anna Micińska (Warsaw: Państwowy Instytut Wydawniczy, 1969), pp. 530–32; J. Z. Jakubowski, "Znalazłem Nauczyciela Przewodnika—Listy Szaloma Asza do Stanisława Witkiewicza," *Przegląd Humanistyczny*, no. 3, 1959; Stanisław Pigon, "Listy Szaloma Asza," *Nasz Głos*, nos. 1–4, 1960. Witkiewicz's son became a very prominent writer. For a book in English about this son, see Daniel C. Gerauld, *Tropical Madness: Four Plays by Stanisław Ignacy Witkiewicz* (New York: Winter House, 1972).

30. The classic example in fiction is how the Jew Jankiel is introduced in Adam Mickiewicz's *Pan Tadeusz*. For a more recent example, which also illustrates it in reference to actual people, see Jan Michalski, *55 Lat Wśród Książek—Wspomnienia, Wrażenia, Rozważania* (Wrocław, 1950). To some extent the negative connotation of the Polish term for Jew might be a result of Russian influences. In the Russian language *Zhid* is definitely an insulting expression. The term for Jew is *Evrii*.

31. Wiktor Alter, *O Żydach i Antysemityzmie* (Warsaw: 1936), p. 9.

32. Abraham Joshua Heshel, "The Inner World of the Polish Jew," in Roman Vishniac, *Polish Jews—a Pictorial Record* (New York: Schocken Books, 1947), p. 7.

33. Celia Stopnicka Heller, "Deviation and Social Change in the Jewish Community of a Small Polish Town," *American Journal of Sociology*, September, 1954, p. 179.

34. See: J. Lestchinsky, "Di Shprakn bay Yidn in Umophengikn Poyln." YIVO Bleter, 22 (Nov.–Dec., 1943): 147–62; L. Hersch, "Shprakhlikhe Asimilirtkeyt bay di Yidishe Studentn fun di Varshever Hokhshuln," *ibid.*, vol. 2 (1931): 441–44.

35. The Ukrainians charged that the Polish Government intended to weaken the Ukrainian element by creating a division between those Ukrainians who spoke Ukrainian and those who did not. The Jewish Caucus in Poland's Parliament contended that the omission of the direct question concerning nationality "will have an unfavorable effect on the proceedings, objectivity and clearness of the census, for a statistical study of the nationality problem is of first-class importance not only to the nationalities concerned, but also to the whole state." *The Polish and Non-Polish Populations of Poland—Results of the Population Census of 1931* (Warsaw: Institute for the Study of Minority Problems, 1932), pp. 7, 27.

36. Jakow Willer, "Żargon Żydowski na Ziemiach Polskich," *Język Polski, Z Uwzględnieniem Języków na Ziemiach Polskich, Encyklopedya Polska,* vol. 3, part 2 (1915), p. 396. The author of the article gave this as the reason why Yiddish, "a language with its rules," was "disparagingly called a jargon." Nevertheless, the title of his article is "The Jewish Jargon on Polish Lands." Interestingly, the article about Hebrew in the same volume bears the title: "The Hebrew Language in Poland." See: Mojżesz Szor, "Język Hebrajski w Polsce," *Język Polski, Z Uwzględnieniem Języków na Ziemiach Polskich, ibid.,* pp. 425–44. (The volume, published by the Polish Academy of Arts and Sciences, aimed to synthesize the research on the Polish language, its historical development, and its relation with the languages of other nationality groups on Polish territories.)

37. Erving Goffman, *Stigma,* p. 49.

38. Frantz Fanon, *Black Skin, White Masks,* Charles Lam Markmann, trans. (New York: Grove Press, 1967), pp. 115–16. For the same idea expressed by an American historian, see Carl N. Degler, *Neither Black or White* (New York: Macmillan, 1971), p. 288.

39. The anthropologist Arthur Keith has suggested a scheme of classifying the grades of visibility among groups: (1) Pandiacritic, every individual recognizable; (2) Macrodiacritic, 80 percent or more recognizable; (3) Mesodiacritic, 30 percent to 80 percent recognizable; (4) Microdiacritic, less than 30 percent recognizable. Gordon Allport, *The Nature of Prejudice* (Reading, Mass.: Addison-Wesley, 1954), p. 132.

40. In 1945, two black sociologists, St. Clair Drake and Horace Cayton, estimated that each year at least 25,000 Negroes enter white society and pass for whites. In addition, there are many whose passing is situational; for example, those who are known as whites at work but return to the black community after work. See St. Clair Drake and Horace Cayton, *Black Metropolis* (New York: Harcourt, Brace, 1945), p. 160. For a fictional treatment of Negroes passing as whites, see: Sinclair Lewis, *Kingsblood Royal* (New York: Random House, 1947).

41. These are two of the subdivisions of the Caucasoid race, classified by physical anthropologists on the basis of a number of associated anatomical characteristics. For studies of the comparative distribution of various types among Jews and Poles, see: Henryk Szpidbaum, "Struktura Rasowa Żydow Polskich," in I. Schiper, A. Tartakower, A. Haftka, eds., *Żydzi w Polsce Odrodzonej* (Warsaw, 1935), vol. 2, pp. 165–84; Salomon Czortkower, *Komunikat z Badań i Dotychczasowych Resultatów Analizy Rasowej Żydów z Wileńszczyzny,* 193–ff; Salomon Czortkower, "Z Badań nad Problemami Rasowymi Żydów," *Miesięcznik Żydowski,* 4 (1934): 97–109; Jan Czekanowski, "Anthropological Structure of the Jewish People in the Light of Polish Analyses," *Jewish Journal of Sociology,* 2 (Nov. 1960): 236–43.

42. Helene Deutsch, *Confrontations with Myself—An Epilogue* (New York: W. W. Norton & Company, 1973), p. 22.

43. Jacob Lestchinsky, "The Industrial and Social Structure of Inter-bellum Poland," *YIVO Annual of Social Science*, 11 (1956–57): 254–58. Arjeh Tartakower, "Zawodowa i Społeczna Struktura Żydów w Polsce Odrodzonej," in *Żydzi w Polsce*, vol. 2, p. 363. Bernard Dobrzyński, "Żydzi w Rolnictwie na Terenie Byłej Kongresówki i Kresów Wschodnich," in *ibid.*, pp. 408–23; I. Schiper, "Żydzi w Rolnictwie na Terenie Małopolski," in *ibid.*, pp. 424–31; Ya'akov Levavi (Babitsky), "Ma'ama-dah Shel Hahaklaút Ha-yehudit Be-Polin Ba-shanim 1918–1939," *Gal-Ed*, 2 (1975): 179–207.

44. Otto D. Tolischus, "Nationalism Casts Polish Jews Aside," *New York Times*, February 8, 1937, p. 9.

45. Simon Segal, *The New Poland and the Jews*, p. 141.

46. E. Ringelblum, "Stosunki Polsko-Żydowskie w Czasie Drugiej Wojny Światowej," *Biuletyn Żydowskiego Instytutu Historycznego*, no. 28 (Oct.–Dec., 1958): 4–37.

III. The Pattern of Oppression

1. *The Jews of Poland—Official Reports of the American and British Investigating Missions* (Chicago: The National Polish Committee of America, 1920); *Report by Sir Stuart Samuel on his Mission to Poland, Presented to Parliament*, Miscellaneous No. 10 (London: His Majesty's Stationery Office, 1920).

2. M. K. Dziewanowski, *Joseph Piłsudski—A European Federalist, 1918–1922* (Stanford: Hoover Institution Press, 1969), especially ch. 5; Józef Lewandowski, *Federalizm: Litwa i Białoruś w Polityce Obozu Bel-wederskiego* (Warsaw, 1962); Piotr S. Wandycz, "Polish Federalism 1919–20 and its Historical Antecedents," *East European Quarterly*, 4 (March 1970): 25–39.

3. See: Andrzej Micewski, *Roman Dmowski* (Warsaw, 1971). The other Polish intermediary at the Peace Conference was Ignacy Jan Paderewski who seemed to lean toward federalism. Piotr S. Wandycz, "Ignacy Jan Paderewski as a Federalist," paper delivered at Second Congress of Polish American Scholars, New York City, April 24, 1971; Wiktor Sukiennicki "Amerykański Memoriał Ignacego Paderewskiego," *Zeszyty Historyczne*, 26 (1973): 166–86.

4. M. K. Dziewanowski, *Joseph Piłsudski*, p. ix.

5. From the analysis of Hołówko's ideas by Wincenty Rzymowski, *W Walce i Burzy—Tadeusz Hołówko na Tle Epoki* (Warsaw, 1933), p. 293. Not long before his death, in a speech before the Diet concerning the Eastern part of Poland (*kresy*), heavily inhabited by Ukrainians and Belorussians, he pleaded: "We do not want any assimilation, we do not want Polonization by force. We want to raise good citizens of the Polish state. There lies the tremendous difference." Tadeusz Hołówko, "Przemówienie w Sprawie Kresów Wygłoszone Dnia 9 Lutego, 1931r.," in *Ostatni Rok* (Warsaw, 1932), p. 87. Assassinated by an Ukrainian extreme nationalist in August 1931, he did not live to see the idea of equality in Polish citizenship betrayed by leading members of the Piłsudski camp who came into power after the Marshal's death.

6. For a concise summary of the ideology of this form of nationalism, see J. Salwyn Schapiro, *The World in Crisis* (New York: McGraw-Hill, 1950), pp. 136–45.

7. Calculations based on official census data from the 1931 Census: *Mały Rocznik Statystyczny* (Warsaw, 1939), pp. 23, 25; For a listing and discussion of interwar studies about ethnic groups in Poland, see Konstanty Symonolewicz, "The Study of Nationalism and Nationality Between the Two Wars (1918–1939)—A Bibliographical Survey," *Quarterly Bulletin of the Polish Institute of Arts and Sciences in America*, October, 1943, pp. 57–125.

8. The first slogan is catchy in Polish: *Polska jest narodowa, nie narodowościowa*. See "Przemówienie Posła Dr. Wygodzkiego na Posiedzeniu Sejmu . . . ," *Budżet Państwa Polskiego na 1929–30r a Żydzi—Mowy W Sejmie i Senacie*, Biuletyn 3 Klubu Posłów i Senatorow Żydowskiej Rady Marodowej (Warsaw, 1929), p. 66.

9. Quoted in Aharon Moshe Rabinowicz," The Jewish Minority," in *The Jews of Czechoslovakia* (Philadelphia: The Jewish Publication Society, 1968), vol. 1, p. 164. To what extent Masaryk's philosophy was affected by the objective condition (so different from the one in Poland) that the two main populations, the Czechs and Slovaks, were nearly equal in number would be important to consider in a thorough comparison of ethnic relations in the two countries.

10. He made this declaration at the Jewish National Celebration organized by Jewish students, which he honored with his presence. As quoted in: Aharon Moshe Rabinowicz, "The Jewish Party," in *The Jews of Czechoslovakia* (1971), vol. 2, p. 263.

11. It seems that Piłsudski, who abhorred anti-Semitism, in his passionate Polish patriotism showed certain mixed feelings toward Jews: on one hand, his warm remembrance and approval of those Jews who con-

tributed to Polish independence, and on the other his hurt resentment of those in the border areas who cooperated with or supported the Bolsheviks. In the previously quoted letter to Paderewski, he wrote about the difficulty with the latter Jews who "during Bolshevik rule constituted a ruling stratum." His dilemma expresses itself dramatically in an interview conducted by an experienced Polish journalist of the Piłsudski camp, Zygmunt Sachnowski, and which appeared in the pro-Piłsudski paper, *Kurier Poranny* (August 29, 1920). According to this reporter, Piłsudski was discussing the war with the Bolsheviks when, unprovoked by any specific question, he turned to the reporter and said energetically: "The Jews did not behave badly everywhere. In [the towns of] Łomża and Mazowiecki they bravely opposed the Bolsheviks. . . . But strange, as many things in Poland are, in the neighborhood [of Łomża], in [the towns of] Łóków, Siedlce, Kałuszyn, Białystok, Włodawa, there were numerous, even massive betrayals on part of Jews." See the reprinted interview in Piłsudski's collected writings: "Wywiad Korespondenta Kuriera Porannego," in Józef Piłsudski, *Pisma Zbiorowe* (Warsaw, 1937), vol. 5, pp. 165–67. Piłsudski's resentment of those who sided with the Russians dated back to the end of the nineteenth century. As a young socialist, he had published an appeal in 1893 "To the Jewish Socialist Comrades in the dislodged Polish provinces." He warned about the rising anti-Semitism among Poles as a result of the Russification of the Jewish intelligentsia, especially in the former Grand Duchy of Lithuania. And he blamed the leaders of the Bund and other members of the Jewish revolutionary intelligentsia for mistakenly leading the Jewish proletariat in that area along a separate path instead of the joint road with Poles toward Poland's freedom. (The appeal appeared in the socialist paper, *Przedwit*, May, 1893 and was reprinted in *Pisma Zbiorowe*, vol. 1, pp. 28–33.) For more on Piłsudski's relation to Jews see P. Szwarc, *Yuzef Pilsudski, Zayn Batsiung Tsu Der Yidn-Frage Un Zayn Kamf Kegn Bund* (Warsaw, 1936), p. 240; Józef Zygmuntowicz, ed., *Józef Piłsudski o Sobie—Z Pism, Rozkazów i Przemowień Komendanta* (Warsaw, 1929); Józef Piłsudski, *Poprawki Historyczne* (Warsaw, 1931); Jan Weiss, "Józef Piłsudski and the Jews," *Program and Abstracts of Papers*, Second Congress of Polish American Scholars and Scientists, April 1971, pp. 47–48. (The complete paper could not be located.) Israel Cohen wrote of his audience with the Marshal in "Documents—My Mission to Poland (1918–19)," *Jewish Social Studies*, 13 (April 1951): 167–68.

12. Aleksander Hertz, "O Małości Pana Zagłoby," *Wiadomości Literackie*, no. 1226, September 28, 1969, pp. 3–4; Ludwik Hirszfeld, *Historia Jednego Życia* (Warsaw: Czytelnik, 1946), p. 352.

13. See, for example, the speeches of the Jewish representatives in the Parliament of Poland and the reactions of Polish members toward them.

Many Polish representatives walked out and others shouted down the declarations of the Jewish representatives (which hailed Polish independence, proclaimed loyalty to the Polish state, and asserted the rights of Jewish *nationality*). See Leopold Halpern, *Polityka Żydowska w Sejmie i Senacie, 1919–33* (Warsaw, 1933) (Odbitka ze "Spraw Narodowościowych"), especially the speeches and reactions in the First Diet of 1919 before the signing of the Minorities Treaty, pp. 9–14. See also *Budżet Państwa Polskiego na 1929–30r a Żydzi—Mowy W Sejmie i Senacie*, Biuletyn 3 Klubu Posłów i Senatorów Żydowskiej Rady Marodowej (Warsaw, 1929), p. 66; *Sytuacia Żydowstwa Polskiego w Świetle Przemówień*, Biuletyn 5 Klubu Posłów i Senatorów Żydowskiej Rady Narodowej (Warsaw, 1930). For an early analysis of the resentment by Poles of Jewish claims to national rights, see Arnold Margolin, "The Jewish Problem in Eastern Europe," *Current History*, 17 (March 1923): 962–67.

14. He was thus described in the Cracow Jewish newspaper, on the occasion of his death at the beginning of 1939. Part of the article is reprinted in "Po Zgonie Ś. P. Romana Dmowskiego," *Nasz Przegląd*, January 4, 1939, p. 5. For the quotation from the conversation with Dmowski on October 6, 1919, which Marshall wrote down soon after to assure authenticity, see "A Conversation between Roman Dmowski and Louis Marshall," in: *Louis Marshall, Champion of Liberty—Selected Papers and Addresses*, ed. Charles Reznikoff (Philadelphia: Jewish Publication Society, 1957), vol. 2, p. 588. For an attempt at a dispassionate appraisal of Dmowski in a Jewish newspaper on the occasion of his death, see: "Ś. P. Roman Dmowski—Wspomnienie Pośmiertne," *Nasz Przegląd*, January 3, 1939, p. 9. For a critical post-World-War II study of his political ideology and activities, see Andrzej Micewski, *Roman Dmowski* (Warsaw, 1971).

15. Hubert M. Blalock, Jr., *Toward a Theory of Minority-Group Relations* (New York: Wiley, 1967), pp. 78–79, 209.

16. Aleksander Hertz, "The Social Background of the Pre-War Polish Political Structure," *Journal of Central European Affairs*, 2 (July 1942): 146–61.

17. Adam Próchnik, *Pierwsze Piętnastolecie Polski Niepodległej*, (2nd ed.: Warsaw, 1957); Kazimierz Kumaniecki, "Konstytucja Rzeczypospolitej Polskiej—Ustawa z Dnia 17 Marca 1921r," *Odbudowa Państwowości Polskiej—Najważniejsze Dokumenty 1912-Styczeń 1924* (Warsaw: Czernicki, 1924), pp. 507–29.

18. The Jews were politically divided concerning the appropriateness of joint political action with the territorial minorities, the Ukrainians, Belorussians and Germans, who were members of the Bloc. For details concerning those Jewish parties which refused to join the National Minorities' Bloc, see ch. 8.

19. This was expressed in the second lecture in honor of the slain president, delivered by Piłsudski on August 25, 1923. It was reprinted later in Józef Piłsudski, "Wspomnienia o Gabrielu Narutowiczu—Wykład Drugi," *Pisma Zbiorowe* vol. 6, p. 134. See also Piłsudski's first lecture, *ibid.*, pp. 36–60. The same observations were also made by Mr. Hołówko: Tadeusz Hołówko, *Ostatni Rok* (Warsaw, 1932), p. 21. See also *Gabrjel Narutowicz, Księga Pamiątkowa* (Warsaw, 1925).

20. Andrzej Ajnenkiel, *Od "Rządów Ludowych" do Przewrotu Majowego—Zarys Dziejów Politycznych Polski, 1918–1926* (Warsaw, 1964).

21. Quotation from: Lord Kennet, "Piłsudski," in W. F. Reddaway *et al.*, *The Cambridge History of Poland—From August II to Piłsudski* (Cambridge: At the University Press, 1951), vol. 2, p. 612. See also William Zukerman, "The Polish Election," *The Nation*, March 7, 1928, pp. 278–80; Andrzej Micewski, *W Cieniu Marszałka* (Warsaw, 1968).

22. Aleksander Hertz, "The Social Background of the Pre-War Polish Political Structure," *Journal of Central European Affairs*, 2 (July 1942); 157.

23. It vested in the President the right to appoint the Prime Minister and an additional Chief Leader (*Wódz Naczelny*), to nominate one third of Senate members, and to dissolve Parliament and to issue decrees. See Wacław Kornicki, *Ustrój Państwowy Rzeczypospolitej Polskiej* (London, 1947) Book I, pp. 39, 45–46.

24. From a letter to S. Strakacz, quoted in Tadeusz Jędruszczak, *Piłsudczycy bez Piłsudskiego—Powstanie Obozu Zjednoczenia Narodowego w 1937r* (Warsaw, 1963), p. 30.

25. Quoted in: Edward D. Wynot, Jr., " 'A Necessary Cruelty': The Emergence of Official Anti-Semitism in Poland, 1936–39," *The American Historical Review*, 76, no. 4 (October 1971): 1049.

26. Jędruszczak, *Piłsudczycy bez Piłsudskiego*, pp. 6–8, 40–47; See also Wynot, "Necessary Cruelty," pp. 1035–58; Jerzy Szapiro, "New Polish Party Appeals for Unity," *New York Times*, February 22, 1937, p. 9. For the text of the ideological declaration: *Deklaracja Ideowo Polityczna OZN* (2nd Edition, Palestine, 1946).

27. Janusz Jędrzejewicz, *W Służbie Idei—Fragmenty Pamiętnika i Pism* (London, 1972), p. 237.

28. Hertz, "Social Background of the Pre-War Polish Political Structure," p. 157.

29. Otto D. Tolischus, "Nationalism Casts Polish Jews Aside—Drive Similar to that in Reich," *New York Times*, February 8, 1937, p. 9. *Diplomat in*

Berlin, 1933–1939—Papers and Memoirs of Józef Lipsky, Ambassador of Poland (New York: Columbia University Press, 1968).

30. K. Bartel, *Mowy Parlamentarne* (Warsaw, 1928), p. 43.

31. Hertz. "Social Background," p. 151.

32. Wincenty Rzymowski, *W Walce i Burzy,* p. 25.

33. Karol Niezabytowski was made Minister of Agriculture, Aleksander Meysztowicz, Minister of Justice. See Antony Polonsky, *Politics in Independent Poland, 1921–39—The Crisis of Constitutional Government* (London: Oxford University Press, 1972), p. 222. See also J. Michał-owski, *Wieś nie ma Pracy* (Warsaw, 1935); Irena Kostrowicka, Zbigniew Landau and Jerzy Tomaszewski, *Historia Gospodarcza Polski XIX i XX Wieku* (Warsaw, 1966), pp. 283–85, 300–2, 305–11; Simon Segal, *The New Poland and the Jews* (New York: Lee Furman, Inc., 1938), pp. 45, 95–104; Wincenty Rzymowski, *W Walce i Burzy—Tadeusz Hołówko na Tle Epoki* (Warsaw, 1933), pp. 248, 254.

34. "To Leon Berenson," in *Louis Marshall, Champion of Liberty,* vol. 2, p. 632.

35. Many issues of the organization's organ, *Przegląd Handlowy,* contained articles on this theme. See, for example, "Przemówienie Prezesa A. Gepnera, Wygłoszone na Walnym Dorocznym Zebraniu CZK," *Przegląd Handlowy,* July 15, 1936, pp. 4–5.

36. For example: M. Zajdenman: "Nasza Odpowiedź," *Przegląd Handlowy,* July 15, 1938, pp. 9–10.

37. T. K., "Agospodarcza Psychologia Narodu," *Gazeta Polska,* December 20, 1938, p. 1; Aleksander Hertz, "The Case of an Eastern European Intelligentsia," *Journal of Central European Affairs,* 11 (Jan.–Apr. 1951): 10–26.

38. Segal, *The New Poland and the Jews,* p. 118.

39. S. Bronsztejn, "The Jewish Population of Poland in 1931," *The Jewish Journal of Sociology,* 6 (July 1964): 5.

40. Robert Zylbersztajn, "Problematyka Gospodarcza Żydów w Polsce," *Przegląd Handlowy,* September 15, 1936, pp. 7–11; Szyja Bronsztejn, *Ludność Żydowska w Polsce w Okresie Międzywojennym—Studium Statystyczne* (Wrocław: 1963), pp. 236–37.

41. "Patologiczne Objawy Atmosfery Etatycznej," *Przegląd Handlowy,* January 15, 1936, p. 5; Jewish Telegraphic Agency Bulletin, September 8, 1924; "Przemówienie Senatora Szabada na 29 posiedzeniu z dn. II marca 1930r. do budżetu Ministerstwa Pracy i Opieki Społecznej," *Sytuacja*

Żydowstwa Polskiego w Świetle Przemówień, Biuletyn No. 5 Klubu Posłów i Senatorów Żydowskiej Rady Narodwej (Warsaw, 1930); Marian Drozdowski, *Klasa Robotnicza Warszawy, 1918–39* (Warsaw, 1968), pp. 245–56.

42. M. Zajdman, "Udział Żydów w Handlu Polski Odrodzonej," in *Żydzi w Polsce Odrodzonej* (Warsaw, 1935), vol. 2, pp. 464–74. Marian Drozdowski, *Polityka Gospodarcza Rządu Polskiego, 1936–39* (Warsaw, 1963), pp. 283–84; *Sytuacja Żydowstwa Polskiego w Świetle Przemówień*, Biuletyn No. 5 Klubu Posłow i Senatorów Żydowskiej Rady Narodowej (Warsaw, 1930).

43. Jerzy Tomaszewski, "Robotnicy Żydowscy w Polsce (1921–39)," *Biuletyn Żydowskiego Instytutu Historycznego*, no. 51 (Aug.–Sept. 1964): 24–26; M. Zajdman, "Udziały Żydów w Handlu Polski Odrodzonej," in *Żydzi w Polsce Ordrodzonej* (Warsaw, 1935), vol. 2, pp. 464–73; Jerzy Gliksman, *Struktura Zawodowa i Społeczna Ludności Żydowskiej w Polsce* (Warsaw, 1931); A. Tartakower, "Ma'Avakam Hakalkali shel Yehude Polin ben Milḥamah Le-milḥamah," *Gal-Ed*, 2 (1975): 145–77.

44. Szyja Bronsztejn, *Ludność Żydowska w Polsce, w Okresie Międzywojennym—Studium Statystyczne* (Wrocław, 1963), p. 80. The author of this statistical study arrived at this figure on the basis of the distribution of Jewish communal fees. See also S. Bronsztejn, "The Jewish Population of Poland in 1931," *Jewish Journal of Sociology* 6 (July 1964): 25; J. Borenstein, "Zagadnienia Pauperyzacji Ludności Zydowskiej w Polsce," in I. Schiper, A. Tartakower, A. Haftka, eds., *Żydzi w Polsce Odrodzonej* (Warsaw, 1935), vol. 2, pp. 395–407.

45. Szyja Bronsztejn, *Ludnośc Żydowska w Polsce*, p. 81. According to 1931 Census figures 28.2 percent of Jewish workers were unemployed as compared with 21.2 percent among non-Jews. For example, in Warsaw the unemployment rate among Jews was 34.4 percent as compared with 20.4 among Poles. See Marian Drozdowski, *Klasa Robotnicza Warszawy, 1918–39* (Warsaw, 1968), pp. 249–54.

46. Jewish Telegraphic Agency Bulletin, December 18, 1924.

47. Simon Segal, *The New Poland and the Jews*, p. 131.

48. Tadeusz Hołówko, *Ostatni Rok* (Warsaw, 1932), p. 131.

49. "Przemówienie Posła Gruenbauma na Posiedzeniu Komisji Budżetowej Sejmu w Dniu 24 XI, 1928 do Budżetu Ministerstwa Spraw Wewnętrznych," *Budżet Państwa Polskiego na 1929–30r a Żydzi—Mowy W Sejmie i Senacie*, Biuletyn 3 Klubu Posłów i Senatorow Zydowskiej Rady Narodowej (Warsaw, 1929), p. 27.

50. A. Prowalski, *Spółdzielczość Zydowska w Polsce—Odbitka ze Spraw Narodowościowych* (Warsaw, 1933), p. 37.

51. *Dziennik Ustaw Rzeczypospolitej Polskiej*, No. 68, *Pozycja* 493 (Warsaw, 1936).

52. YIVO Diaries. Also: "Burza Przeciwpodatkowa," *Warszawska Informacja Prasowa—Wiadomości Codzienne z Prasy Żydowskiej*, April 24, 1928, p. 1; A. Sztolcman, "Słuszny Protest," *Przegląd Handlowy*, April 1, 1936, p. 11; "Kronika Żydowska," *Nasz Przegląd*, July 20, 1938, p. 11.

53. *Sytuacja Żydowstwa Polskiego*, Biuletyn 5 Klubu Posłów i Senatorów Żydowskiej Rady Narodowej (Warsaw, 1930), pp. 26–27; J. Borenstein "Zagadnienia Pauperizacji Ludności Żydowskiej w Polsce," in *Żydzi w Polsce Odrodzonej*, Warsaw, 1935, vol. 2 pp. 400–1; Elimelekh Rak, *Zikhroynes fun a Yidishn Handverker-tver* (Buenos Aires, 1958), pp. 124–27.

54. Raphael Mahler, "Jews in the Public Service and the Liberal Professions in Poland, 1919–39," *Jewish Social Studies*, 6 (October 1944): 291–350, especially pp. 313–14, 325.

55. Aleksander Hertz, "Social Background of the Pre-war Polish Political Structure," p. 153; Mahler, "Jews in Public Service," pp. 291–350; Janusz Żarnowski, *Struktura Społeczna Inteligencji w Polsce w Latach 1918–39* (Warsaw, 1964), pp. 170–72; "Systematyczne Rugowanie Nauczycieli Żydów w Szkołach Powszechnych dla Dzieci Zydowskich," *Nasz Przegląd*, October 6, 1938, p. 9.

56. "Przemówienie Senatora Koernera," *Budżet Państwa Polskiego na 1929–30r a Żydzi, Mowy w Sejmie, Senacie*, Biuletyn 3 Klubu Posłów i Senatorów Żydowskiej Rady Narodowej (Warsaw, 1929), p. 131.

57. "Ekonomiczna Strona Zagadnienia Uboju Rytualnego," *Przegląd Handlowy*, February, 1936, pp. 3–6; "Dyskusja Narodowościowa w Sejmie," *Nasz Przegląd*, December 5, 1938, p. 10; December 10, 1938, p. 5.

58. E. Kwiatkowsky, *Postęp Gospodarczy Polski* (Warsaw, 1927), p. 30; Stanisław A. Kempner, *Rozwój Gospodarczy Polski od Rozbiorów do Niepodległości* (Warsaw, 1924), p. 13. "Związek Kupców Polskich Zainicjował Nową Akcję Anty-Żydowską na Terenie Stolicy," *Nasz Przegląd*, August 6, 1938, p. 26; "Kronika Żydowska," *Nasz Przegląd*, July 24, 1938, p. 25. D. Stanley Eitzen, "Two Minorities: the Jews of Poland and the Chinese of the Philippines," *Jewish Journal of Sociology*, 10 (December, 1968): 221–38.

59. T. K., "Agospodarcza Psychologia Narodu," *Gazeta Polska*, December 20, 1938, p. 1.

60. Tadeusz Lepkowski, *Polska—Narodziny Nowoczesnego Narodu, 1764–1870* (Warsaw: Państwowe Wydawnictwo Naukowe, 1967), pp. 165–72.

61. See articles 114 and 115 of the 1921 Constitution: Kazimierz Kumaniecki, *Odbudowa Państwowości Polskiej—Najważniejsze Dokumenty 1912–Styczeń 1924* (Warsaw: Czernicki, 1924), p. 519. For provisions of the 1935 Constitution, see: Wacław Komarnicki, *Ustrój Państwowy Rzeczypospolitej Polskiej* (London: 1943), pp. 231–34 (mimeographed).

62. Wiesław Mysłek, *Kościół Katolicki w Polsce w Latach 1918–39* (Warsaw: Książka i Wiedza, 1966), p. 17. See also pp. 13–22; For Concordat, pp. 26–55.

63. Article 4 in: *Decklaracja Ideowo Polityczna OZN* (2nd Edition, Palestine, 1946), p. 11.

64. Janusz Jędrzejewicz, *W Służbie Idei*, p. 134. See also Antony Polonsky, *Politics in Independent Poland*, pp. 209–12.

65. Ks. J. Rostoworowski, "Sprawozdanie z Ruchu Religijnego, Naukowego i Społecznago," *Przegląd Powszechny*, no. 6 (1936): 59. For another expression of the fears of secularization, see the unsigned article by a supposed Jewish convert to Catholicism: "Konwertyta w Sprawie Żydowskiej," *Przegląd Powszechny*, nos. 7–8 (1938): 26–35. According to this author Jewish atheists are characterized by an "uncontrolled burning hate against Christianity, and religion in general to a much higher degree than the atheists of other nations. They form an inexhaustible reservoir for the atheist movement among almost all nations."

66. *Haynt*, March 16, 1937.

67. "Majątki i Dochody Kościoła," in: Wiesław Mysłek, *Kościół Katolicki w Polsce w Latach 1918–39* (Warsaw: Książka i Wiedza, 1966), pp. 100–142. Some concessions concerning the Church's property were formalized in the decree of February 1928: *Dziennik Ustaw Rzeczypospolitej Polski*, 1928, no. 16, pp. 218–19.

68. Wiesław Mysłek, *Kosciół Katolicki w Polsce*, pp. 264–65.

69. Ks. Józef Kruszynski, *Talmud Co Zawiera i Co Naucza* (Lublin, 1925). His other books and pamphlets were: *Rola Światowa Żydowstwa; Dążenia Żydów w Dobie Obecnej* (1921); *Antysemityzm, Antyjudaizm, Antygoizm* (Włocławek, 1924); *Żydzi a Polska* (Poznań, 1921).

70. Ks. Stanisław Trzeciak, *Program Światowej Polityki Żydowskiej— Konspiracja i Dekonspiracja* (Warsaw, 1936); He also wrote: *Mesjanizm a Kwestja Żydowska* (Warsaw, 1934). His influence is reflected in the defense of various cases brought to court for anti-Jewish excesses. See, for example: "Bij Żydów, Ratuj Polskę—Przywódca Pikieciarzy na Ławie Oskarżonych—Obrona Powołuje się na Ks. Trzeciaka," *Nasz Przegląd*, September 2, 1938, p. 11.

71. Tadeusz Zaderecki, *Talmud w Ogniu Wieków* (Warsaw: F. Hoesicka, 1936).

72. The author of this calendar was brought to trial in the town of Grudziąc for insulting religion. Father Trzeciak testified in his defense. See "Proces o Obrazę Religji Zydowskiej," *Nasz Przegląd*, December 7, 1938, p. 4 and "Wyrok," *Nasz Przegląd*, December 8, 1938, p. 9.

73. Autobiography 3816, YIVO Archives.

74. In 1920, Captain Wright of the British Mission to Poland—who was considered biased in favor of the Poles by Jewish leaders (including Louis Marshall)—wrote: "There is a general belief among all classes of Poles that Jews practice ritual murder." See *Report by Sir Stuart Samuel*, p. 14. At that time it might have been to a large extent the aftermath of the Beilis case in Russia. (The apprehension of a Jew in 1911 for ritual murder of a Russian boy and his trial in 1913 which attracted world attention. It inspired Bernard Malamud's novel *The Fixer*.) Nevertheless, the belief that Jews practiced such murder prevailed during the interwar period. Parenthetically, "Beilis" became a hate name for Jew, and throughout that period Jewish children were commonly taunted with this name by Polish children.

75. From the pastoral letter of February 29, 1936: August Cardinal Hlond, *Listy Pasterskie* (Poznań, 1936), pp. 192–93.

IV. Organized Terror and Abuse

1. J. Salwyn Schapiro, "Integral Nationalism," in *The World in Crisis* (New York: McGraw-Hill, 1950), p. 137.

2. Przemysław Burchard, "Przyczynki do Zagadnienia Żydowskich Rzemiósł Ludowych w Dawnej Polsce," *Biuletyn Żydowskiego Instytutu Historycznego*, no. 37 (January–March, 1961): 66–80.

3. S. Chmielewski, "Rozmiary i Charakter Akcji 'Odżydzania' Handlu w Polsce," *Przegląd Handlowy*, no. 6 (June 15, 1937): 8–9.

4. Wanda Wasilewska, "Ciemna Fala," in *Prawda o Antysemityzmie*, (Warsaw: Henryk Mroczek, 1936), pp. 9–11.

5. "Dwa Dokumenty o Pogromie w Brześciu," *Biuletyn Żydowskiego Instytutu Historycznego*, no. 49 (Jan.–Mar., 1964): 58–66.

6. Otto D. Tolischus, "Jews Face Crisis in Eastern Europe," *New York Times*, February 7, 1937, p. 34; For a report on one of the later incidents in the same region, in the market town of Suraż, see "Zaczęło się od bicia Żydów—Skończyło się Napaścią na Policję," *Nasz Przegląd*, October 28, 1938, p. 7. For a report of the various tactics to create a pogrom see "Co się Działo w Goniądzu—Gdy Wołanie o Odruch nie Odnosi Skutków, Rzuca się Kalumnię na Żydów," *Nasz Przegląd*, August 31, 1938, p. 13.

7. See, for example: "Proces o Zajścia Antyżydowskie w Brańsku," *Nasz Przegląd*, September 15, 1938, p. 10; "Zajścia Antyżydowskie w Kadzidle Przed Sądem Okręgowym w Lomży'," *Nasz Przegląd*, September 28, 1938, p. 13; "Sala Sądowa Coraz Częściej Zamienia sie w Widownię Walk Politycznych—Przemówienie Posła dra Sommersteina," *Chwila*, February 19, 1938, p. 7.

8. "Memoriał Związku Nauczycieli Polskich," *Nowe Życie*, February 1, 1939, p. 6.

9. The Jewish Congress Bulletin, October 29, 1937.

10. *Żydowski Dom Akademicki w Warszawie, 1924–26*, (Warsaw, 1928). Before independence, one of the first university dormitories for Jewish students established in Europe was in Lvov (1910).

11. Aleksander Hertz, "The Case of an Eastern European Intelligentsia," *Journal of Central European Affairs*, Jan.–Apr. 1951: pp. 13–14.

12. Daily News Bulletin, Jewish Telegraphic Agency, February 28, 1925.

13. He cited examples such as the forced entry of the police at Warsaw University, without previous consultation with its administration, when some students held an antigovernmental demonstration and tore down the portait of the head of state: "Przemówienie Senatora Dr. Dawidsohna...z dn. 21 lutego 1930r," *Sytuacja Żydowstwa Polskiego w Świetle Przemówień*, Biuletyn 5, Klubu Poslów i Senatorów Żydowskiej Rady Narodowej (Warsaw, 1930), pp. 39–41.

14. Daily News Bulletin, Jewish Telegraphic Agency, February 28, 1925. See also: Saul Langnas, *Żydzi a Studia Akademickie w Polsce w Latach 1921–31—Studium Statystyczne* (Lvov, 1933).

15. "Antysemickie Zajścia na Wyższych Uczelniach w Warszawie," *Czas*, October 22, 1936, p. 4; "Zamknięcie Uniwersytetu J. Piłsudskiego," *Czas*, November 27, 1936, p. 4; "Z Frontu Akademickiego—Dzień bez Żydów, Uniwersytet J. Piłsudskiego," *Nasz Przegląd*, November 27, 1938, p. 10. For an example of the Jewish students defiance of the "Jewless week" at the Dental Academy, Warsaw, see "Po Zawieszeniu Zajęć na Uniwersytecie," *Nasz Przegląd*, December 2, 1938, p. 10.

16. Autobiography 3722, YIVO Archives.

17. "Ławki—Getto na Wyższych Uczelniach," *Myśl Socjalistyczna*, October 15, 1937, p. 1.

18. Diary 3599, YIVO Archives.

19. "Oświadczenie min. Świętosławskiego o Ostatnich Zajściach na Wyższych Uczelniach," *Czas*, October 28, 1936, p. 3; See also W. Alter "Czy Znajdą sie tacy Ludzie?" *Nowe Życie*, February 1, 1939, p. 2.

20. From part of his declaration reprinted in "Głosy Światłych Polaków," *Głos Gminy Żydowskiej*, 1, no. 4 (October 1937): 80.

21. See for example how perturbed he was with the killing of Jewish students, an effect of the concessions. "Min. Świętosławski Wzywa do Potępienia Zbrodni Dokonanej na Terenie Politechniki Lwowskiej—Apel do Profesorów i Młodzieży," *Nasz Przegląd*, June 11, 1939, p. 7.

22. "Przeciwko 'Gettu Ławkowemu' na Wyższych Uczelniach—Dalsza Akcja Żydowskiej Młodzieży Akademickiej," *Nasz Przegląd*, August 26, 1938, p. 12.

23. Professor Rimmer, at the Higher School of Commerce in Warsaw, set such a condition. "Numerus Nullus dla Studentów," *Nasz Przegląd*, October 25, 1938, p. 7; "Usunięcie Studentów Żydow z Sali Wykładowej na Uniwersytecie J. Piłsudskiego," *Nasz Przegląd*, October 26, 1938, p. 11; "Zajścia na Politechnice Warszawskiej," *Nasz Przegląd*, November 6, 1938, p. 7; "50 Wawelberczyków poza Uczelnią," *Nasz Przegląd*, December 13, 1938, p. 12; Wanda Wasilewska, "Młodości, ty nad Poziomy—Wybryki Antysemickie w Szkole Wawelberga," *Robotnik*, January 5, 1939.

24. "W Sprawie Bezpieczeństwa Na Wyższych Uczelniach i Popełnianych na ich Terenach Ciężkich Zbrodniach—Interpelacja Posła Dr. Emila Sommersteina do p. Prezesa Ministrów jako Szefa Rządu i Ministra Spraw Wewnętrznych i p. Ministra Wyznań Religijnych i Oświecenia Publicznego," *Nasz Przegląd*, November 30, 1938, p. 5. "Zawieszenie Wykładów i Zajęć na Akademii Stomatologicznej," *Nasz Przegląd*, December 4, 1938. p. 11; "Pogrzeb Tragicznie Zmarłego Studenta Samuela Prowellera," *Nasz Przegląd*, December 8, 1938, p. 18.

25. Autobiography 3837, YIVO Archives.

26. Antoni Sobański, "Kwestji Żydowskiej-Niema?" *Wiadomości Literackie*, 36 (August 29, 1937), p. 3; *Nowe Życie*, February 1, 1939, p. 4; "Morderstwo Włoskie," *Nowe Życie*, June 10, 1939.

27. Stefan Babad, "Spowiedź Chłopskiego Syna," *Nasza Trybuna-Żydowski Dwutygodnik Socjalistyczny*, November 5, 1937, p. 5.

28. "Skutki Akcji 'Ławkowej' na Terenie Szkolnym—Znane Gimnazjum Utraciło Prawa Szkół Państwowych," *Nasz Przegląd*, September 4, 1938, p. 7.

29. Henryk Rolicki, *Zmierzch Izraela* (3rd edition, Warsaw: Myśl Narodowa, 1933).

30. Isaac Deutscher, *The Non-Jewish Jew and other Essays* (London: Oxford University Press, 1968), p. 55.

31. For instance, the work *Hellenism and Judaism*, by the prominent philologist Tadeusz Zieliński, was thus exploited, contrary to his intention. (In this work the author developed his thesis that the Christian religion grew out of Greco-Roman culture and was impregnated with its elements. The lesser influence of Judaism on certain important aspects of the Christian religion was stressed there.) See Tadeusz Zieliński, *Hellenizm a Judaizm* (Warsaw: J. Mortkowicz, 1927); Tadeusz Zieliński, "Nauka i Sentyment Wobec Hellenizum i Judaizmu," *Przegląd Współczesny*, 7, no. 24 (1928): 353–70.

32. All this was implied in the Polish word *zażydzenie*. See: Mieczysław Wardziński, "Antysemityzm-Daltonizmen Państwowym," *Wiadomości Literackie*, 28 (August 4, 1937).

33. From the reprinted speech: "Płk. Wenda Uzasadnia Program OZN w Sprawie Żydowskiej," *Nasz Przegląd*, December 23, 1938.

34. For the fluctuation in the anti-Semitic attack on Tuwim see: Janusz Stradecki, *Julian Tuwim: Bibliografia* (Warsaw, 1959). Also: Magnus J. Kryński, "Politics and Poetry: The Case of Julian Tuwim," *The Polish Review*, 18, no. 4 (1973): 3–33.

35. It was coined by Władysław Rabski, a well-known Warsaw journalist: *"Tuwim nie pisze po polsku, tylko w polskim języku."* Stradecki, *Julian Tuwim: Bibliografia*, p. 93. Ironically, as was the case in a number of other instances, Rabski was married to a woman of Jewish ancestry, Suzanna Kraushar. Her father, Aleksander Kraushar—the historian and author of a famous work on the Frankists—converted to Catholicism. As for Tuwim, he considered himself a Pole and a Polish writer. In 1934 in a letter to a newly discovered cousin abroad, Tuwim wrote about his Polishness and Jewishness: "I and my sister Irena (four years younger than I) *were raised in the Polish spirit, mainly due to my mother*. Irena when she married became converted to Christianity. I remained with the ancestral faith" (italics supplied). See Moshe Altbauer, "Saga Rodu Tuwimów,"*Nowy Kurier* (Israel), September 20, 1964. For a discussion of Tuwim's self-identity as a Pole, see Madeline G. Levine, "Julian Tuwim: 'We, the Polish Jews,' " *The Polish Review*, Autumn 1972, pp. 82–89.

36. For the attack see Zygmunt Wasilewski, "Wampiryzm Poezji Semickiej," *Myśl Narodowa'*, no. 6 (1934). For a discussion of the "deep trauma" the anti-Semitic attack produced in Tuwim, see Magnus Kryński, "Politics and Poetry," pp. 3–33. For the refutation see the analysis of Tuwim's work by the Yiddish poet and essayist Samuel J. Imber. In a work written in Polish, Imber demonstrated that Tuwim's poetry's characteristics did not differ from those of other contemporary poets who were not of Jewish descent. S. J. Imber, *Asy Czystej Rasy* (Cracow, 1934), p. 25.

37. Andrzej Stawar, "Jeszcze o Antysemityzmie," *Wiadomości Literackie,* May 23, 1937, p. 3.

38. Jacob Lestchinsky, "The Anti-Jewish Program: Tsarist Russia, the Third Reich and the Independent Poland," *Jewish Social Studies,* 3 (April 1941): 155.

39. Aleksander Hertz, "The Case of an Eastern European Intelligentsia," p. 25.

40. Janusz Żarnowski, *Struktura Społeczna Inteligencji Polskiej w Latach 1918–39* (Warsaw, 1964), pp. 182–84, 222–24, 244–47; Ludwik Honigwill, "Nowinki Średniowieczne," *Nowe Życie,* February 1939, p. 3; Tadeusz Jędruszczak, *Piłsudczycy bez Piłsudskiego—Powstanie Obozu Zjednoczenia Narodowego w 1937r* (Warsaw, 1963), pp. 140–44.

41. Bolesław Drobner, *Bezustanna Walka—Wspomnienia* (Warsaw, 1965), vol. 2, pp. 21–22; Feliks Gross, *World Politics and Tension Areas* (New York: New York University Press, 1966), p. 139; Jędruszczak, *Piłsudczycy bez Piłsudskiego,* p. 37.

42. Speech of Communist Sejm Deputy, in *Unter der Fon fun KPP* (Warsaw, 1959), pp. 37–41; *Dokumenty Komunistycznej Partii Polskiej, 1935–39* (Warsaw, 1968). He and another deputy were elected in 1922 on the ticket put forth by the Communist Party under the name "The Proletariat of Town and Country." It received 1.5 percent of the votes cast in that election. See Adam Próchnik, *Pierwsze Piętnastolecie Polski Niepodległej* (Warsaw, 1937), pp. 133–35. See also M. K. Dziewanowski, *The Communist Party of Poland,* (Cambridge, Mass.: Harvard University Press, 1959).

43. Joel Cang, "The Opposition Parties in Poland and their Attitude towards the Jews and the Jewish Problem," *Jewish Social Studies,* (April 1939): pp. 248–49; Edward Wynot, " 'A Necessary Cruelty': The Emergence of Official Antisemitism in Poland, 1936–39," *The American Historical Review,* 76, no. 4 (October 1971): 1041; Gross, *World Politics and Tension Areas,* p. 139.

44. For reprints of the declarations and articles of a number of these Poles who were friendly to Jews see *Polacy o Żydach* (Warsaw, 1937).

45. Reprinted as: "Ład Serca," *Nasz Przegląd,* December 11, 1938, p. 7.

46. For the attack on Jews see "Memoriał Związku Nauczycieli Polskich," *Nowe Życie,* February 1, 1939, p. 6; Gross, *World Politics and Tension Areas,* pp. 141–43. For a moving defense of Jews see Emil Zegadłowicz: "Poza Dyskusją," *Wiadomości Literackie,* 20 (May 9, 1937): 2–3. See also the exchange between Józef Łobodowski and Stanisław Piasecki, *Wiadomości Literackie,* 33 (August 6, 1939): 6.

47. See, for example, the report of some Christian passers-by who helped Jewish pedestrians who had been attacked on a Warsaw street by nationalist radicals: "Pobicie Przechodniów Żydowskich," *Nasz Przegląd*, December 6, 1938, p. 13.

48. YIVO Archives, Diary 3516.

49. M. K. Dziewanowski, "Social Democrats versus 'Social Patriots': The Origins of the Split of the Marxist Movement in Poland," *The American Slavic and East European Review*, 10 (February 1951): 14–25.

50. See, for example, the statement of a Polish officer of the famous Piłsudski Legion who, recalling some Jewish comrades who gave their lives for Polish independence, asked the rhetorical question how he could possibly be an anti-Semite in light of these experiences: Bogumił Rembowski, "Jak Mogę Być Racistą—ze Wspomnien b. Oficera Legionów," *Nasz Przegląd*, July 29, 1938.

51. He was the author of the following book, which was translated into English as *On the High Uplands—Sagas, Tales, and Legends of the Carpathians* (New York: Roy, 1955).

52. Aleksander Hertz, *Żydzi w Kulturze Polskiej* (Paris: Instytut Literacki, 1961, pp. 238–48; Ksawery Pruszyński, "W Największym Skrócie," *Wiadomości Literackie*, 21 (May 16, 1937): 3.

53. " 'Żydokomuna' jako Argument Agitacji Antysemickiej—Wywody Posła Miedzińskiego w Świetle Dzieła Marszarłka Piłsudskiego," *Nasz Przegląd*, July 1, 1938, p. 6. Samuel Ettinger, *Diaspora and Unity* (Jerusalem, 1969), pp. 17–37; Wiktor Alter, *O Żydach i Antysemityzmie* (Warsaw, 1936).

54. Benedykt Hertz, *Żydowska Krew* (Warsaw: Ludwik Fiszer 193–), p. 6.

55. Aleksander Świętochowski, "Antysemityzm," in "Pisarze Polscy o Kwestji Żydowskiej," *Wiadomości Literackie*, 16 (April 1, 1937): 3.

56. Jechiel Halpern, "Konsolidacja i Orientacja," *Nasza Trybuna*, November 5, 1937, p. 1.

57. It reflects on the atmosphere that prevailed in Poland that the priest found it proper to send a *speedy* refutation to the Catholic Press Agency in which he "categorically" denied ever having declared himself of non-Polish nationality. "I always considered myself a Pole," he underlined. For father Puder's declaration: "Komunikat Katolickiej Agencji Prasowej w Sprawie Napaści na Księdza Pudra," printed verbatim in: *Nasz Przegląd*, July 5, 1938, p. 6. For reports of occurrence reprinted from leading Polish newspapers—*Nasza Rzeczypospolita, Mały Dziennik, Dziennik Ludowy*—in "Prasa Polska o Napaści na Ks. Pudra," *Nasz Przegląd*, July 5,

1938, p. 11. Also, "KAP Wciąż nie Kapuje," *Oko w Oko*, August, 1938, pp. 6–8.

58. Mackiewicz's statement reproduced in "W Młynie Opinii," *Nasz Przegląd*, July 15, 1938; Part of the article from "Self-Defense of the Nation" was reproduced in "Echa Napaści na Księdza Pudra," *Nasz Przegląd*, July 11, 1938, p. 13.

59. From part of the article reproduced in: "Programowe Wypowiedzenie się Środowiska Legionowego w Sprawie Zydowskiej," *Nasz Przegląd*, September 3, 1938, p. 8.

60. E. Szerer, "Istota Emigracjonizmu," *Nowie Życie*, February 1939; Józef Haller, *Pamiętniki* (London, 1964), p. 310; "Poland and Jewry," *Commonweal*, 26 (September 3, 1937): 440; Emmanuel Melzer, "Hadiplomatiyah Hapolanit Ube'ayat Ha-hagirah Ha-yehudit Ba-shanim 1935–1939," *Gal-Ed*, 1 (1973): 211–49 (English summary, pp. xviii–xx); Jędruszczak, *Piłsudczycy bez Piłsudskiego*, pp. 205–6.

61. "Przemówienie Ministra Becka," *Czas*, December 20, 1936, p. 4; See also: "Możliwości Kolonialne Polski—Odczyt Profesora Hipolita Gliwicy," *Czas*, November 9, 1936, p. 5; P. Wasserman, "Polityka Kolonialna Polski a Problem Emigracji Żydowskiej do Palestyny," *Czas*, October 26, 1936, p. 4.

62. From the speech delivered on December 3, 1938: "Wytyczne Prac OZN w Parlamencie—Mowa Szefa OZN, Gen. St. Skwarczyńskiego," *Gazeta Polska*, December 4, 1938, p. 1. Entire speech also reproduced in "Declaracja Generała Skwarczyńskiego—Antyżydowskie Tezy Ozonu Znajdują Wyraz w Inicjatywie Ustawodawczej," *Nasz Przegląd*, December 4, 1938, pp. 4, 6.

63. "O Własciwe Postawienie Sprawy," *Gazeta Polska*, December 2, 1938, p. 1.

64. The parliamentary question was raised by General Stanisław Skwarczyński, a deputy. For the text of the answer, see Felicjan Sławoj Składkowski, "Do Pana Marszałka Sejmu Rzeczypospolitej," in *Sprawy Narodowościowe*, 13, nos. 1–2 (Warsaw: Instytut Spraw Narodowościowych, 1939), pp. 101–3.

65. Otto D. Tolischus, "Nationalism Casts Polish Jews Aside—Drive Similar to that in Reich," *New York Times*, February, 8, 1937, p. 9.

66. "Zabójstwo Studenta-Żyda we Lwowie," *Nasz Przegląd*, May 28, 1939, p. 7; "Nad Swieżą Mogiłą—Głosy z Prasy," *Nasz Przegląd*, June 9, 1939, p. 14.

67. Kryński, "Politics and Poetry," p. 12.

68. These were the words of one of the prominent publicists, Tadeusz

Bielecki, in a lecture sponsored by the nationalist daily, *Dziennik Narodowy*. From part of the lecture reproduced in: "W Młynie Opinii—Endecja o Sytuacji Politycznej," *Nasz Przegląd*, May 23, 1939, p. 5.

69. Melzer, "Hadiplomatiyah Hapolanit," p. xix–xx.

70. From the interview with Skwarczyński, reproduced in: "W Młynie Opinii," *Nasz Przegląd*, May 10, 1939, p. 5.

V. The Jewish Jews: Orthodox in Faith, Traditional in Culture

1. In the first general election in 1922, out of the 35 candidates of Jewish organizations who were elected to the Sejm, 11 were from the two organizations of Orthodox Jewry: Agudat Israel (6) and Mizrachi (5). Since the Polish electoral system was that of proportional representation, we can tentatively deduce from this that about one-third of the adult population was Orthodox-traditionalist. (For the subsequent two elections [1928 and 1930] no absolute figures are available but of the entire vote cast for Jewish organizations, 21 percent went to the Agudat Israel. However, the Mizrachi figure is not given.) See: A Haftka, "Zycie Parlamentarne Żydów w Polsce Odrodzonej," in I. Schiper, A. Tartakower, A. Haftka, eds., *Żydzi w Polsce Odrodzonej*, vol. 2 (Warsaw, 1935), pp. 293, 305. Perhaps it should be added that my estimated proportion of Orthodox-traditionalists is similar to the educated guess of Harry M. Rabinowicz, in *The Legacy of Polish Jewry* (New York: Thomas Yoseloff, 1965), pp. 108–17.

2. Some of the forthcoming discussion is based on: Celia Stopnicka Heller, "How the Polish Jew Saw His World," *Commentary*, 18 (July 1954): 70–76.

3. J. L. Orlean, "Shabesdikeyt un Vokhedikeyt," *Beys-Yankev Zhurnal*, no. 144, 1937.

4. For a very sympathetic and lovely rendition of the spirit of Hasidism, see Abraham Joshua Heschel, *The Earth is the Lord's—the Inner World of the Jew in East Europe* (New York: Schuman, 1950), pp. 75–82; quotation, p. 75). See also: H. Rabinowicz, "Music and Dance in Hassidism," *Judaism*, 8 (Summer 1959): 252–57. Interestingly, Stanisław Vincenz, a Pole with an unusual knowledge of and sympathy for Jewish traditional life captured the holiday spirit in a novel. One of its characters, a Jew, explains: "Our holy *rebe*, our hasidic *rebe* teaches: When sadness cries in the corner during a holiday, one ought to embrace her, hug her, and whisk her to dance. . . . Let sadness also dance." Stanisław Vincenz, *Zwada* (London, 1970; reissue), p. 33.

5. For more detail, read Rabinowicz, *Legacy of Polish Jewry*, pp. 126–46. The author, the scion of a hasidic dynasty, traces the genealogy of the Polish rebes who headed various hasidic groups in interwar Poland.

6. Abraham Joshua Heschel, "The Inner World of the Polish Jew," in Roman Vishniac, *Polish Jews—A Pictorial Record* (New York: Schocken Books, 1947), p. 8.

7. For a systematic treatment of the bases of status in the traditional community, on which part of the above discussion is based, see: Celia Stopnicka Heller, "Social Stratification of a Jewish Community in a Small Polish Town," *American Journal of Sociology*, 59 (July 1953): 1–11.

8. For a thorough case study of a Polish heder see Yekhiel Shtern, "A Kheyder in Tyszowce" (Tishevits), *YIVO Annual of Jewish Social Science*, 5 (1950): 152–71.

9. A. M. Rogowy, "Di Rekhtlikhe Lage fun Khadorim," *Der Yud*, June 24, 1927, p. 4. H. Seidman, *Dos Yidishe Religyeze Shulvezn in di Ramen fun der Poylisher Gezetsgebung* (Warsaw, 1934).

10. A. Z. Frydman, "Zadanie i Cele Organizacji Szkolnej Ortodoksyjno-Żydowskiej 'Chorew'," in *Almanach Szkolnictwa Żydowskiego w Polsce*, vol. 1 (Warsaw, 1938), pp. 296–99.

11. Stanisław Mauersberg, *Szkolnictwo Powszechne dla Mniejszości Narodowych w Polsce w Latach 1918–1939* (Wrocław: Ossolineum, 1968), pp. 172–73.

12. The first appear in Samuel Chmielewski, "Stan Szkolnictwa Wśród Żydów w Polsce," *Sprawy Narodowościowe*, nos. 1–2 (Warsaw, 1937): 73; The latter are reproduced in Nathan Eck, "The Educational Institutions of Polish Jewry, 1921–39," *Jewish Social Studies*, 9, no. 1 (January 1947): 20.

13. Miriam Eisenstein, *Jewish Schools in Poland, 1919–39—Their Philosophy and Development* (New York: Kings Crown Press, 1950), pp. 79–80.

14. I derive this information from interviews and from the YIVO autobiographies (e.g., no. 3834).

15. Significantly, some articles of this journal were written in Polish, as girls from middle class Orthodox homes often did not know how to read Yiddish. Quote from Pesa Walk, "O Obowiązkach Kobiety Żydowskiej," *Beys-Yankev Zhurnal*, August 1924.

16. Yitzhak Meyer Lewin, "Der Matsev in der Arbet fun Agudas Yisroel," *Der Yud*, no. 38, November 2, 1928, pp. 5–6.

17. Eck, "Educational Institutions of Polish Jewry," p. 24. Also "Ruch Religijno—Wychowawczy 'Bajs Jakow,'" in *Almanach Szkolnictwa Ży-*

dowskiego w Polsce, vol. 1 (Warsaw, 1938), pp. 316–20; Y. Rosenstein "Tsvantsik Yor Beys-Yankev," Beys-Yankev Zhurnal, no. 143 (May–June, 1937).

18. "Wyższe Kursy Nauczycielskie 'Bajs Jakow'," in *Almanach Szkolnictwa Żydowskiego w Polsce*, vol. 1, pp. 321–22.

19. Eck, "Educational Institutions of Polish Jewry," p. 23; Meyer Shapira, "Limed Hatoyre, Yeshives un Yeshivas Khakhmey Lublin," *Der Yud*, no. 38, November 2, 1928, pp. 7–8. Also H. Seidemann, *Szlakiem Wiedzy Talmudycznej* (Warsaw, 1934).

20. Heller, "How the Polish Jew Saw His World," pp. 70–76.

21. Heller, "Social Stratification of a Jewish Community in a Small Polish Town," pp. 1–11.

22. See: "Przemówienie Posła Gruenbauma na Posiedzeniu Komisji Budżetowej Sejmu w d 24, XI, 1928 do Budżetu Ministerstwa Spraw Wewnętrznych," *Budżet Państwa Polskiego na 1929–30r a Żydzi—Mowy w Sejmie i Senacie*, Biuletyn 3 (Warsaw, 1929), p. 32; Józef Dawidsohn, *Gminy Żydowskie* (Warsaw: Nakładem Posłów Sejmowych Żydowskiej Rady Narodowej, 1931); Leon Brandes, "Der Rekhtlikher Matsev fun Yidn in Poyln Tsvishn Beyde Velt Milkhomes," *YIVO Bleter*, 43 (1962): 147–71.

23. By 1919, the secular Jewish parties were being accused in the Agudat Israel newspaper of capturing the relief sent by American and English Jews and using it for political purposes, "pressuring the Orthodox in a way that one would never have expected from fellow Jews." "Der Kamf kegn der Ortodoksie—Tsu di Onfaln Af Haraf Perlmuter un Horav Khaim Oyzer Grodzinski," *Der Yud*, December 19, 1919, p. 4.

24. Yizhak Meyer Lewin, "Der Matsev in der Arbet fun Agudas Yisroel," p. 9.

25. "Der Pilsudski Dekret Benegege Di Yidishe Kehiles," *Der Yud*, no. 192, June 19, 1972, p. 9. Concerning the legal status of Jews, the term used in the above law was that they constituted "*Związek Religijny, publiczno-prawny*," See Michal Ringel, "Ustawodawstwo Polski Odrodzonej o Gminach Żydowskich," in Schiper, et al. *Żydzi w Polsce Odrodzonej*, 2: 242–48, especially p. 245.

26. The case here cited is from a long interview with the plucky board member who spoke up. Another case which points to resistance to government supervision, is the study of the kehilla in the larger city of Częstochowa, cited in William M. Glicksman, *A Kehillah in Poland During the Inter-War Years* (Philadelphia: Advertisers Press, 1970), pp. 69–80.

27. Jacob Lestchinsky, "Economic Aspects of Jewish Community Organi-

zation in Independent Poland," *Jewish Social Studies*, 9, no. 4 (October 1947): 334.

28. *Ibid.*, pp. 330–31, 334.

29. Zosa Szajkowski, "Budgeting American Jewish Overseas Relief, 1919–1939," *American Jewish Historical Quarterly*, no. 59 (1969): 92–97, 112.

30. For the Warsaw kehilla, see Maurycy Mayzel, "O Planach Naszej Działalności," *Głos Gminy Żydowskiej*, 1, no. 1 (July 1937): 2–3; for the kehillot in general, see Maurycy Mayzel, "O Działalności Gmin Żydowskich w Dziedzinie Opieki Społecznej," *Głos Gminy Żydowskiej*, 2, no. 4 (April 1938): 75–76.

31. For an example of debts in a large community, see Mayzel, "O Działalności Gmin Żydowskich," pp. 75–76. For a case study providing insight into the effect of such debts on factional antagonisms, see Glicksman, *A Kehilla in Poland*, pp. 111–12.

32. Dawidsohn, *Gminy Żydowskie*, p. 22. For a case study, documenting such interference by the authorities, see Glicksman, *A Kehillah in Poland*, pp. 33, 73–74.

33. Since the formulation was regarded by many as vague and lending itself to political misuse, I cite the key words in Polish: "którzy wystepują przeciw wyznaniu mojżeszowemu," quoted in Ringel, "Ustawodawstwo Polski Odrodzonej," pp. 242–48.

34. For an example, see Glicksman, *A Kehillah in Poland*, pp. 41–42.

35. See, for example, Rabbi Schorr who while outlining the situation of the Jews, devoted his speech to "the economic degradation of Polish Jewry and the hardships connected with the struggle for a bare existence." Rabbi M. Schorr, *The Present Position of Jews in Poland—An Address before London Ort*, at Woburn House, January 14, 1935. (Warsaw, n.d.), p. 3.

36. Judith R. Kramer, *The American Minority Community* (New York: Thomas Y. Crowell, 1970), p. 21.

37. Heller, "How the Polish Jew Saw His World," p. 74. Subsequently, Fanon noted a similar phenomenon among the oppressed Africans, describing how to them the "zombies are more terrifying than the settlers." His explanation, too, is similar: the oppressed Blacks "perceive that all is settled by a permanent confrontation on the phantasmic plane." See: Franz Fanon, *The Wretched of the Earth* (New York: Grove Press, 1968), p. 56.

38. For a brief review of this role of the court-Jew in Europe, see: Werner J. Cahnman, "Pariahs, Strangers and Court-Jews: Conceptual Clarifica-

tion," *Sociological Analysis*, 35, no. 3 (Fall 1974): 161–63. Also Selma Stern, *The Court Jew* (Philadelphia: The Jewish Publication Society), 1950.

39. Feliks Gross, in his discussion of ethnic relations in Poland, underlines the difference between intergroup and interpersonal relations. To paraphrase, he notes that often the person who could express antagonism against an entire ethnic group could still be friendly with a single member of that group. Gross, *World Politics and Tension Areas* (New York: New York University Press, 1966), pp. 133–44.

40. A. Gotesdiner, *Af Unzere Vegn* (Warsaw, Toyre Vaavoyde, 1934).

41. Rabinowicz, *The Legacy of Polish Jewry*, p. 132

42. Leopold Halpern, *Polityka Żydowska w Sejmie i Senacie 1919–31* (Warsaw, 1933), pp. 8–9.

43. Isaac Lewin, "Di Politishe Oryentatsye," in *Tsu der Geshikhte fun "Agudas Yisroel"* (New York: Orthodox Library, 1964), pp. 29–30.

44. Quoted in Ezra Mendelsohn, "Agudas Yisroel in Poland," in *Soviet Jewish Affairs*, 2, no. 2 (1972): 51. This article represents an important breakthrough in the treatment of the subject. The author has brought to his subject a measure of objectivity heretofore not encountered in the writings about Agudat Israel.

45. From *Der Yud*, November 1, 1922, quoted in *ibid.*, p. 59, n. 20.

46. Wrote Sartre: "For a Jew, conscious and proud of being Jewish, asserting his claim to be a member of the Jewish community without ignoring on that account the bonds which unite him to the national community, there may not be so much difference between the anti-Semite and the democrat. The former *wishes to destroy* him as a man; . . . the latter wishes to destroy him as a Jew and leave nothing in him but the man, the abstract and universal subject of the rights of man and the rights of the citizen" (italics supplied). Jean-Paul Sartre, *Antisemite and Jew*, tr. George J. Becker (New York: Schocken Books, 1948), p. 57.

47. The main part of this declaration is reproduced in Halpern, *Polityka Zydowska w Sejmie i Senacie*, pp. 9–10; Lewin, "Di Politishe Oryentatsye," p. 20.

48. Their conception is simply expressed in the Polish section of an issue of the Agudah journal for women, aimed at educating young women from Orthodox homes who were unable to read the Yiddish section: "Judaism is something more than just a nation and something more than just a religion. Therefore, various national and religious theories applied to the Jewish people cannot but miss their mark." See "Religja a Nacjonalizm w Zydostwie," *Beys-Yankev Zhurnal*, no. 32, May 1928.

49. Mendelsohn, "Agudas Yisroel in Poland," p. 49.

50. Isaac Lewin, "Di Politishe Oryentatsye," p. 20. My statement about Rabbi Halpern's mastery of the Polish language is based on interviews with individuals who have heard him speak, as well as members of his family. For his defense of the Talmud, see, for example, the report in the pro-Zionist independent Yiddish daily: "Di Nekhtige Zitsung fun Seym," Der Moment, December 3, 1920, p. 7.

51. M. A. Hartglas, Na Pograniczu Dwóch Światow—Pamiętniki, 1952 (unpublished). (Permission to quote was generously granted by Professor S. Simonsohn, Rector of Tel-Aviv University.)

52. The quote is from the declaration. See: Dr. Filip Friedman, "Dzieje Żydow w Polsce Odrodzonej (1918–1938)," Głos Gminy Żydowskiej, vol. 2, nos. 10–11 (Warsaw, Oct.–Nov. 1938): 249.

53. From part of the resolution reproduced in Halpern, Polityka Żykowska w Sejmie Senacie, p. 33.

54. In this election, the Jewish parties ran four separate tickets, in addition to the Zionists of former Congress Poland, who were part of the National Minorities' Bloc ticket. It is difficult to estimate how many Jewish votes were cast on that ticket. The total vote of the ticket led by the "Galician" Zionists (240,780 votes) substantially exceeded that of the Agudah (171,987) but the Bund polled less than half that amount (80, 219 votes). Ibid., pp. 33–34.

55. Ibid., p. 33; Friedman, "Dzieje Żydów w Polsce Odrodzonej, p. 250; Yitzhak Meyer Lewin, "Der Matsev in der Arbet fun Agudas Yisroel," pp. 2–6.

56. Yitzhak Meyer Lewin, "Der Matsev in der Arbet fun Agudas Yisroel," p. 6.

57. Isaac Lewin, "Di Politishe Oryentatsye," p. 34. The then president of the Agudah, in describing the 1928 campaign said: "Accusations which the greatest anti-Semites would not allow themselves to make were hauled at us." Yitzhak Meyer Lewin, "Der Matsev in der Arbet fun Agudas Yisroel," p. 6.

58. Yitzhak Meyer Lewin, "Der Matsev in der Arbet fun Agudas Yisroel," pp. 5–6.

59. Dos Yidishe Togblat, January 5, 1934, p. 5. As quoted in Mendelsohn, "Agudas Yisroel in Poland," p. 55.

60. A. Friedman, "In Tsaytn fun Shvere Nisyoynes," in Beys-Yankev Zhurnal, no. 140 (1937); P. Wasserman, "W Obronie Sumienia," Głos Gminy Żydowskiej, 2, no. 3 (Warsaw, March 1938): 52.

61. Mendelsohn, "Agudas Yisroel in Poland," p. 53.

62. From part of the speech reproduced in: Isaac Lewin, "Di Politishe Oryentatsye," p. 29.

63. Mendelsohn, "Agudas Yisroel in Poland," p. 57.

64. Celia Stopnicka Heller, "Deviation and Social Change in the Jewish Community of a Small Polish Town," *American Journal of Sociology*, September 1954, pp. 177–81.

VI. Assimilationists: Poles in Culture and Self-Identity

1. For more on their history, see: Celia Stopnicka Heller, "Poles of Jewish Background—The Case of Assimilation without Integration in Interwar Poland," in Joshua A. Fishman, ed.: *Studies on Polish Jewry, 1919–1939*, (New York: YIVO Institute for Jewish Research, 1974), pp. 244–50.

2. Israel Cohen, "Documents—My Mission to Poland (1918–19)," *Jewish Social Studies*, no. 13 (April 1951): 159.

3. *Pamiętnik Pierwszego Walnego Zjazdu Zjednoczenia Mojżeszowego Wszystkich Ziem Polskich* (Warsaw 1919). Quotes in the order they appear in the text from pages 4, 54–55.

4. Leopold Halpern, *Polityka Żydowska w Sejmie i Senacie 1919–31* (Warsaw, 1933), p. 9.

5. It is exemplified by the 1924 occurrence in the Warsaw kehilla, which was once the epitome of assimilationist influences. In the election of a new board, all assimilationist candidates were defeated, whereupon the Polish government claimed the right to nominate three additional members (by reason that the board had to represent all tendencies among Jews) and proceeded to do so. But the newly elected members of the board, irrespective of their political affiliation, voted not to seat anyone appointed by the government. *Bulletin*, Jewish Telegraphic Mail Service, June 22, 1924.

6. "Alliance Israelite Organ on Elimination of Assimilationists in Poland," *Jewish Telegraphic Mail Service*, Paris, January 8, 1928.

7. A. Lewiński, "Od Słow do Czynów," *Zjednoczenie*, vol. 2, no. 2 (February 15, 1932): 1–2. See also: A. G., "Aktualna Sprawa," *Zjednoczenie*, 1, no. 3 (November 15, 1931): 12. The name of the organization for which the initials ZAMZ stood was *Związek Akademicki Młodzieży Zjednoczeniowej*.

8. E. Pechnik, "Zjednoczenie 'na Przełomie'?" *Zjednoczenie*, 2, no. 4 (April 15, 1932): 6. This article presents a succinct rendition of the ide-

ology of the "neoassimilationists." It was reflected in all of the issues of the same periodical, the official mouthpiece of the ZAMZ, which began publishing in September 1931 and carried the masthead: "The monthly dedicated to the cause of uniting the Jews with the Polish state and nation" (hence its name, *Unity*.) For an article explaining the resolutions taken at the national convention in 1928, including the one against Jewish "clericalism" and the kehillot, see: *Zjednoczenie*, 2, No. 1 (January 15, 1932): 14. For the term "neoassimilationists," see Leo Belmont, "Neoasimilacja czyli rzecz o Semi-Polakach," *Zjednoczenie*, 2 (July–September 1932): 1. About a year later he concretized thus the difference between this group and the old type of assimilationists, "the Poles of Mosaic faith": "they do not base themselves on the theological principle and admit to its ranks even declared non-believers or individuals completely neutral on the question of religious faith." Belmont, "Nie 'W Obronie Mechesów,' " *Zjednoczenie*, 3, nos. 6–7 (June–July 1933): 6–7.

9. Benedykt Hertz, *Żydowska Krew* (Warsaw: Ludwik Fiszer, 193–), p. 14.

10. According to the 1921 census (the only census in interwar Poland that carried the entry for nationality as well as religion) 9.8 percent of Poland's population declared themselves "of Mosaic faith" but only 8.6 percent said that they were of Jewish nationality. The 1.2 percent of Poland's population who considered themselves of "Mosaic faith" but of Polish nationality probably comprised some others but most were assimilationists. *Mały Rocznik Statystyczny* (Warsaw, 1939), pp. 23, 24; *The Polish and non-Polish Populations of Poland* (Warsaw: Institute for the Study of Minority Problems, 1932), Jan Szczepański, *Polish Society* (New York: Random House, 1970, p. 27).

11. Aleksander Hertz, *Żydzi w Kulturze Polskiej* (Paris: Instytut Literacki, 1961), p. 132.

12. Marian Drozdowski, *Polityka Gospodarcza Rządu Polskiego, 1936–39* (Warsaw, 1963), p. 94.

13. For the development of the sociological concept of identificational assimilation as distinct from cultural assimilation, see Milton M. Gordon, *Assimilation in American Life* (New York: Oxford University Press, 1964), pp. 52–54, 68–71.

14. Janusz Żarnowski, *Społeczenstwo Drugiej Rzeczypospolitej, 1918–39* (Warsaw, 1973), p. 393.

15. The Jewish Telegraphic Agency in a special bulletin thus commented on their lack of religiosity while reporting on an article which appeared in the *Paix et Droit*, (organ of the Alliance Israélite Universelle in Paris): "At bottom, in a country where nationality is still merged in religion, where

the Pole is Catholic and the German Protestant, their position of Pole of the Mosaic Faith was false, all the more false as many of these Poles of the Mosaic Faith had no faith, and this inner contradiction sapped their whole position. The recrudescence of Polish anti-Semitism has brutally given the lie to their dream of civic fraternization." Reported in a special bulletin of the Jewish Telegraphic Agency: "Alliance Israelite Organ on Elimination of Assimilationists in Poland," *Jewish Telegraphic Agency Mail Service,* Paris, January 8, 1928.

16. Horace M. Kallen, "The Foundations of Jewish Spiritual and Cultural Unity," *Judaism,* 6 (Spring, 1957): 110–18.

17. Pechnik, "Zjednoczenie 'na Przełomie'?" pp. 4–5. For a report on the reactions of the Jewish press to the first issue of the above publication, see: "Przegląd Prasy," *Zjednoczenie,* 1, no. 4 (December 15, 1931): 10.

18. On the occasion of the death of an older champion of assimilation who had acted as an adviser to and consultant for this young group, the article from which these quotes come pointed up the distinguishing characteristics of these young assimilationists. See "Kazimierz Sterling," *Zjednoczenie,* 3, no. 5 (May 1933): 1–3.

19. See, for example: Ezra Mendelsohn, "Jewish Assimilation in Lvov: The Case of Wilhelm Feldman," *Slavic Review,* 28 (December 1969): 583–84.

20. This can be illustrated historically with the cases of prominent families. Take for example, the case of the very rich Matiasz Berson. An avowed assimilationist, he nevertheless set up the first Jewish museum and heavily supported Jewish institutions. His daughter Jadwiga converted. Her daughter, Zuzanna Kraushar, a poet, was married to a Polish nationalist, Władysław Rabski, who during the interwar period systematically attacked Jews in the newspaper, *Kurier Warszawski,* to which he was a steady contributor. Another example is the case of Jan Bloch (1836–1901), a financier and railway contractor. Although he converted as a young adult, he showed much concern for the Jewish community and supported Jewish institutions. In his testament he wrote: "I was my whole life a Jew and I die as a Jew." But his son and four daughters were completely estranged from Jews and the Jewish community. See the eulogy written on Bloch's death by Nahum Sokolow: "The Loyal Convert," in Lucy S. Dawidowicz, ed., *The Golden Tradition,* (New York: Holt, Rinehart and Winston, 1967), pp. 345–49. For the information on Berson's activities reflecting pride in Jewish culture, see: M. Bałaban, *Zabytki Historyczne Żydow w Polsce* (Warsaw, 1931), p. 26.

21. Janusz Korczak, "Mośki, Joski, i Srule, in *Na Koloniach Letnich* (Warsaw, 1946), p. 54. See also Janusz Korczak, *Wybór Pism* (Warsaw: Nasza Księgarnia, 1957). From an assimilationist family, this famous writer and

educator of the interwar period was also known for his work with Jewish disadvantaged children. With the rise of Hitler and the advent of official anti-Semitism in Poland, his Jewish consciousness deepened. During World War II, as head of a Jewish orphanage, he refused to part from his charges and shared their death. For a biographical note, see *Encyclopedia Judaica*, 1971, vol. 10, pp. 1200–1201; For a moving article about him, see James Feron, "Awarding of West German Peace Prize Stirs Memories of Wartime Martyr of the Warsaw Ghetto," *The New York Times*, Oct. 1, 1972, p. 14.

22. At the national convention of the "Association of Poles of Mosaic Faith," meeting shortly after independence was declared speaker after speaker bemoaned that Jews were still using the "jargon." For example, Kazimierz Sterling, a judge, said: "the tongue of a significant part of the Jewish masses is the jargon, which is nothing else but spoiled German." Kazimierz Sterling, "Przeszłość i Stan Dzisiejszy Sprawy Żydowskiej w Polsce," *Pamiętnik Pierwszego Walnego Zjazdu Zjednoczenia Mojżeszowego Wszystkich Ziem Polskich* (Warsaw, 1919), p. 29. For a series of articles in the organ of the neoassimilationists, which expressed the same attitude to Yiddish, dismissed the Yiddish novels as unworthy of the name literature, and bemoaned a newly published translation of a book by Sholem Aleichem because the "ghetto" types in it would increase the revulsion that Poles felt toward Jews, see Leo Belmont, "Służący Odrodzonego Ghetta," *Zjednoczenie*, vol. 1, no. 3 (November 15, 1931): 5–9. (The article continued in the next few issues.)

23. M. A. Hartglas, *Na Pograniczu Dwóch Światów—Pamiętniki*, 1952 (unpublished). For further insight into this social divide, see: A. Tartakower, "W Walce o Pracę Żydowską," *Nasza Trybuna*, Warsaw, November 20, 1937, p. 3; Jerzy Tomaszewski, "Robotnicy Żydowscy w Polsce (1921–39)," *Biultetyn Żydowskiego Instytutu Historycznego*, no. 51 (Aug.–Sept., 1964): 28–29, A. Tartakower, "Mur Bojkotu," *Nasza Trybuna*, Warsaw, December 20, 1937, p. 4.

24. This is also reflected in the autobiographical writings of prominent assimilationists, even political radicals. For example, Feliks Kohn, the renowned Communist leader, began his book thus: "I was born in Warsaw, May 30, 1864. My parents were Jews devoted to the cause of Poland's liberation. Mother took a direct part in the uprising of 1863. . . . When I recall my childhood days, to this time I see my mother, sitting at the table and telling of Poland's suffering, of men who rose in Poland's defense." Feliks Kohn, *Pod Sztandarem Rewolucji* (Moscow, 1931). See also: Bolesław Drobner, *Bezustanna Walka—Wspomnienia*, vol. 1 (Warsaw: Państwowy Instytut Wydawniczy, 1962), pp. 16–17. I do not necessarily accept these statements as factual; they may have been politically or socially motivated.

25. See Carl N. Degler, *Neither Black nor White—Slavery and Race Relations in Brazil and the United States* (New York: Macmillan, 1971), pp. xii, 107–10.

26. See S. J. Imber, *Asy Czystej Rasy* (Cracow, 1934), especially p. 25; Mieczysław Wardzinski, "Antysemityzm-Daltonizmem Państwowym," *Wiadomości Literackie*, August 4, 1937; Aleksander Hertz, *Żydzi w Kulturze Polskiej*, p. 219.

27. For a historical illustration, see the first example in note 20. The pattern is also depicted in a number of Yiddish novels, notably: I. J. Singer, *The Brothers Ashkenazi* (New York: Alfred Knopf, 1936), p. 178.

28. For example, Boleslaw Drobner, a leading socialist, who officially declared himself *bezwyznaniowy*, without religious affiliation, wrote that he sent his children for Protestant rather than Jewish religious instruction in order to conform to the rule of compulsory attendance at religious classes. See Drobner, *Bezustanna Walka*, vol. 2 (Warsaw, 1965), p. 278.

29. A. Tartakower, "Stan Liczebny i Rozwój Naturalny Ludności Żydowskiej w Polsce," in I. Schiper, *et al.*, *Żydzi w Polsce Ordrodzonej* (Warsaw, 1935), vol. 2, p. 222.

30. Significantly, in the discussion in the "neoassimilationist" youth publication about the increasing conversions it is stated: "We must admit that the so called renegades come from our [assimilationist] milieu rather than those close to Zionism or Orthodoxy." See: Nina Heromanówna, "W Obronie Mechesów—Artykuł Dyskusyjny,"*Zjednoczenie*, 3, no. 5 (May 1933): 11.

31. S. H., "Typy 'Mechesów,' " *Zjednoczenie* vol. 3, no. 5 (May 1933): 8. For an example of a case of the extremely rare conversion of a nonassimilated Jew, the sculptor Marek Szwarc, see the book written by his daughter, Tereska Torres, *The Converts* (New York: Alfred A. Knopf, 1970).

32. Hertz, *Zydzi w Kulturze Polskiej*, p. 111.

33. See: S. H., "Typy 'Mechesów,' " pp. 7–10; Nina Heromanówna, "W Obronie Mechesów, pp. 10–11; Leo Belmont, "Nie 'W Obronie Mechesów,' " pp. 6–7. An example of a typical pragmatic conversion can be found in Helen Deutsch's autobiography. She describes candidly the case of her brother who failed to show in school "the least trace of his father's intellect or character." The father therefore "decided to let Emil be baptized. Only in this way would he be able to make a career for himself in civil service. Accordingly Emil was baptized and made his career, later marrying the daughter of a Polish general." Helene Deutsch, *Confrontations With Myself—An Epilogue* (New York: W. W. Norton, 1973), p. 37.

34. Ksawery Pruszyński, "W Najwiekszym Skrócie," *Wiadomości Literackie*, 21 (May 16, 1937). For nineteenth-century assimilation "which as a rule was connected with conversion to Catholicism or Lutheranism," see: Tadeusz Lepkowski, *Polska—Narodziny Nowoczesnego Narodu, 1764–1870* (Warsaw: Państwowe Wydawnictwo Naukowe, 1967), p. 170.

35. An earlier historical example might be that of the historian, Aleksander Kraushar and his wife Jadwiga who became converted in 1883. When she died in 1912, the Polish press paid tribute to her as "a shining example of Polishness." *Bibloteka Warszawska*, the oldest Polish monthly (founded with the help of wealthy Jews) wrote of her on this occasion: "Born and reared in the Jewish faith, she embraced Catholicism at a mature age in order to bind herself to Poland by the strongest ties. This she did as a result of genuine faith. From then on she remained a devout and convinced Catholic until the end of her days." Her funeral was the talk of Warsaw. More than a hundred priests, headed by the bishop, joined the cortege. Her husband, according to Shatzky, "came to believe that Catholicism and Polonism were synonymous." See: Jacob Shatzky, "Alexander Kraushar on his Road to Total Assimilation," *YIVO Annual of Jewish Social Science*, 7 (1952): 148, 172.

36. However, such deviation in practice from their ideology, seems to have been not at all uncommon. An article devoted to the problem of increased conversions among the young, which appeared in *Unity*, designates such radicals as a distinctive type among the converts: "The radical type: Of course, he does not recognize any religious beliefs, and especially religious superstitions. He is an enemy of clericalism, he is a free thinker, a progressive, . . . even a revolutionary. But he thinks that '*just in case,*' it is better to have 'Roman Catholic' than 'Mosaic' faith stamped in one's personal documents. . . . To declare himself officially without a religion also does not appeal to him. *One thing is theory and another practice.* Parenthetically, in certain leftist circles such 'just in case' conversions are well regarded, which in turn results in the proliferation of such radicals who convert." S. H., "Typy 'Mechesów,' " p. 10.

37. This part of the Declaration is reproduced in: *Zjednoczenie*, 2, no. 1 (January 15, 1932): 14.

38. Through centuries of contact a substantial amount of amalgamation occurred. Teodor Jeske-Choiński, in his anti-Semitic and incomplete work, nevertheless presents fairly reliable evidence (based on years of searching in local church archives) tracing 500 Polish families with Jewish mixture. This book served as a source of information for those attempting to expose the Jewish ancestry of political opponents. See: Teodor Jeske-Choiński, *Neofici Polscy* (Warsaw, 1905). For the question of the reliability of his data, see: Benedykt Hertz, *Żydowska Krew*, p. 26. For

another work, by a Jew, see Matthias Mieses, *Polacy Chrześcijanie Pocho-dozenia Żydowskiego*, 2 volumes (Warsaw, 1938). For the extent to which the phenomenon of "unmasking" Jewish ancestry continued in postwar Communist Poland, see: Celia Stopnicka Heller, " 'Anti-Zionism' and the Political Struggle within the Elite of Poland," *The Jewish Journal of Sociology*, 11, no. 2 (December 1969): 133–50.

39. For example, a sensation was caused when Wojciech Wasiutyński, known for his anti-Semitic and racist articles, took a man to court for impugning his reputation in public by asserting that his grandfather, Józef Buchbinder, was a Jew; Wasiutyński claimed this was not true. The court ruled that it was not libel since he was in fact a Jew. The presiding judge, Leszczyński, who exemplifies those too often forgotten Poles who were revolted by and ashamed of such doings, declared in court: "Not wealth, not origin, testify to a man's worth but his spirit, character, and personal traits." "W Świetle Logiki i Dokumentów," *Wiadomości Literackie*, 22 (May 23, 1937): 7.

40. From part reprinted in: "W Młynie Opinii," *Nasz Przegląd*, August 3, 1938, p. 5.

41. "W Młynie Opinii—'Tragedia' Wychrztów," *Nasz Przegląd*, July 20, 1938, p. 6.

42. Gordon, *Assimilation in American Life*, pp. 52–54, 68–71.

43. For an example of such attacks, and how they supposedly affected his psyche and in turn his political posture, see the carefully documented study about Tuwim by Magnus J. Kryński, "Politics and Poetry: The Case of Julian Tuwim," *The Polish Review*, 18, no. 4 (1973): 3–33. For the integrated intellectual circles, see: Feliks Gross, *World Politics and Tension Areas* (New York: New York University Press, 1966), p. 140.

44. See Hirszfeld's memoirs, written during the war: *Historia Jednego Życia* (Warsaw: Czytelnik, 1946), p. 164.

45. See for example the study of Jews in coal mining. Jewish small mine owners or contractors, as well as Jews employed in mining, were driven out of the industry by anti-Semitism. But the large mine owners "shortly after accumulating a fortune broke completely with their environment . . . . an expression of this was the common pattern of change in religion. . . . The large capitalists were able to hold on to their enterprises to the beginning of World War II." Jerzy Jaros, "Wiadomości o Żydach Czynnych w Polskim Przemyśle Węglowym," *Biuletyn Żydowskiego Instytutu Historycznego*, Warsaw, no. 35 (July–August 1960), p. 99.

46. Professor Hirszfeld, speaks in his memoirs of the aversion that the assimilationists felt toward the Jewish masses. See *Historia Jednego Życia*,

pp. 256–59. Such sentiments are also recalled by Arthur Rubinstein in *My Young Years* (New York: Alfred A. Knopf, 1973), p. 363. He assures us in the Foreword to his book, that he is endowed with an "uncanny memory" for past events and conversations. He admits: "My point of view was that anti-Semitism [dislike of Jews] in many ways, was justifiable." He tells how as a young man in Warsaw, while involved in a discussion of anti-Semitism he argued: "When I see these rich Jews and wives behaving in public the way they do . . . I can understand the indignation of the Gentiles." To the objection that these were but a small minority among Jews, he replied: "but what have we on the other hand? The ghettos? These masses of meek little men with their beards and side curls, afraid of everything and everybody? Why don't they use their born gifts and intelligence for something better than buying and selling old clothes? It infuriates me when anti-Semitic Poles slander us, calling us Jews usurers and thieves. I know that we have, fortunately a highly cultured elite, too . . . but it is too small—it is unable to offset the bad effect of the rest." He points out, however, that his views have changed since then; he became proud of being a Jew.

47. Erving Goffman, *Stigma: Notes on the Management of Spoiled Identity* (Englewood Cliffs, N.J.: Prentice Hall, 1963), pp. 43–44.

48. Eric H. Erikson, "Autobiographic Notes on Identity Crisis," *Daedalus*, Fall 1970, pp. 730–59.

49. The poems were entitled "Stockbrokers" and "The Bank." Ironically his poetry was attacked even more vehemently by Polish anti-Semites. See Kryński, "The Case of Julian Tuwim," p. 7.

50. Since this may appear doubtful to those who know the author by his moving poem of regret about the absence of Jews in the small towns of post–World War II Poland, I present a typical quote: "One of the cardinal and most characteristic Jewish traits is making light of the most sacred accomplishments of the human spirit. They make light of everything: they murder the language [Polish] when they speak it; they disregard the purity of language, body and heart but they overvalue . . . the meaning of money." He attacked the "touchiness" of Jewish nationalists "who cry about their *mangy* pride" and asserted that if they really had national pride, they would get out of Poland, "a country where the word Jew is considered on insult." But they stay on, to make money. Antoni Słonimski, "O Drażliwosci Żydów," *Wiadomości Literackie*, no. 35, 1924, p. 3. Significantly, this article was utilized by Władyslaw Gomułka when in 1968 he launched his "anti-Zionist" campaign against assimilationist Jews in Communist Poland. See: *Trybuna Ludu*, March 20, 1968, p. 4. Also: Heller, " 'Anti-Zionism' and the Political Struggle within the Elite of Poland," pp. 133–50.

51. Sartre sees in such manifestations a certain consciousness of being a Jew: "At that very moment when he is forcing himself by his whole conduct to deny the traits ascribed to him, he feels that he can see these traits in others, and thus they return to him indirectly . . . he affirms that he is only one man among others, and like others, yet he feels himself compromised by the demeanor of the first passer-by, if that passer-by is a Jew." See: Jean-Paul Sartre, *Anti-Semite and Jew*, tr. George J. Becker (New York: Schocken, 1948, p. 106); Kurt Lewin, "Self-Hatred among Jews," *Contemporary Jewish Record*, 4 (June 1941): 225. For similar manifestations among blacks in the United States, see E. Franklin Frazier, *Black Bourgeoisie* (New York: The Free Press, 1957).

52. Albert Memmi, *The Colonizer and the Colonized* (New York: The Orion Press, 1965), p. 121.

53. Sartre, *Anti-Semite and Jew*, pp. 90, 136–37.

54. The strength of the Polish self-identification of assimilationists is dramatically illustrated in the autobiography of Helen Deutsch, one of the first in the pioneering group of women analysts surrounding Freud. She had left Poland as a young girl, and, after a passionate love affair with Herman Lieberman (one of the founders of the Polish Socialist Party) ended, she married a Zionist. Still, in her old age, when she wrote her autobiography, she continued to adhere to her self-identity as a Pole. She wrote: "This love of Polish [patriotic] poets lasted all my life and always formed a bond with my country after I left it for good, and even after its increasing anti-semitism." And later she confessed: "As the story of my childhood indicates, I always identified myself intensely with Poland. Felix [her husband] and I had stereotyped discussions on the subject which never solved the disagreement between us: he regarded my nationality as Jewish, I, as Polish. . . . Felix's death brought me closer to his Jewish ideology." Deutsch, *Confrontations With Myself*, pp. 67, 196–97.

55. Aleksander Gurewicz, "Echo z Zaświatów," *Zjednoczenie*, 2, no. 5 (May 1932): 10.

56. See the article by his wife: Pola Apenszlak, "Nasz Przegląd," in *Di Yidishe Prese Vos Iz Geven* (Tel-Aviv: World Association of Jewish Journalists, 1975), pp. 223–31.

57. A pre-independence case, is that of Alfred Nossig, the first editor of the Lvov assimilationist organ, *Ojczyzna*, who broke with assimilationism and embraced Zionism. See Ezra Mendelsohn, "From Assimilation to Zionism in Lvov. The Case of Alfred Nossig." *The Slavonic and East European Review*, 49, no. 117 (October 1971): 521–34.

58. Hartglas, *Na Pograniczu Dwóch Światów—Pamiętniki.*

59. Reprinted speech of Prof. Dr. Zdzisław Zmigryder-Konopka,

"W Rocznicę Sprawiedliwości Dziejowej, Przemówienie Wygłoszone na Akademji XX-lecia Odrodzenia Polski, Urządzonej przez Związek U-czestników Walk o Niepodległość Polski," *Nasz Przegląd,* November 27, 1938, p. 21. On another occasion, he explained that as one appointed to the Senate by the President, he considered himself as representing in this body not assimilationists, but all Jews. See "Obywatel w Ramach Państwa—Odczyt Sen. Dr. Zmigrydera-Konopki," *Nasz Przegląd,* June 12, 1939, p. 9. Convinced that the artist is often able to capture with his intuition new trends before others are aware of them, I would like to quote a Yiddish writer, Szymon Horończyk, who announced at the end of 1937 his intention to deal in his future work with the crisis of assimilationist youth. This writer of proletarian novels declared that he aimed "to open up in a series of short stories and novels the life of the assimilated Jewish youth, which has lost the ground under its feet and wants now to return to Jewry and yet cannot bring itself to a definite decision." *Nasza Trybuna,* November 5, 1937, p. 5. He had no chance to realize his aim; he committed suicide in 1939 after his son was killed.

60. Sartre, *Anti-Semite and Jew,* p. 92; see also pp. 136–38.

VII. Between Tradition and Assimilation

1. The romanticizing of that culture is even evidenced in studies that aim to be objective. See, for example, Mark Zborowski and Elizabeth Herzog, *Life Is with People—The Culture of the Shtetl* (New York: Schocken, 1952).

2. Lewis S. Feuer, "Generational Struggle as a Universal Theme of History," in *The Conflict of Generations* (New York: Basic Books, 1969), pp. 27–35.

3. For the difference between cultural and identificational assimilation, see Milton M. Gordon, *Assimilation in American Life* (New York: Oxford University Press), 1964, pp. 52–54, 68–71.

4. M. Bałaban, "Nasi Poprzednicy i Nauczyciele—Prasa Żydowska w XIX Wieku," *Nasz Przegląd,* September 18, 1938, p. 3.

5. Arieh Tartakower, "Yidishe Kultur in Polyn Tsvishn Tsvey Velt Milkhomes," *Gedank un Lebn* 4 (April–June, 1946):22–24; Pola Apenszlak, "Nasz Przegląd," *Di Yidishe Prese Vos Iz Geven* (Tel-Aviv: World Association of Jewish Journalists, 1975), pp. 223–31; David Lazer, "Nowy Dziennik—1918–39," *ibid.,* pp. 301–15; I. Remba, "Hebreishe Prese in Poyln Tsvishn Beyde Velt Milkhomes," *ibid.,* pp. 352–92; David Flinker—Moshe Ron, "Di Yidishe Prese in Poyln Tsvishn Beyde Velt Milkhomes,"

in *Yearbook*, vol. 2 (Tel Aviv: World Federation of Polish Jews, 1967), pp. 266–324.

6. For example, in an analysis of statistical data about the home language of Jewish university students, the author referred to the "tremendous linguistic assimilation of our professional (*diplomite*) intelligentsia" as "an important but dark corner of our life." See: L. Hersch, "Shprakhlikhe Asimilirtkeyt bay di Yidishe Studentn fun di Varshever Hokhshuln," *YIVO Bleter*, 2 (1931): 441. See also J. Lestchinsky, "Di Shprakhn bay Yidn in Umophengikn Poyln," *ibid.*, vol. 22, Nov.–Dec., 1943, pp. 147–62; and Tartakower's reference to linguistic assimilation: "Yidishe Kultur in Poyln," p. 7.

7. Menahem Mirkin, "Yidishe Talmidim in Mitlshuln in Poyln," *Yidishe Ekonomik*, no. 4–5 (1939), p. 265.

8. L. Hersch, "Shprakhlikhe Asimilirtkeyt," p. 441.

9. This is vividly demonstrated by Aleksander Hertz in his book, "The Jews in Polish Culture," (by now also available in English translation): *Żydzi w Kulturze Polskiej* (Paris: Instytut Literacki, 1961), especially pp. 264–70.

10. In Moshe Mishkinski, "Regional Factors in the Formation of the Jewish Labor Movement in Czarist Russia, *YIVO Annual of Jewish Social Science*, 14 (1969): 45.

11. Tartakower, "Yidishe Kultur," p. 6; See also Shlomo Schweizer, "Dos Yidishe Kulturlebn Tsvishn Beyde Velt Milkhomes," *Yearbook*, vol. 2, pp. 112–209.

12. Stanisław Mauersberg, *Szkolnictwo Powszechne dla Mniejszości Narodowych w Polsce w Latach 1918–1939* (Wrocław: Ossolineum, 1968), pp. 187–190.

13. Simon Segal, *The New Poland and the Jews* (New York: Lee Furman, 1938), p. 193.

14. *Budżet Państwa Polskiego na 1929–30r a Żydzi—Mowy w Sejmie i Senacie w Dyskusji Budżetowej*, Biuletyn 3 Klubu Posłow i Senatorów Żydowskiej Rady Narodowej (Warsaw, 1929), p. 158. See also Nathan Eck, "The Educational Institutions of Polish Jewry, 1921–39," *Jewish Social Studies*, 9. no. 1 (January 1947): 6.

15. Gedo Hecht, "20 Lat Szkolnictwa Żydowskiego w Polsce," *Almanach, Rocznik Naszego Przeglądu* (Warsaw, 1938), p. 58.

16. *Budżet Państwa Polskiego*, pp. 33, 47 (Gruenbaum), p. 66 (Wygodzki).

17. CYSHO distinguished itself by the imaginative use of modern educational methods. Its monthly publication, *Shulvegn*, attempted to guide and

coordinate its schools. But the organization was split into ideological factions, which managed to gain control of specific schools. For a thorough treatment in English of the various Jewish school systems see Eck, "The Educational Institutions of Polish Jewry," pp. 3–32. For one in Yiddish, see Tartakower, "Di Yidishe Shul in Poyln Tsvishn di Tsvey Velt Milkhomes," *Yearbook*, vol. 2 pp. 210–65.

18. Eck, "The Educational Institutions of Polish Jewry, pp. 4–6.

19. Samuel Chmielewski, "Stan Szkolnictwa Wśród Żydow w Polsce," *Sprawy Narodowościowe*, nos. 1–2 (Warsaw, 1937): 32–74.

20. Mauersberg, *Szkolnictwo Powszechne dla Mniejszości Narodowych*, pp. 168–71.

21. Moses Kligsberg, "Child and Adolescent Behavior under Stress—Terminal Progress Report," YIVO Institute for Jewish Research, 1965, p. 16 (unpublished). For a thorough case study of a heder in Poland, see Yekhiel Shtern, "A Kheyder in Tyszowce (Tishevits)," *YIVO Annual of Jewish Social Science*, 5 (1950): 152–71.

22. The white eagle is the national symbol of Poland. The verse in Polish: Kto ty jesteś? Polak mały. Jaki znak twój? Orzeł biały.

23. YIVO Autobiographies, No. 3587.

24. YIVO Autobiographies, No. 3716.

25. YIVO Autobiographies, No. 3815.

26. Harry M. Rabinowicz, *The Legacy of Polish Jewry* (New York: Thomas Yoseloff, 1965), pp. 89, 128. The theme of stronger Polish influences on Jewish women is found in Polish novels. (G. Zapolska, *Małka Szwarcenkopf* [Warsaw, 1903] or J. Stryjkowski, *Głosy w Ciemności*, postwar ed., Warsaw, 1957); and in Yiddish novels. (There are English translations of I. J. Singer, *The Brothers Ashkenazi* [New York: Alfred A. Knopf, 1956] and Joseph Opatoshu, *In Polish Woods* [Philadelphia: Jewish Publication Society of America, 1938].)

27. Arieh Tartahower, "Yidishe Kultur," p. 19.

28. YIVO Autobiographies, No. 3837.

29. Mirkin, "Yidishe Talmidim," p. 258.

30. *Ibid.*, p. 261; Chmielewski, "Stan Szkolnictwa Wśród Żydów w Polsce," p. 46; S. Bronsztejn, "The Jewish Population of Poland in 1931," *The Jewish Journal of Sociology*, 6, no. 1 (July 1964): 18–19.

31. Chmielewski, "Stan Szkolnictwa Wśród Żydow w Polsce," pp. 52–53.

32. Eck, "The Educational Institutions of Polish Jewry," pp. 6–12, 26–27; Tartakower, "Yidishe Kultur," pp. 5, 8.

33. Mirkin, "Yidishe Talmidim," pp. 262–65.

34. Also to a larger extent than elsewhere, the Jewish intelligentsia in these areas remained Yiddish-speaking. See Schweizer, "Dos Yidishe Kulturlebn," p. 115; Nathan Eck, "The Educational Institutions of Polish Jewry," p. 16.

35. Celia Stopnicka Heller, "Deviation and Social Change in the Jewish Community of a Small Polish Town," The American Journal of Sociology, 60 (September 1954): 177–81.

36. YIVO Autobiographies, No. 3822.

37. YIVO Autobiographies, No. 3597.

38. YIVO Autobiographies, No. 3577.

39. Tartakower, "Yidishe Kultur," p. 20. See also Jeremiasz Frankel, "Znaczenie Nauczania Religji i Wychowania Religijnego," Miesięcznik Żydowki, July–December, 1932, pp. 238–39.

40. Much has been written about this earlier conflict. See, for example: Shmarya Levin, Youth in Revolt (New York: Harcourt Brace, 1930). For a concise treatment, based on such writings see Feuer, The Conflict of Generations, (New York: Basic Books, 1969), pp. 154–72.

41. Max Weinreich, Der Veg Tsu Undzer Yugnt, Vilno: YIVO, 1935; Also his "Studium o Młodzieży Żydowskiej," Przegląd Socjologiczny, vol. 3 (1935): 30–83.

42. For more detailed information on the importance of children, see Zborowski and Herzog, Life Is with People, pp. 308–360.

43. YIVO Autobiographies, No. 3598.

44. Bernard Singer, Moje Nalewki (Warsaw: Czytelnik, 1959), p. 128.

45. Our understanding of the impact of unemployment on the authority of the father in the family is furthered by such works as Marie Jahoda, Paul F. Lazarsfeld and Hans Zeisel, Die Arbeitslosen von Marienthal (Bonn: Verlag fuer Demoskopie, 1960); Mirra Komarovsky, The Unemployed Man and His Family (New York: The Dryden Press, 1940); E. Wright Bakke, Citizens without Work (New Haven: Yale University Press, 1940), pp. 154–225.

46. YIVO Autobiographies, No. 3581.

47. Max Weinreich, Der Veg Tsu Undzer Yugnt, also his "Studium o Młodziezy Żydowskiej," pp. 44–45.

48. YIVO Autobiographies, No. 3597.

49. YIVO Autobiographies, No. 3716.

50. YIVO Autobiographies, No. 3737.

51. Eric H. Erikson, "Autobiographic Notes on Identity Crisis," *Daedalus*, Fall 1970, pp. 730–59.

52. For special insights into the anxiety resulting from being culturally uprooted, see Richard Hoggart, *The Uses of Literacy* (New York: Oxford University Press, 1970), pp. 238–59.

53. Isaac Deutscher, *The Non-Jewish Jew and other Essays* (London: Oxford University Press, 1968), pp. 46–47; see also p. 44. The same sentiment is expressed by Sholem Asch through the mouth of the fictional Polish Jew, Shachliner: "The religion whose praises you're singing is no romantic tradition from the past. . . . It's the Chinese shoe that cramps us. . . . You people who have never lived in the 'mansions' that the Jewish religion has built for us . . . begin to have longings for 'indigenous values' when you're fed up with your luxuries and thrown out of your mansions; well, just come and live the 'indigenous' life among us, and then you'll see where the shoe pinches!" Sholem Asch, *Three Cities* (New York: Putnam, 1933), pp. 327–28.

54. YIVO Autobiographies, No. 3739.

55. For a theoretical discussion of identity as a "psychosocial" concept, see: Erikson, "Autobiographic Notes on Identity Crisis," pp. 730–59; for the role of ideology in the pre-World War II world, see: Karl Mannheim, *Ideology and Utopia* (New York: Harcourt, Brace & World, 1936); on the question of universal human needs: Celia S. Heller, "Toward the Conceptualization of Needs," Paper presented at the Annual Meeting of the American Sociological Association," St. Louis, August, 1961 (unpublished).

VIII. Jewish Resistance to Oppression

1. It began with the resolution against anti-Semitism at the first convention after its founding and continued with various resolutions and appeals against the "national oppression" of Jews. See, for example: *Unter der Fon fun KPP* (Warsaw: 1959), p. 21.

2. The above figure is higher than the one based on the sources of the Polish government of that time, which kept a close tab on the Communists. See Tadeusz Jędruszczak, *Piłsudczycy bez Piłsudskiego—Powstanie Obozu Zjednoczenia Narodowego w 1937r* (Warsaw, 1963), p. 32. For the data on the percentages of Jews, see Julian Auerbach, "Niektóre Zagadnienia Działalności KPP w Srodowisku Zydowskim w Latach Kryzysu (1929–1933)," *Biuletyn Żydowskiego Instytutu Historycznego*, no. 55 (Aug.–Sept. 1965), p. 42. A few active Communists of that period whom I interviewed estimated the proportion of Jews to have been be-

tween one-fourth to one-third of the total membership and even higher in the elite.

3. When the government embarked on official anti-Semitism, its spokesman utilized this theme: " 'Żydokomuna' jako Argument Agitacji Antysemickiej—Wywody Posła Miedzińskiego w Świetle Dzieła Marszałka Piłsudskiego," *Nasz Przegląd,* July 1, 1938, p. 6. For an example of its use in respectable Catholic publications, see the following article in the Jesuit periodical: J. Skaliński, "Reorganizacja Partji Komunistycznej w Polse," *Przegląd Powszechny* (October 1938), pp. 47–63.

4. Significantly this fact has been used in Communist Poland to fault the Jews of interwar Poland: See, for example: Jan Borkowski, "O Społeczeństwie Drugiej Rzeczypospolitej," *Przegląd Humanistyczny,* Warsaw, 18, no. 7 (1974): 126–28.

5. Celia Stopnicka Heller, "Deviation and Social Change in the Jewish Community of a Small Polish Town," *American Journal of Sociology,* 60 (September 1954): 177–81.

6. For the Soviet model, see: Zvi Y. Gitelman, *Jewish Nationality and Soviet Politics: The Jewish Sections of the CPSU, 1917–30* (Princeton: Princeton University Press, 1972). For the Polish Communist Party's stand: *KPP: Uchwały i Rezolucje* (Warsaw: 1953), 1: 54; 3: 209–39; Stanisław Mauersberg, *Szkolnictwo Powszechne dla Mniejszości Narodowych w Polsce w Latach 1918–1939* (Wrocław: Ossolineum, 1968), pp. 35, 41, 202–3; Auerbach, "Niektóre Zagadnienia Działalności KPP," pp. 35–36, 54. M. K. Dziewanowski, *The Communist Party of Poland,* (Cambridge: Harvard University Press, 1954), pp. 105, 128–29; Antony Polonsky, *Politics in Independent Poland, 1921–39—The Crisis of Constitutional Government,* (London: Oxford University Press, 1972), pp. 364–65. For the "autonomous" Ukrainian and Belorussian Communist parties in Poland: M. Szczyrba, "Komunistyczna Partia Zachodniej Ukrainy," *Nowe Drogi,* no. 1 (1959): 79–86; S. Bergman et al., "Komunistyczna Partia Zachodniej Białorusi," *ibid.,* no. 5, pp. 86–93.

7. Auerbach, "Niektóre Zagadnienia Działalności KPP," p. 47.

8. *Unter der Fon fun KPP,* Warsaw, 1959, p. 265.

9. Auerbach, "Niektóre Zagadnienia Działalności KPP," p. 56, see also pp. 35–36, 54.

10. YIVO Autobiographies, No. 3598.

11. The new Communist battle cry of a united front against fascism was first signaled by Stalin in January 1934 at the Congress of the Bolshevik Party and was adopted by the Seventh Congress of the Comintern in 1935. See Dziewanowski, *The Communist Party of Poland,* pp. 141–49;

Bernard K. Johnpoll, *The Politics of Futility—The General Jewish Workers Bund of Poland, 1917–1943* (Ithaca: Cornell University Press), pp. 177–78; Polonsky, *Politics in Independent Poland*, p. 365.

12. "Whoever, directly or indirectly, puts forward the slogan of Jewish 'national culture' is (whatever his good intentions may be) an enemy of the proletariat, a supporter of all that is *outmoded* and connected with *caste* among the Jewish people; he is an accomplice of the rabbis and the bourgeoisie. . . . It is the Jewish nationalists in Russia in general, and the Bundists in particular, who vociferate most about Russian orthodox marxists being 'assimilators.'. . . The Jews in the civilized world are not a nation, they have in the main become assimilated. . . . What do these facts prove? It is that only Jewish reactionary philistines, who want to turn back the wheel of history, and make it proceed, not from the conditions prevailing in Russia and Galicia to those prevailing in Paris and New York, but in the reverse direction—only they can clamour against 'assimilation.' " V. I. Lenin, *Critical Remarks on the National Question and the Right of Nations to Self-determination* (Moscow: Progress Publishers [Scientific Socialism Series], 1971), pp. 14–17. See also Hyman Lumer, ed., *Lenin on the Jewish Question* (New York: International Publishers, 1947); Bertram D. Wolfe, *Three Who Made a Revolution* (New York: Dial Press, 1964), pp. 578–90.

13. Dziewanowski, *The Communist Party of Poland*, p. 154.

14. For similar manifestations among German Jews, see Martin Jay, *The Dialectical Imagination: A History of the Frankfurt School and the Institute of Social Research, 1923–50* (Boston: Little, Brown, 1973).

15. In the aftermath of the splits in that group in 1918, 1920, and 1921, the party succeeded in winning over some of its most prominent leaders, as for example: Gershon Dua-Bogen, S. Zachariasz, Józef Lewartowski (pseudonyms—Grynberg, Arański), and Saul Amsterdam (pseudonyms—Henrykowski, Sandecki) who was eventually killed by the Communist Party. Some of the defectors who knew Yiddish were assigned to the "Jewish street" and some others were sent to Palestine to organize party activities there. *Unter der Fon fun KPP*, Warsaw, 1959; Nachum Nir Rafalkes, *Tsu di Yidn Frage in Poyln*, 1920? (unpublished manuscript, discovered by Dr. Elkana Margalit of Tel-Aviv University); *Arbayter Tsaytung (Tsentral Organ fun Yidishe Sotsial Demokratishe Parteyen in Poyln)*, September 12, 1919, October 8, 1919, November 7, 1919.

16. Isaac Deutscher, *The Non-Jewish Jew and other Essays* (London: Oxford University Press, 1968), p. 33. This was noted early by the Left Poale Zion leader, Nachum Nir Rafalkes. See his article under the pseudonym: A. Szawski, "Epes fun di Iberloyfers," *Unzer Velt*, October 28, 1921.

17. Polish students, too, were radicalized but in the direction of the extreme right. See: Janusz Żarnowski, *Spoleczeństwo Drugiej Rzeczypospolitej, 1918–39* (Warsaw, 1973), p. 221.

18. At the Second Congress of the Polish Communist Party (1923), 30 percent of all delegates were Jews by ascription. However, two-thirds of these identified themselves as "Poles of Jewish descent." See Moshe Mishkinski, "Communism—in Poland," *Encyclopedia Judaica* (Jerusalem: Macmillan, 1971), Vol. 5, p. 804.

19. The term was used by Mieczysław Manelli in his unpublished paper "Antisemitism, an Element of Bureaucratic Communist Ideology." (The paper is in Professor Manelli's possession.)

20. In 1917, in a letter she criticized her friend Mathilde Wurm: "Why do you come with your special Jewish sorrows? I feel just as sorry for the wretched Indian victims in Putamayo, the Negroes in Africa. . . . I cannot find a special corner in my heart for the ghetto." J. P. Nettl, *Rosa Luxemburg* (London: Oxford University Press, 1966), vol. 2, p. 860.

21. For example, the PPS leader, Bolesław Drobner, was from a fairly traditional home. After independence was won, he actively agitated among socialist-Zionists to abandon Zionism and join the PPS. He argued that it was their duty as socialists to take this step "even if it was unpopular, and ostensibly not in the interest of the people to whom they *felt* closest [the Jewish people]. In such an instance one must arm himself with rational arguments, and not with *short-sighted sentiment.*" See: Boleslaw Drobner, "Kilka Słów o Pecekach," *Naprzód*, December 13, 1919 (as quoted in his autobiography: *Bezustanna Walka—Wspomnienia*, Warsaw: Państwowy Instytut Wydawniczy, 1965], vol. 2, pp. 14–15); for PPS recruiting activities among Jewish workers at the turn of the century and the difficulties that such recruits faced while making their break with Orthodoxy, see Mojżesz Kaufman, "Przyczynki do Historji Żydowskiej Organizacji PPS," *Niepodległość*, 12, no. 1 (1935): 22–25. See also: J. Żarnowski, *Polska Partia Socjalistyczna w Latach 1935–1939* (Warsaw, 1965).

22. Jacob S. Hertz, "The Bund's Nationality Program and Its Critics in the Russian, Polish and Austrian Socialist Movements," *YIVO Annual of Jewish Social Science*, vol. 14 (1969): 53–67.

23. It seems that a similar manifestation occurred earlier, at the end of the nineteenth century among the assimilated intelligentsia. Hilary Nussbaum, an ideologue of assimilation, lamented in his book: "It has come to this—the Jewish intelligentsia, seeing the love of the backward masses for the jargon [Yiddish], have begun to use it as a means to serve them healthy spiritual food in an unclean vessel." Hilary Nussbaum, *Żydzi w*

Polsce, Historya Żydów od Mojżesza do Epoki Obecnej, vol. 5 (Warsaw, 1890): 447–48.

24. Max Weinreich, *Geshikhte fun der Yidisher Shprakh* (New York: YIVO, 1973), vol. 1, p. 295. Chaim N. Bialik, "Tsvey Reydes—di Shprakhn-frage Bay Yidn" (Kovno: Tarbut, 1930), pp. 1–15.

25. Deutscher, *The Non-Jewish Jew*, p. 44. The political activities of Deutscher (1907–67), who joined the Communist Party in 1927, concentrated on Jewish workers. As he explained later: "I spent my best years, my politically active years among Jewish workers. . . . As Marxists we tried theoretically to deny that the Jewish labour movement had an identity of its own, but it had all the same." "Who Is a Jew?" in: *Ibid.*, p. 45. He was expelled from the Polish Communist Party in 1932 as an "agent of social-fascism" because he criticized the party for refusing to cooperate with the groups in Centrolew which opposed the Piłsudski regime. See Polonsky, *Politics in Independent Poland*, pp. 364–65. For the educational and cultural activities of the Bund, see Chaim S. Kazdan, *Di Geshikhte fun Yidishn Shulvezn in Umophengikn Poyln* (Mexico City: 1947); and *Di Geshikhte fun Bund* (New York, 1972), vol. 4, pp. 287–388.

26. Vilno had eight Yiddish elementary schools and one of the three Yiddish high schools in Poland. See: A. Tartakower, "Yidishe Kultur in Poyln Tsvishn Tsvey Velt Milkhomes," *Gedank un Lebn*, (April–June 1946): 10; Nathan Eck, "The Educational Institutions of Polish Jewry, 1921–39," *Jewish Social Studies*, 9, no. 1 (January 1947): pp. 9–10.

27. A. Tartakower, "Mur Bojkotu," *Nasza Trybuna*, Warsaw, December 20, 1937, p. 4. See also Tartakower, "W Walce o Pracę Żydowską," *Nasza Trybuna*, Warsaw, November 20, 1937, p. 7; Jerzy Tomaszewski, "Robotnicy Żydowscy w Polsce w Latach 1921–39," *Biuletyn Żydowskiego Instytutu Historycznego*, no. 5 (Aug.–Sept., 1964, pp. 28–29; Marian Drozdowski, *Polityka Gospodarcza Rządu Polskiego, 1936–1939* (Warsaw, 1963), p. 284.

28. In a speech before the Sejm, on November 13, 1928, Representative Y. Gruenbaum spoke about the economic problems: "Sirs, the Jewish masses which are becoming proletarianized ought to be able to join the ranks of labor. These Jewish masses want to work in factories, but are excluded." A Polish representative interjected, "even in Jewish factories?" and the speaker continued: "Yes, even in Jewish factories. If you want, I shall tell you why. When in Łódź a brave Jewish capitalist existed who hired one Jew to his factory, he was threatened with a strike." *Budżet Państwa Polskiego, na 1929–30r a Żydzi—Mowy w Sejmie i Senacie w Dyskusji Budżetowej*, Biuletyn No. 3 Klubu Posłów i Senatorów Żydowskiej Rady Narodowej (Warsaw, 1929), pp. 19–20.

29. The greater docility of Polish workers was discussed by the Polish Communist theoretician J. B. Marchlewski, *Antysemityzm a Robotnicy*, Wydział III (Warsaw, 1920), p. 51. For more on discriminatory hiring in Jewish enterprises: J. Lestchinsky, "Der Yidisher Proletaryat in Poyln," *YIVO Bleter*, 15 (January–February 1940): 26–27.

30. Henryk Ehrlich, *Der Iker fun Bundizm* (New York: Der Bundisher Klub, 1935); I. Hertz, "Der Bund in Umophengikn Poyln, 1918–25," in *Di Geshikhte fun Bund* (New York, 1972), vol. 4, pp. 219–87; Wiktor Alter, *O Żydach i Antysemityźmie* (Warsaw, 1936), pp. 8–28; Leonard Rowe, "Politics Under Stress: The Jewish Response in Poland," *The Bennington Review*, 4 (Spring 1968): 45.

31. Mordechai V. Bernstein, "Der 'Bund' in Poyln," *Yearbook*, 1 (New York: American World Federation of Polish Jews, 1964), p. 172.

32. The Zionists, too, aimed at transforming the kehillot into organs of national autonomy. On Bund's activities, see: *ibid;* K. Walski, "Tsi Iz Nisht Tsu Fri (Tsu di Kehile Diskusye)," *Unzer Tsayt*, 4 (June 1929): 26–31; B. Shefner, "A Klap in Tir- (Vegn Unzer Vayterdiker Batsiung Tsu der Yidisher Kehile)," *Unzer Tsayt*, 3 (March 1929): 32–41.

33. He went on to explain: "I am at heart of Jewish nationality and I am aware of my emotional solidarity, which binds me with the Jewish masses. But no less do I feel the strings of solidarity with the workers of all other nations and humanity as a whole." W. Alter, "Czy Znajdą się Tacy Ludzie," *Nowe Życie*, February 1, 1939, p. 2.

34. One of the first issues to which the Bund addressed itself in independent Poland was the question of achieving power. The left faction (joined by the center) favored a "dictatorship of the proletariat"; the right opposed any form of dictatorship in a socialist state. Related to this, the most persistent issue—among the many over which the factions differed—was whether to affiliate with the Socialist International, the Comintern, or not to affiliate. The central committee of the Bund, as well as the editorial boards of all its official publications, included members of the different factions in proportion to the number of delegates elected to the last national convention of the organization. See Bernstein, "Der 'Bund' in Poyln," pp. 172, 177; K. Johnpoll, *Politics of Futility*, pp. 8–11, 189–93; Leon Oler, "Di Tsvayer in Poylishn Bund," *Unzer Tsayt*, 17 (November–December, 1957), pp. 52–54.

35. Bernstein, "Der 'Bund' in Poyln," pp. 184–90; A. Haftka, "Życie Parlamentarne Żydow w Polsce Odrodzonej," in I. Schiper, A. Tartakower, A. Haftka, eds., *Żydzi w Polsce Odrodzonej*, vol. 2 (Warsaw, 1935), pp. 293, 305.

36. Johnpoll, *Politics of Futility*, p. 193.

37. For general treatments of Zionism, see: Ben Halpern, *The Idea of a Jewish State* (Cambridge: Harvard University Press, 1969); Walter Lacqueur, *A History of Zionism* (New York: Holt, Rinehart and Winston, 1972); Yigal Elam, *Mavo Lehistoriyah Tsiyonit Aheret* (Tel-Aviv: Lewin-Epstein, 1972).

38. From it derives the largest party in Israel, the Mapai. For the range of Jewish political parties in interwar Poland see: I. Schwarzbart, *Tsvishn Beyde Velt-milkhomes* (Buenos Aires: 1955), pp. 279–357; Haftka, "Żydowskie Stronnictwa Polityczne w Polsce Odrodzonej," pp. 249–85; N. Kantorowicz, "Di Tsionistishe Arbayter Bavegung in Poyln," *Yearbook*, 1 (New York: American Federation of Polish Jews, 1964), pp. 110–57.

39. During the 1930 parliamentary election, it got only 2.7 percent of the total vote cast for Jewish parties: Haftka, "Życie Parlamentarne w Polsce Odrodzonej," p. 305. After the split, the Left Poale Zion proposed to the Polish Communist Party that it be incorporated into the Communist Party as its Jewish section. It was told that first it had to break with Zionism. See: *Głos Komunistyczny*, no. 2 (Warsaw, 1922). (Reprinted in: *Unter der Fon fun KPP;* Warsaw, 1959, p. 266.) It was also unsuccessful in its effort to enter the Comintern without renouncing its Zionism.

40. *Plan Pracy, Haszomer Hacair*, Lvov, 1932 (mimeographed instruction book for leaders of groups); Elkana Margalit, *Shomer Hatsair Me'adat Neurim Le-marksizm Mehapkhani (1919–1936)* (Tel Aviv: Tel Aviv University Press, 1971). For its early history see Margalit's: "Social and Intellectual Origins of the Hashomer Hatzair Youth Movement, 1913–20," *Journal of Contemporary History*, 4, no. 2 (April 1969): 25–46.

41. YIVO Autobiographies, No. 3735.

42. YIVO Autobiographies, No. 3834.

43. Leib Spizman, *Khalutsim in Poyln* (New York, 1959), vol. 1, pp. 8, 25, 153, 328–37, 545–62. A. Lewinson, "52-lecie Hapoel Hacairu," *Miesięcznik Żydowski*, April 1933, pp. 356–63. W. Glicksman, "The Halutz Ideology and Experience as Reflected in the Yiddish Novel in Poland, 1919–1939," *YIVO Annual of Jewish Social Science*, 14 (1969): 270–84.

44. Spizman, *Khalutsim in Poyln*, pp. 229–248, 339–438. For a report on the best model farm using the newest agricultural method (located in the Lvov district): *Żydowska Farma Rolnicza w Czyżykowie—Sprawozdanie na Rok 1937* (unpublished).

45. YIVO Autobiographies, No. 3706.

46. YIVO Autobiographies, No. 3516; For an example of wide protest of Polish Jewry against Britain's action, see the resolution passed by the Częstochowa kehilla: William M. Glicksman, *A Kehillah in Poland During*

the *Inter-War Years* (Philadelphia: the Advertisers Press, 1970), pp. 106–7.

47. YIVO Autobiographies, No. 3739.

48. For the concept of "thresholds" of social systems, see Kenneth E. Boulding, "The Learning Process in the Dynamics of Total Societies," in Samuel Z. Klausner, ed. *The Study of Total Societies*, (New York: Frederick A. Praeger, 1967), pp. 107–8.

49. This *Sejm* (1922–27) which came into being as a result of the first general election, was referred to as the Second *Sejm*, the first being a provisional body. In the Third Sejm (1928), there were 15 Jewish representatives; in the Fourth Sejm (1930), 10; in the Fifth (1935), 6. In the 1928 election the total number of voters for Jewish parties decreased by 30 percent as compared with 1922 (710,191 and 1,043,283 votes respectively). The decline was evenly distributed among the parties. Both in the 1928 and 1930 elections, the Agudat Israel's candidates were elected on the ticket of the Non-party Bloc of Cooperation with the Government. The 1935 election was boycotted by most Jewish parties in former Congress Poland (with the exception of the Agudat Israel and the Association of Merchants). The Galician Zionists, however, participated. See: Haftka, "Życie Parlamentarne Żydów w Polsce Odrodzonej," in: I. Schiper, et al., eds., *Żydzi w Polsce Odrodzonej* (Warsaw, 1935), pp. 293, 305, 311, 335. J. Shatzky, "Yidishe Politik Tsvishn di Tsvey Velt-milkhomes," *Algemeyne Entsiklopedye*, Supplementary volume: *Yidn*, 4, pp. 236–37. Also: Leopold Halpern, *Polityka Żydowska w Sejmie i Senacie 1919–31* (Warsaw, 1933): Haftka, "Działalność Parlamentarna i Polityczna Posłow i Senatorów Żydowskich w Polsce Odrodzonej," vol. 2, pp. 313–59; Yakov Wygodzki, *In Sambatyen (Zikhroynes fun Tsveytn Seym)* (Vilno, 1931); Janusz Żarnowski, *Społeczenstwo Drugiej Rzeczypospolitej, 1918–39* (Warsaw, 1973), pp. 392–93.

50. Leopold Halpern, *Polityka Żydowska*, pp. 18–19; Schwarzbart, *Tsvishn Beyde Velt-milkhomes*, pp. 220–23; Ezra Mendelsohn, "The Dilemma of Jewish Politics in Poland: Four Responses," in Bela Vago and George L. Mosse, eds. *Jews and Non-Jews in Eastern Europe, 1918–45*, (New York: John Wiley, 1974), pp. 203–19.

51. The participation of Galician Jews in parliamentary politics dates back to 1848, when three Jews from Galicia were elected to the Vienna Parliament—Abraham Halpern, Isaac Manheimer, and Rabbi Dov Berush Meisels. See: *Encyclopedia Judaica*, vol. 3, p. 895, s.v. "Austria."

52. Halpern, *Polityka Żydowska*, pp. 18–19; Schwarzbart, *Tsvishn Beyde Velt-milkhomes*, pp. 220–23.

53. Herman Bernstein, "The Polish-Jewish Pact to End Anti-Semitism,"

Current History, October 1925, pp. 77–8; *Daily New Bulletin*, Jewish Telegraphic Agency, vol. 6, nos. 149, 155; June 30 and July 7, 1925; Ezra Mendelsohn, "Reflections on the 'Ugoda,' " in Sh. Yeivin, ed., *Studies in Jewish History—Presented to Professor Raphael Mahler on his Seventy-Fifth Birthday* (Merhavia, 1974), pp. 87–102.

54. Halpern, *Polityka Żydowska;* Schwarzbart, *Tsvishn Beyde Velt-milkhomes;* Marian Drozdowski, *Polityka Gospodarcza Rządu Polskiego, 1936–39* (Warsaw, 1963), p. 284; Wygodzki, *In Sambatyen;* Simon Segal, *The New Poland and the Jews* (New York: Lee Furman, 1938), pp. 30–3. Pavel Korzec, "Heskem Memshelet Grabski im Hanetsigut Haparlamentarit Ha-yehudit," *Gal-Ed*, vol. 1 (1973: 175–210; "Tekst Porozumienia Rządu z Kołem Żydowskim Zawaretgo 7 lipca 1925 a Ogłoszonego 6 V 1923 przez Koło Zydowskie," *ibid.*, pp. 203–7.

55. "Przemówienie Posła Dr-a Wygodzkiego na Posiedzeniu Sejmu z Dnia 7/11/29r . . . ," *Budżet Państwa Polskiego na 1929–30r a Żydzi—Mowy w Sejmie i Senacie* (Warsaw, 1929), p. 69.

56. "Przemówienie Senatora dr. Dawidsohna na Posiedzeniu Senatu z dn. 6 marca 1929r," *ibid.*, p. 146.

57. "Przemówienie Senatora Rabina Rubinsteina na Posiedzeniu Senatu z dn. 9 marca 1929r," *ibid.*, p. 155.

58. Quoted in Ezra Mendelsohn, "Agudas Yisroel in Poland," *Soviet Jewish Affairs*, vol. 2, no. 2 (1972): 60f.

59. From the declaration reproduced in: Edward D. Wynot, Jr., " 'A Necessary Cruelty': The Emergence of Official Antisemitism in Poland 1936–39," *The American Historical Review*, 76, No. 4 (October 1971): 10053.

60. M. A. Hartglas, *Na Pograniczu Dwóch Światów—Pamiętniki*, 1952 (unpublished).

61. The great American Zionist, Justice Louis Brandeis, in 1919 opposed this policy embarked on by the Zionists in Europe as inconsistent with the objectives of Zionism. On this issue he clashed with Chaim Weizmann. See David Rudavsky, "Louis D. Brandeis at the London International Zionist Conference of 1920," *YIVO Annual of Jewish Social Science* 15 (1974): pp. 145–48.

62. *Encyclopedia Judaica*, vol. 13, p. 751, s.v. "Poland."

63. YIVO Diaries, No. 3833.

64. Samuel Hirszhorn, "Kwestia Żydowska w Diasporze w Roku 1937," *Almanach—Rocznik Naszego Przeglądu*, Warsaw, 1938, p. 50.

65. The percentage of Jews in the total emigration from Poland in dif-

ferent periods: 1921–1925, 39.3%; 1926–1930, 10.5%; 1931–1935, 36.6%; 1936, 31.2%. These figures appear in Menachem Linder, "Zagadnienia Emigracji Żydowskiej w Polsce Odrodzonej," Głos Gminy Żydowskiej, vol. 2, nos. 10–11 (October–November 1938): pp. 274–5. See also S. Bronsztejn, Ludność Żydowska w Polsce w Okresie Między-Wojennym (Wrocław, 1963), pp. 91–102; 263; ibid., "The Jewish Population of Poland in 1931," The Jewish Journal of Sociology, 6, no. 1 (July 1964): 5; Mały Rocznik Statystyczny (Warsaw, 1939), p. 53; Henryk Rosenberg, "Emigracja Żydów z Polski do Stanów Zjednoczonych w latach 1925–29," Miesięcznik Żydowski, May–June 1933, pp. 526–29; A. Tartakower, Emigracja Żydowska z Polski (Warsaw, 1939); ibid., "The Migrations of Polish Jewry in Recent Times," Yearbook, 1 (New York: World Federation of Polish Jews, 1964), pp. 7–27.

66. "Wychodźctwo Według Wyznania," Rocznik Statystyczny, 15, (Warsaw: Główny Urząd Statystyczny, 1936), p. 51.

67. YIVO Diaries, No. 3599.

68. This designation is used by Ezra Mendelsohn in Encyclopedia Judaica, vol. 13, p. 751, s.v. "Poland."

69. For an example of the Zionist attacks on Revisionists as fascists, see the pamphlet: "Prawda o Rewizjoniźmie," Lvov: Hitachdut Poalej Sion, 1938.

70. "Manifest Kongresu," Myśl Socjalistyczna, November, 20, 1937, pp. 2–3. For one of the latest expressions of the Bund's anti-immigration stand, see its bimonthly publication in Polish: E. Szerer: "Istota Emigracjonizmu," Myśl Socjalistyczna, February 1, 1939, p. 1. See also Tartakower, "The Migrations of Polish Jewry," pp. 26–27.

71. "Batalia Wyborcza do Rady Miejskiej w Łodzi—5 List Kandydackich na Ulicy Żydowskiej," Nasz Przegląd, December 7, 1938, p. 9; J. Shatzky, "Yidishe Politik Tsvishn di Tsvey Velt-milkhomes," Algemeyne Entsiklopedye Yidn, vol. 4, p. 241; Marian Drozdowski, Klasa Robotnicza Warszawy (Warsaw, 1968), pp. 249–50; Leonard Rowe, "Politics Under Stress: The Jewish Response in Poland," Bennington Review, 4 (Spring 1968): 46.

72. "Dyskusja z Powodu Porażki Wyborczej," Nasz Przegląd, January 4, 1939, p. 5.

73. For example, among the sources that we have used, in a statistical study of social characteristics of high school students, the author interjects a remark on the lack of unity and comments: "Can we justly blame others, when things are not in order among ourselves?" Menahem Mirkin, "Yidishe Talmidim in Mitlshuln in Poyln," Yidishe Ekonomik, No. 4–5

(1939): 265. Or an earlier specialized article on the economic situation of Jews: Roman Zylbersztajn, "Problematyka Gospodarcza Żydów w Polsce," *Przegląd Handlowy*, no. 10 (September 15, 1936), pp. 7–8.

74. I. Schwarzbart, "O Zjednoczenie Żydów w Polsce," *Nasz Przegląd*, September 29, 1938, p. 13. At the same time, on the occasion of the Jewish New Year, the greatly respected rabbi and professor, Moses Schorr, thus appealed to the Jewish people to preserve their national dignity: "At this moment, the greatest expression of dignity is unity. . . . . There is no place now for division and fragmentation into parties and factions—each must stretch out a hand to the other, all must unite." Rabin Prof. Dr. Mojżesz Schorr, "Godność Narodu—Refleksje do Święta Rosz Haszana 5699," *Głos Gminy Żydowskiej*, 2, no. 9 (September 1938): 202.

75. This comment appears after the partially reprinted text of the *Moment* article, whose author lamented the lack of unity at a time when Jewish politics "could be characterized as a struggle for life." See: "W Młynie Opinii," *Nasz Przegląd*, December 31, 1938.

76. One of the six organizers who was a socialist-Zionist was called a hypocrite, "a proponent of national unity for Jews but class struggle for others." See: "Konsolidacja Burżuazji Żydowskiej," *Myśl Socjalistyczna*, October 1, 1937, p. 1.

77. Rowe, "Politics Under Stress," p. 47.

77. YIVO Diaries, No. 3599.

79. *Great Britain and Palestine, 1915–1945*, Report prepared for the Royal Institute of International Affairs, no. 20, London, 1946.

80. J. Leshtchinsky, "Der Pshitiker Pogrom" (written July 1, 1936), reprinted in: Dov Shtokfish, ed.: *Sefer Pshitik* (Tel Aviv, 1973), pp. 177–78. Two Jews were killed and a number were wounded. However, a Polish peasant was killed, when a young Jew shot back; an attempt was made to depict the Jews as having provoked the violence. An anti-Semitic tract peddling this line is by Stefan Niebudek, *Wielki Proces Polaków z Żydami* (3rd edition, revised, Warsaw: Sprawa Narodowa, 1936). Significantly, in Communist Poland, this thesis of Jewish culpability in the Przytyk pogrom was revived: See: Jan Borkowski, "O Społeczeństwie Drugiej Rzeczypospolitej," *Przegląd Humanistyczny*, vol. 18, no. 7, (1974): 132.

81. See, for example "Sala Sądowa Coraz Częściej Zmienia sie w Widownię Walk Politycznych—Przemówienie Posła dra Sommersteina," *Chwila*, February 19, 1938, p. 7; "Proces o Zajścia Antyżydowskie w Brańsku," *Nasz Przegląd*, September 15, 1938, p. 10; "Zajścia Antyżydowskie w Kadzidle przed Sądem Okręgowym w Łomży," *Nasz Przegląd*, September 28, 1938, p. 13; "Proces o Obrazę Religji Żydowskiej," *Nasz Przegląd*, December 7, 1938, p. 4; "Wyrok," *Nasz Przegląd*, December, 1938, p. 9.

82. From the recollection of a member of this self-defense group, Yitzhak Friedman, "Unzer Zelbshuts," in *Sefer Pshitik*, pp. 197–99. See also Israel Tsimbalista, "Mir Hobn Gegreyt a Vidershtand," in *ibid.*, pp. 200–2.

83. Leonard Rowe, "Jewish Self-Defense: A Response to Violence," in Joshua A. Fishman, ed. *Studies on Polish Jewry, 1919–1939* (New York: YIVO Institute, 1974), p. 106.

84. For recollections from the memoirs of the third President of Israel, see: Schneur Zalman Shazar, "Defenders of the City," in Lucy Dawidowicz, *The Golden Tradition* (New York: Holt, Rinehart, 1964), pp. 383–88.

85. Rowe, "Jewish Self-Defense," pp. 105–149. The author used the method of "oral history" as well as memoirs published after World War II. For an earlier and less complete treatment, see: Bernstein, "Der Bund in Poyln," pp. 211–17.

86. Rowe, "Jewish Self-Defense," p. 110.

87. Quoted in *ibid.*, p. 119.

88. Ibid., pp. 124–25.

89. P. Rybak, "Wspomnienia o Walce KPP przeciwko Pogromom Antyżydowskim," *Biuletyn Żydowskiego Instytutu Historycznego*, no. 13–14 (January–June, 1955): 268–73.

90. The prominent Polish novelist Maria Dąbrowska, in her highly autobiographical last novel, has one of her heroines, Sabina, commenting at the time of rising anti-Semitism: "The Jews are grateful, for every manifestation of sympathy. . . . They are grateful, as nobody else in the world. Impossibly grateful." Maria Dąbrowska, *Przygody Człowieka Myślącego* (Warsaw, 1972), p. 292.

91. Adam Próchnik, "Udział Żydów w Działalnośći Bojowej pod Sztandarem PPS," *Głos Gminy Żydowskiej*, vol. 2, no. 10–11 (Oct.–Nov. 1938): 242–44.

92. Interesting reminiscences of the contacts with Polish socialists which facilitated defense operations are found in the book written by the head of the *Ordener-grupe*, the Bund militia: Bernard Goldstein, *Tsvantsik Yor in Varshever Bund* (New York: Verlag Unser Tsayt, 1960). For the growing cooperation between the Bund and PPS, see Johnpoll, *The Politics of Futility*, pp. 214–220.

93. Zosa Szajkowski, " 'Reconstruction' vs. 'Palliative Relief' in American Jewish Overseas Work (1919–1939)," *Jewish Social Studies*, 32 (1970): 14–43.

94. YIVO Autobiographies, No. 3837.

95. YIVO Diaries. No. 3599.

Epilogue: The Jewish Remmant in Post-War Poland

1. F. Friedman, *Zagłada Żydów Polskich w Latach 1939–45*, Biuletyn Głownej Komisji Badania Zbrodni Niemieckiej w Polsce, 1946, p. 206. Also: Lucy S. Dawidowicz, *The War Against the Jews, 1933–1945* (New York: Holt, Rinehart and Winston, 1975); Emanuel Ringelblum, *Polish-Jewish Relations During the Second World War*, ed. by Joseph Kermish and Samuel Krakowski (Jerusalem: Yad Vashem, 1974).

2. See, for example, Władysław Bartoszewski and Zofia Lewin, *The Samaritans—Heroes of the Holocaust*, (New York: Twayne Publishers, 1966); Philip Friedman, *Their Brothers Keepers* (New York: Holocaust Library, 1978); Moshe Bejski, "The Righteous Among the Nations and Their Part in the Rescue of Jews," in Yisrael Gutman and Livia Rothkirchen, eds., *The Catastrophe of European Jews* (Jerusalem: Yad Vashem, 1976), pp. 582–607; Nechama Tec, *When Light Pierced the Darkness: Christian Rescue of Jews in Nazi-Occupied Poland* (New York: Oxford University Press, 1986); Gay Block and Malka Drucker, *Rescuers: Portraits of Moral Courage in the Holocaust* (New York: Holmes and Meier Publishers, New York, 1992); Mordechai Paldiel, *The Path of the Righteous: Gentile Rescuers of Jews During the Holocaust* (Hoboken: Ktav Publishers, 1993).

3. Stanisław W. Dobrowolski, *Memuary Pacyfisty* (Cracow: Wydawnitwo Literackie, 1989), pp. 194–201, 202–3. Also see the review of this book in English by Celia Stopnicka Heller, *The Polish Review*, New York, 37, no. 3, 1992, pp. 360–62; Alicia Appleman-Jurman, *Alicia—My Story* (New York: Bantam Books, 1988); Blanca Rosenberg, *To Tell at Last—Survival Under False Identity, 1941–45*, (Urbana: University of Illinois Press, 1993). Also read the heartbreaking short recollections of a Jewish child survivor among Polish peasants: Renee Kuker, "Lets' Throw Her in the Well," *The Hidden Child*, Newsletter, ADL, 3, no. 1, Spring 1993, p. 3.

4. This information is from my interviews conducted in Silesia shortly after the war and later in the United States.

5. Jeff Schatz, *The Generation—The Rise and Fall of the Jewish Communists in Poland* (Berkeley: University of California Press, 1991); Dobrowolski, *Memuary Pacyfisty*, pp. 238–42.

6. Lucjan Dobroszycki, "Restoring Jewish Life in Post-War Poland," *Soviet Jewish Affairs*, 3, no. 2, (1973) pp. 58–72.

7. Celia S. Heller, "Philosemites Counter Anti-Semitism in Catholic Poland," in: Frederick M. Schweitzer and Marvin Perry, editors, *Jewish-Christian Encounters Over Centuries* (New York: Peter Lang Publishing, 1993).

8. Jerzy Surdykowski, *Duch Rzeczypospolitej* (New York: Bicentennial Publishing Corporation, 1989) p. 21.

9. We do not know how many survivors were shot crossing borders illegally. But in the Cracow Jewish cemetery, for example, a grave exists, marked in Hebrew, for 17 members of the Jewish youth organization *Gordonia* who were killed by a Polish terrorist *Ogień* band when they tried to cross the "green line." See: Artur Sandauer, *Publicystyka, Pisma Zebrane*, vol. 3 (Warsaw: Czytelnik, 1985). Also see; Carl Schrag, "Polish-Israelis: Not Much Regret," *Jerusalem Post*, International Edition, May 24, 1991, p. 7.

10. Celia S. Heller, "'Anti-Zionism' and the Political Struggle Within the Elite of Poland," *Jewish Journal of Sociology*, II, no. 2 (December, 1969), pp. 133–50; Robert S. Wistrich, ed., *The Left Against Zionism: Communism, Israel and the Middle East* (London, 1979); Z. Kozik, "O Wydarzeniach Marcowych 1968 r.," *Nowe Drogi*, no. 2, 1988, pp. 60–75; Jerzy Eisler, *Marzec 1968—Geneza, Przebieg, Konsekwencje* (Warsaw: Panstwowe Wydawnictwo Naukowe, 1991).

11. Gustaw Kerszman, "Książka o Marcu," *Zeszyty Historyczne*, no. 99, Paris 1992, p. 157.

12. Celia S. Heller, The Polish 'Maranos': A Post–World War II Social Phenomenon," paper prepared for the Eleventh World Congress of Jewish Studies, Jerusalem, June 27, 1993.

13. Heller, "'Anti-Zionism' and the Political Struggle Within the Elite of Poland."

14. For the analysis of these themes, see ibid., pp. 143–145.

15. J. Holzer, "Doświadczenia Marca 68," *Kierunki*, May 17, 1981.

16. Iwona Irwin-Zarecka, *Neutralizing Memory* (New Brunswick. Transaction Press, 1989).

17. Bogumiła Żongołłowicz, "Prof. Bartoszewski w Australii," *Nowy Dziennik*, April 17–18, 1993, p. 4.

18. Jerzy Ficowski, *A Reading of Ashes* (London: The Menard Press, 1981), p. 2. The quotes are from the foreword to the book by the poet Zbigniew Herbert, p. 1.

19. He took the title from a poem by Czeslaw Miłosz, the Nobel Prize Winner. For the article in English translation, see: Jan Błoński, "The Poor Poles Look at the Ghetto," in Anthony Polonsky, ed., *My Brother's Keeper—Recent Polish Debates on the Holocaust* (London, 1990), pp. 35, 42–43.

20. Michael T. Kaufman, "Debate Over the Holocaust Stirs Poles," *The New York Times*, March 8, 1987, p. A4. Some of the articles are reproduced in: Polonsky, *My Brother's Keeper.*

21. As quoted in: Kaufman, "Debate Over the Holocaust."

22. Wojciech Górecki, "Rozmowa z Markiem Edelmanem," *Życie Warszawy*, April 18, 1993.

23. From the translated quotations in Celia S. Heller, "The Philosemites of Poland," *Midstream*, January, 1992, p. 30.

24. "Walesa Vows to Fight Anti-Semitism," *The New York Times*, March 26, 1991, p. A3; Leon Wieselter, "Washington Diarist—The Milkcan," *The New Republic*, April 22, 1991, p. 47; "At Museum Ceremony, Walesa Vows to Combat Polish Anti-Semitism," *Newsletter*, The United States Holocaust Memorial Museum, May 1991, pp. 1, 4–5.

25. Dan Izenberg and David Makovsky, "Walesa Seeks Reconciliation with Jews," *The Jerusalem Post*, International Edition, June 1, 1991, p. 3; Joel Brinkley, "Walesa in Israel Regrets Poland's Anti-Semitism, *The New York Times*, May 21, 1991, p. A5.

26. "Przezydent Izraela w Polsce," *Nowy Dziennik*, May 27, 1992, p. 2; Stanisław Krajewski, "Polish-Israeli Relations: Excellent, But Are They Normal?" *The American Jewish Committee's Report from Poland*, March 1993; "Prezydent Izraela w Krakowie i Tykocinie," *Nowy Dziennik*, May 28, 1992, p. 2.

27. Jane Perlez, "At Warsaw Ghetto, Poles and Jews Bound by Hope," *The New York Times*, April 20, 1993, p. A3; "Holocaust Recalled," *The Jewish Week*, April 23–29, 1993, p. 46; Kalman Sultanik, "50th Anniversary of the Warsaw Ghetto Uprising," *Midstream*, May 1993, p. 31; Stanisław Krajewski, "Fiftieth Anniversary of the Warsaw Ghetto Uprising," *The American Jewish Committee's Report from Poland*, March 1993.

28. "Przełom w Stosunkach Polsko-Żydowskich," *Nowy Dziennik*, April 22, 1993, p. 1.

29. Quoted in Steve Lipman, "Warsaw 1993: Monuments and Memories Survive," *The Jewish Week*, April 16–22, 1993, p. 3.

30. The quote is from the sensitive article Wieselter, "Washington Diarist—The Milkcan."

31. See, as an example of the longing for the Polish landscape, the poems of Anna Frajlich, which have been characterized as "poetization of her autobiography." Particularly moving is the poem "One Needs a Meadow": Anna Frajlich, *Between Dawn and the Wind—Selected Poetry* (Austin: Host Publication, 1991), pp. 10–11 (in Polish and in English translation). Frajlich left Poland in 1969 because of the "anti-Zionist" campaign. Also see Simon Schama, "Stopping by Woods—The discovery of history in a Polish forest," *The New Republic*, October 26, 1992, pp.

31–37. The quote is from his lovely description of his travels in Poland, a study of landscape and memory, p. 37.

32. Jerzy Turowicz, "Chrześcijanie, Polacy, Żydzi," *Tygodnik Powszechny*; reprinted in: *Nowy Dziennik*, Section 2, March 7, 1991, p. 1.

Index

ABC, 115

Accommodation, traditional, 167–73, 174–78, 181–82, 237, 276; youth's view of, 181

Acculturation: historical background, 20, 44, 64–66; linguistic, 66–69, 215; process of, 143, 212–32; as distinct from assimilation, 184, 212, 215; non-purposive, 217; conscious, 218, 227; and mobility aspirations, 218, 227; *see also* Language distribution; Polonization; Values, Polish-Jewish shift toward

Agriculture, Jews in, 72–73

Agudat Israel: schools of, 156–58, 178–79; its kehilla politics, 163–64, 178–79; its support of Piłsudski, 163, 177–79, 278; its relation with *Sanacja* regime, 167–68, 177–80, 278; its attitudes to Zionism, 173, 175, 180–81; its Council of Sages, 173; its politicization, 173–81; its parliamentary politics, 174–80, 341 *n*54; and radical Polish parties, 175

Aid to the needy, 159–61, 166–67, 291; to German refugees, 291–92

Alexander II of Russia, 37, 38

Alexander rebe, 153, 173

Aliyah, see Palestine, emigration to

Altbauer, Moshe, 332 *n*35

Alter, Abraham Mordechai, 173

Alter, Wiktor, 264

Anti-Semitic climate, 133–36, 203

Anti-Semitic literature, 111–12; 125–27

Anti-Semitic slogans, 44–45, 116, 117, 123, 139, 281

Anti-Semitic slurs, 59–60, 62, 70, 113, 145, 225, 318 *n*30, 329 *n*74

Anti-Semitism: origin, 15–17, 19–21, 76, 107; of the Church, 15–16, 19, 21, 109–14; economic factors in, 16, 84–85, 107–8; class variation in, 16–17, 19–21, 85, 107–8, 116, 128, 133; responses to, 26, 37, 44–45, 133–34, 171–73, 181, 202–4, 207–9, 244, 255, 264, 265, 278, 284–93; of the press, 38, 44, 52, 108, 110–11, 135, 137–38, 200, 203–4; against "Litvaks," 43; election to Duma, 43–44; economic, 44, 83, 93, 97–109, 113, 203, 348 *n*45; greeting independence, 47–53; racist elements in, 64, 113–14, 126–27, 134–35, 203; political manifestations of, 76, 77, 84–86, 88, 115–29, 135, 206; official, 86, 91–93, 97, 98–109, 126, 135–39, 180, 195; Polish opposition to, 93, 111, 116–17, 122–23, 129–33, 133–34, 204,